Just what I have been long[...] that brings the Words ar[...] tures are from every boo[...] with every page focused on [...], the miracles He did or of those who follow Him. Jacqie's in-depth study and knowledge of biblical truths, Christianity, and its history shines through making this an excellent educational resource for Christian leaders and intercessors.

She shares personal testimonies of answered prayers (from home and abroad) for salvation, deliverance, healing, and revival.

You will be given hope to believe that truly all things are possible with God and what Jesus taught is still available for you today. It's every day with Jesus but MORE. Dare to be inspired!

—APRILE HUNT, DIRECTOR
KENTUCKY PRAYER COALITION
KY-NATIONAL GOVERNORS PRAYER TEAM
KY-GOVERNMENTAL SPECIALIST,
HEARTLAND APOSTOLIC PRAYER NETWORK

It's never been more important to watch what you put before your eyes and ears. The things we look at or listen to are deposited into our hearts and affect our lives. Finding resources that will feed instead of undermine your faith are hard to come by. That's why I'm excited to recommend *Manna and Miracles*. Grounded thoroughly in the Word of God, each daily devotion is filled with faith-building stories, practical insights for living a victorious life in Christ, and bold biblical prayers. This devotional will expand your capacity to believe for and receive the miraculous.

—ART HEINZ, PhD, SENIOR PASTOR
HOPE HARBOR CHURCH, MURRAY, KY

MANNA & Miracles

A DAILY DEVOTIONAL

MANNA
&
Miracles

A DAILY DEVOTIONAL

JACQUELYN KRUGER

MANNA AND MIRACLES: A DAILY DEVOTIONAL
by Jacquelyn Kruger
Published by Manna and Miracles, LLC
198 Gentle Drive, Almo, KY 42020

Unless otherwise noted, all Scripture quotations are taken from the New Spirit Filled Life Bible, New King James Version, © 2002 by Thomas Nelson, Inc.

Scripture quotations marked KJV are from the King James Version of the Bible.

Scripture quotations marked NIV are taken from the Holy Bible, New International Version®, NIV®. Copyright © 1973, 1978, 1984, 2011 by Biblica, Inc.™ Used by permission of Zondervan. All rights reserved worldwide. www.zondervan.com. The "NIV" and "New International Version" are trademarks registered in the United States Patent and Trademark Office by Biblica, Inc.™

Scripture quotations marked NLT are from the Holy Bible, New Living Translation, copyright © 1996, 2004, 2007. Used by permission of Tyndale House Publishers, Inc., Wheaton, IL 60189. All rights reserved.

Scripture quotations marked TLB are from The Living Bible. Copyright © 1971. Used by permission of Tyndale House Publishers, Inc., Wheaton, IL 60189. All rights reserved.

Scripture quotations marked TPT are from The Passion Translation®. Copyright © 2017 by BroadStreet Publishing® Group, LLC. Used by permission. All rights reserved. ThePassionTranslation.com.

International Standard Book Number: 978-1-7352282-5-9
E-book ISBN: 978-1-7352282-6-6

20 21 22 23 24 — 987654321
Printed in the United States of America

This book is lovingly dedicated

to

Our three wonderful daughters:

Janine Kruger, Jennifer Revell, and JoEllyn
Leimola, who have always been there to
give unconditional love, prayer support,
and practical suggestions and advice.

CONTENTS

ACKNOWLEDGMENTS

THANKS TO MY wonderful husband, who has been my most faithful cheerleader and helper in this project. His prayers, wise advice, and computer skills have been invaluable, and without which this devotional would not have been written.

Thanks also to my sister-in-law, Vicky Bossom for her excellent and knowledgeable content editing skills, and also to Susan Davis for her proofreading and editing skills.

FOREWORD

ONE OF THE most delightful honors a friend can bestow is to ask one to write a foreword to the book the author has spent endless hours planning, preparing, and verifying their presentation to the reader for now and for generations to come.

This is such a book!

Writing a devotional guide for a year day by day following the calendar, leading the reader through chosen scriptures for the day with the author's interpretation being applied in only a one-page presentation, with testimonies illustrating through extraordinary examples of application using the designated scriptures for that particular day, is an amazing feat. Jacqie, as her friends call her, has been a mentor through these past years without her even realizing this fact. She and Jim, her husband, have become dear friends to me and many here in the Commonwealth of Kentucky after moving from Minneapolis, Minnesota. They are ministers in the Assemblies of God denomination and are video school facilitators with Elijah House, which was founded by John and Paula Sandford. Their son Mark has carried on this amazing ministry to pastors and their wives since his parents' passing.

Both Jacqie and Jim are teachers, and since retirement, they are busier than ever, leading prayer initiatives with passion in their home of Murray, Kentucky, and throughout this Commonwealth of Kentucky. They both are adept at ministering to those of other religions the biblical truths that draw people into a converted committed walk of newly found faith. They birthed the Kentucky Prayer Coalition five years ago and now six major ministries leaders (plus many others) pray daily together for the needs of this state and the nation and the nations of this earth.

Her forefathers came to America on ships that were sailing with William Penn and were pioneers in this new nation with a depth of the Word of God dwelling in each as they settled in community in the State of Pennsylvania. These new settlers were sustained by the richness of God's Word in their lives and were able to remain and be strong for Jesus in this New World.

Our author, Jacquelyn Kruger of *Manna and Miracles* has many surprises awaiting all readers, and one that leaped from the pages for me was from March 1, "Be Opened." She shares from one of their many missionary journeys as a couple in 2017. That same example was gloriously reenacted by a father bringing his mute son and after he was prayed for Jacqie told the boy to say, "Hallelujah," and he was loosed to say it again and again as a sign and a wonder in Bangladesh where miracles signs and wonders are so desperately needed.

As I read this, I was reminded how in 1990 Reinhart Bonnke came to Whitley City, Kentucky, and hosted a time of healing at a gathering there. His team was moving those still needing healing to the back for continuing prayer. He was stopped by an interpreter for the deaf right in front of me with a deaf mute who was sixty-eight years old having lived a lifetime this way who shouted aloud, "HALLELUJAH, HALLELUJAH, HALLELUJAH!" What joy she must have felt to hear her voice for the first time shouting a word that is the same in every spoken language.

This devotional book is filled with truth and hope and Father's love from one who is a devoted Christian patriot and will be a blessing to all ages of readers. May this literary devotional volume be given to many and become a classic from our day.

SINCERELY,
MARY JEAN WARLEN
(MAMA BUNNY)
HAPN KENTUCKY
RPN KENTUCKY
REDEMPTIVE GIFT SPECIALISTS FOR HAPN/GAPN

JESUS REVEALED

*"Behold, the virgin shall be with child, and bear a Son and they shall
call His name Immanuel," which is translated, "God with us."*
—Matthew 1:23; read also Matthew 1

Isaiah, the prophet, in Isaiah 7:14, prophesied these
words seven hundred years before Jesus was born. Mary was the
virgin about whom Isaiah prophesied. All came to pass just
as the prophet had spoken, and they named the child Jesus.

Jesus was first revealed in Genesis 3:15 when the Lord spoke to the
serpent who had deceived Eve. "And I will put enmity between you
and the woman, and between your seed and her Seed; He shall bruise
your head, and you shall bruise His heel." This is speaking of Jesus,
who would later crush the head of the enemy. When Adam and Eve
disobeyed God and ate the fruit in the garden, sin was introduced
into the human race.

In Romans 5:19, we read, "For as by one man's disobedience
(Adam), many were made sinners, so also by one Man's obedience,
(Jesus Christ), many will be made righteous." Then in Romans 6:23,
we read, "For the wages of sin is death, but the gift of God is eternal
life through Christ Jesus our Lord." Through these words, we see that
God had a plan for our restoration from the very beginning through
His Son, Jesus.

Julia Ward Howe wrote "The Battle Hymn of the Republic" after a
visit to a Union Army camp in 1862. The 3rd verse of the song alludes
to Genesis 3:15 when she wrote this: "I have read a fiery gospel writ
in burnished rows of steel: 'As ye deal with my contemners (despised
ones), so with you, my grace shall deal; Let the Hero, born of woman,
crush the serpent with His heel, Since God is marching on.'"[1]

Prayer: *Thank You, Lord, that You had a plan to rescue, restore, and
redeem us from the beginning of time. Your truth is marching on! Glory
hallelujah! Come into our lives and hearts today, and have Your way!
Amen!*

January 2

GIVER OF LIFE

When they saw the star, they rejoiced with exceedingly great joy. And when they had come into the house, they saw the young Child with Mary, His mother, and fell down and worshiped Him. And when they had opened their treasure, they presented gifts to Him: gold, frankincense, and myrrh. Then being divinely warned in a dream that they should not return to Herod, they departed for their own country another way.

—MATTHEW 2:10–12; READ ALSO MATTHEW 2

Wise men from the East came to Jerusalem to find the King of the Jews because they had seen His star in the East and had come to worship Him.

After they left, the Lord appeared to Joseph in a dream and told him to escape to Egypt because Herod would seek to kill the young child. This was also prophesied in Hosea 11:1, where it is written, "Out of Egypt, I called My Son."

Then Herod "sent forth and put to death all the male children who were in Bethlehem and in all its districts, from two years old and under, according to the time which he had determined from the wise men" (v. 6). Jeremiah prophesied about this in Jeremiah 31:15: "A voice was heard in Ramah, lamentation and bitter weeping, Rachel weeping for her children, refusing to be comforted for her children because they are no more."

PRAYER: *Lord, help us to be like the wise men who came from far away to seek Jesus! And as they rejoiced when they found Him, let us also rejoice with great joy that we too have found this great treasure: the One who is the Life-Giver! Through faith in Christ Jesus, we support life from its very beginning in the womb. Let us be people of life and not death; and let us elect leaders who promote life and not death. In Jesus' name. Amen.*

THE POWER OF REPENTANCE

*The voice of one crying in the wilderness: "Prepare the way of the
LORD; Make His paths straight."*
— Matthew 3:3; read also Matthew 3

This prophecy quoted from Isaiah 40:3 spoke of John the Baptist.
John was the cousin of Jesus. He was clothed in camel's hair, with
a leather belt around his waist; and his food was locusts and wild
honey. His message was, "Repent, for the kingdom of heaven is at
hand!" (v. 2).

This is a message that is still relevant today! How we need to repent
of our sins! As it says in 2 Chronicles 7:14: "If my people which are
called by My name will humble themselves and pray and seek My
face and turn from their wicked ways, then will I hear from heaven,
and will forgive their sin and heal their land." It was this scripture,
along with others, that was a catalyst for establishing the National
Day of Prayer.

On January 25, 1988, while under President Ronald Reagan's
administration, a joint resolution of the one hundredth US Congress declared the first Thursday of each May to be recognized as
a National Day of Prayer. Prayer is the recipe to bring about the
healing of our land.

Prayer will heal—the divisions, the strife, the murders, the poverty, the broken marriages and homes, the addictions, the sickness,
the worship of false gods, and death. Yes, our prayers and genuine
repentance will make a difference and will heal our land.

Prayer: *Lord, I do with all my heart repent of all my sins. (It must
start with us.) I also repent on behalf of my family, my city, my state,
and my nation. Forgive us and heal our land as You promised. Then
baptize me with Your Holy Spirit and Your fire and use me for Your
glory! We long to hear Your voice speaking over us as You spoke over
Your Son: "This is My beloved son/daughter, in whom I am well pleased"
(Matthew 3:17). Amen.*

EATING THE BREAD OF LIFE

Then Jesus was led up by the Spirit into the wilderness to be tempted by the devil. And when He had fasted forty days and forty nights, afterward He was hungry.
—Matthew 4:1–2; read also Matthew 4

In the first four verses of Matthew 4, we see Satan coming to tempt Jesus after He had fasted forty days and forty nights in the wilderness. First of all, Satan tempted Jesus to command the stones to become bread.

But Jesus answered and said that we (mankind) should not live by bread alone, but that we would live by every word that comes from the mouth of God. This refers not only to physical bread but also to the spiritual bread of revelation. "Open my eyes today, Lord, that I may behold wondrous things from Your law" (Psalm 119:18). "Give us a spirit of wisdom and revelation in the knowledge of You" (Ephesians 1:18).

The devil tempted him to eat bread, but Jesus is the Bread of Life! We eat this bread by reading and meditating on His Word. As we eat this bread, we receive healing and any miracle that we need. This is because the Bible has promises that apply to any need that we may have.

And then, beginning in verse 23, it says: "And Jesus went about all Galilee, teaching in their synagogues, preaching the gospel of the kingdom, and healing all kinds of sickness and all kinds of disease among the people."

Psalm 103:2–3 says, "Bless the Lord O my soul, and forget not all His benefits: Who forgives all your iniquities, Who heals all your diseases." Matthew 8:17 says, "He Himself took our infirmities and bore our sicknesses." This fulfilled the word spoken by Isaiah the prophet (Isaiah 53:4–5).

Prayer: *This is from an old song. "Thank You, Lord, for saving my soul. Thank You, Lord, for making me whole. Thank You, Lord, for giving to me, thy great salvation so rich and free." Thank You, Lord, that "by Your stripes, I was healed" (1 Peter 2:24). In Jesus' name. Amen.*

LET YOUR LIGHT SHINE

You are the light of the world. A city that is set on a hill cannot be hidden. Nor do they light a lamp and put it under a basket, but on a lampstand, and it gives light to all who are in the house. Let your light so shine before men, that they may see your good works and glorify your Father in heaven.
—MATTHEW 5:14; READ ALSO VV. 1–26

Jesus also said, "I am the light of the world. He who follows Me shall not walk in darkness, but have the light of life" (John 8:12).

If we follow Him, we reflect His light everywhere we go. That light cannot be hidden unless we choose to put it under a basket. But if we let His light shine through us, it gives light to everyone around us. Our good works will give glory to God.

Peter Bulkley (1583–1659) was the Puritan leader who founded Concord, MA. In his book, *The Gospel Covenant*, he stated: "We are as a city set upon a hill, in the open view of all the earth... We profess ourselves to be a people in covenant with God..."[2] He also said that if we walk contrary to the covenant, it would bring shame upon us. President Reagan in his farewell address to the nation in 1989, mentioned "the shining city upon a hill." Presidents George H. W. Bush and Harry S. Truman both placed their hands on this scripture as they took the presidential oath in 1989 and 1949, respectively.

We are the light of the world, and our nation is the city that is set on a hill. The Pilgrims who landed in America on November 11, 1620, dedicated this nation for "the glory of God and the advancement of the Christian faith."[3]

PRAYER: *Lord, help us to be shining lights for You. As our forefathers dedicated America for the glory of God and the advancement of the Christian faith, let us follow in their footsteps, taking the light of Christ wherever we go. In Jesus' name. Amen.*

January 6

CHOOSING TO FORGIVE

You have heard that it was said, "You shall love your neighbor and hate your enemy." But I say to you, love your enemies, bless those who curse you, do good to those who hate you, and pray for those who spitefully use you and persecute you, ... Therefore you shall be perfect, just as your Father in heaven is perfect.
—MATTHEW 5:43–44, 48; READ ALSO VV. 27–48

Jesus said we should love our enemies and do good to those who hate us. One amazing example of this is Corrie ten Boom.

Corrie's family helped Jews escape the Nazi holocaust in World War II. It is estimated that they saved over eight hundred people. They hid them in the Beje house in Haarlem, Netherlands. Since her father was a watch maker, and their home was a watch shop, it was a perfect façade for hiding the Jews. On the outside, it looked like a totally normal business. On the inside, there was a hiding place for the Jews.

In February 1944, a Dutch informant told about their activities, and all members of the ten Boom family were arrested. Corrie and her sister Betsie were taken to the Ravensbruck concentration camp.

Betsie died there in December 1944, and Corrie was miraculously released 12 days later. She then began a rehabilitation center for concentration camp survivors. And, in loving her enemies, she also took in those who cooperated with the Germans during the occupation.

One day she spoke at a church in Munich, and the guard who had been so cruel to Betsie at Ravensbruck was there. He came up afterward and told her he had become a Christian, and would she forgive him. She struggled greatly and asked for Jesus' help, but when she took his hand, the love and warmth of God literally flowed through her hand to his. She had truly forgiven him.[4]

PRAYER: *Father, we can't make forgiveness happen, and we can't forgive without Your grace. We choose to forgive from our hearts all who have hurt us. In Jesus' name. Amen.*

PRAYING TO THE FATHER

Our Father in heaven, Hallowed be Your name.
—MATTHEW 6:9; READ ALSO VV. 1–18

Jesus taught His disciples to pray this prayer, which can be expanded upon in the most powerful way to cover all that is needful every day:

Our Father in heaven—Here we realize that we are in a relationship with a loving heavenly Father who is not like our earthly fathers, but one Who is perfect in every way.

Hallowed be Your name. Here we can praise Him and lift up His redemptive names: Jehovah Jireh—provider; Jehovah Nissi—banner of victory; Jehovah Shalom—our peace; Jehovah Shammah—He is present constantly; Jehovah Tsidkenu—our righteousness; Jehovah Rohi—the Lord and Shepherd of the sheep; Jehovah Rophe—our healer; etc.

Your kingdom come. Your will be done on earth as it is in heaven. There is no sickness, poverty, death or relationship problems (divorce) in heaven, so we don't accept these things on earth. We declare His will to be done on earth as it is in heaven.

Give us this day our daily bread. We declare Philippians 4:19 that God will provide for all our needs—spirit, soul, and body. "The Lord is my shepherd; I shall not want" (Psalm 23:1). We read and study the Word of God because it is our daily bread. "Man does not live by bread alone, but by every word that proceeds out of the mouth of God" (Matthew 4:4). Jesus said that He had food to eat of which the disciples did not know (John 4:32). It was the bread of obedience to the will of God and to finish the work God had given Him.

Lead us not into temptation, but deliver us from the evil one. This is a prayer of protection against deception and the thief who comes to "steal, kill, and destroy" (John 10:10).

For thine is the kingdom, and the power, and the glory forever." Amen.

PRAYER: *The Lord's Prayer* (Matthew 6:9–13; Luke 11:2–4).

DON'T WORRY

Therefore I say to you, do not worry about your life, what you will eat or what you will drink; nor about your body, what you will put on. Is not life more than food and the body more than clothing? Look at the birds of the air for they neither sow nor reap nor gather into barns; yet your heavenly Father feeds them. Are you not of more value than they?...But seek first the kingdom of God and His righteousness, and all these things shall be added to you. Therefore do not worry about tomorrow, for tomorrow will worry about its own things. Sufficient for the day is its own trouble.
—MATTHEW 6:25–27, 33–34; READ ALSO VV. 19–34

Jesus here commands us not to worry. When we worry, we are expressing doubt in Him, and this is a sin! Do the birds worry about their food? God takes care of them. Aren't we more valuable than they are? Jesus says that we are, indeed, more valuable.

These verses are supported by Philippians 4:6: "Don't be pulled in different directions or worried about a thing. Be saturated in prayer throughout each day, offering your faith-filled requests before God with overflowing gratitude. Tell him every detail of your life, then God's wonderful peace that transcends human understanding, will make the answers known to you through Jesus Christ" (TPT).

Then Jesus instructs us what we are to do instead of worrying. "Seek first the kingdom of God and His righteousness, and all these things will be added to you."

It's what we spend our time thinking about that affects us. If we focus on our troubles, we will worry, and the troubles will seem to grow bigger and bigger. If we focus on God and how big He is and what we can do to please Him, the problems will grow smaller and smaller in comparison to His greatness. He will add to us everything we need.

PRAYER: *Father in heaven, forgive us for focusing on our problems. Fill us with Your faith and help us to focus on the solution—which is Your provision, Your love, and how great You are! Amen!*

January 9

A NATION OF PRAYER

Ask...seek...knock.
—MATTHEW 7:7–9; READ ALSO MATTHEW 7

We are a nation of prayer. When the first Congress of the United States met on September 7, 1774, it began with prayer. Reverend Jacob Duché, Rector of Christ Church in Philadelphia, prayed this prayer after reading Psalm 35:

> O Lord our Heavenly Father, high and mighty King of kings and Lord of lords, who dost from Thy throne behold all the dwellers on earth and reignest with power supreme and uncontrolled over all the kingdoms, empires and governments; look down in mercy, we beseech Thee, on these our American States, who have fled to Thee from the rod of the oppressor and thrown themselves on Thy gracious protection, desiring to be henceforth dependent only on Thee...
>
> Be Thou present, O God of wisdom, and direct the councils of this honorable assembly; enable them to settle things on the best and surest foundation. That the scene of blood may be speedily closed; that order, harmony, and peace may be effectually restored, and truth and justice, religion and piety, prevail and flourish amongst the people. Preserve the health of their bodies and vigor of their minds; shower down on them and the millions they here represent, such temporal blessings as Thou seest expedient for them in this world and crown them with everlasting glory in the world to come. All this we ask in the name and through the merits of Jesus Christ, Thy Son, and our Savior. Amen.[5]

God answered this prayer for America! Surely God showed them His "gracious protection." He has a destiny for America.

PRAYER: *Today Lord, we thank You for the powerful men of God who prayed and sacrificed everything so that we could have a free nation. Help us to keep it free by putting You first. "Seek first the kingdom of God and His righteousness, and all these things will be added to you" (Matthew 6:33). Amen.*

LORD MAKE ME WHOLE

When evening had come, they brought to Him many who were demon-possessed. And He cast out the spirits with a word, and healed all who were sick, that it might be fulfilled which was spoken by Isaiah the prophet, saying: "He Himself took our infirmities and bore our sicknesses."
—MATTHEW 8:16–17; READ ALSO VV. 1–17

These verses were a fulfillment of the Isaiah 53:4 prophecy: "Surely He has borne our griefs and carried our sorrows."

Notice that Jesus healed all who were sick; He didn't say to some that it was not His will to heal them. No, as it says in verse 2 when the leper came and said, "Lord, if You are willing, You can make me clean," He said, "I am willing; be cleansed." Immediately his leprosy was cleansed. Jesus is always willing.

In Matthew 12:15, we are told that "great multitudes followed Him and He healed them all." Here in Matthew 8:14–15, we see His love for the individual. Peter's mother-in-law was lying sick with a fever. How did Jesus respond to this? He touched her hand and the fever left her! Then she arose and served them.

God revealed Himself to the people of Israel as a healer God, Jehovah Rapha. He promised to keep disease from them if they would obey His Word. "…If you diligently heed the voice of the Lord your God and do what is right in His sight, give ear to His commandments and keep all His statutes, I will put none of the diseases on you which I have brought on the Egyptians. For I am the Lord who heals you" (Exodus 15:26).

The words to a wonderful song that we used to sing say this: "He touched me, oh, He touched me. And oh, the joy that floods my soul. Something happened and now I know, He touched me and made me whole." We saw a pastor's wife in northeast India rise up and walk and be completely made whole as we were singing this song over her.

PRAYER: *Holy Spirit come. According to Your word, I have been made whole because You are the Lord who heals me. You took my infirmities and bore my sicknesses so I wouldn't have to. I give You praise and thanks for touching me and making me whole! Amen!*

January 11

FOLLOWING CHRIST

... Then a certain scribe came and said to Him, "Teacher, I will follow You wherever You go." And Jesus said to him, "Foxes have holes and birds of the air have nests but the Son of Man has nowhere to lay His head." Then another of His disciples said to Him, "Lord, let me first go and bury my father." But Jesus said to him, "Follow Me and let the dead bury their own dead."
—MATTHEW 8:19–22; READ ALSO VV. 18–34

One person who heard Jesus say, "Follow me," was Lillian Trasher, missionary to Asyut, Egypt, as well as the founder of the first orphanage in Egypt.

She was engaged to marry a minister when she heard a missionary from India speak. Because of that message, she knew that the Lord had called her to Africa. Didn't Jesus say that if you love your family more than Me, you are not worthy of Me? When she read Acts 7:34 where it says: "I have surely seen the oppression of My people who are in Egypt..." she knew she must go. She broke the engagement ten days before the wedding because her fiancé did not share her call. She left for Egypt with her sister, despite the protest of her parents. When she and her sister arrived, they were given a malnourished baby girl whose mom had just died. She soon began an orphanage, which eventually took care of over eight thousand orphans and forgotten people from 1911 to 1961. She went without furlough when the Nazis ruled during World War II.

One of her adventures was taking all one hundred orphans to hide in a brick kiln during the war of Egyptian independence. But when they got there, two of the children were missing! Having the children pray for her protection, she went out in the midst of the fighting, hid in a ditch while soldiers were after her, found the children, and returned to the brick kiln safely.[6]

PRAYER: *Father in heaven, we are so challenged to read of saints like Lillian Trasher who gave all to serve You. We also want to give our lives for the One who gave His life for us! Amen!*

WORSHIPPING OUR BRIDEGROOM KING

And Jesus said to them, "Can the friends of the bridegroom mourn as long as the bridegroom is with them?"
—MATTHEW 9:15; READ ALSO VV. 1–17

The End-Time prayer movement will have a relational focus, which will be reflected in our singing of the wonders of God's love for us and our response of love for Him. We will begin to have an understanding of Jesus as our Bridegroom King and of the body of Christ as His cherished bride. Before the Lord returns, the church will see herself as a bride crying out to her Bridegroom King to come to her. We will begin to relate to Jesus as "friends of the Bridegroom."

"As the bride of Christ, we are positioned to experience God's heart—His desire for us. The Bridegroom message is focused on Jesus's emotions for us, His beauty, and His commitment to share His heart, home, throne, secrets, and beauty with us."[7]

Isaiah connected the revelation of Jesus as the Bridegroom with the end-time prayer movement that will continue night and day until the Lord returns to make Jerusalem a praise in the earth (Isaiah 62:4–7).

The Bridegroom was taken away physically for two thousand years, but He is returning for His church. The Spirit and the bride (church) are saying "Come Lord Jesus!" (Revelation 22:20).

The "friends of the bridegroom are Shulamites—lovers of God. In the Song of Solomon, we read, "Draw me into your heart. We will run away together into the king's cloud-filled chamber" (Song of Solomon 1:4, TPT). The Hebrew text literally means "the king's chamber inside of a chamber." This points us to the Holy of Holies inside the temple chamber.[8]

PRAYER: *Jesus, in these last days, may we come to know and worship You as our Bridegroom King. Amen.*

LABORERS IN GOD'S VINEYARD

Then Jesus went about all the cities and villages, teaching in their syna-gogues, preaching the gospel of the kingdom, and healing every sickness and every disease among the people. But when He saw the multitudes, He was moved with compassion for them, because they were weary and scattered, like sheep having no shepherd. Then He said to His disciples, "The harvest truly is plentiful, but the laborers are few. Therefore pray the Lord of the harvest to send out laborers into His harvest."
—MATTHEW 9:35–38; READ ALSO VV. 18–38

As we look at our Savior and how He went about evangelizing the lost, we notice several things:

1. He went about all the cities and villages, teaching, preaching, and healing every sickness and every disease among the people.
2. He was moved with compassion for the people.
3. He told us to pray to the Lord of the harvest to send out laborers into His harvest.

Of course, when we pray that He'll send out laborers, who is He going to send? He will send US! He will also use us to pray for the lost to come to Him.

Do you have lost loved ones? Do you have friends and neighbors that do not know Christ? Here are some Scriptures to pray for these people:

1. Acts 26:18: "Pray that God will turn them from darkness to light and from the power of Satan to God that they would receive forgiveness of sins…"
2. Colossians 4:3: "God would open to us a door for the word, to speak the mystery of Christ…"
3. 2 Thessalonians 3:1: "Pray for us, that the word of the Lord may spread rapidly and its glory be recognized everywhere."
4. 2 Corinthians 4:4: "Open the eyes of those that the god of this age has blinded…"

PRAYER: *Lord, mobilize Your army to pray for laborers, and follow the Great Commission and "Go!" Amen!*

SPREADING THE GOSPEL

The kingdom of heaven is at hand. Heal the sick, cleanse the lepers,
raise the dead, cast out demons. Freely you have received, freely give.
—MATTHEW 10:7–8; READ ALSO VV. 1–20

When Jesus sent the disciples out, He told them what to preach and what to do. Are we preaching and doing this today?

Then in verses 11–16, He told them to go to the cities and towns, ask who in it is worthy, and stay there till they were to leave. He said that whoever would not receive them or hear their words, to shake off the dust from their feet, and depart; that it would be more tolerable for the land of Sodom and Gomorrah in the day of judgment than for that city!

In the early American frontier, we had amazing pioneers that followed these words. Francis Asbury, a Methodist circuit rider, traveled more than three thousand miles on horseback and preached more than sixteen thousand sermons from 1771 to 1816 to spread the Gospel. He and other circuit riders braved the cold weather and lack of roads and dangers of Indian attacks to bring the Gospel to the pioneers. The Methodists grew in number from only three hundred members and four ministers to over two thousand members and two thousand ministers in that span of time.[9]

At the same time, the Baptists sent out their "farmer preachers." With an emphasis on the need for personal conversion and salvation from sin through faith in Jesus Christ, these ministers spread the Gospel far and wide.[10]

It was in the early 1900s at the Azusa Street revival in California that people began receiving the baptism of the Holy Spirit and the healings, miracles, signs, and wonders began. And they continue today as Jesus taught in Matthew 10!

PRAYER: *Father, we pray in Jesus' name that we could again hear Your words, obey Your commands, and do the works You taught Your early disciples to do. Amen.*

PRAYING FOR THE PERSECUTED

Now brother will deliver up brother to death, and a father his child; and children will rise up against parents and cause them to be put to death. And you will be hated by all for My name's sake. But he who endures to the end will be saved.
—MATTHEW 10:21–23; READ ALSO VV. 21–42

In the book "10 Amazing Muslims" by Faisal Malick, the story was told of Steven Masood, a Muslim from northwest Pakistan.[11] Someone gave him a New Testament at age thirteen, which he read. His father and his friends almost beat the man to death who had given the Scriptures to his son, a Muslim.

This led Steven to a search for truth. At eighteen, he became a Sunni Muslim. But in all his studies, he found it was impossible to know if he was going to hell or not. Even Muhammad said to his followers, "None of you will enter paradise through his good works. Not even me, unless Allah covers me with his grace and mercy." The Koran could not answer his question.

He eventually became a Christian, and three years later was brought to his parents who planned an "honor killing." His father pulled out a sword to kill him, but the donkey he was on kicked and took off running, and he was spared.

Later at the university, he was kidnapped for being a Christian and was buried alive. But God sent a monsoon, and the water washed him up out of the grave. God provided a tree for him to grab hold of and be rescued. His amazing story of multiple rescues from death shows God's love and mercy to a faithful witness!

PRAYER: *Lord, let us be willing to take up our cross and follow You! Let us be like Job who said, "Though he slay me yet will I trust Him." We pray for the persecuted church. We pray that You will strengthen them. We pray that You provide for them and their families. We pray You will miraculously make a way of escape for them as You did for Steven. We pray for them to be filled with Your Spirit and be courageous! Amen!*

THE GREATEST, MOST POWERFUL PLEA

Assuredly, I say to you, among those born of women there has not risen one greater than John the Baptist; but he who is least in the kingdom of heaven is greater than he. And from the days of John the Baptist until now, the kingdom of heaven suffers violence, and the violent take it by force.
—MATTHEW 11:11–12; READ ALSO MATTHEW 11

According to Wesley Duewel, in his book *Mighty Prevailing Prayer*, Charles Spurgeon said, "It is the habit of faith, when she is praying, to use pleas"[12]...

Perhaps the greatest, most powerful, most answerable plea of all is the blood of Jesus. No more prevailing argument can we bring before God than the sufferings, blood, and death of His Son. We have no merit of our own. Bring before the Father the wounds of Jesus. Remind the Father of the agony of Gethsemane. Recall to the Father the strong cries of the Son of God as He prevailed for our world and for our salvation. Remind the Father of earth's darkest hour on Calvary, as the Son triumphed alone for you and me. Shout to Heaven again Christ's triumphant cry, 'It is finished!' Pray until you have the assurance of God's will. Then plead the blood of Jesus. The name of Jesus and the blood of Jesus—glory in them, stake your all on them and use them to the glory of God and the routing of Satan. Let there be a generation of people arise who are consumed with this passion, with this vision of the blood of Jesus.[13]

Revelation 12:11 says: "They overcame him by the blood of the Lamb and the word of their testimony and they loved not their lives unto death."

PRAYER: *Teach us the power of the Blood and name of Jesus in overcoming Satan. You made a way for us to be victorious. You always lead us in a triumphal procession and through us diffuse the fragrance of His knowledge in every place. Amen.*

January 17

A HOUSE UNITED WILL STAND

No wonder he can cast out demons. He gets his power from Satan,
the prince of demons.
　　　　—MATTHEW 12:24, NLT; READ ALSO VV. 1–32

Jesus was accused of getting His power from Satan after He had healed a demon-possessed man who was blind and mute.

Jesus knew their thoughts and replied, "Any kingdom at war with itself is doomed. A city or home divided against itself is doomed (cannot stand.) And if Satan is casting out Satan, he is fighting against himself. His own kingdom will not survive" (v. 25, NLT). Jesus said that His casting out demons showed the supremacy of the Kingdom of God over the kingdom of Satan.

In 1858 Abraham Lincoln delivered his "a house divided against itself cannot stand" speech in the Lincoln-Douglas debates. He said the Dred Scott decision in 1857 had opened the door to slavery in the north as well as all the US territories. This decision said Dred Scott was not free and was not a citizen. Lincoln said, "I believe this government cannot endure permanently half slave and half free. I do not expect the Union to be dissolved—I do not expect the house to fall—but I do expect it will cease to be divided. It will become all one thing or all the other." His strong anti-slavery stand got him nominated and then elected as president in 1860.[14] (The Dred Scott decision was later reversed by the Supreme Court.)

God has had a plan for America to be the home of the "free and the brave." Abraham Lincoln also said in the Gettysburg address: "Fourscore and seven years ago, our fathers brought forth on this continent a new nation, conceived in liberty and dedicated to the proposition that all men are created equal…that we here highly resolve that these dead shall not have died in vain, that this nation under God shall have a new birth of freedom, and that government of the people, by the people, for the people shall not perish from the earth."

PRAYER: *Lord, we pray that our marriages, our homes, our states, and our nation will be a "house united" in love and truth and justice and not be a "house divided" against itself. Amen.*

January 18

THE POWER OF THE TONGUE

Either make the tree good, and its fruit good, or else make the tree bad and its fruit bad; for a tree is known by its fruit. Brood of vipers! How can you, being evil, speak good things? For out of the abundance of the heart the mouth speaks. A good man out of the good treasure of his heart brings forth good things, and an evil man out of the evil treasure brings forth evil things. But I say to you that for every idle word men may speak, they will give account of it in the Day of Judgment. For by your words you will be justified, and by your words you will be condemned.

—MATTHEW 12:33–37; READ ALSO VV. 33–50

It will only take a minute before you know what a person has been putting into his heart because what he has been putting into his heart will come out his mouth. If he has been filling his heart with the Word of God, that wisdom will come out of his mouth. If he has been meditating on worry, hate, fear, or reading books or watching movies that are full of lies and cursing, these are the things that will come out of his mouth since it has been deposited into his heart…

When Dr. Kevin Zadai was lying on a hospital bed going through a dental procedure, he died and was taken to heaven. During this time, he met Jesus and was talking to Him. One of the most powerful things he heard was when Jesus stepped very close to him and said, "You know I meant what I said when I said you would give an account of every idle word you said on the day of judgment."[15]

PRAYER: *Father, You said in Your word that the power of life and death is in the tongue (Proverbs 18:21). You said it defiles the whole body and sets on fire the course of nature; and it is set on fire by hell (James 3:7). We ask for forgiveness for every idle word we have spoken and declare it will produce no fruit. Give us a new awareness of the power of the words we speak. In Jesus' name. Amen.*

January 19

GOOD SOIL

Behold, a sower went out to sow.
—MATTHEW 13:3; READ ALSO VV. 1–30

In the explanation of the parable of the sower, Jesus said that when anyone hears the word of the kingdom of God and does not understand it, then the wicked one comes and snatches away what was sown in his heart. This is the word sown by the wayside. The seed sown on the stony ground is he who hears the word and receives it joyfully, but when trouble or persecution arises, the person stumbles. The one who receives the seed among the thorns hears the word, but it is choked out because of the cares of this world and the deceitfulness of riches. But he who receives seed on the good ground is he who hears the word, truly accepts God's message and produces a huge harvest—thirty, sixty, or even a hundred times as much as had been planted.

The four types of soil represent different responses to God's message. People respond differently because they are in different states of readiness. Some are hardened, others are shallow, many are contaminated by distracting worries, and some are receptive. What kind of soil are you? What kind of soil do you want to be? Do you want to produce thirty, sixty, or even a hundred times as much as has been planted? If so, you will be able to do *"exceedingly abundantly above all that we ask or think according to the power that works within us, to Him be glory in the church by Christ Jesus to all generations, forever and ever. Amen"* (Ephesians 3:20–21).

PRAYER: *Father in heaven, prepare the soil of my heart to receive Your word and produce a huge harvest for You—thirty, sixty, or even a hundred times as much as has been planted. Give me a soft heart to hear Your voice and a desire to be obedient immediately. "Create in me a clean heart, O God, and renew a right spirit within me. Cast me not away from your presence and take not thy Holy Spirit from me. Restore unto me the joy of thy salvation and uphold me with thy free spirit"* (Psalm 51:10–12, KJV). Amen.

January 20

SOWING GOOD SEED

He who sows the good seed is the Son of Man. The field is the world, the good seeds are the sons of the kingdom, but the tares are the sons of the wicked one. The enemy who sowed them is the devil, the harvest is the end of the age, and the reapers are the angels. Therefore as the tares are gathered and burned in the fire, so it will be at the end of this age. The Son of Man will send out His angels, and they will gather out of His kingdom all things that offend, and those who practice lawlessness, and will cast them into the furnace of fire. There will be wailing and gnashing of teeth. Then the righteous will shine forth as the sun in the kingdom of their Father. He who has ears to hear, let him hear!
—Matthew 13:36–42; read also vv. 31–58

In this chapter, we hear Jesus tell the parable about the wheat and the tares. There was a man who sowed good seed in his field, but his enemy came and sowed tares.

Here we have a simple explanation of who sows the good seed (Jesus) and who sows the tares (false grain or weeds). The tares are sown by the devil and his children. Yes, there are the children of God and the children of the devil. Jesus told the religious leaders in John 8:44: *"You are of your father the devil, and the desires of your father you want to do."*

Jesus goes on to say there will be a harvest at the end of the age. He will send out His angels, and they will throw those who practice lawlessness into the eternal fire, but the righteous will shine forth as the sun.

There is a way to become children of God, and that is to give your heart to Jesus and ask Him to come in and be the Lord of your life. The Bible is very clear that this is a conscious decision we make and does not happen automatically. As Corrie ten Boom is often quoted as saying, "If you are a mouse in the cookie jar, it does not automatically make you a cookie!"

PRAYER: *We say what the Christmas hymn says, "Oh come to my heart Lord Jesus. There is room in my heart for You!" Let me be a son/daughter of the kingdom planting good seed! In Jesus' name. Amen!*

MIRACULOUS PROVISION

*Then He commanded the multitudes to sit down on the grass. And
He took the five loaves and the two fish, and looking up to heaven,
He blessed and broke and gave the loaves to the disciples; and the
disciples gave to the multitudes.*
—MATTHEW 14:19–21; READ ALSO VV. 1–21

The multitudes were following Jesus. He had compassion on them
and healed their sick. When it was evening, the disciples said to send
the multitude away so they could go to the villages and buy food. But
Jesus said, "*They do not need to go away. You give them something to eat*"
(v. 16). But they said that they only had five loaves and two fish. After
Jesus prayed and gave thanks, the food was multiplied. When they
took up the left-over fragments, they filled twelve baskets full. There
were about five thousand men, plus women and children.

God is able to produce and multiply anything we need. Marilyn
Hickey, an American Bible teacher in her late 80's, tells of needing
thirty thousand dollars for a trip to Pakistan. She was in a hotel in
Indonesia waiting for a ride to the airport when a gentleman she did
not know came up to her and asked her if she had need of money! She
said, "Yes, thirty thousand dollars." He told her he had it and gave it
to her! She arrived in Pakistan with the money she needed. God is a
miracle working God! [16]

Jerry Savelle tells another story of miraculous provision. As he was
driving home late one night with his wife and two small children, an
animal ran into the car and tore a hole in the gas tank. The gas ran
out, and they were stranded. In the middle of the night, a man came
by, picked them up, towed the car to a nearby gas station. There he
fixed the gas tank and filled it with gas. When Jerry stopped through
that little town a little later to thank the man, he was told that no
one had been in that station for years and years. God miraculously
supplied!

PRAYER: *Father in heaven, I have need of _____. If You can
multiply the two fish and five loaves, You can meet my need according to
Your riches in glory by Christ Jesus. Amen.*

January 22

NOTHING IS TOO HARD FOR GOD

Now in the fourth watch of the night Jesus went to them, walking on the sea. And when the disciples saw Him walking on the sea, they were troubled, saying, "It is a ghost!" And they cried out for fear. But immediately Jesus spoke to them, saying, "Be of good cheer! It is I; do not be afraid."
—Matthew 14:25–27

So He said, "Come." And when Peter had come down out of the boat, he walked on the water to go to Jesus. But when he saw that the wind was boisterous, he was afraid; and beginning to sink, he cried out, saying "Lord, save me!" And immediately Jesus stretched out His hand and caught him and said to him, "O you of little faith, why did you doubt?" And when they got into the boat, the wind ceased.
—Matthew 14:29–32; read also vv. 22–36

Here we have a demonstration of Jesus' love, mercy, and power over nature. First, we see Jesus Himself walking on water! Then we see Peter walking on water until he took his eyes off of Jesus and became afraid. After this, we see Jesus grabbing Peter by the hand, pulling him out of the water, and bringing him into the boat. It was after they got into the boat that the wind ceased.

Our Lord had many miracles with water in the Old Testament as well. Remember how He opened the Red Sea as the Israelites were leaving Egypt. *"Then Moses stretched out his hand over the sea; and the Lord caused the sea to go back by a strong east wind all that night, and made the sea into dry land, and the waters were divided. So the children of Israel went into the midst of the sea on dry ground, and the waters were a wall to them on their right hand and on their left"* (Exodus 14:21–22).

From just these two examples, we can see that absolutely nothing is *too hard* for the Lord. He is Lord over all circumstances.

Prayer: *Father in Heaven, we bring our concern before You right now that in man's eyes seems to be impossible. But if You can create the seas, divide the Red Sea, and walk on water, You can do a miracle in this situation. We give You praise in advance for the miracle You are doing! We consider it done! Amen!*

FILLING YOUR HEART WITH GOOD THINGS

Jesus said, "Hear and understand: Not what goes into the mouth defiles a man; but what comes out of the mouth, this defiles a man."
—MATTHEW 15:10

Do you not yet understand that whatever enters the mouth goes into the stomach and is eliminated? But those things which proceed out of the mouth come from the heart, and they defile a man. For out of the heart proceed evil thoughts, murders, adulteries, fornications, thefts, false witness, blasphemies. These are the things which defile a man, but to eat with unwashed hands does not defile a man.
—MATTHEW 15:16–20; READ ALSO VV. 1–15

For out of the abundance of the heart, the mouth speaks.
—MATTHEW 12:34

Whatever we are reading, watching, or listening to is what we are putting into our hearts. This is what is influencing us, and we will talk about these things. Whoever we spend time with also will affect our speech.

It also says in Joshua 1:8: "This book of the law shall not depart from your mouth, but you shall meditate in it day and night, that you may observe to do according to all that is written in it. For then you will make your way prosperous, and then you will have good success." This then is the secret to success and prosperity. This is the antidote for the evil thoughts not being in our hearts. Start memorizing the Bible.

PRAYER: *Father in heaven, I come to You in Jesus' name and thank You that You have given a solution to the problem of putting the wrong thing in our hearts. Thank You for good Bible teachers and Christian music that abounds on the internet. Thank You for the freedom to even have a Bible! Help me to take advantage of all that You have provided for me! Give me wisdom as to how to fill my heart with the good things, and to say "No" to evil and worthless things. Amen.*

THE CHILDREN'S BREAD

Lord, help me!
—MATTHEW 15:25; READ ALSO VV. 21–39

In the region of Tyre and Sidon, a Gentile woman came to Jesus crying out to Him to heal her daughter who was severely demon possessed. He said that He was only sent to the lost sheep of the house of Israel and that it was not right to take the children's bread and throw it to the little dogs. She could have been offended, but instead, she said, *"Yes, Lord, yet even the little dogs eat the crumbs which fall from their masters' table"* (v. 27). Then Jesus commended her on her faith and healed her daughter. This shows that healing is "the children's bread."

Jesus also provides bread to eat! After this story, we see again Jesus feeding four thousand with seven loaves and a few little fishes.

George Mueller was a man of great faith. By May 1870, he was caring for 1,722 children within five homes in England. Mueller never asked for financial support, nor did he go into debt, even though the five homes cost more than one hundred thousand pounds to purchase.

Many times, he received unsolicited food donations only hours before they were needed to feed the children, further strengthening his faith in God. Mueller was in constant prayer that God touch the hearts of donors to make provisions for the orphans. On one well-documented occasion, thanks was given for breakfast when all the children were sitting at the table, even though there was nothing to eat in the house. As they finished praying, the baker knocked on the door with sufficient fresh bread to feed everyone, and the milk man gave them plenty of fresh milk because his cart broke down in front of the orphanage.[17]

PRAYER: *Praise to You, O Lord, for You are a God who answers prayer! You supply every need. "Oh, fear the LORD, you His saints! There is no want to those who fear Him. The young lions lack and suffer hunger; but those who seek the LORD shall not lack any good thing"* (Psalm 34:9–10). *Amen.*

January 25

AUTHORITY IN CHRIST

When Jesus asked the disciples, "Who do you say I am?" Simon Peter answered and said, "You are the Christ, the Son of the living God."
—MATTHEW 16:15–16; READ ALSO MATTHEW 16

The Passion Translation gives Jesus' response like this: "I give you the name Peter, a stone. And this truth of who I am will be the bedrock foundation on which I will build my church—my legislative assembly, and the power of death will not be able to overpower it! I will give you the keys of heaven's kingdom realm to forbid on earth that which is forbidden in heaven, and to release on earth that which is released in heaven" (v. 18–19).

This passage is the great passage that tells us of our authority in Christ. Who is really in charge—God or the devil? Who has the authority, and who has the power? Where God and Satan are concerned, the issue is not power. God is all powerful. Satan was kicked out of heaven in a flash of God's power. It is a question of authority.

Dutch Sheets in his book, *Authority in Prayer*, points out that if Jesus stripped Satan of his power at the cross, then we no longer need to be concerned about him—he can no longer affect or control us. We can ignore him. "If on the other hand Jesus dealt with Satan's authority—the right to use his power or abilities—then we would need to deal with him as a usurper, a rebel, a thief that has no *right* to steal, kill, or destroy, but *will* if not stopped." [18]

Luke 10:19 says, *"Behold I have given you authority to tread upon serpents and scorpions, and over all the power of the enemy, and nothing shall injure you."* He says in Matthew 16:19 that we have authority to "bind" the forces of hell. I bound the spirit of death when my husband had his heart attack and released life and health. God heard and answered!

PRAYER: *Lord, teach us the authority we have in Your Name and give us revelation of how to bind and loose to see Your kingdom come on earth. In Your Name. Amen.*

January 26

PRAYER AND FASTING

However, this kind does not go out except by prayer and fasting.
—Matthew 17:21; read also Matthew 17

Here we see a man who came to Jesus asking for mercy for his son who was an epileptic and often fell into the fire or into the water. Jesus' disciples had been unable to cure him.

> Jesus answered and said, "O faithless and perverse generation, how long shall I be with you? How long shall I bear with you? Bring him here to Me." Jesus rebuked the demon and it came out of him and the child was cured from that very hour.
>
> —Matthew 17:17–18

Then the disciples wondered why they could not cast it out. Jesus said it was because of their unbelief. He said if they had faith as a grain of mustard seed, nothing would be impossible for them. But some demons only leave when you are fasting.

What does it mean to fast? Fasting is a deliberate act. It means to turn from food or other personal appetites so that we might focus our attention on God. It is abstaining from food for spiritual purposes. Fasting is a sacrifice. Sacrifice releases power for a display of God's blessing.

The purpose of fasting is to discipline the body and quiet the soul so that one can hear from God. Although the Scriptures show us that prayer and fasting are linked together, fasting doesn't buy us anything from God; rather, it aligns us with His purposes and will.[19]

Fasting was part of early American revival movements. John Wesley would not ordain a man to ministry unless he practiced fasting two days a week. Jonathan Edwards fasted before he preached his famous sermon: "Sinners in the Hands of An Angry God." In the mid-1800s, Christians fasted in order to attend lunch-hour prayer meetings. Charles Finney would retreat and fast to regain the Spirit's anointing.

Prayer: *Lord, help us to seek You and obey like the early revivalists in the area of fasting, so we can see the same results. Amen.*

PRAYING TOGETHER

Again I say to you that if two of you agree on earth concerning any-
thing that they ask, it will be done for them by My Father in heaven.
For where two or three are gathered together in My name, I am there
in the midst of them.
—MATTHEW 18:19–20; READ ALSO VV. 1–20

We have a powerful secret to answered prayer in these verses! I personally have stood on these verses alone and seen hundreds if not
thousands of answers to prayer. We have seen prodigals return to
Christ, wives and husbands reunited, and the sick with incurable diseases healed. We have seen the smallest prayer answered to locate
the lost book before the bus came. We have also witnessed the blind
seeing, the lame walking, and the mute speaking in answer to prayer.

What an unspeakable privilege united prayer is and what a power
it might be:

1. If the believing husband and wife knew that they were joined
    together in the name of Jesus to experience His presence and
    power in united prayer.

2. If friends believed what mighty help two or three praying
    together could give each other.

3. If in every prayer meeting, the coming together in His name,
    faith in His presence, and the expectation of the answer were
    of foremost importance.

4. If in every church, united, effective prayer were regarded as one
    of the chief purposes for which they are banded together and
    the highest exercise of their power as a church.[20]

PRAYER: *We agree in prayer right now according to Matthew 18 for*
the homes and marriages of all who are reading this devotional entry.
We agree for peace and protection for families, churches, our state and
nation. We agree for a great outpouring of Your Spirit and this 3rd
Great Awakening to come to our lives, our families, our churches, and
our nation. In Jesus' name. Amen.

January 28

FORGIVE AND BE FORGIVEN

Then Peter came to Him and said, "Lord, how often shall my brother sin against me, and I forgive him? Up to seven times?" Jesus said to him, "I do not say to you, up to seven times, but up to seventy times seven."
—MATTHEW 18:21–22; READ ALSO vv. 21–35

Jesus went on with a parable. There was a certain king who wanted to settle accounts with his servants. One of his servants owed him ten thousand talents. He could not pay, so the king commanded that he be sold with his wife and children and all that he had, and that payment be made. When the servant fell down before him and asked that he be patient, and that he would pay all, the master had mercy on him and forgave him his debt.

But then that servant went out and found a fellow servant who owed him a hundred denarii. He took him by throat and demanded payment. When his fellow servant couldn't pay, he would not have mercy on him, but demanded that he be thrown into prison until he could pay all.

When the master heard about this, he called his servant in and said how wicked he was, because his debt had been canceled, but that he had had no compassion on his fellow servant and demanded that he pay all. The master delivered him to the torturers until he should pay all that was due to him.

Jesus said, "So My heavenly Father also will do to you if each of you, from his heart, does not forgive his brother his trespasses" (v. 35).

This parable shows the seriousness of unforgiveness. If we do not forgive, we will not be forgiven.

PRAYER: *Father in heaven, as an act of my will, I do forgive
_____ for what they have done to me. (Be specific.) They owe me nothing. I give up my right to be the judge and jury and turn that over to You. Forgive me also for the part that I had in this situation. I release it to You! Bless them now in every way! In Jesus' name. Amen.*

THE JOY OF BEING WHO GOD MADE YOU

And He answered and said to them, "Have you not read that He
who made them at the beginning made them male and female," and
said, "For this reason a man shall leave his father and mother and be
joined to his wife, and the two shall become one flesh?"
—MATTHEW 19:4–5

The Pharisees came to Jesus and asked Him if it were lawful for a man to divorce his wife for just any reason. The answer He gave above, also addresses many difficult questions which people in today's society are asking.

1. In the beginning, God created the heavens and the earth (Genesis 1:1). He created the heavens and the earth and everything in it in six days. He is God. He can do that. There is no other mention of a length of time in creation. No mention of apes gradually becoming people. Everything reproduces after its kind.

2. On the sixth day, He created male and female. In Psalm 139, the Bible says, "*My frame was not hidden from You, when I was made in secret,… Your eyes saw my substance, being yet unformed. And in Your book they all were written, the days fashioned for me, when as yet there were none of them.*" He created two genders and told them to go and multiply and fill and subdue the earth. He had a plan from the beginning of time for each one of us.

Tony Perkins shares about how there is a growing concern over a radical ideology sweeping through our educational institutions. The LGBT movement is actively promoting dangerous transgender policies in our schools that attack the biblical view on sexual morality and gender identity.[21] There is great joy in fulfilling who God created you to be and great confusion when you don't!

PRAYER: *May the truth of Your word be shouted from the housetops to save this wicked and perverse generation. May we always base our lives on the truth of Your word! Amen!*

GOD'S GRACE AND GENEROSITY

So the last will be first, and the first last...
—MATTHEW 20:16; READ ALSO VV. 1–16

This is a parable of the vineyard workers, and it goes like this: an owner of an estate went out early one morning to hire workers for his vineyard. He agreed to pay the normal daily wage and sent them out to work.

At 9:00 a.m., he was passing through the marketplace and saw some people standing around doing nothing. So, he hired them and told them he would pay them what was right at the end of the day. He did the same thing around noon and 3:00 p.m. and 5:00 p.m.

In the evening, he told the foreman to call the workers in and pay them, beginning with the last workers first. He ended up paying the ones who only worked one hour the same as the ones who worked the whole day. The people who worked the whole day thought that was unfair.

But the owner said, *"I haven't been unfair! Didn't you agree to work all day for the usual wage? Take it and go. I wanted to pay this last worker the same as you...Should you be angry because I am kind?"* (v. 13–15, NLT).

> Now you can understand what I meant when I said that the first will end up last and the last will end up being first. Everyone is invited, but few are the chosen.
>
> —MATTHEW 20:16, TPT

This parable is not about rewards but about salvation. It is a strong teaching about grace, God's generosity. We shouldn't begrudge those who turn to God in the last moments of life, because, in reality, no one deserves eternal life. The criminal who repented as he was dying will be there, along with people who have believed and served God for many years. Will we resent God's gracious acceptance of the despised, the outcast, and the sinners who have turned to him for forgiveness?

PRAYER: *Lord, we are so **thankful** for Your great mercy. That person that turns to You in the last moments just may be our child, our spouse, our parent, or our friend. We are thankful that **anyone** who chooses You will be saved. Amen.*

THE WAY OF THE HUMBLE

But Jesus called them to Himself and said, "You know that the rulers of the Gentiles lord it over them, and those who are great exercise authority over them. Yet it shall not be so among you; but whoever desires to become great among you, let him be your servant. And whoever desires to be first among you, let him be your slave—just as the Son of Man did not come to be served, but to serve, and to give His life a ransom for many."
—MATTHEW 20:25–28; READ ALSO VV. 17–34

Jesus demonstrated humility. Meditate on these teachings about humility from Jesus' words:[22]

1. "Blessed are the poor in spirit for theirs is the kingdom of heaven…Blessed are the meek [humble], for they shall inherit the earth" (Matthew 5:3–5).
2. "Learn from Me, for I am gentle [meek, humble] and lowly in heart, and you will find rest for your souls" (Matthew 11:29).
3. "Whoever humbles himself as this little child is the greatest in the kingdom of heaven" (Matthew 18:4).
4. "Whoever desires to become great among you, let him be your servant. And whoever desires to be first among you, let him be your slave" (Matthew 20:26–27).
5. "He who is greatest among you shall be your servant" (Matthew 23:11).
6. "For whoever exalts himself will be humbled, and he who humbles himself will be exalted" (Luke 14:11).

PRAYER: *Lord, Your WORD says, "He guides the humble in what is right and teaches them His Way" (Psalm 25:9, NIV). Teach us first to have humility before You, and then we will have humility in personal relationships. We want You to teach us Your ways and guide us in what is right. Above all, we want to be like You in everything. Amen.*

LORD OF PURITY, PRAISE, AND POWER

Hosanna to the Son of David! Blessed is he who comes in the name of the Lord! Hosanna in the highest!
—MATTHEW 21:9; READ ALSO VV. 1–22

The whole city was shaken up and stirred up and asked, "Who is this?" And the crowds answered that He was the prophet from Nazareth in Galilee. He is Lord of the prophetic.

Next, He went to the temple and drove out all who were buying and selling there. He overturned the tables of the money changers and the benches of those selling doves. He is the Lord of purity.

He said that it was written, "My house will be called a house of prayer, but you are making it a 'den of robbers.'" He is the Lord of prayer.

The blind and the lame came to him at the temple, and he healed them. He is the Lord of power.

When the chief priests and the teachers of the law saw the wonderful things he did and the children shouting in the temple area, "Hosanna to the Son of David," they were very upset and indignant. He is the Lord of praise. He said in Psalm 8:2, "Out of the mouth of babies and nursing infants you have ordained strength, (or perfected praise), because of Your enemies, That You may silence the enemy and the avenger."

PRAYER: *We do praise You, Lord that You are the Lord of the prophetic! Your gifts also have never stopped functioning. You still speak prophetically through Your servants. We praise You that You are the Lord of purity, prayer, power, and praise. You are Alpha and Omega, the God who never changes. You purify us, pray through us, give us Your power, and we praise You now and throughout all generations! Amen!*

JESUS, OUR CORNERSTONE

The stone rejected by the builders has now become the cornerstone.
This is the Lord's doing, and it is marvelous to see.
—MATTHEW 21:42, NLT; READ ALSO VV. 23–46

In this parable, there was a landowner who planted a vineyard, set a hedge around it, dug a winepress in it, and built a tower. He leased it to tenant farmers and went far away. Now when it was time for the grape harvest, he sent his servants to collect his share of the crop. But the farmers grabbed his servants, beat one, killed one, and stoned another.

Finally, the owner sent his son thinking they will surely respect him. But when the farmers saw him, they said, "Here comes the heir to the estate. Let's kill him and get the estate for ourselves!" So, they grabbed him and killed him.

Jesus asked what the owner would do to the farmers. The religious leaders said, "He will put them to a horrible death and rent the vineyard to others who will give him his share of the crop after each harvest (v. 41, NLT). Then Jesus quoted from Psalm 118:22 about Him being the cornerstone that the builders rejected.

Jesus said that this meant the Kingdom of God would be taken away from them and given to the nation that would produce the proper fruit. He added, "Anyone who stumbles over that stone will be broken to pieces, and it will crush anyone on whom it falls" (v. 44, NLT).

In this parable, the son spoken of is Jesus, the prophets are the servants, and the farmers are the religious leaders. Jesus shows that "the stone" will affect people in different ways. Many will trip over it. At the last judgment, God's enemies will be crushed by it. In Daniel 2:34–35, the stone cut out without hands strikes the kingdoms of power and breaks them to pieces, and it becomes a great mountain and fills the earth.

PRAYER: *Lord, let us listen and learn! We declare that You are the Cornerstone, like the song says, "Jesus is the Cornerstone, came for sinners to atone, though rejected by His own, Jesus is the Cornerstone!" Lord, You are our Cornerstone, the Rock of our salvation! Amen!*

AN OPEN INVITATION

Come to the wedding feast for my son and his bride…
—MATTHEW 22:4, TPT; READ ALSO VV. 1–22

There once was a king who arranged an extravagant wedding feast for his son. He sent out his servants to summon all the invited guests, but they chose not to come. On the day of the feast, he sent out even more servants to inform the guests that the feast was ready!

But the invited guests were preoccupied with other things. And the rest seized the king's messengers and shamefully mistreated them, and even killed them. This infuriated the king, so he sent his soldiers to execute those murderers and had their city burned to the ground. (This was fulfilled by the Roman prince Titus).

So, the servants were told to go and invite the good and bad alike until the banquet hall was crammed with people!

God is the King who prepares His kingdom feast for His Son, Jesus Christ. The servants are the prophets. This parable is all about the marriage of the Lamb to the bride of Christ. God has a glorious feast prepared for us!

Now the banquet hall was crammed with people, and when the king entered it, he looked with glee over all his guests. But then he noticed a guest who was not wearing the wedding robe provided for him. So, he asked why he was not wearing the wedding garment. The man was speechless.

The king said to his servants, "Tie him up and throw him into the outer darkness, where there will be great sorrow, with weeping and grinding of teeth. For everyone is invited to enter in, but few respond in excellence" (v. 13–14, TPT). [Or, few are worthy, pure, or chosen.]

The wedding robe is a picture of the garment of righteousness. When we make Jesus Lord of our lives, He exchanges our "filthy rags" for a robe of righteousness. We become the righteousness of Christ (2 Corinthians 5:21).

PRAYER: *Thank You, Lord for the open invitation to come to the wedding feast of the Lamb and spend eternity with You. Amen.*

LOVING OTHERS AS CHRIST LOVES YOU

"Teacher, which is the great commandment in the law?" Jesus said to him, "'You shall love the Lord your God with all your heart, with all your soul, and with all your mind.' This is the first and great commandment. And the second is like it: 'You shall love your neighbor as yourself.' On these two commandments hang all the Law and the Prophets."
—MATTHEW 22:36–40; READ ALSO VV. 23–46

On August 8, 1975, Bob Jones, mightily respected for accurate prophecies, died. Following is his testimony, paraphrased. After he died, he found himself in a line. To his left were a lot of people on something like a conveyor belt, where they were rolling past him. There was a huge number of people in that line. There were not many in his line. As he looked at the other line, there were many people who slid off the conveyor and went into darkness, where there would never be light again. Then, in his line, he saw a big black woman who had nearly a hundred angels with her. He asked the Lord why she had so many angels, and the Lord said it was because she was a great minister and these angels helped her do great things for God. When she approached the Lord, He looked at her and said, "Did you learn to love?" And she said, "Yes, Lord!" She threw her arms up, and He put His arms around her and kissed her and pulled her and her angels in with Him.[1]

With all the great works she had done, there was one question the Lord had for her. "Did you learn to love?" It is as the Bible says in 1 Corinthians 13:13: *"And now these three remain: faith, hope and love. But the greatest of these is love."*

PRAYER: *Lord, help us to love like You love. Were we to face You one day after we die, and You ask us, "Did you learn to love?" we could answer immediately that, "Yes, we learned to love!" We learned to love You more, and we learned to love people more. Amen.*

TITHERS' RIGHTS

Woe to you, scribes and Pharisees, hypocrites! For you pay tithe of mint and anise and cummin and have neglected the weightier matters of the law: justice and mercy and faith. THESE YOU OUGHT TO HAVE DONE, WITHOUT LEAVING THE OTHERS UNDONE. *Blind guides, who strain out a gnat and swallow a camel!*
—MATTHEW 23:23–24; READ ALSO VV. 1–24

Here we have a clear example that tithing is mentioned by Jesus in the New Testament. He said that we can't be obsessed with peripheral issues and ignore the most important things like justice, mercy, and faith. But He also said we were not to leave the tithing undone.

The Bible says in Malachi 3:10 that we are to bring all the tithes into the storehouse that there might be food in His house—so the bills, salaries, missions, etc., could be taken care of. If we do what He says, He will open up the windows of heaven and pour out a blessing that we cannot contain. And He will rebuke the devourer for our sakes. This means we won't be spending money on things that break down, lawyer's bills, doctor's bills, etc. He will fight the devil and his strategies to rob us if we tithe.

The evangelist/teacher Mark Barclay tells of a story where his grandson drowned. When they brought him up from the bottom of the pool, he was no longer breathing. When Mark's son-in-law came out and saw the situation, he yelled, "Tither's rights!" His little boy began breathing again! God fought for his family that day and upheld His Word about rebuking the devourer!

PRAYER: *Thank You, Lord, for the promises in Your Word! Thank You that You defend us as we are obedient to You. As we tithe and walk in justice, mercy, and faith in Your promises, You show Yourself strong! You never fail us or forsake us! Amen!*

February 6

CHRIST PAID FOR OUR TRANSGRESSIONS

O Jerusalem, Jerusalem—you are the city that murders your prophets! You are the city that stones the very messengers who were sent to deliver you! So many times I have longed to gather a wayward people, as a hen gathers her chicks under her wings—but you were too stubborn to let me. And now it is too late, since your city will be left in ruins. For you will not see me again until you are able to say, "We welcome the one who comes to us in the name of the Lord."
—MATTHEW 23:23–24, TPT; READ ALSO VV. 25–39

In His great love, Jesus laments over the faithlessness of His countrymen. He laments that they will not reach their destiny, and He grieves over the rejection of the prophets, the apostles, and of Himself, their Messiah. He wept over Jerusalem; He would have gathered them like a hen gathers chicks under her wings, but they would not come to Him. "But you were not willing" is a sad statement of judgment given when Jesus left the temple.

"This scene reminds us of Ezekiel's picture of the glory of God leaving the temple (Ezekiel 11:23). God became concretely real on earth in Jesus. God took the initiative in coming (John 1:14) but, as in Jeremiah 7:25–27, Jerusalem refused the grace of God." [2]

Jesus said they would not see Him again until He came in His glory. Then they would say, "Blessed is He who comes in the name of the Lord." This speaks of the prophecy of Psalm 118:26. That event is yet to come, for after His resurrection, He only appeared to His believing disciples. But when He comes again, the unbelievers will see Him in His glory for "at the name of Jesus every knee shall bow...and every tongue shall confess..." (Philippians 2:10–11).

PRAYER: *Lord, You were despised and rejected of men, a man of sorrows and acquainted with grief. You were wounded for our transgressions and bruised for our iniquities; the chastisement for our peace was upon You and by Your stripes, we are healed (Isaiah 53:3–5). Thank You for what You have done for us! We confess that Jesus Christ is Lord! Amen!*

February 7

SIGN OF END TIME

This gospel of the kingdom will be preached in all the world as a witness to all the nations, and then the end will come.
—MATTHEW 24:14; READ ALSO VV. 1–31

This is the chapter of the signs of the times and the end of the age. Jesus said deception would abound, and many would claim, "I am the Christ." He said there would be wars and rumors of wars, famines, pestilences, and earthquakes. He said we would be hated by all nations for His name's sake; lawlessness would abound, and the love of many would grow cold; but that "he who endures to the end shall be saved" (v. 13).

He spoke of His second coming: "the sign of the Son of Man will appear in heaven, and then all the tribes of the earth will mourn, and they will see the Son of Man coming on the clouds of heaven with power and great glory. And He will send His angels with a great sound of a trumpet, and they will gather together His elect from the four winds, from one end of heaven to the other" (v. 31). This speaks of the "rapture" of the church—the catching away of the saints. (See 2 Thessalonians 4:16–17).

We may ask, "What is the gospel of the kingdom?" In Matthew 4:17, 23–24, Jesus preached, "Repent, for the kingdom of heaven is at hand..." and "...went about all Galilee, teaching in their synagogues, preaching the gospel of the kingdom, and healing all kinds of sickness and all kinds of disease among the people." This gospel includes signs, wonders, and miracles.

Peter on the day of Pentecost preached, "Therefore let all the house of Israel know assuredly that God has made this Jesus, whom you crucified, both Lord and Christ" (Acts 2:36). The people that heard this were cut to the heart and asked what they should do. Peter said, "Repent and be baptized in the name of Jesus Christ for the remission of sins; and you shall receive the gift of the Holy Spirit. For this promise is to you, your children, and to all who are afar off, as many as the Lord our God will call."

PRAYER: *Use us to preach the gospel to the nations, and to cover the earth with this gospel message. Then You said the end would come. Maranatha! Come quickly, Lord Jesus! Amen!*

February 8

MEANINGFUL RELATIONSHIP WITH GOD

But of that day and hour no one knows, not even the angels of heaven, but My Father only. But as the days of Noah were, so also will the coming of the Son of Man be. For as in the days before the flood, they were eating and drinking, marrying and giving in marriage, until the day that Noah entered the ark, and did not know until the flood came and took them all away, so also will the coming of the Son of Man be. Then two men will be in the field: one will be taken, and the other left. Two women will be grinding at the mill: one will be taken, and the other left. Watch therefore, for you do not know what hour your Lord is coming.
—MATTHEW 24:36–42; READ ALSO VV. 32–51

While Jesus was certain of His return, He didn't know the exact time. Therefore, His primary emphasis was on watchfulness. This section is a call for faithfulness as we live in hope. We need to have a meaningful relationship with Him and not a fear of the end. Jesus calls us to be disciples in the world, to serve in the world, to evangelize the world—not to stand apart, waiting for His coming.

The reference to Noah is important. Jesus' point is that life went on as always. God patiently waited for one hundred and twenty years while Noah prepared the ark and preached to the people. But he was ignored; they did not listen. Then suddenly, the flood came, and the people couldn't say, "If only He had waited a bit longer, we would have repented." We will not be able to say that either. It has been two thousand years since the Lord told us to be ready for His coming!

Christ's coming will be swift and sudden. There will be no opportunity for last-minute repentance or bargaining. The choice we have already made will determine our eternal destiny.

PRAYER: *Now is the time for us to get ready, live ready, and as much as lies within us, to get our families and loved ones ready. We need to "watch." Help us to all be ready for that day! Amen!*

BE WATCHFUL AND READY

The Kingdom of Heaven can be illustrated by the story of ten brides-maids (virgins) who took their lamps and went to meet the bride-groom. Five of them were foolish, and five were wise. The five who were foolish took no oil for their lamps, but the other five were wise enough to take along extra oil. When the bridegroom was delayed, they all lay down and slept. At midnight they were roused by the shout, "Look, the bridegroom is coming! Come out and welcome him!"
—Matthew 25:1–6, nlt; read also vv. 1–30

This parable is about a wedding that was traditionally held in Israel. On the wedding day the bridegroom went to the bride's house for the ceremony; then the bride and groom, along with a great procession returned to the groom's house, where a feast took place, often lasting a full week.

These ten bridesmaids in the parable were waiting to join the procession, and they hoped to take part in the marriage feast. But when the groom didn't come at the expected time, five of them were out of lamp oil. By the time they had purchased extra oil, it was too late to join the feast.

Upon their return to join in the feast, they found the door shut, and when they asked the bridegroom to open the door for them, he said, "I do not know you." Three of the saddest sayings in the parables of Jesus are found here: 1) "Our lamps are gone out"; 2) "The door was shut"; 3) "I do not know you."

When Jesus returns to take His people to heaven, we must be ready, for spiritual preparation cannot be bought or borrowed at the last minute. Our relationship with God must be our own.

Jesus says in verse 13: "So stay awake and be prepared, because you do not know the day or hour of my return."

Prayer: *Our Father in heaven, our greatest desire is to be found doing what You called us to do on earth and watching for Your return. We want to "occupy till You come" (Luke 19:13). Then we will be ready for Your coming. When the midnight cry comes, help us to be found watching and ready! Amen!*

THE LEAST OF GOD'S CREATURES

Assuredly, I say to you, inasmuch as you did it to one of the least of these My brethren, you did it to Me.
—MATTHEW 25:40; READ ALSO VV. 31–46

At the end of this age, Jesus will separate sheep nations from goat nations. To the sheep nations, Jesus said, "Come you blessed of My Father, inherit the kingdom prepared for you from the foundation of the world: for I was hungry and you gave Me food; I was thirsty and you gave Me drink; I was a stranger and you took Me in; I was naked and you clothed Me; I was sick and you visited Me; I was in prison and you came to Me" (v. 35–36).

Henry Hyde served thirty-two years in the House of Representatives and was a powerful defender of the unborn and of American freedom. On July 16, 1993, he stated:

> That all men are created equal and are endowed by their Creator—human beings upon creation, not upon birth. That is where our human dignity comes from. It comes from the Creator. It is an endowment, not an achievement. By membership in the human family, we are endowed by our Creator with "inalienable rights." They can't be voted away by a jury or a court. "Among which are life"—the first inalienable right, the first endowment from the Creator.
>
> It is the unborn who are the least of God's creatures. We have been told that whatsoever we do for the least of these, we do unto Jesus.[3]

He sponsored the Hyde Amendment which forbids federal funds to pay for abortions with certain exceptions.

PRAYER: *Lord, forgive us as a nation for the millions of abortions we have done, cutting short the destiny and plan that You had for Your little ones! How many presidents, pastors, apostles, prophets, and inventors who would discover cures for cancer, etc., did we decide needed to die? Help us to protect and defend these innocent, helpless ones! Help us to be a sheep nation who is blessed of You because we took care of "the least of these!" In Jesus' name. Amen!*

FESTIVAL OF PASSOVER

This is My body…this is My blood.
—MATTHEW 26:26, 28; READ ALSO VV. 1–35

In this passage, Jesus institutes the Lord's supper. On the first day of the Feast of Unleavened Bread, Jesus sent His disciples into the city to prepare for the Passover feast.

At the Passover meal, Jesus took bread, blessed and broke it, and gave it to the disciples. *"Take, eat; this is My body."* Then He took the cup and gave thanks, and gave it to them saying, *"Drink from it, all of you. For this is My blood of the new covenant, which is shed for many for the remission of sins"* (v. 27–28). Then He said he would not drink of the fruit of the vine again until He drinks it with us in His Father's kingdom.

The first of God's festivals is Passover. It is a celebration of God's love and power in delivering His people out of Egypt. The Israelites were told to kill a lamb, drain the blood, and put the blood of the lamb on their doorposts. The death angel passed over their homes because God accepted the lamb's death in place of Israel's firstborn. Egypt's firstborn were all killed. This plague finally made Pharaoh let the people go.

The Messianic Jews and Christians see Jesus in the Passover Feast. Part of the feast includes three matzos—unleavened bread which is pierced and striped with a pointed tool. The matzos are covered with a napkin. The Jewish father takes the middle cake out and breaks it in two. This breaking speaks of Jesus' broken body. One half of the matzo (the afikomen) is wrapped in a napkin and hidden, picturing Jesus' burial. Later, after it is found, it is unwrapped and held up for all to see. This symbolizes the resurrection of Jesus. Elijah's cup which is full of wine/grape juice, is also part of the feast and represents the cup of Redemption. At this point in the Passover, Jesus lifted the cup and said, *"This is the new covenant in my blood; do this, whenever you drink it, in remembrance of me"* (1 Corinthians 11:25).

PRAYER: *We are so amazed at the perfect fulfillment of the prophetic picture in Passover. Thank You for forgiving our sins and that "by your stripes, we are healed" (1 Peter 2:24). Thank You that Your blood cleanses us from all sin. Amen.*

BE FREE FROM THE TRAP OF HATE

*Then Jesus came with them to a place called Gethsemane, and said
to the disciples, "Sit here while I go and pray over there." And He
took with Him Peter and the two sons of Zebedee, and He began to
be sorrowful and deeply distressed. Then He said to them, "My soul
is exceedingly sorrowful, even to death. Stay here and watch with
Me...."*

*He went a little farther and fell on His face and prayed, saying, "O
My Father, if it is possible, let this cup pass from Me; nevertheless, not
as I will, but as You will."*
—Matthew 26:36–39; read also vv. 36–75

Then Jesus went a second time and then a third time praying the same
words. He asked His disciples why they were still sleeping. He said
the hour of the Son of Man to be betrayed was upon them, and the
betrayer was at hand.

In the Garden of Gethsemane, Jesus entered into prayer, identifying with those who hated Him. He began to drink the cup of our
sins. He began to reap in His own body all the consequences of each
and every sin committed in the past, present, and future. He felt the
full penalty of every murder, rape, perversion, lie, and betrayal. He
bore this in His body to the extent that it caused His capillaries to
burst.

His agony was not just physical, but spiritual and emotional as
well. Later, on the cross He cried out, "Why have You forsaken me?"

Just like Jesus identified with those who hated Him, we also need
to go to that garden and pray something like the following prayer
asking forgiveness for ourselves and forgiving others.

PRAYER: *"Lord, in compassion identify me with the heart of my
offender, with his hurts and wounds Bring to death in me that which
would declare him as sinful and me as righteous. I am not better than he.
I am one with him at the foot of the cross. 'Forgive us!' Set us free from
the traps of hate. End all one-upmanship. Enable me to identify with
the person You created him to be. Restore us, oh Lord."*[4] *In Jesus'* name.
Amen.

CRUCIFIED FOR OUR SIN

Pilate said to them, "What then shall I do with Jesus who is called Christ?" They all said to him, "Let Him be crucified!" Then the governor said "Why, what evil has He done?" But they cried out all the more, saying, "Let Him be crucified!" When Pilate saw that he could not prevail at all, but rather that a tumult was rising, he took water and washed his hands before the multitude, saying, "I am innocent of the blood of this just Person. You see to it." And all the people answered and said, "His blood be on us and on our children." Then he released Barabbas to them; and when he had scourged Jesus, he delivered Him to be crucified.
  —MATTHEW 27:22–26; READ ALSO 1–26

The horrible act of crucifixion was now underway. Pilate had Jesus scourged, a most terrible torture in which the prisoner was tied to a post with His back bent, and a whip with long leather thongs studded with sharp pieces of bone and pellets of lead was used. The pain was so severe that men died under it or broke with loss of their senses. Fragments of flesh would be torn from the victims.[5]

Isaiah the prophet prophesied about this in Isaiah 53:4–5; "Surely He has borne our griefs and carried our sorrows; Yet we esteemed Him stricken, smitten by God, and afflicted. But He was wounded for our transgressions, He was bruised for our iniquities; The chastisement for our peace was upon Him, and by His stripes we are healed."

It was these stripes on His back that purchased our healing. In 1 Peter 2:24, the Bible says, "By His stripes we were healed." When we take communion, the bread is the symbol of the broken body of Jesus. If we take this communion in faith, we will receive healing.

PRAYER: *Our Father in heaven, as we take this communion, we are believing this bread is a symbol of Your body given for our healing. This wine is a symbol of forgiveness of sins. We receive both healing of our bodies and forgiveness of our sins. Amen.*

TRUE SON OF GOD

Truly this was the Son of God!
—MATTHEW 27:54; READ ALSO VV. 27–66

The crucifixion story is so horrific, it defies imagination. It tells how they beat and mocked Jesus—how they stripped Him and put a scarlet robe on Him. They twisted a crown of thorns and put it on His head; they put a reed in His right hand and said, *"Hail, King of the Jews"* (v. 29). They spit on Him, took the reed and struck Him, and led Him away to be crucified. He paid a debt He did not owe. We owed a debt we could not pay. He took the punishment we deserved.

Now, after He was crucified, it was dark over all the land from the 6th to the 9th hour. Then Jesus cried out, "My God, My God, why have You forsaken Me?" (v. 46). This was a fulfillment of Psalm 22:1. Then Jesus cried out again with a loud voice and yielded up His spirit.

At that moment, the veil of the temple was torn in two from top to bottom; and the earth quaked, the rocks were split, and the graves were opened. Many of the saints who had died were raised and came out of their graves after His resurrection.

When the centurion and those with him saw these things, they were greatly afraid and said that He was the Son of God!

What did Jesus do then? The apostle Peter in 1 Peter 3:18–20 said He went down into the heart of the earth where He preached to the spirits in prison that were disobedient in the days of Noah. After this, since death could not hold Him, He seized the keys of death and of hell (Revelation 1:18). From there in Ephesians 4:8–11 we read, He ascended up on high and led captivity captive. He led the righteous dead who had been held captive in paradise up into the presence of God, or the third heaven. From there, He gave gifts of apostles, prophets, evangelists, pastors and teachers.

PRAYER: *How can we ever thank You enough for what You have done for us! You truly are the Alpha and Omega, the beginning and the end! You paid the ultimate price so that we could be saved and forgiven, if we would put our trust in You! We acknowledge that You are Lord. Come to our hearts, Lord Jesus! There is room in our hearts for You! Amen!*

HE IS RISEN!

Now after the Sabbath, as the first day of the week began to dawn, Mary Magdalene and the other Mary came to see the tomb. And behold, there was a great earthquake; for an angel of the Lord descended from heaven, and came and rolled back the stone from the door, and sat on it. His countenance was like lightning, and his clothing as white as snow. And the guards shook for fear of him, and became like dead men. But the angel answered and said to the women, "Do not be afraid, for I know that you seek Jesus who was crucified. He is not here; for He is risen, as He said. Come, see the place where the Lord lay. And go quickly and tell His disciples that He is risen from the dead, and indeed He is going before you to Galilee."
—MATTHEW 28:1–7; READ ALSO VV. 1–8

Mary Magdalene had an encounter with Jesus in which she was delivered of seven demons. As a result, she became completely devoted in her love for her Savior. She, and others, were so dedicated to Jesus and His ministry that they supported Him out of their own personal resources.

Throughout the Gospels, Mary Magdalene never seems to be far from Jesus. She followed Jesus all the way to Calvary and watched Him breathe His last breath. She went to bring spices to anoint His body on resurrection morning (Mark 16:9).

Mary had the honor of being the first to witness His resurrection. She was among the first to hear the most revolutionary words in history: "He is risen!" She was the first to hear the Lord, speak her name, the first to whom He revealed Himself, and the first to hear Him issue the call to spread the good news that He is alive! God chose a woman!

PRAYER: *Father in heaven, if You made such a difference in Mary Magdalene's life, and healed her from her past so as to be the first to witness Your resurrection, and the first to spread the good news that You are alive, then please do that in my life! Amen!*

February 16

PREACHING THE GOSPEL OF SALVATION

He is not here; for He is risen, as He said.
—MATTHEW 28:6; READ ALSO VV. 9–20

The greatest day in all of history is when the angel rolled back the stone and told the women who came to see His tomb, *"He is not here, for He is risen, as He said."* Jesus met the women and told them to tell His brothers to go to Galilee, and there they would see Him.

On the mountain of ascension Jesus spoke to them, "All authority has been given to Me in heaven and on earth. Go therefore and make disciples of all the nations, baptizing them in the name of the Father and of the Son and of the Holy Spirit, teaching them to observe all things that I have commanded you; and lo, I am with you always, even to the end of the age" (v. 18–20).

The 1628 charter of the Massachusetts Bay Company stated that a chief purpose of this New England colony was "to win the natives of the country to the knowledge and obedience of the only true God and Savior of mankind."[7] Its seal pictured a native American and the Macedonian's call to Paul from Acts 16:9, "Come Over and Help Us."

John Eliot, known as the "Apostle to the Indians," learned the Algonquian language. He saw many of these native Americans put their faith in Christ and leave their pagan ways behind. He translated the entire Bible into Algonquian. This was the first Bible printed in America. Many others began to reach out to native Americans. Dartmouth University was started through a Puritan man who trained these young men to preach the Gospel.

PRAYER: *Our Father in heaven, help us to always be mindful of the great commission, to be faithful to share the Gospel wherever we go. "For I am not ashamed of the gospel of Christ, for it is the power of God to salvation, for everyone who believes, for the Jew first and also for the Greek" (Romans 1:16). Amen.*

VOICE OF TRUTH

The voice of one crying in the wilderness: prepare the way of the
LORD; make straight in the desert a highway for our God. Every
valley shall be exalted and every mountain and hill brought low; the
crooked places shall be made straight and the rough places smooth.
—ISAIAH 40:3–4; READ ALSO MARK 1:1–22

It was John the Baptist who said, "The voice of one crying in the wilderness: 'Prepare the way of the LORD; Make His paths straight'" (v. 3). From Isaiah 40:4: "Every valley shall be exalted and every mountain and hill brought low; the crooked places shall be made straight and the rough places smooth..." God has always had His prophets preparing His way and making His paths straight.

One such prophet in American history was Martin Luther King Jr. He was a powerful driving force in the push to end racial discrimination and segregation through non-violent means. In 1964 he delivered his unforgettable speech, "I Have a Dream," at the Lincoln Memorial.

Now is the time to rise from the dark and desolate valley of segregation to the sunlit path of racial justice...Now is the time to make justice a reality for all of God's children...

I have a dream that one day this nation will rise up and live out the true meaning of its creed: 'We hold these truths to be self-evident: that all men are created equal.'

...From every mountainside, let freedom ring. And when this happens, when we allow freedom to ring, when we let it ring from every village and every hamlet, from every state and every city, we will be able to speed up that day when all of God's children, black men and white men, Jews and Gentiles, Protestants and Catholics, will be able to join hands and sing in the words of the old Negro spiritual, "Free at last! Free at last! Thank God Almighty, we are free at last!" [8]

PRAYER: *Lord, we pray along with Martin Luther King, Jr. against racial division and strife. We pray 1 Corinthians 1:10: "Now I plead with you..., by the name of our Lord Jesus Christ, that you all speak the same thing, and that there be no divisions among you, but that you be perfectly joined together in the same mind and in the same judgment." In Jesus' Name. Amen.*

ONE MORE TOUCH

*Now a leper came to Him, imploring Him, kneeling down to Him
and saying to Him, "If You are willing, You can make me clean." Then
Jesus, moved with compassion, stretched out His hand and touched
him, and said to him, "I am willing; be cleansed." As soon as He had
spoken, immediately the leprosy left him, and he was cleansed.*
—MARK 1:40–42; READ ALSO VV. 23–45

Many people have experienced loneliness and rejection; but think
about this leper. He is an outcast forbidden to enter society because of
a flesh-eating disease. His condition prevented him from approaching
Jesus. What rejection, despair, and hopelessness must have weighed
upon that sad man! He kept hearing shouts of healing and victory
across the valley, yet he was left out.

Then he got a thought that he really didn't care what people
thought anymore and rushed down into the midst of that crowd and
reached out to Jesus while the crowds were crying out, "Unclean!
Unclean!" He threw himself at Jesus' feet. He knew He could heal
him, but would He do it? Jesus answered the question forever of: "Are
you willing to heal me?" He said, "Yes, I am willing." Jesus touched
the leper. "Be made whole," He said.

> The man needed much more than just physical restoration, … he needed
> an inner work of healing power for his mind and emotions. He needed
> the entire complex of his very being to be touched and transformed. He
> needed the confidence of God Himself poured into his character. He
> needed wholeness for his entire self: spirit, soul and body.[9]

PRAYER: *Dear Jesus, if You can heal a leper in one touch physically,
spiritually, and emotionally, would You touch me? I know what the
answer is: "I am willing. Be made whole." Forever and ever, your answer
is "I am willing!" Amen.*

POWER OF FAITH

Son, your sins are forgiven you.
—MARK 2:5; READ ALSO MARK 2

When Jesus was in Capernaum, many gathered together. Then four men carrying a paralytic came to Him. Because the crowd was so great, they uncovered the roof where Jesus was and let down the bed on which the paralytic was lying.

When Jesus saw their faith, He said to the paralytic that his sins were forgiven. When the scribes questioned His ability to forgive sins, He asked which was easier, to forgive sins or to command the man to take up his bed and walk. Jesus said to the paralytic, "'I say to you, arise, take up your bed, and go to your house.' Immediately he arose, took up the bed, and went out in the presence of them all, so that all were amazed and glorified God, saying, 'We never saw anything like this!'" (v. 11–12).

This blessed influence of Jesus has touched many men and women through the years. William Cullen Bryant (1794–1878), was known as the "Father of the American Poets." He wrote:

> The very men who, in the pride of their investigations into the secrets of the internal world, are not aware how much of the peace and order of society, how much the happiness of households, and the purest of those who are the dearest to them, are owing to the influence of that religion extending beyond their sphere...
>
> In my view, the life, the teachings, the labors, and the sufferings of the blessed Jesus, there can be no admiration too profound, no love of which the human heart is capable too warm, no gratitude too earnest and deep of which He is justly the object.[10]

PRAYER: *We praise You that You are the same yesterday, today, and forever. You are always moved by men's faith. Release the gift of faith in us today. You said that whoever believes in You would do greater works because You go to the Father. And that whatever we would ask in Your Name, You would do it. May we spread Your miracles everywhere! Amen!*

February 20

DIVINE AUTHORITY

*Then He appointed twelve, that they might be with Him and that He might send them out to preach, and to have **power** to heal sicknesses and to cast out demons.*
—MARK 3:14–15; READ ALSO VV. 1–19

The word for power here is *exousia*, which means the authority or right to act. Jesus had the *exousia* to forgive sin, heal sicknesses, and to cast out devils. He gave us that authority also.

In the book *Authority in Prayer*, Dutch Sheets gives this testimony by Will Ford. Using this authority, they averted death.

> My wife Michelle had an elderly uncle who had been ill and had suddenly taken a turn for the worse. The family was called in to meet with the doctor and was informed that her uncle wouldn't live to see the morning. His vital signs were shutting down
>
> My wife and I were praying at home, and just when we were about to accept what was happening to him due to his age, we both heard the Holy Spirit say her uncle's time on earth was not yet finished. We believed the Lord was instructing us to take authority over the spirit of death and speak life to her uncle. When the two of us prayed in this manner, we felt the presence of God and His authority released through us in a powerful way. It was the first time we had experienced praying and using a clear word of knowledge from the Holy Spirit.[11]

The next morning their uncle was alive and well and eventually made a full recovery. He reconciled with family members and spent the time he had missed out on with his daughters. Two years later, he went home to be with the Lord.

PRAYER: *We praise You Lord for the authority You have given us in this life to overcome all the power of the enemy. We take authority over _____ now in Jesus' name. Amen.*

February 21

SURRENDERING OUR LIVES TO GOD

Who is My mother, or My brothers?
—MARK 3:33; READ ALSO VV. 20–35

When Jesus' brothers and His mother came to speak to Jesus, the multitude told Him that His mother and brothers were outside seeking Him.

> But He answered them, saying, "Who is My mother, or My brothers?" And He looked around in a circle at those who sat about Him, and said, "Here are My mother and My brothers! For whoever does the will of God is My brother and My sister and mother."
> —MARK 3:33–35

Missionary Jim Elliot is a wonderful example of this. In the summer of 1950, he was at Camp Wycliffe to learn how to transcribe a language for the first time. He met a missionary who told him about the "Auca" (savage) people of Ecuador, and he felt called by God to go there. Elliot and four other missionaries made contact from their airplane using a speaker and basket to hand out gifts. The natives met them, apparently wanting a ride in their airplane. When they landed in January 1956, all five were killed by the Auca Indians, and their bodies were found downstream.

His journal entry for October 28, 1949 expressed his belief that work dedicated to Jesus was more important than his life. "For whosoever will save his life shall lose it: but whosoever will lose his life for my sake the same shall save it" (Matthew 16:25, KJV). He wrote, "He is no fool who gives what he cannot keep to gain that which he cannot lose." [12]

After his death, his wife along with other missionaries went back to those same people who had killed her husband to work with them and win them to Christ. This time, they succeeded in their mission.

PRAYER: *So many have given their lives for You and we are so humbled by their sacrifice and obedience. Help us also to do Your will and be considered as Your brother or sister. We offer ourselves to You today. In Jesus' name. Amen.*

DEEPER UNDERSTANDING
THE WORD OF GOD

*But when He was alone, those around Him with the twelve asked
Him about the parable. And He said to them, "To you it has been
given to know the mystery of the kingdom of God; but to those who
are outside, all things come in parables, so that "Seeing they may see
and not perceive, and hearing they may hear and not understand; lest
they should turn. And their sins be forgiven them."*
—MARK 4:10–12; READ ALSO VV. 1–20

To Jesus' disciples, a parable was intended to unveil the truth, but to
the Pharisees, the parable dropped a curtain of mystery over their
eyes.

"Despite its outward innocence, a parable is a teaching tool that
divides believers and unbelievers. To believers, it unveils the mystery
of the Kingdom of God; to unbelievers a parable drops an opaque
curtain upon their understanding."[13]

The "mystery of the kingdom of God" means that the kingdom of
God has come in the Person of Jesus of Nazareth, in His words and
works. This "mystery" can only be solved by divine revelation.

Jesus' followers will understand the lessons taught by parables or
will be stimulated to probe for deeper understanding. Those who
have already shut their eyes and ears to the truth will not realize the
significance of what they are seeing and hearing.

PRAYER: *Father, we pray that You would give us a spirit of wisdom
and revelation to understand Your teachings! We pray the eyes of our
understanding would be opened, so that we could know the hope of our
calling and what are the riches of the glory of Your inheritance in the
saints, and what is the exceeding greatness of Your power towards us
(Ephesians 1:17–19). In Jesus's name. Amen!*

SPEAKING TO THE STORMS IN OUR LIVES

Peace, be still!
—MARK 4:39; READ ALSO VV. 21–41

We read in this chapter about a great storm arising on the sea and Jesus being asleep. So, His disciples went to awaken Him and ask Him if He cared that they were perishing.

Then He arose and rebuked the wind and said to the sea "Peace, be still!" And the wind ceased and there was a great calm. And the disciples feared exceedingly, and said to one another, "Who can this be that even the wind and the sea obey Him!" (v. 41).

Ezra Stiles, president of Yale College (1778–1795) related this story to what happened in the Revolutionary War:

In our lowest and most dangerous state, in 1776 and 1777, we sustained ourselves against the British Army of sixty thousand troops commanded by...the ablest generals Britain could procure throughout Europe, with a naval force of twenty two thousand seamen in above eighty men-of-war.

Who but a Washington, inspired by heaven, could have conceived the surprise move upon the enemy at Princeton—that evening when Washington and his army crossed the Delaware?

Who but the Ruler of the winds could have delayed the British reinforcements by three months of contrary ocean winds at a critical point of the war?

Or what but "a providential miracle" at the last minute detected the treacherous scheme of traitor Benedict Arnold, which would have delivered the American army, including George Washington himself, into the hands of the enemy? [14]

PRAYER: *Lord, You spoke to the winds and waves and said, "Peace, be still" and the storm stopped. You held back the winds to help our nation during the Revolutionary War. Lord we speak to the storms in our life and say, "Peace, be still!" We speak to the storms in our nation and say "Peace, be still!" In Jesus' name. Amen!*

AUTHORITY OVER PRINCIPALITY
AND POWER

When he (the Gadarene demoniac) saw Jesus from afar, he ran and worshiped Him. And he cried out with a loud voice and said, "What have I to do with You, Jesus, Son of the Most High God? I implore You by God that You do not torment me." For He said to him, 'Come out of the man unclean spirit!' Then He asked him, 'What is your name?' And he answered, saying, 'My name is Legion; for we are many.' Also he begged Him earnestly that He would not send them out of the country." Now a large herd of swine was feeding there near the mountains. So all the demons begged Him, saying, 'Send us to the swine, that we may enter them.' And at once Jesus gave them permission. Then the unclean spirits went out and entered the swine (there were about two thousand); and the herd ran violently down the steep place into the sea and drowned in the sea."
—MARK 5:6–13; READ ALSO VV. 1–20

What is a demon? A demon is a fallen angel. When Satan, who was the very highest angel, rebelled against God, he took a large number of the angels with him (Isaiah 14:12–15; Revelation 12:3–4). When their rebellion failed, they were cast out of heaven. Those angels are now demons. Demons torment and harass people leading them away from God and His truth. The sins of the flesh listed in Galatians 5:19–21 can also be expressions of demonic activity in the lives of people. Any type of occult activity is especially subject to demonic activity.

Just as there are archangels and higher powers, the demons have what are called "principalities and powers" (Ephesians 6:12). There is a conflict in the invisible world between God's angels and demonic hosts. Amazingly, God uses the prayers of His people as a restraint against demonic activity, inviting the presence of God to intervene in the course of human events.[15]

PRAYER: *Thank You that through Your Name and blood, we have authority over and protection from all demons! Amen!*

February 25

RAISING THE DEAD TO LIFE

Who touched me?
—MARK 5:31; READ ALSO VV. 21–43

One day a leader of the local synagogue, Jairus, came and fell down before Jesus and pleaded with Him to heal his little daughter who was about to die. Jesus went with him. On the way, a woman with an issue of blood met Him. She had had this condition twelve years and had suffered many things from physicians and instead of getting better, she only got worse. She said, *"If only I may touch His clothes, I shall be made well"* (v. 28). When she did touch Him, the bleeding stopped immediately, and she could feel that she had been healed! Jesus realized at once that healing power had gone out from Him, so He turned around and asked, *"Who touched me?"*

In fear and trembling, she told Him the truth, that she had been healed. One touch from Jesus and she was healed. He said to her, *"Daughter, your faith has made you well. Go in peace and be healed of your affliction"* (v. 34).

At this point, Jesus heard that Jairus' daughter was dead. He said, *"Do not be afraid; only believe."* When He got to the ruler of the synagogue's home, many were there weeping and wailing loudly. He asked why they were making such a commotion because the child was not dead; she was only sleeping. They ridiculed Him, but He put them all outside and said to the child, *"Little girl, I say to you, arise."* Immediately the girl arose and walked. She was twelve years old. Jesus never said, "No, I cannot or will not heal you." He healed everyone.

Even today, Jesus raises the dead to life. David Hogan, missionary to Mexico for over forty years, has raised thirty seven people from the dead. His first person was a little boy of 9 years old. When David and the dad got to the hut in the jungle, they found the boy had been dead for five hours. He prayed and the Lord brought him back to life.[16] David appeared on Sid Roth, "It's Supernatural," (ISN), on October 6, 2019.

PRAYER: *Increase our faith to walk in signs, wonders, and miracles, that the world might believe that Jesus is Lord! Amen!*

FAITHFUL UNTO DEATH

And when Herodias' daughter herself came in and danced, and pleased Herod and those who sat with him, the king said to the girl, "Ask me what ever you want, and I will give it to you." "I want you to give me the head of John the Baptist on a platter."
—MARK 6:22, 25; READ ALSO VV. 1–29

History is full of examples of Christian martyrs. One example is Polycarp, the Christian bishop of Smyrna. Polycarp was a disciple of John the apostle who ordained him as bishop of Smyrna. These are the words of his disciple, Iranaeus:

> I could tell you the place where the blessed Polycarp sat to preach the word of God. It is yet present to my mind with what gravity he everywhere came in and went out; what was the sanctity of his deportment, the majesty of his countenance; and what were his holy exhortations to the people. I seem to hear him now relate how he conversed with John and many others who had seen Jesus Christ, the words he had heard from their mouths.[17]

After refusing to burn incense to the Roman Emperor, he was tied to a stake. He said on the day of his death, "Eighty and six years I have served Him, and He has done me no wrong. How then can I blaspheme my King and Savior? You threaten me with a fire that burns for a season, and after a little while is quenched; but you are ignorant of the fire of everlasting punishment that is prepared for the wicked." He assured those executing him that he would stand immoveable during the fire. He was burned at the stake. The flames encircled him, but did not touch him, so the executioner pierced him with a sword and his blood put out the fire.

PRAYER: *Lord, You said to the church of Smyrna, "Be faithful unto death, and I will give you the crown of life" (Revelation 2:10). May we, Your present-day church, be faithful unto death. Amen.*

February 27

DO NOT BE AFRAID

And when He had sent them away, He departed to the mountain to pray. Now when evening came, the boat was in the middle of the sea; and He was alone on the land. Then He saw them straining at rowing, for the wind was against them. Now about the fourth watch of the night He came to them, walking on the sea, and would have passed them by. And when they saw Him walking on the sea, they supposed it was a ghost, and cried out; for they all saw Him and were troubled. But immediately He talked with them and said to them, "Be of good cheer! It is I; do not be afraid."
—MARK 6:46–50; READ ALSO VV. 30–56

Jesus is always telling us to "Fear not." Fear is the opposite of faith. God tells us in His Word that "without faith it is impossible to please God, for he who comes to God must believe that He is, and that He is a rewarder of those who diligently seek him" (Hebrews 11:6). We also read that "faith comes by hearing and hearing by the Word of God" (Romans 10:17).

When we find the promises of God in the Word, we find the will of God. If you have need of healing, the Word says, "by His stripes you were healed" (1 Peter 2:24). If you have need of finances, the Bible says, "For my God shall meet all of your need according to His riches in glory" (Philippians 4:19). If you are afraid, the Bible says, "Don't worry about anything, instead, pray about everything; tell God your needs, and don't forget to thank him for his answers. If you do this, you will experience God's peace, which is far more wonderful than the human mind can understand. His peace will keep your thoughts and your hearts quiet and at rest as you trust in Christ Jesus" (Philippians 4:6–7, TLB).

"This is the confidence that we have in Him, that if we ask anything according to His will, He hears us. And if we know that He hears us, whatever we ask, we know that we have the petition that we have asked of Him" (1 John 5:14–15).

PRAYER: *Since You have plainly said that we are not to worry about anything but to tell You all that is on our hearts, we give You all our burdens and fears and needs right now. Amen.*

SOW HONOR, REAP HONOR

*For Moses said, "Honor your father and your mother;" and, "He
who curses father or mother, let him be put to death." But you say, "If
a man says to his father or mother, 'Whatever profit you might have
received from me is Corban'"—(that is, a gift to God).*
—MARK 7:10–11; READ ALSO VV. 1–23

Here we see Jesus upholding the words spoken by Moses in Deuteronomy 5:16: "Honor your father and your mother, as the Lord your
God has commanded you, so that you may live long and that it may
go well with you in the land the Lord your God is giving you."

What does it mean to honor? The Hebrew word for honor is *kabad.*
It means to be or make heavy; abounding in glory; noble; very great!
It means to place high value or price upon; to give a good report; to
bless. We honor our parents because of their position and authority.

To dishonor means to make light of, or to place a low value or price
upon. It means to refuse, reject, consider invalid or illegitimate. Jesus
said they were dishonoring parents.

According to John Sandford, every area where we could consciously or unconsciously honor our parents, life will go well with us.
In every area where we judged or dishonored our parents consciously
or unconsciously, life will not go well with us. When we sow seeds
of "dishonor" we will reap in the same way. When we sow seeds of
honor, we will reap honor in the same way. In other words, if we have
honored our parents, we will reap honor from our children, and if we
have dishonored them, we will reap that from our children.[18]

PRAYER: *Help us to obey Your word and reap that life of honor from
others. Forgive us where we have dishonored and are reaping the same
things. We bless our parents in Jesus' name. We say good things about
them! We are so thankful for the parents You have given us for they
have given us life! Amen!*

March 1

BE OPENED

Be opened!
—MARK 7:34; READ ALSO VV. 24–37

Some people brought to Jesus a deaf man with a severe speech impediment. They pleaded with Jesus to place His hands on him and heal him.

So, Jesus led him away from the crowd to a private spot. Then He stuck His fingers into the man's ears and placed some of His saliva on the man's tongue. Then He gazed into heaven, sighed deeply, and spoke to the man's ears and tongue, *"Ephphatha,"* which is Aramaic for *"Open up, now!"*

"At once the man's ears opened and he could hear perfectly, and his tongue was untied and he began to speak normally. Jesus ordered everyone to keep this miracle a secret, but the more he told them not to, the more the news spread! The people were absolutely beside themselves and astonished beyond measure. And they began to declare, 'Everything he does is wonderful! He even makes the deaf hear and the mute speak!'" (v. 34–37, TPT).

According to some commentators, the people were praising Him and realizing that this was a fulfillment of the Isaiah 35:5–6 prophecy: *"Then the eyes of the blind shall be opened, and the ears of the deaf shall be unstopped. Then the lame shall leap like a deer, and the tongue of the dumb sing…"*

While I was in Bangladesh in 2017 on a mission trip, a father brought his mute son to me to pray for him. I commanded the mute spirit to leave as Jesus did. It did. Then I told the boy to say, "Hal-le-lu-jah!" He repeated it many times and this was a sign and a wonder to the people around us. His father especially was so excited and in awe and wonder at this miracle!

PRAYER: *We praise You, Lord, that You are the same yesterday, today, and forever. You are the healer. You are MY healer. You are Lord over every situation. You are worthy of all of our praise. Amen.*

BELIEVE IN GOD

Then He charged them, saying, "Take heed, beware of the leaven of the Pharisees and the leaven of Herod."
—MARK 8:15; READ ALSO VV. 1–21

Since the disciples had only brought one loaf with them in the boat, they thought He was talking about the bread. But actually the *"leaven of the Pharisees and of Herod"* is their unbelief. Jesus was amazed at their unbelief and asked them, *"Having eyes, do you not see? And having ears, do you not hear? And do you not remember?"* (v. 18).

He then reminded them of the time when He broke the five loaves for the five thousand. He asked how many baskets of fragments they picked up. *"Twelve,"* they replied. Then He asked about the seven loaves for the four thousand, and how many large baskets of fragments they took up. They said, *"Seven"* (v. 19–20).

If He did that, then why were they concerned that they only had one loaf with them? Why could they not connect the "leaven" with the fact that they had taken up seven large baskets of fragments just before they got into the boat.

Jesus is concerned about our faith. He has been modeling through all the miracles of the loaves and fishes, the walking on the sea, the healing of every sick person that came to Him, including raising the dead girl to life, how to function in the realm of the kingdom. He had been teaching them that God has authority over everything, even that which cannot be seen. He had told them, *"And whatever things you ask in prayer, believing, you will receive"* (Matthew 21:22).

Lift up in prayer those impossible situations and circumstances, and watch God turn them around.

PRAYER: *Father, we lift up our nation to You. We lift up all who are in authority. We pray You give them a spirit of wisdom and revelation. We pray for unity in our nation. We pray for that Third Great Awakening in Jesus' name. We believe You are able to save America and fulfill its destiny and purpose. Amen.*

March 3

DIVINE CALL

Whoever desires to come after Me, let him deny himself, and take up his cross, and follow Me. For whoever desires to save his life will lose it, but whoever loses his life for My sake and the gospel's will save it. For what will it profit a man if he gains the whole world, and loses his own soul? Or what will a man give in exchange for his soul? For whoever is ashamed of Me and My words in this adulterous and sinful generation, of him the Son of Man also will be ashamed when He comes in the glory of His Father with the holy angels.
—MARK 8:34–38; READ ALSO VV. 22–38

Jesus is speaking here of giving up all to follow Him. He has a unique calling for each person and will reveal that calling to each and every individual.

One man who has had a very unique calling by "carrying the cross" is Arthur Blessitt. He has literally carried the cross to *every* nation and *every* island group—324 nations. He has walked over forty-three thousand miles which adds up to over eight-three million steps. The length of the cross is twelve feet, and the width is six feet. It weighs forty-five pounds. He started in 1968, has been carrying the cross fifty-one years, and is now seventy-eight years old. He has shared the Gospel every place he went.

Two of the scariest times he faced were when he was in front of a firing squad in Nicaragua and also when he was stoned and beaten in Morocco. Half of the churches where he wanted to leave the cross overnight said "No," but the bars and nightclubs always said "Yes." He has been arrested twenty-four times, and he was most likely to be arrested in the USA.[19]

PRAYER: *Lord, show us our calling, and thank You for Your promise that "we can do all things through Christ who strengthens us" (Philippians 4:13). Thank You that "We are more than conquerors through Him who loved us" (Romans 8:37). Thank You that "God is able to make all grace abound toward us, so that in all things at all times, having all that we need, we will abound in every good work" (2 Corinthians 9:8, NIV). Amen.*

March 4

DIVINE NATURE OF JESUS CHRIST

Jesus went on to say, "I assure you that some of you standing here right now will not die before you see the Kingdom of God arrive in great power!" Six days later Jesus took Peter, James, and John to the top of a mountain. No one else was there. As the men watched, Jesus' appearance changed, and his clothing became dazzling white, far whiter than any earthly process could ever make it. Then Elijah and Moses appeared and began talking with Jesus.

—MARK 9:1–4, NLT; READ ALSO VV. 1–29

Peter thought it was wonderful, but not really knowing what to say because they were all afraid, he said they would make three shrines—one for Jesus, one for Moses, and one for Elijah. Then a voice came to them from the cloud and said *"This is my beloved Son. Listen to him"* (v. 7). When they looked around, only Jesus was there and then He told them not to tell anyone what they had seen until He had risen from the dead.

The transfiguration revealed Christ's divine nature. God's voice exalted Jesus above Moses and Elijah as the long-awaited Messiah with full divine authority. Moses represented the law, and Elijah, the prophets. Their appearance showed Jesus as the fulfillment of both the Old Testament law and the prophetic promises. It also reminds us of Daniel's vision of the Ancient of Days who sat down to judge. His clothing was as white as snow, his hair like whitest wool (Daniel 7:9, NLT).

Jesus was not a reincarnation of Elijah or Moses. He was not merely one of the prophets. As God's only Son, He far surpasses them in authority and power.

PRAYER: *Lord, many voices try to tell us how to live and how to know God personally. Some of these are helpful, many are not. Help us to first listen to the Bible, and then evaluate all other authorities in light of God's revelation. Help us to know the Christ as Prophet, Priest, and King of kings and Lord of lords. Amen.*

March 5

UNITY IN CHRIST

*"Teacher, we saw someone who does not follow us casting out demons
in Your name, and we forbade him because he does not follow us."
But Jesus said, "Do not forbid him, for no one who works a miracle
in My name can soon afterward speak evil of Me. For he who is not
against us is on our side. For whoever gives you a cup of water to
drink in My name, because you belong to Christ, assuredly, I say to
you, he will by no means lose his reward."*
—MARK 9:38–41; READ ALSO VV. 30–50

In our reading today, Jesus forbids sectarianism or narrow exclusivism in the church.

There is no place for narrow exclusivism in the church. All genuine Christians are to be tolerant toward their fellow believers, regardless of their denomination. A crucial test in determining true service is the motive. Is the work being done for the sake of Christ and for His glory? Is it in line with His Word?

Jesus was teaching His disciples not to be sectarian in His three-part response to their comments in verse 38. Each sentence in His response is introduced by "for." 1) For the one who does miracles in the power of My name proves he is not My enemy. 2) For whoever is not against us is for us. 3) For whoever gives you a cup of water because you carry the name of Christ will never lose his reward.

It is very clear in the seventeenth chapter of John that Jesus desires unity in His body. He says in verse 21:... *"that they all may be one, as You, Father, are in Me and I in You; that they also may be one in Us, that the world may believe that You sent Me."*

PRAYER: *Father, we come to You in Jesus' name that as You pour
out Your Spirit in these last days, we will be in unity so the world may
believe that You, Father, have sent Your Son Jesus. We also pray we will
be in unity in the true faith taught in the Word of God, that there is
no other Name by which we can be saved other than the Name of Jesus
(Acts 4:12). Amen.*

NOTHING IS IMPOSSIBLE WITH GOD

With men it is impossible, but not with God; for with God all things are possible.
—MARK 10:27; READ ALSO VV. 1–3

The disciples asked Jesus who could be saved. Jesus said that with men it is impossible, but with God all things are possible. He said that if we leave family or lands for His sake, we'll receive a hundred-fold now and eternal life as well.

Dr. David Yonggi Cho, pastor of the world's largest Pentecostal church is an amazing example. He was raised as a Buddhist in North Korea. When war broke out in 1950, he went to South Korea with other refugees. He contracted tuberculosis and his right lung was completely destroyed by it. The doctor gave him no hope, saying that he had less than a month to live.

In desperation, he cried out to God when he realized Buddha had not helped him at all. God heard his prayer and sent a young girl with a Bible to him. He told her to leave, but she kept coming back and continued to witness to him. He read about Jesus healing the sick. He asked Christ to forgive him and heal him. Next, he found a church and he was the first to come to the altar. He had never known such joy and peace. The pastor was an Assemblies of God missionary.

After this, he went home but was excommunicated from the family. His uncle called him an "unholy Christian dog." He went back to the pastor, and they took him in. He learned the Bible, and God completely healed him. He wanted to meet with Jesus and "have a consultation" with Him about his future. In the night, Jesus came into his room as a bright light. His face was as bright as the sun. He was filled with the Holy Spirit and began praying in tongues. After this, he went to a Bible school and started a church. Now Yoido Full Gospel Church has more than eight hundred thousand people attending.[2]

PRAYER: *Truly with You, God, nothing is impossible. We lift up this seemingly impossible situation to You now _____. Thank You for intervening! In Jesus' name. Amen!*

March 7

BE HUMBLE

Whoever desires to become great among you shall be your servant.
—Mark 10:43; read also vv. 32–52

"Don't break your arm patting yourself on your back." We've often heard that when someone was praising or promoting himself. James and John did that in this chapter. They came up to Jesus and told Him to do for them whatever they asked! So, He asked them what they wanted. They asked to sit on His right hand and His left hand in His glory! Jesus said that they didn't know what they were asking and asked if they were able to be baptized with the baptism that He was going to be baptized with. (This was a baptism of suffering.) They said they were able, and He agreed with them. (James in Acts 12:2 was put to the sword by King Herod. John was exiled to the Island of Patmos for his faith. It is said they tried to boil him in oil, but the Lord protected him.)

The other disciples were very upset with James and John. Jesus used this to teach them all that *"whoever desires to become great among you shall be your servant"* (v. 43).

In his 1989 Inaugural Address, George H. W. Bush stated that his first act as President was to pray. He prayed as he asked them to bow their heads:

Heavenly Father, we bow our heads and thank You for Your love. Accept our thanks for the peace that yields this day and the shared faith that makes its continuance likely. Make us strong to do Your work, willing to heed and hear Your will, and write on our hearts these words: 'Use power to help people.' For we are given power not to advance our own purposes, nor to make a great show in the world, nor a name. There is but one just use of power, and it is to serve people. Help us to remember it, Lord. Amen.[3]

Prayer: *Father, help us to learn the humility that Your Son Jesus our Lord demonstrated. For He did not come to be served, but to serve, and to give His life a ransom for many. Help us to follow this model, for it will bring much joy. Amen.*

PRAYER AND WORSHIP

Then He taught, saying to them, "Is it not written, 'My house shall be called a house of prayer for all nations'? But you have made it a 'den of thieves.'"
—MARK 11:17; READ ALSO VV. 1–18 AND ISAIAH 56:7

One of the greatest movements of prayer happening today is prayer combined with worship. David instituted a similar form of worship in the tabernacle. It says in Amos 9:11–15 that God would *"raise up the tabernacle of David, which has fallen down, and repair its damages; I will raise up its ruins, and rebuild it as in the days of old; that they may possess the remnant of Edom* [an Islamic nation]*, and all the Gentiles* [nations] *who are called by My name, says the Lord who does this thing…"*

The tabernacle of David was a tent housing the ark of the covenant. King David organized four thousand musicians and two hundred eighty-eight singers to stand before it to minister to God in shifts that continued day and night. (1 Chronicles 23, 25).

Mike Bickle established his International House of Prayer according to this model and it has been going 24/7 since 1999. These prayer meetings combined with worship are one of the keys to refreshing and enjoyable prayer because they have a focus on the beauty of God.

In Psalm 27, David gives us another key that he employed in his tabernacle—inquiring of the Lord. David engaged in strategic prayer, asking to know God's will and the specific plans and strategies to accomplish His will. All over the earth the Lord is raising up prayer ministries that include gazing on God's beauty and encountering His love alongside inquiring about His strategies for the nations—all in a setting of prophetic worship.[4]

PRAYER: *Meditate on Psalm 27 and use it as a prayer guide. Use it to sing a new song to the Lord. Use it to sing spontaneous songs. Sing of His beauty and grace. Amen.*

CONFESS AND BELIEVE

And Jesus answering saith unto them, "Have faith in God. For verily I say unto you, That whosoever shall say unto this mountain, be thou removed, and be thou cast into the sea; and shall not doubt in his heart, but shall believe that those things which he saith shall come to pass, he shall have whatsoever he saith. Therefore I say unto you, What things soever ye desire, when ye pray, believe that ye receive them, and ye shall have them."
—Mark 11:22–24, kjv; read also vv. 19–33

Jesus said, "Have *faith in God.*" If you don't have doubt in your heart, you can speak to any mountain to be removed and cast into the sea and it will be done. In fact, if you have faith, whatever you desire when you pray, if you believe with all your heart, you will have the answer that you desire.

Look at the role the tongue plays in this miraculous answer to prayer you are going to receive. First, you *speak* to the mountain. Then, if you believe what you *say,* you will have whatever you *say.*

If you desire healing, you speak to the sickness or problem and command it to be "cast into the sea or be gone." You must believe what you say, and you will have whatever you say. The faith comes from the Word of God (Romans 10:17).

When our oldest daughter (5 years old) had a skin disease, we took her to the doctor and he said, "Keep her out of water, or it will get worse." We were temporarily moving to California to a motel that had a swimming pool, and we were right across the street from the ocean. Keep her out of water? Right!

I kept confessing Mark 11:23–24 and trying to believe, but still struggling with doubts. One day God said, "Don't you think I can heal her even if she goes swimming?" I knew then that He would heal her. Within three weeks, the disease was gone. God is faithful!

Prayer: *Thank You God, for the gift of faith. Thank You for Your Word that whatever I desire when I pray, if I believe in my heart, I will have it. Thank You for answered prayer! Now thank the Lord in advance for **your** answer to prayer. Amen.*

PRAY FOR THOSE IN AUTHORITY

Is it lawful to pay taxes to Caesar or not?
—MARK 12:14; READ ALSO VV. 1–27

The Pharisees and Herodians came to Jesus with that question. What they really meant was, "Is it right or wrong?" If Jesus answered "Yes," He would alienate the masses and give the Pharisees evidence for their charge of blasphemy. (The image of Caesar on the coin had an inscription calling Caesar divine.) If He answered "No" the twisted allegiance of the Herodian Jews would get the news to Roman authorities that Jesus was an insurrectionist.

Jesus' answer was brilliant, "*Give to Caesar what belongs to him, and to God what belongs to Him.*" His response disarmed both the Pharisees and Herodians; neither side had a case.

Peter Marshall, the chaplain of the US Senate (1947–1949), issued a call to honor God:

> The choice before us is plain: Christ or chaos, conviction or compromise, discipline or disintegration. I am rather tired of hearing about our rights and privileges as American citizens. The time is come—it is now—when we ought to hear about the duties and responsibilities of our citizenship. America's future depends upon her accepting and demonstrating God's government.[5]

The government has a realm of authority and in 1 Timothy 2:1–2, we are commanded to pray for those in authority. Our future depends on it. We must pray for those in leadership every day.

However, God has a realm of authority that takes precedence over secular citizenship. Jesus brilliantly turned the "either-or" question, into a "both-and" answer.

PRAYER: *We come to You today, Father, and ask that you bless our president and all that are in authority with wisdom and strength. Help them see clearly between good and evil, right and wrong, and bitter and sweet. Help us also to always put You and Your kingdom first. In Jesus' name. Amen.*

March 11

JESUS LOVES US

Jesus answered him, "The first of all the commandments is: Hear, O Israel, the LORD our God, the LORD is one. And you shall love the Lord your God with all your heart, with all your soul, and with all your mind, and with all your strength. This is the first commandment. And the second, like it, is this: You shall love your neighbor as yourself. There is no other commandment greater than these."
—MARK 12:29–31; READ ALSO VV. 28–44

Ida Scudder had vowed she would NEVER be a missionary in India like her parents and grandparents. She was going to stay in America, where it is clean and comfortable. She wanted to make plenty of money, and she hated the poverty, dirt, flies, and seeing the beggars. Now that she had been sent to school in America, she was not going to go back.

However, God had other plans. Her mother got sick, so Ida went back to India to care for her. While she was there one evening, there was a knock at the door. It was a young Hindu man who wanted her to come and help his wife. He wanted a woman doctor. She said her father was a doctor, but she wasn't, and she couldn't help him; she would take him to her dad. The man said that their religion forbids women from seeing a man doctor. Two more men came to the door the same night from other religions with the same requests; they were forbidden to see a man doctor. Early the next morning, Ida sent to see how the women were doing and learned that they had all died.

She was not able to sleep that night. "If I were a doctor, I could save the lives of many women and girls here in India. They need a woman doctor, to stop this needless suffering!"[6] Ida became Dr. Ida Scudder who worked for the rest of her life in India. She built several hospitals in the town of Vellore which later became the greatest medical center in all of Asia. She taught the people that Jesus loved them.

PRAYER: *Father, Your Son Jesus gave everything for us. He is our example in every way in loving and giving all. Amen.*

March 12

THE SECOND COMING

Now learn this parable from the fig tree.
—MARK 13:28; READ ALSO VV. 1–20

The Lord said there would be these signs that the end was near: a) many will come in My name and will deceive many; b) there will be wars and rumors of wars; c) earthquakes, famines, pestilences, and troubles. These signs would be markers that He will soon return.

These natural disasters are accompanied by increasing evangelism. This increased evangelism provokes increased persecution and betrayal, even involving family members. Yet, the gospel must be preached to all the nations. *"You will be hated by all for My name's sake. But he who endures to the end shall be saved"* (v. 13).

This period of trouble increases until it becomes the worst possible time in the history of man. *"In those days, there will be tribulation, such as has not been since the beginning of time"* (v. 19).

This fierce pressure will take place because God endeavors to save every single person possible and to destroy every demonic stronghold that has held the human race captive.

"And unless the Lord had shortened those days, no flesh would be saved; but for the elect's sake, whom He chose, He shortened the days" (v. 20).

Jesus said, *"Now learn this parable from the fig tree: When its branch has already become tender, and puts forth leaves, you know that summer is near. So you also, when you see these things happening, know that it is near—at the doors"* (v. 28–29).

Israel, or the fig tree, has been referred to as the "time clock" for the end-times. Watch Israel. She became a nation in 1948. In 1967, following the six-day war, Jerusalem came back under Israeli control. These events speak of the soon coming of our Lord.

PRAYER: *Lord, we see the signs of Your imminent return all around us. Help us to make the most of every opportunity to be a witness for You and help us to be ready to meet You at any moment. Help us keep watch and deliver us from evil. In Jesus' name. Amen.*

WATCH AND PRAY

But of that day and hour no one knows, not even the angels in heaven, nor the Son, but only the Father. Take heed, watch and pray; for you do not know when the time is. It is like a man going to a far country, who left his house and gave authority to his servants, and to each his work, and commanded the doorkeeper to watch. Watch therefore, for you do not know when the master of the house is coming—in the evening, at midnight, at the crowing of the rooster, or in the morning—lest, coming suddenly, he find you sleeping. And what I say to you, I say to all: Watch!
—MARK 13:32–37; READ ALSO VV. 21–37

The New Testament "watch" consisted of four watches of the night and four watches of the day. The first watch begins in the evening at sunset and ends at nine; the second one ends at midnight; the third ends when the rooster crows at three in the morning; the fourth watch ends at dawn. In Mark 6:47–48, Jesus was walking on the water of the Sea of Galilee. *"About the fourth watch of the night he went out to them, walking on the lake"* (v. 48). This would be three A.M.

It is like a man [Jesus], going to a far country [heaven], who left his house and gave authority to his servants [us], and to each his work, and commanded the doorkeeper to watch, [we are also doorkeepers]. He wants us to be found doing what He has assigned us to do when He returns. What has He commanded you to do?

Jesus exhorts us to "watch and pray" because we don't know when He's coming back. Just like Anna, who watched and prayed for fifty years before the Lord's first coming, He wants us to be wise virgins with oil in our lamps so we can be invited to the wedding to be the wife of the Lamb throughout eternity.

PRAYER: *You have called us to be on watch day and night. You have told us in Luke 21:36 to always be on the watch, that we may escape all that is about to happen, and that we will be able to stand before the Son of Man. Teach us how to watch and pray! In Jesus' name. Amen.*

DO WHAT PLEASES GOD

*And being in Bethany at the house of Simon the leper, as He sat at
the table, a woman came having an alabaster flask of very costly oil of
spikenard. Then she broke the flask and poured it on His head. But
there were some who were indignant among themselves, and said,
"Why was this fragrant oil wasted? For it might have been sold for
more than three hundred denarii and given to the poor. And they
criticized her sharply. But Jesus said, "Let her alone. Why do you
trouble her? She has done a good work for Me. For you have the poor
with you always, and whenever you wish you may do them good; but
Me you do not have always. She has done what she could. She has
come beforehand to anoint My body for burial.*
—MARK 14:3–8; READ ALSO VV. 1–26

In John 12, we have a similar story of anointing, and the person
doing it was Mary. In any case, this was a woman who loved Jesus
very much and came and poured precious oil on His head. She risked
being rebuked for coming and doing this. She was, in fact, sharply
criticized, but she was more concerned about showing her love and
loyalty to Jesus, than being afraid of what others thought.

This is like the love David showed to God when he was bringing
the ark of the Lord back to Jerusalem. In 2 Samuel 14, the Bible says.
*"Then David danced before the LORD with all his might; and David was
wearing a linen ephod."*

When Michal, Saul's daughter and David's wife, saw him dancing
in his linen ephod, she despised him in her heart. David, however,
said, *"I will be even more undignified than this and will be humble in
my own sight."*

So, the woman who anointed Jesus in Mark 14 also humbled herself because of her great love for her Lord. *"Assuredly, I say to you,
wherever this gospel is preached in the whole world, what this woman has
done will also be told as a memorial to her"* (v. 9).

PRAYER: *Lord, help us to be like the woman who anointed You for
burial. Help us to be more concerned with what pleases You than what
pleases men. In Your name. Amen.*

PRAYING FOR ALL NATIONS

Then He came and found them sleeping, and said to Peter, "Simon, are you sleeping? Could you not watch one hour? Watch and pray, lest you enter into temptation. The spirit indeed is willing, but the flesh is weak."
—MARK 14:37–38; READ ALSO VV. 27–53

The Lord seems incredulous that they couldn't even watch and pray one hour. That seems to be a minimum of what He expects.

Dick Eastman, of Every Home for Christ, outlines a plan to follow for "the hour that changes the world," by dividing the hour into twelve, five-minute segments:

+ Praise—Recognize God's Nature (Psalms 63:3)
+ Waiting—Silent Soul Surrender (Psalms 46:10)
+ Confession—Temple Cleansing Time (Psalms 139:23)
+ Scripture Praying—Word-enriched Prayer (Jeremiah 23:29)
+ Watching—Develop Holy Alertness (Colossians 4:2)
+ Intercession—Remember the World (1 Timothy 2:1–2)
+ Petition—Share Personal Needs (Matthew 7:7)
+ Singing—Worship in Song (Psalms 100:2)
+ Meditation—Ponder Spiritual Themes (Joshua 1:8)
+ Thanksgiving—Confess My Blessings (1 Thessalonians 5:18)
+ Listening—Receive Spiritual Instruction (Ecclesiastes 5:2)
+ Praise—Conclude with Praise (Psalm 52:9)

Every Home for Christ also puts out a *World Prayer Map* where you can pray for all nations of the world and their leaders every month.[7]

PRAYER: *Help us Lord to partner with You in the harvest of the nations! "This generation of Christians is responsible for this generation of souls on the earth."*
—KEITH GREEN

THE TRUE HIGH PRIEST

*Finally, the chief priest stood up in the middle of them and said to
Jesus, "Have you nothing to say about these allegations? Is what
they're saying about you true?" But Jesus remained silent before them
and did not answer. So the chief priest said to him, "Are you the
anointed Messiah, the Son of the Blessed God?" Jesus answered him,
"I am. And more than that, you are about to see the Son of Man
seated at the right hand of the Almighty and coming in the heavenly clouds!" Then as an act of outrage, the high priest tore his robe
and shouted, "No more witnesses are needed, for you've heard this
grievous blasphemy." Turning to the council he said, "Now, what is
your verdict?" "He's guilty and deserves the death penalty!" they all
answered.*
—MARK 14:60–64, TPT; READ ALSO VV. 54–72

What a dramatic scene! Two high priests are facing each other: the
high priest of the Jewish system and the true High Priest. One is of
the order of Aaron, the other of the order of Melchizedek (Hebrews
7:11–28). One a sinful man; the other, the sinless Son of God. We
learn from Leviticus 21:10 that if a high priest tears his robe he is disqualified from his office. So here Caiaphas is now stepping aside, and
God's true High Priest is taking his place."[8]

The Bible also says in Hebrews 7:24, that Jesus continues forever,
and has an unchangeable priesthood. "Therefore, He is also able to
save to the uttermost (completely) those who come to God through
Him, since He always lives to make intercession for them."

PRAYER: *How amazing that You are seated on the throne, Jesus, at the
right hand of God the Father always interceding for us! You are holy,
harmless, undefiled, separate from sinners, and have become higher than
the heavens. You hear our cries, and You save us from our sins and
sicknesses and protect us from evil. What a great High Priest we serve!
Amen!*

THE MIND OF THE CHRIST

They brought Jesus to the execution site called Golgotha, which means "Skull Hill." There they offered him a mild painkiller, a drink of wine mixed with gall, but he refused to drink it.
—MARK 15:22–23, TPT; READ ALSO VV. 1–25

The Aramaic word is "Golgotha." This is Calvary. David took Goliath's head (Goliath and Golgotha are taken from the same root word) and buried it outside of Jerusalem (1 Samuel 17:54). Some believe this is where the hill got its name, Golgotha (the place of the skull). Jesus died on Goliath's skull and thus made a way for our minds to submit to the revelation of the cross.[9]

He made a way for us to overcome the *"god of this world"* and receive the revelation of the cross. He gave us weapons of warfare that are not carnal but are mighty through God to pull down strongholds and every high thing that exalts itself against the knowledge of God and bring every thought into captivity to the obedience of Christ (2 Corinthians 10:4–5).

The Bible also says in 1 Corinthians 1:30 that we now have *"the mind of Christ."*

Goliath, the champion of the Philistines who dared to taunt the Israelites and rule over them and bring them into captivity, was taken down by King David. Jesus, the Son of David, took down the mind which exalts itself against the knowledge of God and was crucified in that very place where the skull of Goliath was buried. He set us free from being dominated by our minds, so we could humble ourselves and become servants of the King of kings, and Lord of lords.

PRAYER: *Thank You for the cross that won victory for us in the battle for the mind! We are no longer subject to it ruling over us as we submit to You. We can have our minds transformed now by the Word of God. We now can use our minds to the fullest for Your glory! Amen!*

THE SON OF GOD

They nailed his hands and feet to the cross. The soldiers divided his clothing among themselves by rolling dice to see who would win them. [Fulfillment of Psalm 22:18] It was nine o'clock in the morning when they finally crucified him. Above his head they placed a sign with the inscription of the charge against him, which read, "This is the King of the Jews." Two criminals were also crucified with Jesus, one on each side of him. This fulfilled the Scripture that says: "He was considered to be a criminal."

—MARK 15:24–28, TPT; READ ALSO VV. 26–47

In the NKJV the Bible says, "He was numbered with the transgressors, And He bore the sin of many, and made intercession for the transgressors" (Isaiah 53:12). Those who passed by ridiculed Him, telling Him to come down from the cross! Even the ruling priests and the religious scholars joined in the mockery and said, *"Let the 'Messiah,' the king of Israel, pull out the nails and come down from the cross right now. We'll believe it when we see it!'"* (v. 32, TPT).

The Koran says that Jesus did not die, and that He was not risen from the dead. But this is one of the things that history has proven. He died and He rose again! This is the amazing good news that sets Christianity apart from every other religion.

For three hours beginning at noon, darkness came over the earth. Jesus cried out in Aramaic, *"My God, My God, why have you forsaken me?"* (v. 34). This fulfilled the prophetic word in Psalm 22:1. Jesus cried out a second time and breathed His last. At that moment, the veil in the Holy of Holies was torn in two from the top to the bottom. The fact that the veil tore from top to bottom proves that God did this, for the veil was very thick and nearly eighty feet tall. When the Roman military officer saw how He died, he said that there was no doubt that this man was the Son of God!

PRAYER: *Jesus, Savior, Redeemer, Deliverer, Son of God, Risen from the dead, Firstborn from the dead, Pure and spotless Lamb of God, Lion of the tribe of Judah, Son of God, Son of Man. You are our all in all! Amen!*

BAPTIZED IN THE HOLY SPIRIT

And He said to them, "Go into all the world and preach the gospel to
every creature. He who believes and is baptized will be saved; but he
who does not believe will be condemned. And these signs will follow
those who believe: In My name they will cast out demons; they will
speak with new tongues; they will take up serpents; and if they drink
anything deadly, it will by no means hurt them; they will lay hands
on the sick, and they will recover."
—MARK 16:15–18; READ ALSO MARK 16

One powerful example of fulfilling this scripture in our day is the
German-American evangelist, Reinhard Bonnke who is known as the
"Billy Graham of Africa." He died at 79 years on December 7, 2019.

He saw 77 million documented decisions for Christ. In the year
2000, in Lagos, Nigeria, there were 3.4 million decisions in one week
for Christ. The last day over 1 million people got saved.

He surely had the signs following his ministry that Jesus spoke
about in Mark 16. In his meetings, the blind received sight, the lame
walked, people jumped out of wheelchairs, incurable diseases were
healed, and deliverance came for demonic oppression and possession.

In 2001, a Nigerian minister was raised from the dead. His name
is Daniel Ekechukure and he had died in a car crash. After three days,
his wife brought him to the basement of the church where Reinhard
Bonnke was preaching, and he was raised from the dead.

Reinhard Bonnke attributed the success of his ministry to being
baptized in the Holy Spirit.[10]

PRAYER: *Lord, we praise You for the amazing promises in Your word!*
Let them be fulfilled in our lives as You did in the life of Your servant,
Reinhard Bonnke. Fill us anew with Your Holy Spirit! You never change
and Your word is still true today! In Jesus' name. Amen!

March 20

AUTHENTICITY

...it seemed good to me also, having had perfect understanding of all things from the very first, to write to you an orderly account, most excellent Theophilus, that you may know the certainty of those things in which you were instructed.
—LUKE 1:3–4; READ ALSO VV. 1–20

Luke, a physician, writes with the compassion of a family doctor as he carefully documents the perfect humanity of the Son of Man, Jesus Christ. He builds the gospel narrative on the foundation of historical reliability, emphasizing Jesus' ancestry, birth, and early life before moving chronologically through His earthly ministry. Some grew in faith, and some in opposition to the Lord, which led finally to the death of the Son of Man on the cross. But Jesus' resurrection ensures that His purpose of saving the lost is fulfilled.

Christianity welcomes examination into its authenticity, so that we might *"know the certainty"* of its truths. (Luke 1:4). Alexander Hamilton, a signer of the Constitution and one of America's first constitutional lawyers, made such an investigation and concluded:

I have carefully examined the evidences of the Christian religion, and if I was sitting as a juror upon its authenticity, I would unhesitatingly give my verdict in its favor. I can prove its truth as clearly as any proposition ever submitted to the mind of man.[11]

PRAYER: *We thank You, Lord that the authenticity of the birth, death, and resurrection of Jesus are beyond question. We are so thankful for the authenticity of the Bible. It is the Book we can trust and rely on. It shows us how to live successfully in this life, and how to receive eternal life as well! The promise in Psalm 1 is that if we meditate day and night in Your word, we shall be like a tree planted by the rivers of water, that brings forth its fruit in its season, whose leaf also shall not wither; and whatever we do shall prosper. Amen.*

THE BIRTH OF JESUS CHRIST

Now Mary arose in those days and went into the hill country with haste, to a city of Judah, and entered the house of Zacharias and greeted Elizabeth. And it happened, when Elizabeth heard the greeting of Mary, that the babe leaped in her womb; and Elizabeth was filled with the Holy Spirit. Then she spoke out with a loud voice and said, "Blessed are you among women, and blessed is the fruit of your womb! But why is this granted to me, that the mother of my Lord should come to me?"
—LUKE 1:39–43; READ ALSO VV. 21–38

WHEN WAS JESUS born? Some Jewish historians say the calculation of His birth begins with Zacharias, the father of John the Baptist. According to the Jewish *Mishna*, Zacharias, being from the family of Abijah would have had his duty in the Jewish month of Sivan (about June). Elizabeth became pregnant after his duty. John would have been born in the Jewish month of Nisan (about March) the following year during the festivals of Passover, Unleavened Bread, and First Fruits. The Jews expected Elijah to come at Passover.

If John was born at Passover, then Jesus must have been born during the autumn feasts, probably the Feast of Tabernacles (Sukkoth). We know this because in Luke 1:26 and 36 we are told that Jesus was six months younger than John.

When Jesus was born, the shepherds were out in the field when the angel appeared to them; the weather was not so cold at this time of year. Jesus was born in a type of Sukkot or manger where they kept sheep and cattle. There was no room for Him in the inn.

If Yeshua was born in Sukkoth, then He was conceived during Hanukkah, the Festival of Lights which is conveniently around December 25th.

PRAYER: *"Light of the world, You came down into darkness, opened our eyes, let us see. Beauty that made our hearts adore You. All for love's sake became poor."* We worship You for becoming a man, the Savior of the world! Amen!

GOD'S DESTINY FOR US

And Mary sang this song: "My soul is ecstatic, overflowing with praises to God! My spirit bursts with joy over my life-giving God! For he set his tender gaze upon me, his lowly servant girl. And from here on, everyone will know that I have been favored and blessed. The Mighty One has worked a mighty miracle for me; holy is his name!"
—LUKE 1:46–49; READ ALSO VV. 39–56

In verse 47, Mary says, *"And my spirit has rejoiced in God my Savior"* (NKJV). Mary is the first recorded person to call Jesus Savior. She, too, needed a Savior just like every other human being.

God had a profound destiny for a young woman named Mary—a destiny unlike any He has ever allowed or will ever allow another woman to fulfill. He handpicked her for the highest honor ever given to a human being. He chose her to be the earthly mother of His only Son.

What was it about her that qualified her to be the mother of Jesus? We know that Mary possessed enormous purity, humility, devotion, and confidence in God. We know that she was 'highly favored' of the Lord, and we know that when she heard God's holy call, she simply said "yes."[12]

Mary could have said "no." Her situation must have been unsettling and would certainly make her the talk of the town. When she said to Gabriel, *"Let it be to me according to your word"* (v. 38), she did not know how her life would change or whether Joseph would be faithful to her. In fact, she perhaps assumed he would break their engagement. But still, she chose obedience. Essentially, she told Gabriel, "I belong to the Lord. Whatever He says, I'll do it." She placed her entire life on the altar of God's purpose, and then rejoiced, embracing God's destiny for her.

PRAYER: *Lord, help us to be like Mary and say, Lord, "Whatever You ask me to do, I'll do; wherever You ask me to go, I'll go; whatever You ask me to say, I'll say it!" Amen!*

MINISTRY OF JOHN THE BAPTIST

And you, child, will be called the prophet of the Highest; For you will go before the face of the Lord to prepare His ways, to give knowledge of salvation to His people by the remission of their sins, through the tender mercy of our God, with which the Dayspring from on high has visited us; to give light to those who sit in darkness and the shadow of death, to guide our feet into the way of peace.
—LUKE 1:76–79; READ ALSO VV. 57–80

The Passion Translation says it like this concerning the Dayspring: "The splendor light of heaven's glorious sunrise is about to break upon us in holy visitation, all because the merciful heart of our God is so very tender. The word from heaven will come to us with dazzling light to shine upon those who live in darkness, near death's dark shadow" (v. 78–79, TPT).

Some believe this is a quote from Malachi 4:2: *"But to you who fear My name the Sun of Righteousness shall arise with healing in His wings."* He is the dawning light of a new day to this dark world. The *"sunrise"* is the appearing of Jesus, the Messiah.

Jesus is our dazzling light. He is *"the light of the world"* and He has called us *"the light of the world. A city on a hill cannot be hidden"* (Matthew 5:14).

John (God's gracious gift) was born to point the way to the Light of the World, who would bring salvation to all. May we also point all to the Light of the World! He is the One who has healing in His wings, and will bring healing to all—spiritual, physical, and emotional.

PRAYER: *Our Father who is in heaven, we thank You for this wonderful ministry of John the Baptizer who pointed all to the Light of the World. He said that "He must increase while I must decrease." May we be like John and point everyone to the Light of the world, our Savior and Redeemer, Jesus Christ. May He always increase in our lives. May there be more of Him, and less of us! In Jesus' name. Amen.*

PEACE AND RECONCILIATION

Now there were in the same country shepherds living out in the fields, keeping watch over their flock by night. And behold, an angel of the Lord stood before them, and the glory of the Lord shone around them, and they were greatly afraid. Then the angel said to them, "Do not be afraid, for behold, I bring you good tidings of great joy which will be to all people. For there is born to you this day in the city of David a Savior, who is Christ the Lord. And this will be the sign to you: You will find a Babe wrapped in swaddling cloths, lying in a manger." And suddenly there was with the angel a multitude of the heavenly host praising God and saying: "Glory to God in the highest, and on earth peace, goodwill toward men!"
—LUKE 2:8–14; READ ALSO VV. 1–24

These are the unforgettable words President John F. Kennedy was to deliver in a luncheon speech on the day he was assassinated in Dallas, Texas, November 22, 1963:

We in this country, in this generation are, by destiny rather than choice, the watchmen on the walls of world freedom. We ask, therefore, that we may be worthy of our power and responsibility, that we may exercise our strength with wisdom and restraint, and that we may achieve in our time and for all time the ancient vision of *"peace on earth, goodwill toward men."* That must always be our goal. For as was written long ago, "Except the Lord keep the city, the watchman waketh but in vain."[13]

PRAYER: *We pray with all our hearts these words that the angels spoke on the day of the birth of Jesus Christ, our Savior. We pray there will be peace on earth: peace in our nation, peace in our states, peace in our cities, peace in our churches, and peace in our families. We pray for peace and reconciliation. We pray Jesus' words, that we would love one another, for this is the first and greatest commandment. We pray that Your church would fulfill its role as watchman toward this end! In Jesus' name. Amen.*

A PRAYER FOR YOUR CHILDREN

And He said to them, "Why did you seek Me? Did you not know that I must be about My Father's business?" But they did not understand the statement which He spoke to them. Then He went down with them and came to Nazareth, and was subject to them, but His mother kept all these things in her heart. And Jesus increased in wisdom and stature, and in favor with God and men.
—LUKE 2:49–52; READ ALSO VV. 25–52

PRAYER: *Abba Father, we pray verse 52 for our children. First, we pray that they will increase in wisdom. According to Proverbs 4:7–9, we declare that wisdom is the principal thing and that our children will get wisdom. In all their getting, they will get understanding. They will exalt her, and she will promote them. She will bring our children honor, when they embrace her. She will place on their head an ornament of grace; a crown of glory she will deliver to them. We pray Isaiah 54:13 for our children:* "All your children shall be taught by the Lord, and great shall be the peace of your children." *Of course, the greatest source of wisdom is the Bible itself.*

Next, we pray they will increase in stature and be in good health both physically and morally. We praise the Lord with all that is within us and bless His holy name. He forgives all our children's sins and heals all their diseases. He redeems their lives from the pit and crowns them with love and compassion. He satisfies their desires with good things so that their youth is renewed like the eagle's (Psalm 103:1–5).

Lastly, we pray that they will increase in favor with God and man. We pray they will love the Lord with all their heart and soul and mind and strength and seek after Him with all their heart, like Jesus did. We pray that God will bless the righteous, and surround them with favor as with a shield according to Psalm 5:12. We thank You by faith for Your blessing upon our children. Let this divine blessing be evidenced in every area of our children's lives—physically, materially, socially, emotionally, mentally, and spiritually. For Your glory we pray. In Jesus' name. Amen.

DOCTRINE OF TRINITY

When all the people were baptized, it came to pass that Jesus also was baptized; and while He prayed, the heaven was opened. And the Holy Spirit descended in bodily form like a dove upon Him, and a voice came from heaven which said, "You are My beloved Son; in You I am well pleased."

—LUKE 3:21–22; READ ALSO LUKE 3

This is one of the clearest scriptures supporting the Christian doctrine of the Trinity. The Trinity is not three Gods, but Three in One. Here we have Jesus, the Son of God who is being baptized. The Holy Spirit descended upon Him in bodily form like a dove, and a voice (the Father's voice) came from heaven which said, "*You are My beloved Son; in You I am well pleased.*" This is why we baptize in the name of the Father, and of the Son, and of the Holy Spirit.

We also see this in John 14:15–17: Jesus said: "If you love Me, keep My commandments. And I will pray the Father, and He will give you another Helper, that He may abide with you forever—the Spirit of truth, whom the world cannot receive, because it neither sees Him nor knows Him; but you know Him, for He dwells with you and will be in you."

We also see the Trinity in creation in Genesis 1:26: "Let Us make man in Our image, according to Our likeness; . . ."

In Isaiah 48:16, we see Isaiah speaking prophetically of Jesus: "Come near to Me, hear this: I have not spoken in secret from the beginning; from the time that it was, I was there and now the Lord God and His Spirit have sent Me."

We see Jesus in Matthew 6:9–15 praying the Lord's prayer to Father God. "Our Father who is in heaven." This is right after Matthew 4 where the Spirit led Jesus out into the wilderness to be tempted by the devil.

PRAYER: *Dear Heavenly Father, we thank You for revealing Your Son, Jesus, and Your Spirit to us. Fill us anew with Your Spirit and teach us Your ways. Protect us from evil and all false doctrine, for Your Name's sake. Amen.*

OVERCOMING TEMPTATION

And the devil said to Him, "If You are the Son of God, command this stone to become bread." But Jesus answered him, saying, "It is written, Man shall not live by bread alone, but by every word of God."
—Luke 4:3–4; read also vv. 1–15

Jesus refused to turn stones to bread, yet today He transforms the stony hearts of human beings and converts us into living bread to give to the nations.

If Jesus, the living Word, is quoting from the written Word (Deuteronomy 8:3), against the enemy's temptations, how much more do we need the revelation of what has been written so we can stand against all the snares of the devil?

In the third temptation, the devil took Jesus to Jerusalem and set him on the highest point of the temple and tempted him there saying, *"If you really are the Son of God, jump down in front of all the people For it is written in the Scriptures, 'God has given his angels instructions to protect you from harm. For the hands of angels will hold you up and keep you from hurting even one foot on a stone'"* (v. 9–10, TPT).

The devil was quoting from Psalm 91:11–12 but misapplied it. The devil knows scripture and can twist it. Jesus was not deceived. He quoted from Deuteronomy 6:16 and said, *"It is also written in the Scriptures, 'How dare you provoke the Lord your God!'"* (TPT).

Jesus was filled with the Holy Spirit at His baptism and was led by the Spirit out into the wilderness to be tempted. In His humanity, He did not stand in His own strength, but in the strength of the Word of God.

We, too, need the weapons of the Word of God, the power of the Spirit, and the blood of Jesus to overcome temptation.

Prayer: *Father, Your Word says in Revelation 12:11, that "they overcame him (the devil) by the Blood of the Lamb and the Word of their testimony." Help us to use Your weapons to overcome the temptations of the enemy! In Jesus' Name. Amen.*

March 28

MISSION EXTENSION

The Spirit of the Lord is upon Me, because He has anointed me to preach the gospel to the poor; He has sent Me to heal the brokenhearted, to proclaim liberty to the captives and recovery of sight to the blind, to set at liberty those who are oppressed; to proclaim the acceptable year of the Lord.
—LUKE 4:18–19; READ ALSO VV. 16–44

Jesus was reading from Isaiah 61:1–2. Jesus is defining His mission. First, He is anointed to preach the gospel to the poor. In Matthew 10:7–8 He tells His disciples to preach the gospel of the kingdom, which is to heal the sick, cleanse the lepers, raise the dead, cast out demons.

Second, He said He has been sent to heal the brokenhearted. He has been sent to heal broken hearts, broken relationships, broken hopes and dreams, and broken emotions.

Third, He said He has come to proclaim liberty to the captives and give new eyes for the blind.

Fourth, He said He would preach to prisoners this message: *"You are set free! I have come to share the message of Jubilee, for the time of God's great acceptance has begun"* (TPT).

Isaiah continues in verse 3: *"To comfort all who mourn, to console those who mourn in Zion, to give them beauty for ashes, the oil of joy for mourning, the garment of praise for the spirit of heaviness; that they may be called trees of righteousness, the planting of the LORD, that He may be glorified."*

Friends, this is our message. This is our ministry. This is our calling and destiny. Because Jesus lives in us, He is wanting His mission to be extended through us.

PRAYER: *Our Father in heaven, help us to see others the way You do. Help us to see the poor, the sick, the downtrodden, the ones who have lost hope. Help us to see with Your eyes, and hear with Your ears, the cry of the lost. Help us to share the good news with everyone. Help us to see that one person on Your heart today. Help us also to pray as You would for each one. In Jesus' name. Amen.*

FISHER OF MEN

At Your Word, I will let down the net.
—LUKE 5:5; READ ALSO VV. 1–16

This is the story of the miracle catch of fish. Jesus was preaching to a vast multitude of people on the shore of the Sea of Galilee. They were pushing to get close to Jesus. He noticed two fishing boats at the water's edge and Jesus climbed into the boat belonging to Simon Peter and asked him, *"Let me use your boat. Push it off a short distance away from the shore so I can speak to the crowds"* (v. 3, TPT).

Jesus sat down in the boat to teach the people, as was the custom of a rabbi to sit while teaching. When He had finished speaking, He said to Peter, *"Now row out to deep water to cast your nets and you will have a great catch"* (v. 4, TPT).

Peter tried to explain that they had been fishing all night and caught nothing, but he said, *"if you insist, we'll go out again and let down our nets because of your word."* As far as we can tell, Jesus was in the boat with them as He directed this. His presence gave confidence. "It is a blessed thing to see Christ sitting in the boat while you cast out the net. If you catch a glimpse of his approving smile as he watches you, you will work right heartily." [14]

"And when they had done this, they caught a great number of fish, and their net was breaking. So they signaled to their partners in the other boat to come and help them. And they came and filled both the boats, so that they began to sink" (v. 6–7, TPT). It has been estimated that this was a catch of nearly one ton of fish, what was normally caught in two weeks.

"When Simon Peter saw it, he fell down at Jesus' knees, saying, 'Depart from me, for I am a sinful man O Lord!'" (v. 8). Peter was convinced by this miracle that Jesus was the Messiah and his response was to fall on his knees and worship.

Jesus said to not be afraid, for *"from now on you will catch men"* (for salvation). From that moment on, they left *everything* to follow Jesus.

PRAYER: *You are the greatest fisherman of all, Jesus. Amen!*

NEW GARMENT

Then He spoke a parable to them: "No one puts a piece from a new garment on an old one; otherwise the new makes a tear, and also the piece that was taken out of the new does not match the old. And no one puts new wine into old wineskins; or else the new wine will burst the wineskins and be spilled, and the wineskins will be ruined. But new wine must be put into new wineskins, and both are preserved. And no one having drunk old wine, immediately desires new, for he says, 'The old is better.'"
—Luke 5:36–39; read also vv. 17–39

Jesus' point is clear that you can't fit His new life into the old forms. This explains why Jesus did not begin a reform movement within Judaism, working with the rabbinical schools and such. Jesus was saying that He hadn't come to patch up old practices, but that He had come with a whole new set of clothes.

He said that patching up an old garment with a piece of a new garment not only destroys the new garment, but the new garment will pull the old garment to pieces. It will be just as disastrous to adapt the principles of Jesus to the old systems.

"And who pours new wine into an old wineskin? If someone did, the old wineskin would burst and the new wine would be lost. New wine must always be poured into new wineskins. Yet you say, 'The old ways are better,' and you refuse to even taste the new that I bring" (v. 37–39, TPT).

Christ is our new garment (righteousness) and our new wine that is poured into a new wineskin (our new life and divine nature). Many today are trying to patch up their old garments (self-righteousness), hoping their old lives can hold the new wine of the Spirit.

Prayer: *Lord, help us to be willing to leave behind the old life and put on the new life that You provide so freely. Thank You for the Cross and all it means! In Jesus' name, Amen!*

PROTECTION FROM TRAITORS

After Jesus had spent all night in prayer, He chose twelve apostles: Simon, whom He also named Peter, and Andrew his brother; James and John; Philip and Bartholomew; Matthew and Thomas; James the Son of Alphaeus, and Simon called the Zealot; Judas the son of James, (also called Thaddeus) and Judas Iscariot who also became a traitor.
—LUKE 6:14–16; READ ALSO VV. 1–26

Iscariot is not Judas' last name. It could be taken from a Hebrew word meaning lock. Judas the locksmith. Most likely he was chosen to lock the collection bag. Having the key, he could pilfer it when he wanted to.

In a similar way that Judas Iscariot became a traitor, we have an example in our own American history. Benedict Arnold was considered by many to be the best general and the most accomplished leader in the Continental Army during the Revolutionary War. Without his early contributions to the American cause, some historians feel the American Revolution might have been lost. Thanks to his friend George Washington, his rank was adjusted to Major General in February 1777.

After marrying a beautiful young British Loyalist, Peggy Shippen, he fell deeply into debt and became frustrated over perceived lack of recognition. As a result, he negotiated his treason with the British commander, Sir Henry Clinton, and promised to deliver the American stronghold at West Point and its three thousand defenders for about one million dollars in today's currency.

He persuaded Washington to place the fort under his command. Fortunately, the plot was discovered just before the British attack. Arnold was able to escape capture and fled to England where he became a Brigadier General and led devastating attacks against the Americans. After the war, he returned to England, where he died, virtually unknown.[15]

PRAYER: *Lord, protect us and our nation from traitors like Benedict Arnold and Judas Iscariot. We pray for Psalm 91 protection over America. Amen.*

April 1

BUILDING ON THE ROCK OF HIS WORD

But why do you call Me "Lord, Lord," and not do the things which I say? Whoever comes to Me, and hears My sayings and does them, I will show you whom he is like: He is like a man building a house, who dug deep and laid the foundation on the rock. And when the flood arose, the stream beat vehemently against that house, and could not shake it, for it was founded on the rock. But he who heard and did nothing is like a man who built a house on the earth without a foundation, against which the stream beat vehemently; and immediately it fell. And the ruin of that house was great.
—LUKE 6:46–49; READ ALSO VV. 27–49

This warning of Jesus applies to people who speak or say things to Jesus—or about Jesus—but don't really mean it. They say it superficially, while their mind is elsewhere. They believe there is value in the bare words and feel like they are fulfilling some kind of religious duty, but with no heart, no soul, and no spirit. In other words, their spiritual life has nothing to do with their daily life.

Jesus, in this illustration of the two builders, shows that the real foundation of life, homes and marriages is usually hidden and is only proven in the storm. The wise and foolish men both undertook to build houses, and both finished them. One built his house upon the rock, and one built his house upon the sand. When the storms of life arose, the one whose foundation was built upon the rock could not be shaken, but the one who built his house upon the sand crashed, and its ruin was devastating. Merely hearing God's word isn't enough to provide a secure foundation. It is necessary that we also apply the word to our life's circumstances.

Barna research has shown 33 percent of marriages end in divorce. If we build on the Rock of His Word, we will have successful marriages! (Our marriage has lasted fifty-two years!)

PRAYER: *Lord, we want good and faithful marriages and homes built upon Your Word and prayer. Help us to be faithful to our marriages and to always set godly examples. May the family altar be the center of our homes. The family that prays together, stays together. In Jesus' name. Amen.*

JESUS, THE MESSIAH

And that very hour He cured many of infirmities, afflictions, and evil spirits; and to many blind He gave sight. Jesus answered and said to them, "Go and tell John the things you have seen and heard: that the blind see, the lame walk, the lepers are cleansed, the deaf hear, the dead are raised, the poor have the gospel preached to them. And blessed is he who is not offended because of Me."
—LUKE 7:21–23; READ ALSO VV. 1–30

We see in John 1:29–36 that John the Baptist clearly recognized Jesus as the Messiah at His water baptism. John's doubt in the Luke passage might be explained because he himself may have misunderstood the ministry of the Messiah. Perhaps John thought that if Jesus were really the Messiah, He would perform works connected with the political deliverance of Israel—or at least deliver him from prison.

Also, there were Jews who made the distinction between the coming One and the Christ. "Some Jews of that time distinguished between a prophet to come promised by Moses in Deuteronomy 18:15, and the Messiah. Perhaps John's long trial in prison had confused him."[1] The prophet to come was Jesus.

Verse 21, above, was the real power of the Messiah in action; yet performed in personal, even humble ways. Most of these miracles fulfill some promise found in Isaiah, particularly Isaiah 61:1, 11; Isaiah 35:5–6; Isaiah 26:19.

Jesus wanted to assure both John and his disciples that He was the Messiah. However, He did not work in spectacular displays of political deliverance, but in humble acts by meeting people's needs.

Jesus said that the ones not offended in Him would be blessed. He knew that the focus of His ministry was quite offensive to those who longed for political deliverance.

PRAYER: *Jesus, You said that "Greater works than these shall you do, because I go to my Father" (John 14:12). May we walk in love, service, and signs, wonders and miracles! Amen!*

April 3

THE GREATNESS OF GOD'S MERCY

Then one of the Pharisees asked Him to eat with him. And He went to the Pharisee's house and sat down to eat. And behold, a woman in the city who was a sinner, when she knew that Jesus sat at the table in the Pharisee's house, brought an alabaster flask of fragrant oil, and stood at His feet behind Him weeping; and she began to wash His feet with her tears, and wiped them with the hair of her head; and she kissed His feet and anointed them with the fragrant oil. Now when the Pharisee who had invited Him saw this, he spoke to himself, saying, "This Man, if He were a prophet, would know who and what manner of woman this is who is touching Him, for she is a sinner."
—LUKE 7:36–39; READ ALSO VV. 31–50

Simon, the Pharisee, thinks that a genuine prophet could discern the character of the woman. In Jesus' reply, He tells the parable about the creditor who had two debtors. One owed five hundred denarii and the other fifty. When they had nothing to pay, he forgave both of them. Jesus asked Simon which one would love him more. Simon replied that the one who had more forgiven would love him more. Jesus told him he was right.

Jesus then went on to say that when He came into the house, Simon gave Him no water to wash His feet; the woman washed His feet with her tears. Simon gave Him no kiss, but the woman had not ceased to kiss His feet. Simon did not anoint His head with oil; but she anointed His feet with fragrant oil. So, Jesus forgave her because she loved much. *"But to whom little is forgiven the same loves little"* (v. 47).

This parable is a contrast between two debtors: the amount of debt, the forgiveness of the debts, and the contrasting gratitude of them both. Simon's minimal hospitality is contrasted with the woman's lavish devotion.

PRAYER: *Lord Jesus, we see here that the woman was forgiven of her sin and showed her love and thanks to You from her heart. May we realize the depth of our sin like she did, and the greatness of God's mercy and be filled with unending love and thankfulness. In Jesus' name. Amen.*

April 4

LORD OVER THE WEATHER

Now it happened, on a certain day, that He got into a boat with His disciples. And He said to them, "Let us cross over to the other side of the lake." And they launched out.
—LUKE 8:22; READ ALSO VV. 1–25

During their crossing, the Lord fell asleep and a great storm arose. They were terrified and awoke him saying, *"Master, Master, we are perishing!"* (v. 24). Jesus rebuked the wind and the raging of the water, and instantly there was a calm. He then asked them, *"Where is your faith?"* (v. 25).

There was another time in American history during World War II when General Patton asked Chaplain O'Neill to write a prayer for good weather in order to defeat the Germans in the winter of 1944. The Chaplain responded it was not customary to pray for clear weather in order to kill fellow men.

Patton's response was direct, "Chaplain, are you teaching me theology or are you the Chaplain of the Third Army? I want a prayer."

He wrote this prayer, which was used during the Battle of the Bulge and given to about two hundred and fifty thousand men in the 3rd Army:

> Almighty and most merciful Father, we humbly beseech Thee, of Thy great goodness, to restrain these immoderate rains with which we have had to contend. Grant us fair weather for Battle. Graciously hearken to us as soldiers who call upon Thee that armed with Thy power, we may advance from victory to victory, and crush the oppression and wickedness of our enemies, and establish Thy justice among men and nations. Amen.[2]

The next day the weather cleared and remained perfect for about six days while the Third Army pushed North. Upon reviewing the weather, Patton said of the Chaplain, "******! Look at the weather. That O'Neill sure did some potent praying. Get him up here. I want to pin a medal on him." He was given a Bronze Star Medal for his good stand with the Lord and the soldiers. God had miraculously intervened!

PRAYER: *You are Lord over the weather, and our nation! Amen!*

April 5

DELIVERANCE FROM EVIL

*Jesus asked him, saying, "What is your name?" And he said, "Legion,"
because many demons had ventered him. And they begged Him that
He would not command them to go out into the abyss. Now a herd of
many swine was feeding there on the mountain. So they begged Him
that He would permit them to enter them. And He permitted them.
Then the demons went out of the man and entered the swine, and the
herd ran violently down the steep place into the lake and drowned.*
—LUKE 8:30–33; READ ALSO vv. 26–56

This is the story of the Gadarene demoniac who did not wear clothes,
nor did he live in a house, but in the tombs. Jesus commanded the
demons to leave him. Then Jesus asked him (the man) what his name
was, and a demon answered. Jesus gave him (the man), dignity and
identity, by asking him what his name was. He was not asking the
demon to name himself.

The word *possessed* is never found in the Greek text. One term that
is used is "to be demonized" or to be affected by a demon. Demons
specialize in illness and infirmity (Mark 9:17–25); in mental deception,
(1 Timothy 4:1); emotional turmoil (1 Samuel 16:14); relationship troubles (Judges 9:23); and occult activity, e.g. New Age (Acts 16:16).

Areas that open one up to be "demonized" are:[3]

+ Embracing false doctrines (1 Timothy 4:1)
+ Refusal to forgive (Matthew 18:23–35)
+ Sexual perversion (1 Corinthians 5:5)
+ Occult practices (Leviticus 20:27; Deuteronomy 18:9–13)—
  This is especially harmful.

To receive deliverance from the oppression of demons, one must
repent of the sin that gave a demon access.

Jesus told us in Mark 16:17, that one of the signs of a believer was
that we would cast out demons. We have been given authority over
them through our faith in Jesus Christ (Luke 10:19).

PRAYER: *Our Father, we pray that You would deliver us from evil!
Thank You that we are hidden in Christ! Amen!*

AUTHORITY FOR MINISTRY

Then He called His twelve disciples together and gave them power and authority over all demons, and to cure diseases. He sent them to preach the kingdom of God and to heal the sick....So they departed and went through the towns preaching the gospel and healing everywhere.
—Luke 9:1–2, 6; read also vv. 1–17

In these verses, Jesus delegates authority for ministry. Through the flow of Holy Spirit's power, we may expect victory over the powers of darkness and their operations (Luke 10:19). We are assigned to "do business" as authorized representatives of our Lord until He returns (Luke 19:13).

There is an amazing example of this from Bethel School of Supernatural Ministry:

> One student named Jason was ordering a meal inside a fast-food restaurant. Not content to share Christ only with those behind the counter, he began to speak past the cashier to three men in a car at the drive-up window! After receiving his food, Jason left noticing they had parked to eat. He renewed his conversation with them and saw' that the man in the back seat had a broken leg. So, he climbed into the car with them and invited the Holy Spirit to come...and He came. The man began to curse. He had no understanding about the holy fire on his leg. They all jumped out of the car, and the injured man removed his brace and stomped his leg. He was completely healed! The three were so moved by God's goodness that they opened the trunk of their car, which was filled with illegal drugs. They dumped the narcotics onto the pavement, dancing on them and destroying them! Jason brought the three men to the 24-hour prayer house and led them to Christ. The kindness of God led them to repentance. This is the normal Christian life.[4]

Prayer: *Help us not to limit You and Your designated power and authority through our unbelief. Help us to expect You to do amazing miracles today! In Jesus' name, amen!*

April 7

FAITHFUL MARTYRS

Then He said to them all, "If anyone desires to come after Me, let him deny himself, and take up his cross daily, and follow Me. For whoever desires to save his life will lose it, but whoever loses his life for My sake will save it."
—LUKE 9:23–24; READ ALSO VV. 18–36

Vibia Perpetua (181?–203) was an early Christian who lived in Carthage, North Africa. Roman Christians had brought the gospel to that region even though Emperor Severus had banned teaching or making of converts.

Perpetua was well aware of this at the time of her own baptism. She said as she came out of the water, "The Holy Spirit has inspired me to pray for nothing but patience under bodily pain." To add to the intensity of the situation, she was nursing her baby. Her father begged her to recant. Felicitas, her pregnant maidservant, also accepted Christ, and the two were in prison together for their faith. Vibia was allowed to nurse her son while in prison. Felicitas gave birth to a little daughter who was brought up by her sister.

> At last, the day of the martyrs honor and glory came. They were taken to the arena. With joyful countenances they marched from the prison to the arena as though on their way to heaven. If there was any trembling, it was for joy, not fear. Felicitas, too, was joyful because she had safely survived childbirth and was now able to participate in the contest with the wild animals.…Perpetua was tossed first and fell on her back. She sat up, and being more concerned with her sense of modesty than with her pain, covered her thighs with her gown which had been torn down one side. Then finding her hairclip, which had fallen out, she pinned back her loose hair, thinking it not proper for a martyr to suffer with disheveled hair; it might seem that she was mourning in her hour of triumph.…They were both killed by the sword of the gladiators.[5]

PRAYER: *Father in heaven, we are humbled by these brave and faithful martyrs. May we follow their example. Amen.*

April 8

MARKED BY MERCY

Now it came to pass, when the time had come for Him to be received up, that He steadfastly set His face to go to Jerusalem and sent messengers before His face. And as they went, they entered a village of the Samaritans, to prepare for Him. But they did not receive Him, because His face was set for the journey to Jerusalem. And when His disciples James and John saw this, they said, "Lord, do You want us to command fire to come down from heaven and consume them, just as Elijah did?" But He turned and rebuked them, and said, "You do not know what manner of spirit you are of. For the Son of Man did not come to destroy men's lives but to save them."
—LUKE 9:51–56; READ ALSO VV. 37–62

We see here that true greatness is marked by mercy, not judgment. James and John were outraged by the poor reception that Jesus received in this village and offered to destroy the city in spectacular judgment for Jesus' sake.

Interestingly, these men were so confident in their ability to call down fire to destroy a city, but earlier they weren't even able to cast the demon out of a young boy (v. 37–42). Their reaction was purely based in anger.

The offence they picked up on behalf of Jesus was not appreciated, and they received a rebuke. Their failing came in two ways: 1) They didn't know themselves. They thought they were being like Jesus or showing the character of God. They were wrong. They did not represent God or His heart. He loved the Samaritans and wanted them to repent and be saved. 2) They didn't know Jesus and His mission. He came to seek and to save the lost, not to burn them up with fire from heaven.

They learned that following Jesus means being merciful to others instead of being harsh with them. Especially we need to remember that God says, *"Vengeance is Mine, I will repay, says the Lord"* (Romans 12:19).[6]

PRAYER: *Father in heaven, show us Your heart. Give us a heart of mercy. Help us to take up our cross daily and follow You. Help us always to represent Your heart to people! In Jesus' name. Amen.*

April 9

REACHING THE LOST

Whatever house you enter, first say, "Peace be to this house." And whatever city you enter, and they receive you, eat what is set before you; and heal those in it who are sick, and say to them, "The kingdom of God has come near to you."
—LUKE 10:5, 8, 9; READ ALSO VV. 1–24

Here we find Jesus giving a four-step evangelistic method for reaching the lost: 1) Speak peace to them. 2) Fellowship with them. 3) Take care of their needs. 4) Proclaim the good news.

1. Jesus' method of evangelism calls for us to speak peace over the lost. We need to declare peace because we, as Christians, have been at war with the lost. Jesus was glad to be known as a friend of sinners. Ed Silvoso learned of his own belligerence to the lost when he was telling God about everything that was wrong with his neighbors. He talked to Him in disgust about the unwed mother, about the couple who kept them awake arguing and fighting, and about the neighbor whose yard was a disgrace and lowering the real estate values of the neighborhood. He also talked about the teenager on drugs. God said to him, "Ed, I am so glad you have not witnessed to any of these yet." He asked why. God said, "Because I don't want your neighbors to know that you and I are related. I hurt when they hurt....Unless you love them I cannot trust you with their lives."[7] He repented!

2. Have them over for dinner and fellowship with them. Show them acceptance, love, and respect. Fellowship then leads to the third step.

3. Pray for their felt needs. Their most important need is salvation, but they don't know that. But through meeting felt needs, we show them that Jesus is a friend of sinners.

4. Then we share the Gospel with them. This is like pulling up to someone in the desert with cold drinks. You don't need to beg him to come on board. You just open the door.

PRAYER: *Father in heaven, forgive us for the ways we have misrepresented You in winning the lost. Help us to be like You in every way. Help us to be good fishermen! Amen!*

ONE THING

Now it happened as they went that He entered a certain village; and a certain woman named Martha welcomed Him into her house. And she had a sister called Mary, who also sat at Jesus' feet and heard His word. But Martha was distracted with much serving, and she approached Him and said, "Lord, do You not care that my sister has left me to serve alone? Therefore, tell her to help me." And Jesus answered and said to her, "Martha, Martha, you are worried and troubled about many things. But one thing is needed, and Mary has chosen that good part, which will not be taken away from her."
—Luke 10:38–42; read also vv. 25–42

Pay attention: Jesus said, *"One thing was needed."*

Our "one thing," personal devotions, are very important to Jesus. First, make prayer, praise, and devotions a part of your devotional time. Second, read Scripture, devotionals, and biographies of the faithful. Remember Joshua 1:8 says, *"Let not this book of the law depart from your eyes, but you shall meditate in it day and night, that you may observe to do according to all that is written in it. For then you shall make your way prosperous, and then you shall have good success."* Third, you must listen to God: He will speak to you personally, through the Scriptures. It helps to apply and remember what He says when you write it down in a journal. If needed, you can share with a trusted mentor in the faith. God's Word says in John 10:4–5: *"And when he brings out his own sheep, he goes before them; and the sheep follow him, for they know his voice. Yet they will by no means follow a stranger, but will flee from him, for they do not know the voice of strangers."*

Billy Graham said, *"The greatest hindrance to Christianity today is Christians who do not know how to practice the presence of God."* [8]

PRAYER: *Lord and Master, please forgive us for being so busy and distracted like Martha with "much serving." Help us to be like Mary and just sit at Your feet and be known as a person of Your Presence. Amen.*

April 11

NAMES OF GOD

Our Father in heaven, Hallowed be Your name.
—LUKE 11:2; READ ALSO VV. 1–28

Jesus taught us to pray that the Father's name be "hallowed." To hallow God's name means "to sanctify or set apart or praise it."

In the Old Testament, eight names of God are compounded with the covenant name "Jehovah:"[9]

+ Jehovah-Tsidkenu: "the Lord our righteousness" (Jeremiah 23:5–6). As we pray this name, we thank God that Jesus, who is our righteousness, forgave our sin and we stand before God having the free gift of the righteousness of Christ.

+ Jehovah-M'kaddesh: "the Lord who sanctifies" (Leviticus 20:8). As we pray this name, we thank God that He sanctifies us and gives us victory over the power of sin in our lives.

+ Jehovah-Shammah: "the Lord is there" (Ezekiel 48:35). We thank God that He fills us with His presence and will never leave us or forsake us.

+ Jehovah-Shalom: "the Lord is peace" (Judges 6:24). We thank God for giving us peace with God through the cross and for imparting His peace.

+ Jehovah-Rophe: "the Lord who heals" (Exodus 15:26). We thank God for physical and spiritual healing.

+ Jehovah-Jireh: "the Lord who sees to it, or the Lord's provision shall be seen" (Genesis 22:14). We praise God for providing for all our needs, spirit, soul, or body and that we can do all things through Christ (Philippians 4:13).

+ Jehovah-Nissi: "the Lord my banner" (Exodus 17:15). We thank God who gives us victory and makes us conquerors.

+ Jehovah-Rohi: "the Lord my shepherd" (Psalm 23:1, 4, 6). We thank God He feeds, leads, protects, and cares for us.

PRAYER: *We thank You, Lord God for these powerful names that touch every area of our lives. Your Name is above every name, and at the name of Jesus, every knee will bow. Praise Him now for these names and what they mean to you. Amen.*

April 12

HELP OUR UNBELIEF

And while the crowds were thickly gathered together, He began to say,
"This is an evil generation. It seeks a sign, and no sign will be given
to it except the sign of Jonah the prophet. For as Jonah became a sign
to the Ninevites, so also the Son of Man will be to this generation.
The queen of the South will rise up in the judgment with the men of
this generation and condemn them, for she came from the ends of the
earth to hear the wisdom of Solomon; and indeed a greater than Sol-
omon is here. The men of Nineveh will rise up in the judgment with
this generation and condemn it, for they repented at the preaching of
Jonah; and indeed, a greater than Jonah is here."
—LUKE 11:29–32; READ ALSO VV. 29–54

Jesus told us that Jonah became a sign, and Jesus would be a similar sign to this generation. Jonah gave his life to appease the wrath of God which was against his disobedience. But death did not hold him; after three days and nights of being in the belly of the whale, he was alive and free. Jesus also gave His life to appease the wrath of God for our sin and was in the heart of the earth for three days and three nights. Death could not hold Him, and God raised Him from the dead.

He also said the Queen of the South came from the ends of the earth (modern day Yemen) to hear the wisdom of Solomon. When she saw the great works God did for and through Solomon, she praised the God of Israel.

The queen of the South and the men of Nineveh were all Gentiles, but they had hearts more open to the things of God than the religious people of Jesus' day who would not believe and receive the work of God unfolding right before their eyes. The Ninevites converted after the preaching of one prophet. The people of Israel had many prophets throughout their history, and the greatest Prophet of all was now preaching to them, yet they refused to listen.

PRAYER: *Dear God, we are amazed at the unbelief of the Israelites, and yet are we not also guilty of unbelief? Lord, we believe, help our unbelief! May our faith please You! Amen!*

PREPARATION FOR ETERNITY

Jesus then gave them this illustration: A wealthy landowner had a farm that produced bumper crops. In fact, it filled his barns to overflowing! He thought, "What should I do now that every barn is full and I have nowhere else to store more? I know what I'll do! I'll tear down the barns and build one massive barn that will hold all my grain and goods. Then I can just sit back, surrounded with comfort and ease. I'll enjoy life with no worries at all." God said to him "What a fool you are to trust in your riches and not in me. This very night the messengers of death are demanding to take your life. Then who will get all the wealth you have stored up for yourself?" This is what will happen to all those who fill up their lives with everything but God.
—Luke 12:17–21, TPT; READ ALSO VV. 1–31

The man in Jesus' parable was blessed with financial success. In fact, he was so successful that he had trouble managing his resources. "What shall I do?" he said. Sometimes we mistakenly think that to be rich means to be free from anxiety, but this rich man was as full of cares as a beggar. So, he decided the answer to his problems was to build bigger barns.

But God said to him, "*Fool! This night your soul will be required of you*" (v. 20). In one night, all the man's accomplishments and plans were ruined. He was not a fool because he was rich, but because he had forgotten about preparation for *eternity*. This man owed his life and all he had to God. But most of all, he owed his soul to God. God asked him who would those things belong to now? He certainly couldn't take them with him. God said, "*So is he who lays up treasure for himself, and is not rich toward God*" (v. 21).

John Wesley said you should earn as much as you can, save as much as you can, and give as much as you can. He himself lived on 28 British pounds and gave the rest away, even when his salary quadrupled.[10]

PRAYER: *Lord, help us to be rich toward You! Amen!*

DISCERNMENT

Then He also said to the multitudes, "Whenever you see a cloud rising out of the west, immediately you say, 'A shower is coming'; and so it is. And when you see the south wind blow, you say 'There will be hot weather'; and there is. Hypocrites! You can discern the face of the sky and of the earth, but how is it you do not discern this time?"
—LUKE 12:54–56; READ ALSO VV. 32–59

Jesus rebuked the people of His day because they did not discern this time. They should have understood more about the prophecies regarding the first coming of Jesus and appreciate the obvious signs confirming Jesus as the promised Messiah. Jesus wanted everyone to discern this time and be ready for His return.

In our present times, there are many reasons to believe that Jesus is coming soon, adding to our sense of urgency concerning the day in which we live.

The stage is set for a rebuilt temple, which is necessary to fulfill the prophecies of the abomination of desolation (Matthew 24:15).

Since 1948 Israel is a nation again, and hopes of the rebuilt temple continue to rise among certain Jews.

In 1967, Jerusalem came under Israeli control, fulfilling Luke 21:24, which says Jerusalem will be trampled by Gentiles until the times of the Gentiles are fulfilled.

The stage is set for the kind of false religion the Bible says will characterize the very last days (2 Thessalonians 2:4).

Lawlessness is abounding, and the love of many is growing cold (Luke 24:12). The days are as Lot and Noah with the LGBT agenda taking forefront (Luke 17:27–30).

The stage is set for the kind of one-world economic system predicted for the very last days (Revelation 13:15–17).

PRAYER: *We do pray in Jesus' name that we will discern the time and be ready for the Second Coming. We pray we will be in the Word, and not be deceived as the days grow closer for the Son of Man to return! Amen!*

April 15

THE IMPORTANCE OF REPENTANCE

*There were present at that season some who told Him about the Gali-
leans whose blood Pilate had mingled with their sacrifices. And Jesus
answered and said to them, "Do you suppose that these Galileans
were worse sinners than all other Galileans, because they suffered
such things? I tell you, no; but unless you repent you will all likewise
perish. Or those eighteen on whom the tower of Siloam fell and killed
them, do you think that they were worse sinners than all other men
who dwelt in Jerusalem? I tell you, no; but unless you repent you will
all likewise perish."*
—LUKE 13:1–5; READ ALSO VV. 1–22

Jesus mentioned two disasters that were well known in His day. One
was an evil done by the hand of man, and the other was seemingly a
natural disaster when the tower of Siloam fell.

We normally think of some people as good and some people as
bad. We find it easy to believe that God should allow good things to
happen to good people and bad things to bad people, but Jesus cor-
rected this thinking.

It wasn't that the Galileans in question were innocent; His point
was that they were simply not more guilty than the others. All were,
and are, guilty.

It's true that the wicked man sometimes falls dead in the street,
but isn't it true that ministers have fallen dead in the pulpit? [11]

Jesus turned His focus from "Why did this happen?" and turned
it to the question, "What does this mean to me?" It means that we all
may die at any time, so repentance must be a top priority. Repentance
means to change your mind or purpose. It is fully turning to God
without reservation or excuse. Jesus' warning that they must repent
or perish had an immediate, chilling fulfillment. Within a generation, those citizens of Jerusalem, who had not repented and turned to
Jesus, perished in the destruction of Jerusalem in 70 A.D.

PRAYER: *Lord, considering the nearness of Your second coming, may we
all be ready to meet You. Forgive us of our sins. Amen.*

URGENCY TO ENTER THE GATE

*The one said to Him, "Lord, are there few who are saved?" And He
said to them, strive to enter through the narrow gate, for many, I say to
you, will seek to enter and will not be able. When once the Master of
the house has risen up and shut the door, and you begin to stand outside and knock at the door, saying, "Lord, Lord, open for us," and He
will answer and say to you, "I do not know you, where you are from."*
—LUKE 13:23–25; READ ALSO VV. 23–35

Following these verses, the Bible then says that those He is talking to
will reply and tell Him that they dined with Him and walked with
Him as He taught them. But He will reply and say that these people
are not part of His family. He will say *"Now, go away from me! For
you are all disloyal to me and do evil"* (v. 27, TPT).

The real question is not "Will the saved be few? But, "Will it be
you?" This is what He was saying when He said, *"Strive to enter
through the narrow gate."*

Because the way is narrow, it takes both effort and purpose to
enter it. It also implies that we can't bring with us unnecessary things.
Therefore, we must "strive" or "agonize" in order to lay these things
aside and come in.

This is not a call to save yourself by good works. Good works aren't
the right gate. Jesus Himself is the gate; He is the door.

We need to strive to enter because there are many obstacles in the
way. "The world is an obstacle. The devil is an obstacle. Probably the
worst obstacle is our own flesh."[12]

We must have an urgency to enter the gate, because there will
come a time when it is too late to enter. When Jesus speaks of the
"shut door," this means there are limits to His divine mercy, and that
there will be those who will not be able to enter in.

PRAYER: *Dear Father, as the chorus goes: "I have decided to follow
Jesus. No turning back. No turning back. The world behind me, the cross
before me. No turning back, no turning back." In Jesus' name, amen.*

MINISTER TO THE POOR AND BE BLESSED

For whoever exalts himself will be humbled, and he who humbles himself will be exalted. Then He also said to him who invited Him, "When you give a dinner or a supper do not ask your friends, your brothers, your relatives, nor rich neighbors, lest they also invite you back and you be repaid. But when you give a feast, invite the poor, the maimed, the lame, the blind. And you will be blessed, because they cannot repay you; for you shall be repaid at the resurrection of the just."

—LUKE 14:11–14; READ ALSO VV. 1–24

Bill Johnson tells this story in his book *When Heaven Invades Earth:*

Ralph and Colleen, who had a ministry to the poor were getting married. Although it is common for the bride and groom to register for gifts at fine department stores, Ralph and Colleen did so at Target; and all they put on their wish list were coats, hats, gloves, and sleeping bags. These were to be given to their guests. They sent out a bus to pick up everyone. They had asked Bill to be sensitive to the Holy Spirit in case He wanted to heal people during the wedding.

Since they were expecting miracles, they were not disappointed. Luke came, needing a cane to walk. He had braces on each arm and a large brace around his neck. He said his problem was carpel tunnel syndrome. They prayed, and he was totally healed! Then they asked about the braces. He said he had been in an accident and had an artificial shin and hip and had lost half a lung. His one leg was an inch too short. The Lord answered, lengthened his leg and he walked without a limp. Then the Lord healed his neck of cancer and replaced the muscles. (A doctor was praying and commanded the muscles to grow, using the Latin names). He could move his neck. They took off the neck brace. The doctor gave him a clean bill of health! [13]

PRAYER: *"If you ask anything in My name, I will do it"* (John 16:24). Hallelujah! Amen!

April 18

PUT JESUS FIRST

If anyone comes to Me and does not hate his father and mother, wife and children, brothers and sisters, yes, and his own life also, he cannot be My disciple. And whoever does not bear his cross and come after Me cannot be My disciple.
—LUKE 14:26–27; READ ALSO VV. 25–35

The Passion Translation says it like this: "When you follow me as my disciple, you must put aside your father, your mother, your wife, your sisters, your brothers—yes, you will even seem as though you hate your own life. This is the price you'll pay to be considered one of my followers."

What Jesus is saying is this: a true disciple puts Jesus first, and other relationships are definitely of lower priority than faithfulness and obedience to Jesus.

> Napoleon understood this principle when he said, "I know men; and I tell you that Jesus Christ is no mere man. Between him and every other person in the world there is no possible term of comparison. Alexander (the Great), Caesar, Charlemagne, and I have founded empires. But on what did we rest the creations of our genius? Upon force. Jesus Christ founded his empire upon love; and this hour millions of men would die for him."[14]

We see always that Jesus founded His kingdom upon love, yet here He uses the word *hate*. This shows how great the difference must be between our loyalty to Jesus and to everyone and everything else.

Jesus said to the multitudes that we must bear His cross and come after Him. The people knew what He meant. In the Roman world, before a man died on the cross, he had to carry his cross (or at least the beam of it) to the place of execution. Carrying the cross always led to death on the cross; he never came back.

PRAYER: *Lord, help us to understand and take to heart Your words. We are not just asking You to be our Savior, we are asking You to be our Lord and to follow Your commands. This requires us to die to ourselves and live only for You. Amen.*

April 19

LOST SOULS

Or what woman, having ten silver coins, if she loses one coin, does not light a lamp, sweep the house, and search carefully until she finds it? And when she has found it, she calls her friends and neighbors together, saying "Rejoice with me, for I have found the piece which I lost!" Likewise, I say to you, there is joy in the presence of the angels of God over one sinner who repents.
—LUKE 15:8–10; READ ALSO VV. 1–10

One commentator suggested that it was possible that the coin referred to was on a silver chain worn round the head as a mark of a married woman. It was a very precious ornament.

First, the woman in the story brought light. Then, she swept and cleaned the house while searching carefully for the coin. She kept looking until she found the missing coin.

> This is how the church, led by the Holy Spirit, will search for lost souls. First, we put forth the light of God's word, then we must sweep and clean our own house, and then we search carefully for the lost. This points out powerfully the worth of single souls.[15]

Then, when the coin was finally found, the woman was rejoicing! She was happy! In the same way, God is happy when sinners repent. *"As the bridegroom rejoices over the bride, so shall your God rejoice over you"* (Isaiah 62:5). *"The Lord your God in your midst, The Mighty One, will save; He will rejoice over you with gladness. He will quiet you with His love, He will rejoice over you with singing"* (Zephaniah 3:17).

Lost coins, of course, don't repent, so Jesus added this so people would know that repentance is important for lost people.

PRAYER: *Lord, we pray that You would lead us to lost souls! Then we can enter into Your joy, when they repent and come to know You! This is the greatest joy, seeing someone come to You! In Jesus' name, amen.*

RETURN OF THE PRODIGAL

Then He said: "A certain man had two sons. And the younger of them said to his father, 'Father, give me the portion of goods that falls to me.' So he divided to them his livelihood."
—Luke 15:11–12; read also vv. 11–32

Then we read that the younger son went to a far country and wasted his possessions on reckless living. When he had spent all he had, a famine arose and he was in desperate need. In fact, he worked for a man that sent him into his fields to feed swine. Pigs were regarded by the Jews as especially "unclean."

When he came to his senses, he returned home and was going to ask to be made like a servant. He was going to say, "I have sinned against heaven and before you." But when his father saw him a long way off, he met him and had compassion on him and kissed him. He put on him the best robe, put a ring on his finger and sandals on his feet. These gifts were meant to honor his son.

Augustine was such a prodigal. He pursued a life of unabashed depravity, but his mother prayed and wept for him. He fathered a son by a mistress at sixteen, joined a heretical group, and went deeper into sin for nine years. His mother, Monica (331–387), kept praying and left Carthage and went to Rome then Milan where Augustine was. He gave up his mistress of fifteen years—but then took another one! Finally, in desperation he turned his life over to God and, later, along with Bishop Hippo helped strengthen Christianity when the Roman Empire disintegrated. He is one of our heroes of faith.[16]

If there is a prodigal in your life, never give up! Don't look at what your natural eyes see but intercede with eyes of love that see the destiny God has planned within your son or daughter's heart.

Prayer: *God, Your arm is not short, but You can reach every person. You can reach our family members! Nothing is too difficult for You. We claim them for Your purposes! Amen!*

SALVATION AWAITS THE RIGHTEOUS

*Jesus continued. "There once was a very rich man who had the finest
things imaginable, living every day enjoying his life of opulent luxury.
Outside the gate of his mansion was a poor beggar named Lazarus.
He lay there every day, covered with boils, and all the neighborhood
dogs would come and lick his open sores. The only food he had to
eat was the garbage that the rich man threw away. One day poor
Lazarus died, and the angels of God came and escorted his spirit into
paradise. The day came that the rich man also died. In hell (Hades)
he looked up from his torment and saw Abraham in the distance,
and Lazarus the beggar was standing beside him in the glory. So
the rich man shouted, 'Father Abraham!...Have mercy on me. Send
Lazarus to dip his finger in water and come to cool my tongue, for I
am in agony in these flames of fire!'"*
—Luke 16:19–24, tpt; read also Luke 16

Jesus was not telling a parable here, but an actual story of something
that had happened. Before the finished work of Jesus on the cross, the
spirits of the dead went to Hades, some to the righteous compart-
ment (Paradise), and some to the torments of fire. It is reasonable to
think that when Jesus visited Hades as part of His redemptive work
and when He preached in Hades (1 Peter 3:18–19), that Jesus set
the captives in Hades free and took them to heaven with Him. Jesus'
work and preaching offered salvation for those like Lazarus, who in
faith awaited it, and it also sealed the condemnation of the wicked
and unbelieving, like the rich man.[17]

Now, after the resurrection, the righteous go directly to heaven
when they die, because to be absent from the body is to be present
with the Lord (2 Corinthians 5:6–8).

The rich man now became the beggar pleading for someone to go
to his brothers so they wouldn't come to where he was. Abraham said
they had Moses and the prophets. If his brothers wouldn't listen to
them, they wouldn't listen even if one were sent from the dead.

Prayer: *Father, thank You for raising Jesus from the dead! Amen!*

DON'T BE A STUMBLING BLOCK

Then He said to the disciples, "It is impossible that no offenses should come, but woe to him through whom they do come! It would be better for him if a millstone were hung around his neck, and he were thrown into the sea, than that he should offend one of these little ones."
—LUKE 17:1–2; READ ALSO VV. 1–19

"The ancient Greek word used here for offenses is *skandalon*, and it comes from the word for a bent-stick—the stick that springs the trap or sets the bait. It also was used for a stumbling block, something that people trip over." [18]

Division and false teaching bring an offense among God's people, "Now I urge you, brethren, note those who cause divisions and offenses, contrary to the doctrine which you learned and avoid them" (Romans 16:17).

Jesus said that it would be better for him if a millstone were hung around his neck, and he were thrown into the sea, than that he should offend one of these little ones. In other words, Jesus issues a strong warning against being the cause for the apostasy of others, particularly those less mature in years or experience.

First John 2:10 gives the solution to being a stumbling block to others—love. "He who loves his brother abides in the light, and there is no cause for stumbling in him." If we love our brother, we will not bring an offense into his life.

If someone offends you and sins against you seven times in a day, and says "I repent," you are to forgive him, Jesus says. This indicates that we are not permitted to judge another's repentance.

That is when the apostles said to the Lord, "increase our faith!" It takes great faith to get along with people like this.

PRAYER: *Lord, we pray and ask You to accomplish forgiveness in us for every offense. Rip out all the bitter roots. Even if the roots are like the mulberry tree Jesus spoke of, give us the faith for those roots to be pulled up and be planted in the sea. In Jesus' name. Amen.*

CREATED FOR HIS PURPOSE

*And as it was in the days of Noah, so it will be also in the days of the
Son of Man: They ate, they drank, they married wives, they were
given in marriage, until the day that Noah entered the ark and the
flood came and destroyed them all. Likewise as it was also in the days
of Lot: They ate, they drank, they bought, they sold, they planted, they
built; but on the day that Lot went out of Sodom it rained fire and
brimstone from heaven and destroyed them all. Even so will it be in
the day when the Son of Man is revealed.*
—LUKE 17:26–30, TPT; READ ALSO VV. 20–37

We see in Genesis 19 the depravity of Sodom, the city of Lot, Abraham's nephew. Two angels came there, and the men of the city wanted
to abuse Lot's visitors in a sadistic, homosexual manner.

The Bible is very clear about homosexuality. *"You shall not lie with a
male as with a woman. It is an abomination"* (Leviticus 18:22). See also
Jude 7. And yet in June 2015, the Supreme Court legalized gay marriage in Obergefell v. Hodges. Sadly, that night, the White House
was lit with the colors of the rainbow.

Since that day the LGBT agenda has flourished. Our teenagers are
taking hormones and having surgeries to make themselves a different
sex. They do not realize that their heavenly Father created them the
gender they are for His purposes, and that we are to praise Him
because we are fearfully and wonderfully made (Psalm 139:14).

We have also had many court cases where bakers, photographers,
and other businesses were sued for not being willing to endorse gay
marriages, and as a result were forced into bankruptcy. (e.g. Melissa's
Sweet Cakes, 2013).

Jesus said it would be like this in the last day. Sodom and Gomorrah
were destroyed because of their sexually perverse ways. We pray that
America will repent and be saved.

PRAYER: *Lord, as we see Your second coming approaching, let us walk
in true wisdom. Your word says that wisdom pours into us when we
begin to hate every form of evil in our life. Let us take a stand for righteousness now. In Your name, amen.*

PERSISTENT IN PRAYER

Then He spoke a parable to them, that men always ought to pray and not lose heart, saying: "There was in a certain city a judge who did not fear God nor regard man. Now there was a widow in that city; and she came to him saying, 'Get justice for me from my adversary.' And he would not for a while; but afterward he said within himself, 'Though I do not fear God nor regard man, yet because this widow troubles me I will avenge her, lest by her continual coming she weary me.' Then the Lord said 'Hear what the unjust judge said, and shall God not avenge His own elect who cry out day and night to Him, though He bears long with them? I tell you that He will avenge them speedily. Nevertheless, when the Son of Man comes, will He really find faith on the earth?'"

—LUKE 18:1–8; READ ALSO VV. 1–23

Jesus was not saying that God was like the unjust judge, but unlike him. God loves to answer our prayers, and He even helps us as we pray. God is for us as we pray, not against us.

Sometimes it does seem to us that God is reluctant to answer our prayers. Yet the delays in prayer are not needed to change God but to change us. Persistence in prayer brings a transforming element into our lives, building into us the character of God Himself. It is a way that God builds into us a heart that cares about things the same way He does.

Dutch Sheets gives us an example of this as he tells of praying for over a year for a young girl who had been in a coma. He spent up to two hours a week in her room interceding over her. After two and a half years in the coma—God gave her an amazing miracle. To the absolute amazement of the medical community, she was completely restored."[19] Dutch says that his heart was changed as God shared His heart for suffering people during this year. What an amazing miracle!

PRAYER: *Father, change our hearts to care for people the way You do! And help us to keep praying and never give up! May we be found persistent and full of faith in our praying! Amen!*

April 25

TELL GOD YOUR NEEDS

Then it happened, as He was coming near Jericho, that a certain blind man sat by the road begging. And hearing a multitude passing by, he asked what it meant. So they told him that Jesus of Nazareth was passing by. And he cried out, saying, "Jesus, Son of David, have mercy on me!" Then those who went before warned him that he should be quiet; but he cried out all the more, "Son of David, have mercy on me!"
—LUKE 18:35–39; READ ALSO VV. 24–43

Jesus commanded that the blind man be brought to Him, and He asked him what he wanted. Jesus wants us to ask and be specific. The Bible says in James 4:2, *"You have not because you ask not."* He told Jesus he wanted his sight. Jesus knew what he needed and what he wanted, but God still wants us to tell Him our needs as a constant expression of our trust and reliance on Him. Jesus then said, *"Receive your sight; your faith has made you well"* (v. 42).

Then when he received his sight, he glorified God, and all the people when they saw it, glorified God. Jesus is the same yesterday, today, and forever. When His compassion flows through us, the miracles come too!

James Maloney was invited to speak in a retirement community in California. The service was advertised as a miracle service. Bring the sick. Bring the afflicted. At 10 after noon, James was told by the pastor, the people will leave for Wyatt's cafeteria. About halfway through his testimony, people began to leave. All except for a ten years old boy who was visiting and who had very crossed eyes. He came forward and asked if Jesus would help him see straight. When he looked up after the prayer, his eyes were perfect. The people decided to stay instead of beating the crowd to Wyatt's cafeteria! Didn't Jesus say, *"My bread is to do the will of my Father?"* [20]

PRAYER: *Forgive us Lord, for putting our schedules ahead of Yours and missing out on what You are wanting to do. Help us put Your kingdom ahead of our convenience. Amen.*

FRIEND OF SINNERS

*And Jesus said to him, "Today salvation has come to this house,
because he also is a son of Abraham; for the Son of Man has come to
seek and to save that which was lost."*
—LUKE 19:9–10; READ ALSO VV. 1–27

Here we have the wonderful conversion story of Zacchaeus, the hated
tax collector. He was short so he ran ahead and climbed up into a
sycamore tree because Jesus was going to pass that way. And when
Jesus saw him, He looked up and said, *"Zacchaeus, make haste and
come down for today I must stay at your house"* (v. 5). So, he came
down with great joy. Jesus didn't have to teach Zacchaeus about character. Zacchaeus perceived at once that character was of the greatest
importance and told the Lord that he would give half of his goods
to the poor and also restore four-fold to anyone whom he had taken
from wrongly.

It appears that Jesus deals with us individually. With the rich
young ruler, Jesus commanded that he give away everything he had to
the poor. However, with Zacchaeus, it was enough to make restitution to those he had wronged.

Jesus explained why He sought and extended friendship to a notorious sinner like Zacchaeus. Jesus came precisely to save people like
Zacchaeus.

This entire account gives us a remarkable who, what, where, when,
why, and how of receiving Jesus:[21]

+ *Who* Jesus wants to be received by: those lost.

+ *What* Jesus wants with those who receive Him: a relationship.

+ *Where* Jesus wants to go: down to him.

+ *When* Jesus wants you to receive Him: immediately, quickly.

+ *Why* Jesus wants you to receive Him: to be with Him, to connect with Him in life.

+ *How* Jesus wants you to receive Him: joyfully.

PRAYER: *Lord of the Harvest, help us also to seek and save the lost, and
introduce them to You. In Your Name. Amen.*

HOUSE OF PRAYER

Then He went into the temple and began to drive out those who bought and sold in it, saying to them, "It is written, My house is a house of prayer, but you have made it a den of thieves."
—LUKE 19:45–46; READ ALSO VV. 28–48

Dr. Cho has pastored in South Korea since 1958, and prayer has been the key to the church's growth and success. He began ministry in a poor area outside Seoul. He pitched a tent and preached during the day and spent his nights in prayer. Soon over fifty people were gathering to spend entire nights in prayer.

In their church and in most churches in Korea, prayer begins at 5:00 a.m. and lasts for one or two hours before work. On Fridays, they spend the entire night in prayer.

Dr. Cho says on Sundays before each service, there is prayer. He says "this is why the holy and mighty presence of God is in our services. Sinners are convicted by the Holy Spirit even before I get up to preach the gospel. Christian hearts are opened to receive the truth of God's Word by the spirit of prayer among us." [22]

He says that during the Sunday services, the believers pray together. The sound of thousands of Korean believers praying reminds him of the thunderous roar of a mighty waterfall.

They also have a place called Prayer Mountain with individual prayer grottos that are dug right into the side of the hill and are used for complete solitude in prayer. Dr. Cho says they have had as many as twenty thousand fasting and praying at Prayer Mountain.

Now with the threat of nuclear North Korea, the people are still praying earnestly, as well as for loved ones caught there. Today Yoido Full Gospel Church is attended by eight hundred thousand people, with many cell groups. It belongs to the Korean Assemblies of God. It is the world's largest megachurch.

PRAYER: *Heavenly Father, may we not be only hearers of the Word, but doers. May our lives and churches be houses of prayer for all nations! In Jesus' name, amen.*

THE CORNERSTONE

*Then He looked at them and said, "What then is this that is written:
'The stone which the builders rejected has become the chief cornerstone?' 'Whoever falls on that stone will be broken; but on whomever
it falls, it will grind him to powder.'"*
—LUKE 20:17–18; READ ALSO VV. 1–26

Jesus taught them from Psalm 118, because this Psalm described the
coming of the Messiah to Jerusalem, as coming through the gates of
righteousness (Psalm 118:19).

The religious leaders understood the parable immediately and
objected that Jesus had spoken this parable against them. Their hos-
tility showed that this Messianic stone was being rejected, even if He
was initially greeted with hosannas.

Jesus is often likened unto a stone or a rock in the Bible. He is
the rock of provision that followed Israel in the desert (1 Corinthians
10:4). He is the stone of stumbling (1 Peter 2:8). He is the stone cut
without hands that crushes the kingdoms of this world (Daniel 2:45).

> The cornerstone was a stone used at the building's corner to bear the
> weight or stress of the two walls. It would have functioned somewhat
> like a capstone in an arch or other architectural form. It was the stone
> which was essential or crucial to the whole structure.[23]

*"Whoever falls on that stone will be broken; but on whomever it falls,
it will grind him to powder"* (v. 18). This means that anyone who comes
to Jesus will be broken of their pride and self-will, but those who
refuse to come will be crushed by Christ in judgment.

PRAYER: *Father in heaven, we invite Your Son to be our cornerstone.
We invite You, Jesus, to be our rock of provision. We invite You to be
the stone that breaks our pride, for You said, "God resists the proud, but
gives grace to the humble" (1 Peter 5:5). You said if we humble ourselves in the sight of the Lord, You will lift us up. Have Your way in us!
Amen!*

LIFE AFTER RESURRECTION

Jesus answered and said to them, 'The sons of this age marry and are given in marriage. But those who are counted worthy to attain that age, and the resurrection from the dead, neither marry nor are given in marriage; nor can they die anymore, for they are equal to the angels and are sons of God, being sons of the resurrection. But even Moses showed in the burning bush passage that the dead are raised, when he called the Lord the God of Abraham, the God of Isaac, and the God of Jacob. For He is not the God of the dead but of the living, for all live to Him."

—LUKE 20:34–38; READ ALSO VV. 27–47

The Sadducees were questioning Jesus about the resurrection as they did not believe in the resurrection. He is correcting their misunderstanding. First, Jesus reminded them that life in the resurrection is quite different from this life. We know that family relationships will still be known in life in the world beyond, but we will not marry nor be given in marriage. The rich man Jesus described in the afterlife was aware of his family relationships.

Jesus also said that in heaven, we cannot die anymore, but we are equal to the angels. Sadducees also did not believe in angels. He was making a point that angels are real.

He also proves the resurrection from the Torah, the five books of Moses, which were the only books the Sadducees accepted as authoritative. He then referred back to when Moses called the Lord, *"the God of Abraham, the God of Isaac, and the God of Jacob."* Jesus said, *"God is not the God of the dead but of the living..."*

The glory of heaven will surpass anything we have known before. It says in Revelation 21:22–23 that *"I saw no temple in the city, for its temple is the Lord God, the Almighty, and the Lamb. The city has no need for the sun or moon to shine, for the glory of God is its light, and its lamp is the Lamb"* (TPT).

PRAYER: *We praise You Father for the resurrection, for as the apostle Paul said, "Without the resurrection, our faith is vain." We look forward to that glorious day. In Jesus' name, amen.*

April 30

WIDOW'S MITE

And He looked up and saw the rich putting their gifts into the treasury, and He saw also a certain poor widow putting in two mites. So He said, "Truly I say to you that this poor widow has put in more than all; for all these out of their abundance have put in offerings for God, but she out of her poverty put in all the livelihood that she had."
—LUKE 21:1–4; READ ALSO VV. 1–19

Jesus notices how much we give, but He is far more interested in the faith and motive of the heart in giving than simply the amount.

Jesus said that she put in more than all of them—all of them put together. The others gave out of their abundance; she gave sacrificially out of her poverty.

Jesus' principle here shows us that before God, the spirit of giving determines the value of the gift more than the amount. God doesn't want grudgingly given money or guilt money. God loves the cheerful giver.

The widow's gift and Jesus' comment on it also shows us that the value of a gift is determined by what it costs the giver. This is what made the widow's gift so valuable.

We wonder what her reward was as she gave all she had. We know from Malachi 3:10 that we are to *"bring all the tithes into the storehouse that there may be food in My house, and try Me now in this, says the Lord of hosts, If I will not open for you the windows of heaven and pour out for you such blessing that there will not be room enough to receive it. And I will rebuke the devourer for your sakes...."*

If God will open the windows of heaven for us, provide for all our needs, and rebuke the devourer if we tithe, then surely, He provided a wonderful reward for this widow!

PRAYER: *Father in Heaven, help us to be obedient to bring our tithes into Your storehouse. And help us to be like this widow with spectacular contributions when You ask, given from a cheerful heart. You are always watching! Amen!*

May 1

OUR LOVE FOR GOD

But when you see Jerusalem surrounded by armies, then know that its desolation is near. Then let those who are in Judea flee to the mountains, let those who are in the midst of her depart, and let not those who are in the country enter her. For these are the days of vengeance, that all things which are written may be fulfilled. But woe to those who are pregnant and to those who are nursing babies in those days! For there will be great distress in the land and wrath upon this people. And they will fall by the edge of the sword and be led away captive into all nations.

—LUKE 21:20–24; READ ALSO VV. 20–38

This prophetic warning was fulfilled in A.D. 70 when the Roman army encircled Jerusalem, conquered the city, and destroyed the temple. "History records that 1.1 million Jews were killed and another ninety seven thousand were taken captive in one of the worst calamities to strike the Jewish people. When the Romans were done with Jerusalem in 70 A.D., not a single Jew was left alive in the city."[1] The Christians, on the other hand, remembered Jesus' warning and fled across the Jordan River mostly to Pella. Few if any Christians perished in the fall of Jerusalem.

In Deuteronomy 28:15–68, God had warned these things would happen if they were unfaithful and rebellious. This is why Jesus wept over Jerusalem (Luke 19:41–44). He could foresee the massive devastation coming upon the city that He loved so much, and this is why He warned all who would listen how they could flee from destruction. As Pastor Gene Oller has said, "God is a Father, always. A judge when He has to be. He always prefers to be a Father."

PRAYER: *Father God, You said that if we loved You, we would obey You and keep Your commandments. You said if we keep Your word, the love of God is perfected in us (1 John 2:5). Fill us today with Your love and keep us unspotted from the world. In Jesus' name, amen.*

May 2

HOLY COMMUNION

Then He said to them, "With fervent desire I have desired to eat this Passover with you before I suffer; for I say to you, I will no longer eat of it until it is fulfilled in the kingdom of God." Then He took the cup, and gave thanks, and said, "Take this and divide it among yourselves; for I say to you, I will not drink of the fruit of the vine until the kingdom of God comes." And He took bread, gave thanks and broke it, and gave it to them, saying, "This is My body which is given for you; do this in remembrance of Me."
—Luke 22:14–20; read also vv. 1–23

Jesus established the practice we now call "communion" with His disciples on the night when He was about to be betrayed, arrested, and then crucified. This same night was also the annual Jewish celebration of Passover, which had been celebrated in Israel for fourteen hundred years since the time of the actual Passover event.

When Jesus spoke the words in the passage above, He was declaring that He Himself was the Passover Lamb. Within hours, he would literally give His life as the sacrifice, thereby fulfilling the long prophetic history of the Passover meal.

We can look at Communion in this way: the Communion bread is the Word of God in edible form. When we eat it, we are to remember what it illustrates. The Communion cup is the Word of God in drinkable form. When we drink it, we are to remember Him. Jesus said that as often as we eat this bread and drink the cup, we are to remember His death until He comes (1 Corinthians 11:24–26).

Do you know what happened when He hung on the cross? The answers to these questions are the heart of the gospel, and we need to know these answers for they are the very foundation of the Christian faith. The moment Jesus died, He said, *"It is finished!"* His new covenant was established.[2]

Prayer: *Father, thank You for the cross! Thank you that the curtain of the temple was torn in two when Jesus died, and now, we can enter the Holy of Holies. Hallelujah! Amen!*

JESUS, THE INTERCESSOR

Peter, my dear friend, listen to what I'm about to tell you. Satan has demanded to come and sift you like wheat and test your faith. But I have prayed for you, Peter, that you would stay faithful to me no matter what comes. Remember this: after you have turned back to me and have been restored, make it your life mission to strengthen the faith of your brothers.
—LUKE 22:31–32, TPT; READ ALSO VV. 24–46

Jesus is aware of a spiritual battle behind the scenes. Peter, however, was no doubt ignorant of the fact that Satan wanted to completely crush and defeat him.

Apparently, Satan wanted to do much more against Peter than the Lord would allow. Jesus said that Satan wanted to sift Peter like wheat, and in that process no wheat would remain, but that everything would be blown away like chaff. Satan wanted Peter destroyed— like Judas was.

However, Satan did not completely crush Peter, because Jesus had prayed for him. Do we realize that Jesus is praying for us as well? He is our Great Intercessor, seated at the right hand of God always interceding for us. The Bible says in Hebrews 7:25: *"Therefore He is also able to save to the uttermost those who come to God through Him, since He always lives to make intercession for them."* He is our great High Priest.

Jesus prayed that Peter's faith would not fail. Peter's faith did falter, but it didn't fail. Jesus knew that Peter would return to Him, become a mighty man of faith, and be a symbol of hope to strengthen others.

In the Christian life, we may falter, but we must never fail. If we have denied Jesus in some way, then we must return to Him immediately. After we've been restored by His love, we are enabled to help others. It is important to Jesus that we focus not on ourselves, or our shortcomings, but on others.

PRAYER: *Dear Jesus, we are so thankful that You are interceding for us that our faith will not fail. We see how You intervened for Peter, and You will do the same for us. Help us to always comfort and encourage our brothers in the faith! Help us to follow Your example and pray for others. Amen.*

JESUS, THE CHRIST

"If You are the Christ, tell us. But He said to them, 'If I tell you, you will by no means believe. And if I also ask you, you will by no means answer Me or let Me go. Hereafter the Son of Man will sit on the right hand of the power of God.' Then they all said, 'Are You then the Son of God?' So He said to them, 'You rightly say that I am.' And they said, 'What further testimony do we need? For we have heard it ourselves from His own mouth.'"
—LUKE 22:67–71; READ ALSO VV. 47–71

As Jesus stood before the Council during His second trial, the leaders wanted Him to say if He was the Christ. But He said that even if He said "Yes," they would not believe. Their question was merely a formality because they had already illegally passed judgment on Him the night before.

Jesus said that hereafter they would see the Son of Man sitting on the right hand of the power of God. In other words, He was saying, that although they sat in judgment of Him now, He would one day sit in judgment of them—and with a far more binding judgment. How overwhelming it will be to Jesus' foes in the "hereafter." Charles Spurgeon said,

> Now where is Caiaphas? Will he now adjure the Lord to speak? Now, ye priests, lift up your haughty heads! Utter a sentence against him now! There He sits, your victim upon the clouds of heaven. Say now that he blasphemes and hold up your rent rags, and condemn him again. But where is Caiaphas? He hides his guilty head. He is utterly confounded, and begs the mountains to fall upon him.[3]

Jesus said they would see Him on the *"right hand of the power of God."* The apostle John in Revelation 19:11–14, saw Jesus on a white horse and *"He was called Faithful and True and in righteousness He judges and makes war."* He was clothed with a robe dipped in blood, and His name is called The Word of God. And the armies in heaven dressed in fine linen followed him on white horses.

PRAYER: *Dear Father, one day every knee will bow, and every tongue confess that Jesus Christ is Lord! Amen!*

May 5

THE COST OF SALVATION

*Now when Herod saw Jesus, he was exceedingly glad; for he had
desired for a long time to see Him, because he had heard many things
about Him, and he hoped to see some miracle done by Him. Then he
questioned Him with many words, but He answered him nothing.
And the chief priests and scribes stood and vehemently accused Him.
Then Herod, with his men of war, treated Him with contempt and
mocked Him, arrayed Him in a gorgeous robe, and sent Him back
to Pilate. That very day Pilate and Herod became friends with each
other, for previously they had been at enmity with each other.*
—LUKE 23:8–12; READ ALSO VV. 1–25

Herod Antipas had surely heard much about Jesus, but his only
interest was a desire to be amused and entertained. This son of Herod
the Great never took Jesus seriously.

He hoped to see some miracle done by Him. Yet his interest in
Jesus was not sincere and was to his condemnation, not his praise. He
had heard the Word of God from John the Baptist, yet he chose to
continue in his sin and hardened his heart against God. Although he
questioned Him with many words, Jesus did not answer him.

Herod governed over Galilee where Jesus spent most of His ministry. Herod had countless opportunities to hear Him, but he was not
a true seeker after the truth. Herod may have thought "Let's hear an
answer from the Great Teacher! Let's see a miracle from the Miracle
Man!" But Jesus may have thought, "I have nothing for you, the murderer of My cousin John the Baptist."

He who answered blind beggars when they cried for mercy is silent to
a prince who only seeks to gratify his own irreverent curiosity. Then
Herod mocked Him. With the Son of God before him, Herod could
only jest; he even dressed Him in a royal robe.[4]

PRAYER: *Heavenly Father, help us to understand the tremendous price
Jesus paid for our salvation—the emotional pain of mockery, dishonor,
hatred and rejection from leaders. Amen.*

May 6

LAST-MINUTE SALVATION

Then one of the criminals who were hanged blasphemed Him, saying, "If You are the Christ, save Yourself and us." But the other, answering, rebuked him, saying, "Do you not even fear God, seeing you are under the same condemnation? And we indeed justly, for we receive the due reward of our deeds; but this Man has done nothing wrong." Then he said to Jesus, "Lord, remember me when You come into Your kingdom." And Jesus said to him, "Assuredly I say to you, today you will be with Me in Paradise."
—LUKE 23:39–43; READ ALSO VV. 26–56

We see here that one of the criminals joined in the mockery and scorn and blasphemed Him. But the other rebuked him. We see in Matthew and Mark, that at first both criminals mocked Jesus. However, one of the criminals began to see things differently and to actually put his trust in Jesus. In saying, *"Do you not even fear God?"* he acknowledged that Jesus had done nothing wrong. He called out to Jesus when he said, *"Lord."* He believed Jesus was who Jesus said He was because he said, *"remember me when You come into Your kingdom."*

It is truly remarkable that Jesus answered the trust of the second criminal and assured him that he would be with Him in Paradise. His love brought salvation even in suffering.

> This may be the only Biblical example of a last-minute salvation. It is significant that the thief who trusted Jesus at the last moment goes to the same heaven anyone else does. Even though this may not seem fair, it gives glory to the grace of God, not to our earning our salvation. In heaven, we will all be filled to the full with joy and reward; but the degree of our faithfulness now determines how big our reward will be in heaven.[5]

Jesus answered the second criminal far beyond his expectation when He said that he would be with Him, not in some distant time, but TODAY.

PRAYER: *Dearest Father, thank You that You do save at the last moment. Thank You that there are deathbed conversions! Amen!*

May 7

VERIFIABLE PROOF OF CHRIST

Now that same day two of them were going to a village called Emmaus, about seven miles from Jerusalem. They were talking with each other about everything that had happened.
—LUKE 24:13–14, NIV; READ ALSO VV. 1–35

Jesus Himself joined them and began speaking after they told Him that the women had found the tomb of Jesus empty. He said:

"How foolish you are, and how slow of heart to believe all that the prophets have spoken! Did not the Christ have to suffer these things and then enter his glory?" *And beginning with Moses and all the prophets, he explained to them what was said in the Scriptures concerning himself.*
—v. 25–26

"And I will put enmity between your seed and the woman, and between your offspring and hers; he will crush your head and you will strike his heel." Here, at the beginning of the creation, God says He will put enmity (conflict) between Satan's seed (your seed) and God's people, (the woman's seed), especially Jesus Christ (her Seed)."
—GENESIS 3:15

This depicts the struggle between good and evil with God winning through Jesus Christ, the last Adam (1 Corinthians 15:45).

Deuteronomy 18:15 is another prophecy about the Christ from the Old Testament: "The Lord your God will raise up for you a prophet like me from among your own brothers. You must listen to him."

Then in Isaiah 7:14, it says: "Therefore the Lord himself will give you a sign: The virgin will be with child and will give birth to a son, and will call him Immanuel."

Finally, in Isaiah 9:6, it says, "For to us a child is born, to us a son is given, and the government will be on his shoulders. And he will be called Wonderful Counselor, Mighty God, Everlasting Father, Prince of Peace."

PRAYER: *Father God, thank You for Your word and the over three hundred verifiable prophecies which Jesus Christ fulfilled to the very letter. And You said that suddenly the messenger of the covenant whom we desire will come—Jesus, the Christ. You have come, and You will come again, as You said! Amen!*

May 8

JESUS GIVES HIS BLESSING

And He opened their understanding, that they might comprehend the Scriptures. Then He said to them, "Thus it is written, and thus it was necessary for the Christ to suffer and to rise from the dead the third day, and that repentance and remission of sins should be preached in His name to all nations, beginning at Jerusalem...."

"Behold, I send the Promise of My Father upon you; but tarry in the city of Jerusalem until you are endued with power from on high." And He led them out as far as Bethany and He lifted up His hands and blessed them. Now it came to pass, while He blessed them, that He was parted from them and carried up into heaven.
—LUKE 24:44–48, 50–51; READ ALSO VV. 36–53

Here we see the last three things that Jesus did on earth before He ascended to the Father:

1. He opened their understanding and gave them their assignment.
2. He promised to send the Helper to equip and enable them to finish their assignment.
3. He gave them His blessing so they would prosper and succeed in what they were called to do.

First, they were told by the Master what to preach, where to preach it, and how to preach it. They were even told where to begin to preach it: first in Jerusalem, then in Judea and Samaria, and then to the uttermost parts of the earth. They were told to preach it in His name.

Secondly, they could not do it unless they were endued with power from on high, and that power would come from the Holy Spirit.

The last thing we see Him do is bless them! Nothing but blessing had ever come from those hands; yet now, Jesus stands as the eternal High Priest over His people, to bless them. His blessing has power in it, and nothing can reverse the blessing that He gives. He was blessing them as He ascended to heaven!

PRAYER: *Lord, You are amazing! We long for our assignment, the power to finish it, and Your blessing on us! Amen!*

May 9

JESUS IS GOD

In the beginning was the Word, and the Word was with God, and the Word was God. He was in the beginning with God....

And the Word became flesh and dwelt among us, and we beheld His glory, the glory as of the only begotten of the Father, full of grace and truth.

—JOHN 1:1, 14; READ ALSO vv. 1–28

These statements are the core of Christianity. In the beginning refers to the timeless eternity of Genesis 1:1, *"In the beginning, God created the heavens and earth."* When the beginning started, the Word was already there. The Word was with God, and the Word was God. All false religions deny that Jesus is God, but here we see clearly that the Word (Jesus) is God. And we understand that they are two different persons, because Jesus, as the Word, was with God, and yet He is God.

"And the Word became flesh and dwelt among us..." God has come close to us in Jesus Christ. We don't have to struggle to find Him; because He came to us. And He has come full of grace and truth.

We read in verse 9 that He was the true Light which gives light to every man coming into the world. In other words, every human being has a witness of the Light of Christ. The Word says so.

"He was in the world and the world was made through Him, and the world did not know Him. He came to His own and they did not receive Him" (v. 10–11).

This is a very key verse: *"But as many as received Him, to them He gave the right to become children of God, to those who believe in His name"* (v. 12). We need to embrace and receive Him to ourselves. Receiving Him is asking Jesus by faith to come into our hearts and forgive our sins and be the Lord of our life.

PRAYER: *Here is a prayer you can pray: Jesus, I believe that You died for my sins. I confess my sins to You and ask You to forgive me. I want to receive You as my Lord and Savior. I want to spend eternity with You in heaven. Amen.*

BEHOLD, THE LAMB

The next day John saw Jesus coming toward him, and said, "Behold!
The Lamb of God who takes away the sin of the world."
—JOHN 1:29; READ ALSO VV. 29–51

Israel was looking for a political king—a military savior who would free them from the dominating foreign power of Rome. Contrary to their expectation, John the Baptist described Jesus as *"the Lamb of God who takes away the sin of the world!"*

This was not the mighty military king they expected. Yet, the Scriptures had foretold the Lamb from the very beginning:

+ Genesis 4:4—Abel's sacrifice of the firstborn of his flock pleased God.

+ Genesis 22:8—Abraham prepared to sacrifice his own son and foretold God's provision of a sacrifice.

+ Exodus 12:6, 7, 13—At the first Passover, lambs were slain, and their blood applied as protection against the death of the firstborn in all Egypt. Jesus is our Passover Lamb.

+ Isaiah 53:7—Isaiah prophesied the Lamb. *"All we like sheep have gone astray; we have turned, every one to his own way; and the Lord has laid on Him the iniquity of us all."*

+ Revelation 5:8–9—*"Now when He had taken the scroll, the four living creatures and the twenty-four elders fell down before the Lamb…and they sang a new song saying, You are worthy to take the scroll, and to open its seals; for You were slain, and have redeemed us to God by Your blood…."*

Jesus is not only the Lamb of God, but He is the Good Shepherd of Psalm 23. "The Lord is my shepherd, I shall not want. He makes me lie down in green pastures" (v. 1).

PRAYER: *Jesus, You are the Lamb of God, and the Good Shepherd of the sheep. You are also the Lion of the Tribe of Judah, and when You come again, You will reign as "King of kings, and Lord of lords!" Jesus, be the Lord of my life! Amen!*

May 11

THE FIRST MIRACLE

On the third day there was a wedding in Cana of Galilee, and the mother of Jesus was there. Now both Jesus and His disciples were invited to the wedding and when they ran out of wine, the mother of Jesus said to Him, "They have no wine." Jesus said to her, "Woman, what does your concern have to do with Me? My hour has not yet come." His mother said to the servants, "Whatever He says to you, do it."

—JOHN 2:1–5; READ ALSO VV. JOHN 2

The invitation of Jesus to this wedding says something about Jesus' presence at weddings. First, Jesus was always welcome among those having a good time. One commentator, said that Jesus comes to a marriage, and gives His blessing there, that we may know that our family life is under His care. It also says that He blesses marriages and families. This was His plan from the beginning that a *"man should leave his father and mother and be joined to his wife, and the two shall become one flesh."* This is recorded in Genesis 2:24 and quoted in Matthew 19:5. It was never His plan that a man and woman should live together without benefit of marriage.

When His mother told Him, they had run out of wine, He said to her, *"Woman, what does your concern have to do with Me?"* (v. 4). We don't know exactly why she brought this problem to her Son, Jesus. Perhaps she eagerly anticipated the day Jesus would miraculously demonstrate that He was the Messiah. [This would also vindicate Mary, who lived under the shadow of a pregnancy and birth that many people questioned]. But also, in that culture, to not provide for the guests would involve social disgrace.

He spoke to His mother with a term of respect, "Woman," for now at the beginning of His ministry, He would have a different relationship with Mary. Now He would submit to His Heavenly Father for direction, rather than His earthly parents. He then turned the water into wine! This was His first miracle.

PRAYER: *Father, thanks for the wonder of marriages and for Your blessing and provision in miraculous ways. Amen.*

YOU MUST BE "BORN AGAIN"

*There was a man of the Pharisees named Nicodemus, a ruler of the
Jews. This man came to Jesus by night and said to Him, "Rabbi, we
know that You are a teacher come from God; for no one can do these
signs that You do unless God is with him." Jesus answered and said to
him, "Most assuredly, I say to you, unless one is born again, he cannot
see the kingdom of God."*
—JOHN 3:1–3; READ ALSO vv. 1–15

Jesus is talking about the new birth and saying that unless we are
"*born again*" we will not see the kingdom of God. Nicodemus asked
how a man can be "born again." Can he enter his mother's womb a
second time? Jesus answered and said that the wind blows where it
wishes, and you hear the sound of it, but you can't tell where it comes
from and where it goes. It's like that with being "born again."

This is my story about being born again. When I was ten years old,
I went to Baptist Church Camp. There was an evangelist there who
held up a pencil and asked what we could tell him about the pencil. I
raised my hand and said it had an eraser, and that meant that people
made mistakes.

He said I was right. He then went on to say that the Bible says
in Romans 3:23 that all have sinned and come short of the glory of
God. In Romans 6:23 it says that the wages of sin is death, but that
the gift of God is eternal life through Jesus. He then shared 1 John
1:9, that if we confess our sins, He is faithful and just to forgive us
our sins. Then in Revelation 3:20 Jesus says, "*Behold I stand at the
door and knock. If any man opens the door to Me, I will come in and
eat with him.*"

So that night, I realized that I could not be "good enough" to make
it to heaven. I was a sinner. But Jesus shed His blood and died for my
sin, and if I asked Him to forgive my sins and come into my heart, He
would, and He would take me to heaven. I repented and shed many
tears that night! I did give my heart to Jesus that night. The next
morning it was like a veil was off my heart and all the colors outside
were more vivid, and I was filled with love and joy! I was a new creation!

PRAYER: *Here you can pray your own prayer. Amen.*

May 13

SAVE FROM ETERNAL DESTRUCTION

For God so loved the world that He gave His only begotten Son, that whoever believes in Him should not perish but have everlasting life. For God did not send His Son into the world to condemn the world, but that the world through Him might be saved.
—JOHN 3:16–17; READ ALSO VV. 16–36

These are probably the most popular single verses used in evangelism. Jesus' teaching was different from the accustomed way of thinking. Many of the Jews thought that God only loved Israel. But this is a universal offer of salvation and was very revolutionary.

God didn't just feel sorry for the plight of the fallen world. He did something about it by sending His only begotten Son. And the recipient of this gift would be someone who *believed* in Jesus. "Believes in" means much more than intellectual awareness or agreement. It means to trust in, to rely on, and to cling to.

The intention of God's gift was that His love actually saves man from eternal destruction. He didn't send His Son to condemn the world, but to save the world.

It comes down to a choice that man himself must make. Jesus came to bring salvation, but those who reject that salvation condemn themselves.

Jesus goes on to explain what keeps people from faith and rescue in Him. It is because they are drawn to darkness and love it more than the light. There is a critical moral dimension to unbelief. Many opponents of Christianity have a vested interest in fighting against the truth of Jesus because they love their sin and don't want to face it or face a God who will judge their sin. It takes humility to admit one is a sinner and needs a Savior. When we demand to be lord over our own life, that sin is enough to deserve condemnation before God. The good news is that we can choose to walk in His light and love.

PRAYER: *Father, thank You for Your Word that tells us clearly how we can be saved. We choose Your salvation. We choose to walk in the light. We choose Your Son! Amen.*

FRIEND OF SINNERS

Jesus answered and said to her, "If you knew the gift of God, and who it is who says to you, 'Give Me a drink,' you would have asked Him, and He would have given you living water."
—John 4:10; read also vv. 1–26

Jesus said He needed to go through Samaria. This was the divine appointment the Father had given Him. When He got to Jacob's well, he was tired and thirsty. There was a Samaritan woman there and He asked her for a drink. This greatly surprised her, because the Jews had no dealings with Samaritans.

Then Jesus said He could give her living water and that if she drank that water, she would never thirst again. This she really wanted, so she asked Him for this living water. She was wanting Jesus to make her life easier and more convenient. Next, He was going to deal with the sin in her life. He told her to call her husband. She said, "*I have no husband.*" Jesus said, "*You have well said, 'I have no husband,' for you have had five husbands, and the one whom you now have is not your husband; in that you spoke truly.*" When Jesus said this, He showed that living together and marriage are not the same thing. Jesus also showed that just because someone calls a relationship marriage, does not mean that Jesus considers it marriage.

She tried to change the subject here by talking about where one should worship, in Samaria or in Jerusalem. Jesus said plainly, "*Salvation is of the Jews.*" She said she knew the Messiah was coming. Jesus told this woman, a Samaritan woman living in sin, that He was the Messiah. Amazing. He reveals Himself to sinners. Whereupon she told her village to come and meet a man who "*told me all the things that I ever did.*" When the villagers came to meet Him themselves, they were convinced that He was indeed the Christ, the Savior of the world.

Prayer: *Jesus, thank You for being a friend of sinners. Thank You for knowing how to reach lost people by revealing who You are to them in unique and miraculous ways. Amen.*

THE FIELDS ARE WHITE FOR HARVEST

Do you not say, "There are still four months and then comes the harvest?" Behold, I say to you, lift up your eyes and look at the fields, for they are already white for harvest!
—JOHN 4:35; READ ALSO VV. 27–54

God has spoken this very word to His servants, to send them out to their families, churches, cities, states, and nations to do His work. He had said in verse 34 that *"My food is to do the will of Him who sent Me, and to finish His work."* Sometimes we complain about not being "fed" in our churches, but here Jesus said His food was to do His work.

The next verse, (v. 35), is His work. This verse was the very word that God spoke to Lottie Moon. She was only four-foot-three but had a calling to China. She was a Quaker descendent of Robert Barclay, a Scottish man who pioneered with such men as George Fox and William Penn.

She was highly educated and was a tutor, but when her sister left for China, her heart also turned to the mission field. After hearing a sermon based on the above verse, she received her own call to missions and left for China in 1873. She was 33.

She dressed, ate, and lived like the Chinese. She traveled from village to village in a mule litter sharing the love of Jesus and commonly slept in vermin-infested inns. She was fearless during these dangerous trips. She suffered many hardships, including the Boxer Uprising during which she left China and went to Japan to teach. When she returned to China, a revolution broke out in 1911. She gave all she had to feed the poor. When she finally bowed to the pressure to leave China, she died on her trip home. "Ten years earlier, Lottie Moon had said, 'I would that I had a thousand lives, that I might give them to the women of China.' She gave her one life, and its influence was multiplied a thousandfold."[6]

PRAYER: *Father in Heaven, I pray what's written on this wall plaque would be written on our hearts: "Only one life, so soon it will pass. Only what's done for Christ will last." Amen.*

YOU'VE BEEN MADE WHOLE

Now a certain man was there who had an infirmity thirty-eight years. When Jesus saw him lying there, and knew that he already had been in that condition a long time, He said to him, "Do you want to be made whole?" The sick man answered Him, "Sir, I have no man to put me into the pool when the water is stirred up; but while I am coming, another steps down before me." Jesus said to him, "Rise, take up your bed and walk."
—JOHN 5:6–8; READ ALSO VV. 1–24

Now this man suffered from a paralytic condition for a long time and apparently was frequently at the Pool of Bethesda in hope of healing. It was a hope that had been long disappointed. Jesus saw him lying there and selected him among the great multitude of sick people to work a miracle.

It is interesting that there was a multitude of needy people there, yet none looked to Jesus who could heal them. Their eyes were fixed on the water. Since they thought that was the way they were going to be healed, they neglected the true way.

Isn't this true today? "Some wait for a more convenient season. Some wait for dreams and visions. Some wait for signs and wonders. Some wait to be compelled. Some wait for a revival. Some wait for a particular feeling, or a celebrity."[7]

Jesus said, *"Do you want to be made well?"* Jesus wanted to build the faith of this man. The man explained to Jesus that he had no one to put him into the pool when it was stirred up. Someone else always beat him to it. This is an interesting case of hope combined with hopelessness. He had hope, so he was at the Pool of Bethesda. Yet he was hopeless because no one would put him in. Jesus said, *"Rise, pick up your bed and walk."* As the man responded in faith, and did what Jesus told him to do, he was miraculously healed! When Jesus saw him later, He said, *"See, you have been made well. Sin no more, lest a worse thing come upon you"* (v. 14).

PRAYER: *Lord, we fix our eyes on You for our miracle! Thank You for giving us faith when we are full of doubt! Amen!*

May 17

HIS WORD IS EVERLASTING LIFE

Most assuredly, I say to you, he who hears My word and believes in Him who sent Me has everlasting life, and shall not come into judgment, but has passed from death into life. Most assuredly, I say to you, the hour is coming, and now is, when the dead will hear the voice of the Son of God; and those who hear will live. For as the Father has life in Himself, so He has granted the Son to have life in Himself, and has given Him authority to execute judgment also, because He is the Son of Man.

—JOHN 5:24–27; READ ALSO VV. 25–47

Here Jesus is saying that those who heard his word would have everlasting life. They would have the life connected with eternity and have that life now. With these words, Jesus lifted Himself far above the level of any mere man. Think of it. *"Hear My word and have everlasting life."* This was either the babbling of an insane man or the words of God Himself. There is no neutral ground to be found here.

Jesus also said that he who hears His word will not come into judgment but has passed from death into life. The man who doesn't know God lives a dying life, or a living death; but he who believes in the Son of God passes over from death to life.

"The dead will hear the voice of the Son of God and those who hear will live" (v. 25). This can well apply to those who do not know Christ. Declare over lost loved ones, friends and acquaintances that they (spiritually dead) WILL hear the voice of the Son of God and they will live. Lift them up by name.

"Do not marvel at this; for the hour is coming in which all who are in the graves will hear His voice and come forth—those who have done good, to the resurrection of life, and those who have done evil, to the resurrection of condemnation" (v. 29). This is remarkable in that everyone, both good and evil, will live forever, but where we spend eternity is a choice.

PRAYER: *Father, what a glorious future we have in You. "Heaven is a wonderful place; filled with glory and grace. I want to see my Savior's face, 'cuz heaven is a wonderful place." (Children's Sunday School song). Amen!*

May 18

MIRACLE OF MULTIPLICATION

When He had given thanks, He distributed them...
—JOHN 6:11; READ ALSO VV. 1–21

Multiplication. In our passage today, we see that a great multitude was following Jesus. A great many Jews had gathered for Passover, and as Jesus saw them coming, He asked where they would buy food to feed them. Philip said two hundred denarii worth of bread would not be sufficient for them. Andrew said there was a lad there who had five barley loaves and two small fish. That was all the food they had. Jesus told the people to sit down. He took the loaves and gave thanks and began distributing them to the disciples and the disciples to those sitting down. This small lad's lunch fed all five thousand people and they had twelve baskets of fragments left over.

Marilyn Hickey, eighty-nine year-old Bible teacher from Colorado, tells a similar miracle story that happened while she was in Cairo, Egypt a few years ago.

They were hosting a Ministry Training School for pastors and leaders from all over Egypt, and they had boxed lunches to feed three thousand five hundred. However, five thousand people showed up. They had nowhere near enough food to meet their needs!

Exactly thousand five hundred boxed lunches were delivered and counted. And thousand five hundred tickets for the boxed lunches were handed out to attendees. When all the tickets were collected, they still had boxed lunches left. So, they passed out one thousand two hundred more boxes! After those had been handed out, when they counted again, miraculously, another one thousand two hundred boxes were there! [8]

Our God is Jehovah Jireh (the God who provides) and never changes. What He did for Jesus, He will do for us!

PRAYER: *Our Father in heaven, we give thanks to You for Your miracle working provision. Thank You, not only for all the extra food, but also that just as You worked the miracle of feeding the five thousand, You showed You are still the same miracle working God today! Thank You for meeting our need of _____ today! In Jesus' name. Amen.*

THE LIVING BREAD

And Jesus said to them, "I am the bread of life. He who comes to Me shall never hunger, and he who believes in Me shall never thirst. But I said to you that you have seen Me and yet do not believe. All that the Father gives Me will come to Me, and the one who comes to Me I will by no means cast out. For I have come down from heaven, not to do My own will, but the will of Him who sent Me. This is the will of the Father who sent Me, that of all He has given Me I should lose nothing but should raise it up at the last day. And this is the will of Him who sent Me, that everyone who sees the Son and believes in Him may have everlasting life; and I will raise him up at the last day."
—JOHN 6:35–40; READ ALSO VV. 22–40

In the previous verses, Jesus had just fed the five thousand. Here He is hoping to lift up their eyes from material bread to spiritual realities. They needed to put their confidence in Jesus instead of in material bread.

This is the first of Jesus' beautiful "I Am" sayings. *"I am the bread of life. He who comes to me will never hunger, and he who believes in Me shall never thirst."* Coming to Jesus here means to come to Him in prayer with trust, and obedience. Jesus is appealing to each of us to come to Him. This is what faith in Christ is: it is simply coming to Him.

Jesus made it clear that coming to Jesus is first a work of the Father, and He will never "cast out" anyone who comes to Him. This is an election mystery of divine sovereignty (the Father draws) and human responsibility (the one who chooses to come to Jesus).

Jesus says that the will of the Father is that He would lose none the Father sent Him but raise them all up the last day.

John 6:40 says that all who "see" the Son will be saved. Here we see the interconnection of the relationship of the Father and Jesus: Jesus raises the believer to eternal life because this is the will of the Father!

PRAYER: *Lord, we come to You, the living bread, that we may never hunger again. We will put our trust in You. Amen.*

May 20

UNDAUNTED PREACHING

Jesus replied to them, "Listen to this eternal truth: Unless you eat the body of the Son of Man and drink his blood, you will not have eternal life. Eternal life comes to the one who eats my body and drinks my blood, and I will raise him up in the last day. For my body is real food for your spirit and my blood is real drink. The one who eats my body and drinks my blood lives in me and I live in him. The Father of life sent me, and he is my life. In the same way, the one who feeds upon me, I will become his life. I am not like the bread your ancestors ate and later died. I am the living Bread that comes from heaven. Eat this bread and you will live forever!"
—John 6:53–58, tpt; read also vv. 41–71

This language must have been very offensive to the natural Jewish mind, having been taught NEVER to drink blood. And that old command had to do with animals, not the blood or flesh of a person! It must have sounded like cannibalism, hearing those words for the first time.[9]

Such radical statements offend many; in part this was Jesus' intent. The sacrificed life of Jesus is food and drink for the hungry and thirsty soul. When we receive Jesus and Him crucified, we truly abide in Jesus, and He in us. The Bible says in John 15:7: *"If you abide in Me, and My words abide in you, you shall ask what you will, and it shall be done for you."*

John 6:60 records that *"many of His disciples, when they heard this, said 'This is a difficult statement; who can listen to it?'"* Jesus didn't preach just to please His audience. If that were the case, He would have taken back what He just said, after seeing that folks were offended. Jesus then explained to them that the things that He had told them were spiritual things, not fleshly things.

Prayer: *Jesus, Your bread is manna from heaven for us; it is our healing, our provision. You said if we eat this bread, we would live forever. You shed Your blood for our forgiveness. Amen.*

FEAST OF TABERNACLES

Now the Jews' Feast of Tabernacles was at hand. "You go up to this feast. I am not yet going up to this feast, for My time has not yet fully come". But when His brothers had gone up, then He also went up to the feast, not openly, but as it were in secret.
—JOHN 7:2, 8, 10; READ ALSO VV. 1–27

The description of the Feast of Tabernacles, (the feast of rejoicing), is found in Leviticus 23:33–44. This is the last feast of the fall cycle of feasts: Feast of Trumpets (Rosh Hashana), Day of Atonement (Yom Kippur) and Feast of Tabernacles (Sukkot). This final feast celebrates when all of Israel will come to know Messiah as their Savior.

During this feast the Orthodox Jews and some others build booths adjacent to their homes. Today many synagogues build booths next to their synagogues. The Jews go there to have bread and wine and say their prayers. It is to be a kind of temporary shelter, which pictures Israel living in temporary shelters when they left Egypt. They live in these shelters seven days. This tradition also foreshadows God coming down and dwelling in a temporary shelter with them. This was fulfilled in Jesus' earthly advent.

This feast celebrates all five tabernacles where God's glory was manifested. The *first* tabernacle was the Tabernacle of Moses (Exodus 50:33–35). When Moses set up the tabernacle, the glory of the Lord filled it. When His glory came, they had food (manna) and their clothes did not wear out. They had complete protection and total health. There was not a sick one among them.

The *second* tabernacle is the Tabernacle of David, which held the ark of the covenant. David surrounded it with 24/7 praise and God's glory came down. The *third* tabernacle is JESUS. When Jesus came we beheld His glory" (John 1:14). The *fourth* tabernacle is the church (Acts 15:16–17), and the *fifth* is the eternal tabernacle (Revelation 21:3–4).

PRAYER: *Father in heaven, we rejoice in Your sending Jesus and that He tabernacled (dwelt) among us. Show us your glory (miracles) now, even as You did in Exodus and Acts! Amen!*

May 22

RIVERS OF LIVING WATER

On the last day, that great day of the feast, Jesus stood and cried out, saying, "If anyone thirsts, let him come to Me and drink. He who believes in Me, as the Scripture has said, out of his heart will flow rivers of living water." But this He spoke concerning the Spirit, whom those believing in Him would receive, for the Holy Spirit was not yet given, because Jesus was not yet glorified.
—JOHN 7:37–39; READ ALSO VV. 28–53

Every year at the Feast of Tabernacles, the High Priest performed a prophetic act. He would bring water from the pool of Siloam, carry it up to the temple, and pour it out beside the altar. This symbolized an appeal to God for the latter rain to fall on the land. It also symbolized an appeal to God for the outpouring of His Spirit, the "spiritual rain" spoken of in Joel 2:28–29: *"I will pour out My Spirit, on all people. Your sons and your daughters will prophesy, your old men will dream dreams, your young men will see visions."*

This action of pouring out the water from Siloam was repeated every day of the feast. Finally, they came to the last day, the "great day," of the feast. This was the climax of the Feast of Tabernacles, and all the feasts.

As the priest brought water from the pool of Siloam and carried it up to the temple, huge crowds would have accompanied him. As the priest stood beside the altar and prepared to pour out the water, a hush would have fallen over the crowd. But as the priest began to pour out the water, Jesus stood and cried out in a loud voice, *"If any man is thirsty, let him come to Me and drink. He who believes in Me from his innermost being shall flow RIVERS OF LIVING WATER!"* [10]

PRAYER: *Jesus, just as You spoke of the Day of Pentecost and the outpouring of the Holy Spirit upon the one hundred and twenty in the upper room (Acts 2:4), fill us again with Your Holy Spirit with the evidence of speaking in other languages! Amen!*

May 23

GO AND SIN NO MORE

Then the scribes and Pharisees brought to Him a woman caught in adultery. And when they had set her in the midst, they said to Him, "Teacher, this woman was caught in adultery, in the very act. Now Moses, in the law, commanded us that such should be stoned. But what do You say?"

—JOHN 8:3–5; READ ALSO VV. 1–27

The religious leaders brought this woman to Jesus in shame-filled circumstances. To mention the obvious, there was also a man involved in the act of adultery—yet the guilty man was not brought before Jesus, but only the woman. Perhaps this situation was a set up using one of the religious leaders.

"Moses in the law commanded us that such should be stoned." So, they had set a trap for Jesus. If He said, "Let her go," then He would seem to break the Law of Moses. If He said, "Execute her for the crime of adultery," then He would seem harsh and perhaps even cruel. Also, He would break Roman law, because they had taken the right of execution for religious offenses away from the Jews.

But Jesus, stooped down and wrote on the ground with His finger, as though He did not hear. Stooping down indicates humility. He identified with the humiliation of the woman.

He wrote on the ground. Perhaps he wrote in the dust to fulfill Jeremiah's prophecy that those who forsake God (spiritual adultery) will be written in the dust (Jeremiah 17:13).[11]

So, when they continued asking Him, He raised Himself up and said to them, *"He who is without sin among you, let him throw a stone at her first"* (v. 7). Then he stooped down and wrote on the ground again. Gradually, being convicted by their own conscience, they all left, one by one, beginning with the oldest. He asked the woman where her accusers were that condemned her. She said that no one had condemned her. Then Jesus said to her, *"Neither do I condemn you; go and sin no more."*

PRAYER: *Dear Father, Your message is to stop sinning, and yet You lovingly mediate for us against our accusers. Amen.*

NO SOVEREIGN BUT GOD

Then Jesus said to those Jews who believed Him, "If you abide in My word, you are My disciples indeed. And you shall know the truth, and the truth shall make you free." "Therefore, if the Son makes you free, you shall be free indeed."
—JOHN 8:31–32, 36; READ ALSO VV. 28–59

Freedom is one thing that Americans have fought, bled and died for. Patrick Henry in 1775 said, "Give me liberty or give me death!" During the years 1775–76, American colonies had endured taxation without representation, searches and seizures without probable cause, the confiscation of firearms, and on and on. The colonial leaders had tried to remain loyal to the Crown but were finally compelled to break away in revolt.

One amazing example of this is the Lutheran pastor John Muhlenberg. He preached a sermon from Ecclesiastes 3:1, "To everything there is a season…" "There is a time to preach and a time to fight. And now is the time to fight." [12] He then threw off his clerical robes and revealed the uniform of a Revolutionary Army officer. That afternoon, at the head of three hundred men, he marched off to join General Washington's troops and became Colonel of the 8th Virginia Regiment. They were armed with the holy cause of liberty.

Our quest for true protection of human liberties resulted in the Bill of Rights, which are the first ten amendments to the constitution. Without the Bill of Rights, basic human rights such as the freedom of religion and of speech, freedom to assemble and petition, the right to a free press, and the right to bear arms, etc., could have been denied or repressed.

We are still in battles for freedom of religion, for prayer and Bible reading, and for not being forced to hire people with life-styles not lining up to biblical standards, etc.

PRAYER: *Father in heaven, thank You for the freedoms we have enjoyed in America! May we see prayer and Bibles back in our schools! We declare over America: "No Sovereign but God, and No King but Jesus!" Amen!*

May 25

THE LIGHT OF THE WORD

Now as Jesus passed by, He saw a man who was blind from birth. And His disciples asked Him, saying "Rabbi, who sinned this man or his parents, that he was born blind?" Jesus answered, "Neither this man nor his parents sinned, but that the works of God should be revealed in him. I must work the works of Him who sent Me while it is day, the night is coming when no one can work. As long as I am in the world, I am the light of the world."
—JOHN 9:1–5; READ ALSO VV. 1–23

In the context of Jesus' teaching on the light of the world and mankind being in the dark, this miracle of giving sight to the blind man is a powerful proof of Jesus' words. Christ, in His birth, became a man of clay. When He applies this clay over our eyes and we wash in the water of His Word, our spiritual sight is restored.

So, when Jesus said, *"I am the light of the world,"* He spit on the ground and made clay with the saliva; and He anointed the eyes of the blind man with the clay. Then He told him to *"Go, wash in the pool of Siloam"* (v. 11). So he went and washed and came back seeing.

Just as God used the dust of the ground and clay to do a work of creation in Genesis, so Jesus did a work of creation with dust and clay for this man.

Opening the eyes of the blind was prophesied to be a work of the Messiah: *"The eyes of the blind shall be opened"* (Isaiah 35:5). This miracle caused a stir among the religious leaders because He healed on the Sabbath. They didn't believe him and went and asked his parents who said "Yes," their son was born blind. When they asked the man how Jesus opened his eyes, he said, *"Whether this man is a sinner or not I do not know. One thing I know; that though I was blind, now I see."*

PRAYER: *Heavenly Father, God of miracles, we worship You and thank You that You open the eyes of the blind, physically and spiritually. You said we would do even greater works! Amen!*

LORD, I BELIEVE

Jesus heard that they had cast him out; and when He had found him, He said to him, "Do you believe in the Son of God?" He answered and said, "Who is He, Lord, that I may believe in Him?" And Jesus said to him, "You have both seen Him and it is He who is talking with you." Then he said, "Lord, I believe!" And he worshiped Him.
—JOHN 9:35–38; READ ALSO VV. 24–41

The religious leaders rejected the man whom Jesus healed. Jesus then made it a point to meet him and receive him.

Jesus asked him if he believed in him, and he said, *"Lord, I believe."* When the healed man declared his loyalty to Jesus by not denying Him before the hostile religious leaders, he was rewarded with a greater revelation of Jesus as the Son of God. *"You have both seen Him and it is He who is talking with you."*

Jesus dealt with this man differently than most. He met his physical need first, then allowed him to endure persecution, then called him to a specific belief.

"And he worshipped Him." The religious leaders told the man, "You can't worship with us at the temple." Jesus said, "I will receive your worship." The fact that Jesus accepted this worship is another proof that Jesus was and is God, and that He knew Himself to be God.

"And Jesus said, 'For judgment I have come into this world, that those who do not see may see, and that those who see may be made blind.'" (v. 39) He meant that those who admit their spiritual blindness can find sight in Jesus, whereas those who falsely claim to have spiritual sight will be made blind. In other words, the light is there, but if people refuse to avail themselves of it and instead deliberately reject it, how can they be enlightened? As Jesus said, *"Therefore their sin remains."*

PRAYER: *Dear Father, Jesus was sent to be the Light of the world. Help us to shine His light everywhere we go. Give us a spirit of wisdom and revelation in the knowledge of Him! In Jesus' name. Amen.*

THE SHEPHERD

Most assuredly, I say to you, he who does not enter the sheepfold by the door, but climbs up some other way, the same is a thief and a robber. But he who enters by the door is the shepherd of the sheep. To him the doorkeeper opens and the sheep hear his voice; and he calls his own sheep by name and leads them out. And when he brings out his own sheep, he goes before them; and the sheep follow him for they know his voice. Yet they will by no means follow a stranger, but will flee from him, for they do not know the voice of strangers.
—JOHN 10:1–5; READ ALSO VV. 1–21

In this spiritual picture, Jesus said that the door for the sheep pen had a doorkeeper—one who watched who came in and who went out. He would grant the true shepherd access.

In towns of that time, sheep from many flocks were kept for the night in a common sheepfold, overseen by one doorkeeper who monitored the shepherds and the sheep they collected.

One commentator said, "In my youth, some shepherds in the Scottish Highlands not only called their individual sheep by name but claimed that an individual sheep would recognize its own name and respond to it." [13]

"During World War 1, some soldiers tried to steal a flock of sheep from a hillside near Jerusalem. The sleeping shepherd awoke to find his flock being driven off. He couldn't recapture them by force, so he called out to his flock with his distinctive call. The sheep listened and returned to their rightful owner. The soldiers couldn't stop the sheep from returning to their shepherd's voice." [14]

Jesus used the Biblical illustration to show us that if we listen, it is His promise that we will follow His voice and not follow the voice of a stranger. If we need to hear His voice, and get His direction, we can claim this promise from John 10:4–5.

PRAYER: *Dear Heavenly Father, we thank You that Jesus is the Door of the sheep. If anyone enters by Him, he will be saved. We thank You that as Your sheep, we know Your voice. Amen.*

May 28

SEEK AND RELY ON GOD

Now it was the Feast of dedication in Jerusalem, and it was winter.
And Jesus walked in the temple, in Solomon's porch.
—JOHN 10:22–23; READ ALSO VV. 22–42

This feast is also known as Hanukkah and celebrated the cleansing and rededication of the temple after three years of desecration by Antiochus Epiphanes, king of Syria in 165 B.C.

After Antiochus attacked Jerusalem, he instituted a reign of terror upon the Jews of the city. He said that possessing a copy of the Jewish law was punishable by death. Circumcising a child was punishable by death. The temple was turned into a house of prostitution. The great altar of burnt offering was turned into an altar to the Greek god Zeus, and pigs were sacrificed upon it. Eighty thousand Jews were killed.

The rise of the Maccabees ended these horrors. They purified the temple and lit the great seven-branched candlestick. Unfortunately, there was only enough purified oil to light the lamps for one single day. By a miracle, the oil lasted for eight days, until new oil had been prepared according to the correct formula and had been consecrated.[15]

Jesus continued teaching there and said, *"My sheep hear My voice, and I know them and they follow Me. And I give them eternal life, and they shall never perish; neither shall anyone snatch them out of My hand. My Father who has given them to Me is greater than all; and no one is able to snatch them out of My father's hand"* (v. 27–29).

This is a wonderful promise to us, that as we continue to seek the Lord, no one can snatch us out of the Father's hand. Just as Jesus is the good shepherd who gives His life for the sheep, He is able to protect us. *"Even though we walk through the valley of the shadow of death, we will fear no evil"* (Psalm 23:4).

PRAYER: *As we pray through the 23rd Psalm, we praise You Jesus that You are our Good Shepherd. We shall not want. Surely goodness and mercy shall follow us all our lives. Amen!*

May 29

JESUS IS THE RESURRECTION AND LIFE

Jesus said to her, "I am the resurrection and the life. He who believes in Me, though he may die, he shall live. And whoever lives and believes in Me shall never die. Do you believe this?"
—JOHN 11:25–26; READ ALSO vv. 1–29

Josh McDowell writes in his book *A Ready Defense*: "Professor McDowell, why can't you refute Christianity?" I answered, 'For a very simple reason—the resurrection of Jesus Christ.'" [16]

The resurrection of Christ is the core of Christianity. McDowell made several observations of Christianity worth noting. Observation #1: The historical, literary, and legal testimony supports its validity. Gary Habermas in "The Case for the Resurrection of Jesus" looks at one thousand four hundred modern sources in three different languages, both skeptics and Christians and they all agreed on four minimal facts: a) Jesus died by crucifixion and lived. b) Disciples believed He was resurrected. c) The changed life of Saul to the Apostle Paul, and d) The conversion of James, the half-brother of Jesus.

Observation #2: His Resurrection was foretold. Throughout the four Gospels, Christ actually predicted He would rise on the third day.

Observation #3: The resurrection is the very basis for the truth of Christianity. *"But if there is no resurrection of the dead, not even Christ has been raised; and if Christ has not been raised, then our preaching is in vain; your faith also is in vain"* (1 Corinthians 15:13–14).

Observation #4: It is an intelligent faith. It is believing in the light of historical facts, consistent with evidences, on the basis of witnesses. Historically the resurrection is inescapable.

PRAYER: *We praise You Father that Jesus was seen by the disciples for forty days after the resurrection, and then was taken up in a cloud from Mt. Olivet to heaven. Thank You for the angels who said that Jesus will come in like manner as He went into heaven (Acts 1:3–11). Come quickly Lord Jesus! Amen!*

LAZARUS, COME FORTH

Jesus said to her, "Did I not say to you that if you would believe you would see the glory of God?" Then they took away the stone from the place where the dead man was lying. And Jesus lifted up His eyes and said, "Father, I thank You that You have heard Me. And I know that You always hear Me, but because of the people who are standing by I said this, that they may believe that You sent Me." Now when He had said these things, He cried with a loud voice, "Lazarus, come forth!" And he who had died came out bound hand and foot with graveclothes, and his face was wrapped with a cloth. Jesus said to them, "Loose him, and let him go."
—JOHN 11:40–44; READ ALSO vv. 30–57

What an amazing story! When Jesus came to the scene of Lazarus' tomb, Jesus intensely groaned in the spirit. This literally means to snort like a horse—implying anger and indignation. This means that Jesus wasn't so much sad at the scene surrounding the tomb of Lazarus. It is more accurate to say that Jesus was angry. He was angry at the destruction and power of the great enemy of humanity which is death. Jesus would soon break its power.[17]

Jesus wept. He shared in the grief of those who mourned. He related to their pain! Yet He was able to do something about it. He said, *"Take away the stone."* Martha said that by now there would be a great stench. But Jesus reminded her that if she would believe, she would see the glory of God.

Then they took away the stone from the place where the dead man was lying. Then He cried with a loud voice, *"Lazarus, come forth!"* It has been said that it was a good thing He called him by name, or all the people would have come out!

He came out still bound with the grave clothes and Jesus said, *"Loose him, and let him go!"*

PRAYER: *Jesus, You said that we were to heal the sick, and raise the dead, and that we would do greater works than You did. Help us to believe and not doubt! In Your name. Amen.*

May 31

FOLLOW ME

Most assuredly, I say to you, unless a grain of wheat falls into the ground and dies, it remains alone; but if it dies, it produces much grain. He who loves his life will lose it, and he who hates his life in this world will keep it for eternal life. If anyone serves Me, let him follow Me, and where I am, there My servant will be also. It anyone serves Me, him My Father will honor.
—JOHN 12:24–26; READ ALSO VV. 1–26

Just as a seed will never become a plant unless it dies and is buried, so the death and burial of Jesus was necessary to His glorification. Before there can be resurrection power and fruitfulness, there must be death. If this is true of Jesus, it is also true of His followers.

In the passage above, we are called to hate our life, not in the sense that we disregard it, but in the sense that we freely give it up for God. Our life is precious to us, especially because it is something we can give to Jesus. We are to understand that we are mere pilgrims and sojourners on this earth, with our home in heaven (Hebrews 11:13–16). The man whose priorities are right has such an attitude of love for the things of God that it makes all interest in the affairs of this life appear as hatred by comparison.

Next, Jesus said, "*If anyone serves Me, let him follow Me.*" To be a Christian is to serve Jesus. It doesn't mean that you stop working your job or caring for your family or studying at school. It means all you do, you do as a servant of Jesus.

It would be easy for the disciples to think, "Jesus is going to the cross. Thank heaven I don't have to do that." Then Jesus says, "*Follow Me.*"

PRAYER: *Father, there will always be circumstances where what we want and what You want are different. Help us to do what it says in Galatians 2:20: "I have been crucified with Christ; it is no longer I who live, but Christ lives in me; and the life which I now live in the flesh I live by faith in the Son of God, who loved me and gave Himself for me." Amen.*

June 1

THE WORD OF GOD IS THE JUDGE

Jesus said, "And if anyone hears My words and does not believe, I do not judge him; for I did not come to judge the world but to save the world. He who rejects Me, and does not receive My words, has that which judges him—the word that I have spoken will judge him in the last day. For I have not spoken on My own authority; but the Father who sent Me gave Me a command, what I should say and what I should speak. And I know that His command is everlasting life. Therefore, whatever I speak, just as the Father has told Me, so I speak."

—JOHN 12:47–50; READ ALSO VV. 27–50

Here again, we see that Jesus said He did not come to judge the world but to save the world. He said that it is *"the word He speaks"* that will judge us on the last day. It actually is *"the Word"* that people do not receive or believe. The words that Jesus speaks are not from Him, but they are the words the Father has given Him to speak.

This is prophesied by Moses in Deuteronomy 18:18, "I will raise up for them a Prophet like you from among their brethren, and will put My words in His mouth, and He shall speak to them all that I command Him." The Prophet God referred to and raised up was Jesus.

Jesus said in John 3:17: "For God sent not His Son into the world to condemn the world, but that the world through Him might be saved."

"Yet the word that I have spoken will judge him." There are inescapable consequences for rejecting Jesus. Always in the Gospel of John there is this essential paradox: Jesus came in love, yet His coming is still a judgment, in that He exposes sin. The Gospel of John begins with the revelation that Jesus is the very living Word of God: "in the beginning was 'the Word' and the Word was with God, and the Word was God." And then in verse 14 in chapter one, we read, "and the Word became flesh and dwelt among us." This Word that dwelt among us will judge us.

PRAYER: *Dear Father in Heaven, Your Word says that "the fear of the Lord" is the beginning of wisdom. May we honor, respect, and obey Your Word. One day it will judge us. Amen.*

HUMILITY OF SERVANTHOOD

So when He had washed their feet, taken His garments, and sat down again, He said to them, "Do you know what I have done to you? You call Me Teacher and Lord, and you say well, for so I am. If I then, your Lord and Teacher, have washed your feet, you also ought to wash one another's feet."
—JOHN 13:12–14; READ ALSO VV. 1–20

Jesus' entire life was a series of lessons and living examples to the disciples. In this situation, He felt it was important to specifically draw attention to the lesson of what He had just done. He didn't want the understanding of it left to chance.

Jesus commanded them to show the same humble, sacrificial love to one another. This example of Jesus should mark their own attitude and actions.

Charles Spurgeon said, "If there be any deed of kindness or love that we can do for the very meanest and most obscure of God's people, we ought to be willing to do it—to be servants to God's servants."

We, like the disciples would gladly wash the feet of Jesus, but He tells us to wash one another's feet. Anything we do for each other that washes away the grime of the world and the dust of defeat and discouragement is foot washing. It is easy to criticize those with dirty feet instead of washing them. Christ's way is very different. He says nothing but takes the basin and begins to wash away the stain. Do not judge and condemn but seek the restoration and the improvement of the erring.[1]

If we are going to wash one another's feet, we need to be careful of the temperature of the water. It can't be too hot—in our fervency being too zealous. It can't be too cold—being distant in heart to them. Jesus washed us "with the washing of the water of the word." We must follow His example.

PRAYER: *We pray in Jesus' name that we would have that humility of servanthood like Jesus displayed. Servants notice what needs to be done and do it. They don't care who gets the credit. Amen.*

June 3

OLD COMMANDMENT IN A NEW WAY

A new commandment I give to you, that you love one another; as I have loved you, that you also love one another. By this all will know that you are My disciples, if you have love for one another.
—JOHN 13:34–35; READ ALSO VV. 21–38

The new commandment was actually an old commandment but was presented in a new way. We might have thought the new commandment was for us to love Jesus in an outstanding way. Instead, Jesus directed us (not them) to love one another and a special presence of His love was to be among the Believers as a result.

We are to love our neighbor as ourselves. However, we are to love our fellow Christians as Christ loved us, which is far more than we love ourselves.

Jesus said that love would be the identifying mark of His disciples. It wasn't that love for unbelievers in the world was not important, but it wasn't first. The world will mark us as His disciples by our love for one another.

James Maloney tells the story relating to the power of love. He was ministering in a home meeting when parents brought their five-year-old daughter who had cerebral palsy. He felt this flow of compassion from the Lord that rushed out to her. As he was about to lay his hands on her, the Holy Spirit checked him and said to him, "She doesn't need prayer. She needs you to pick her up and just love on her."[2] So he gathered her up in his arms and turned his back on the rest of the group. He cradled her and just loved on her, his spirit oozing out this feeling of compassion. He learned later that he held her about fifteen minutes. She just seemed to soak in that compassion; it just seemed to cover her. When he put her down, he told her to run to Mommy and Daddy. She was completely healed, and he didn't pray a word over her!

PRAYER: *Lord, You said in John 14:14 that if we ask anything in Your name, You would do it. We ask that we could love people like You do! In Jesus' name. Amen!*

THE WAY, THE TRUTH, AND THE LIFE

Let not your heart be troubled; you believe in God, believe also in Me. In My Father's house are many mansions; if it were not so, I would have told you. I go to prepare a place for you. And if I go and prepare a place for you, I will come again and receive you to Myself; that where I am, there you may be also. And where I go you know, and the way you know. Thomas said to Him, "Lord, we do not know where You are going, and how can we know the way?" Jesus said to him, "I am the way, the truth, and the life, No one comes to the Father except through Me."
—JOHN 14:1–6; READ ALSO JOHN 14

Simon Greenleaf was the Royal Professor of Law at Harvard and considered one of the greatest legal minds in Western history. In his *Testimony of the Evangelists,* he stated:

> The religion of Jesus Christ aims at nothing less than the utter over-throw of all other systems of religion in the world; denouncing them as inadequate to the wants of man, false in their foundations, and dangerous in their tendency. It not only solicits the grave attention of all, to whom its doctrines are presented, but it demands their cordial belief, as a matter of vital concernment.
>
> (These are no ordinary claims)…but if they are well-founded and just, they can be no less than the high requirements of heaven, addressed by the voice of God to the reason and understanding of man, concerning things deeply affecting his relations to his sovereign, and essential to the formation of his character and of course to his destiny, both for this life and for the life to come.[3]

Jesus didn't say that He would show us a way; He said that He *is* The Way. He didn't promise to teach us *a* truth; He said that He *is* The Truth. Jesus didn't offer us the secrets to life; He said that He *is* The Life. He is the ONLY way to the Father.

PRAYER: *Father in heaven, thank You for providing the way for us to go to heaven through Jesus, and making it **very** clear. Amen.*

GREATER LOVE

This is my commandment that you love one another as I have loved you. Greater love has no one than this, than to lay down one's life for his friends.

—JOHN 15:13–14; READ ALSO JOHN 15

Shortly before 1 A.M. on February 2, 1943, the American transport ship *Dorchester* was hit by a German torpedo. The ship carried 902 men on its way from Newfoundland to an American base in Greenland. Many were killed in the blast.

Through the pandemonium, four Army chaplains brought hope in despair and light in darkness to the men who struggled to find their way out. They were Lt. George Fox, Methodist; Lt. Alexander Goode, Jewish; Lt John Washington, Roman Catholic; and Lt. Clark Poling, Dutch Reformed.

Men jumped from the ship into lifeboats, overcrowding them to the point of capsizing. As most of the men reached topside, the chaplains opened a storage locker and began distributing life jackets. When there were no more available, the chaplains astonished onlookers, taking off theirs and giving them to four frightened young men. One of the survivors, John Ladd, said, "It was the finest thing I have seen or hope to see this side of heaven."

Then in the darkness, the four chaplains linked arms, grasped the railing of the ship together as it began to slip into the ocean, and began singing and shouting biblical encouragement in English, Hebrew, and Latin to the men in the sea. One man, floating among his dead comrades, later said, "Their voices were the only thing that kept me going."

Of the men aboard the *Dorchester*, 672 died, including the chaplains. Their sacrificial action constitutes one of the purest spiritual and ethical acts a person can make. Their heroic conduct set a vision of greatness that stunned America as did the magnitude of the tragedy.[4]

PRAYER: *We are so amazed Lord at the courage of Your servants and their willingness to give their lives for others! Give us the same kind of love for others as these men had! Amen!*

June 6

CONVICTION OF SIN

And when He has come, He will convict the world of sin, and of righ-
teousness, and of judgment: of sin, because they do not believe in Me;
of righteousness, because I go to My Father and you see Me no more;
of judgment, because the ruler of this world is judged.
—JOHN 16:8–11; READ ALSO JOHN 16

"The Holy Spirit will convict people of sin. Before this conviction, people may say, 'I make a lot of mistakes. Nobody's perfect.' But after the convicting work of the Holy Spirit one may say, 'I'm a lost rebel, fighting against God and His law—I must rely on Jesus to get right with God.' The essence of sin is unbelief, which is not a casual incredulity. It is total rejection of God's messenger and message." [5]

In the great awakening of 1860-61 in Great Britain, a high-ranking army officer described the conviction of sin in his Scottish town. "Many turned from open sin to lives of holiness, some weeping for joy for sins forgiven." [6] When the Holy Spirit is pleased to open a man's eyes to see the real state of his heart, he can see the real foundation upon which he had placed his trust was on his own goodness, and not on Christ.

The Holy Spirit convicts us of righteousness. The ascension of Jesus to heaven demonstrated that He had perfectly fulfilled the Father's will and had proven Himself righteous.

The Holy Spirit convicts the world of judgment, because the ruler of this world is judged. He shows us that Satan is judged and is under our feet. We have authority over him.

"In essence, sin is related to Adam. Righteousness is related to Christ. And judgment is related to Satan, for the pure works of Christ bring judgment on the works of Satan." [7]

PRAYER: *All praise to You, God for sending Jesus who conquered sin, gave us His righteousness, and judged Satan. Amen.*

AUTHORITY OVER ALL FLESH

As You have given Him authority over all flesh, that He should give eternal life to as many as You have given Him. And this is eternal life, that they may know You, the only true God, and Jesus Christ whom You have sent.
—JOHN 17:2–3; READ ALSO JOHN 17

Jesus claimed to have authority over all flesh and to have the ability to give eternal life to mankind. This is a clear and startling claim to deity; no One but God could truthfully and knowingly make this claim. In other words, Jesus claimed authority to determine the ultimate destiny of all men.

Knowing that Jesus has authority over all flesh gives us great hope for evangelism and missionary work. Even for those who reject Jesus or are ignorant of Him, Jesus has authority over them. We can pray in faith and ask Jesus to exercise that authority over those who have yet to repent and believe.

"You have given Him authority over all flesh." Philippians 2:9–10 is a demonstration of this authority. A day will come when everyone, either voluntarily or involuntarily, will recognize the authority of Jesus. We read that *"every knee will bow and every tongue confess that Jesus Christ is Lord."*

Jesus understood that He was and is the One who grants eternal life to those given to Him by the Father. We know that Jesus is God's gift to us, but the Bible says that we are God's gift to Jesus.

"And this is eternal life that they may know You...and Jesus Christ whom You have sent" (v. 3). In 1636 Harvard was founded by the Puritans and adopted the "Rules and Precepts" which stated "Let every student be plainly instructed, and earnestly pressed to consider well, the main end of his life and studies is, to know God and Jesus Christ which is eternal life." [8]

Eternal life is found in an experiential knowledge of God the Father and Jesus Christ, God the Son. Knowing Him this way will affect every aspect of our lives forever.

PRAYER: *Father, we pray that once again, the main end of our lives and studies would be to know Jesus Christ! Amen!*

June 8

I AM

Jesus therefore, knowing all things that would come upon Him, went forward and said to them, "Whom are you seeking?" They answered Him, "Jesus of Nazareth." Jesus said to them, "I am (He)." And Judas, who betrayed Him, also stood with them. Now when He said to them, "I am He," they drew back and fell to the ground.
—JOHN 18:4–6; READ ALSO VV. 1–18

If Judas thought he would surprise Jesus, he was wrong, for Jesus' entire life was prepared for this hour. When Jesus asked whom they were seeking, they said *"Jesus of Nazareth,"* as this was the name He was known by. He answered by saying *"I Am."* ("He" was added by the translators.) With this answer He proclaimed that He was God.

"Now when He said to them, 'I am (He),' they drew back and fell to the ground." When He declared His divine identity, Judas and all the soldiers fell back. There was an awesome display of divine presence, majesty and power in those two words: I AM.

Jesus was completely in control of the situation. In all honesty, He did not have to go with this arresting army. Jesus could have easily overpowered them by His words and escaped. Their falling to the ground reveals His glory. People still fall backwards to the ground in the presence of His glory.

+ Jesus was born as a humble baby, yet announced by angels.

+ Jesus was laid in a manger, yet signaled by a star.

+ Jesus submitted to baptism as if a sinner, but heard the Divine Voice from heaven.

+ Jesus slept when He was exhausted, but awoke to calm the storm.

+ Jesus wept at a grave, then called the dead to life.

+ Jesus surrendered to arrest, then declared "I Am" and knocked all the troops over.

+ Jesus died on a cross, but by it He defeated sin, death, and Satan.[9]

PRAYER: *To God our Savior, who is the Great I AM! Amen!*

June 9

WHAT IS TRUTH?

Pilate therefore said to Him, "Are You a king then?" Jesus answered,
"You say rightly that I am a king. For this cause I was born, and for
this cause I have come into the world, that I should bear witness to
the truth. Everyone who is of the truth hears My voice." Pilate said to
Him, "What is truth?" And when he had said this, he went out again
to the Jews, and said to them, "I find no fault in Him at all."
—JOHN 18:37–38; READ ALSO VV. 19–40

After Pilate sarcastically asked Jesus if He were a king, Jesus
answered that he said rightly that He was a king. He insisted He
was born a king, although He proved to be a different kind of King.
He came to be a King of Truth, that He should bear witness to the
truth. This was the good confession before Pilate that Paul spoke of
in 1 Timothy 6:13.

Our Lord said that He was born a king. This is proof of the incar-
nation of the Son of God.

Pilate then said, "*What is truth?*" This could be genuine, or it could
be a cynical question showing that he thought Jesus' claim to be King
to be a foolish one. It has been said that in Pilate's perspective, soldiers and armies were truth, Rome was truth, Caesar was truth, and
political power was truth.

Many in our day have asked "What is truth?" but from a different
perspective. Some think truth is only personal, individual, and not
authoritative truth from the Word of God. They think there is your
truth, and there is my truth and one is as good as the other. Some
think all truth is relative; the question for them is: "Is that true?"

Jesus said, "I am the truth." His Word never changes. Abortion
will always be wrong. Gay marriage will always be wrong. The ten
commandments are the standard of right and wrong. This is truth
revealed in Jesus. Heaven and earth will pass away, but His Word
will never pass away (Matthew 24:35).

PRAYER: *Heavenly Father, we see that truth is a Man, Jesus Christ,*
and that that truth will never change like shifting sands. One thing will
not be wrong one day, and right the next. Thank You for the stability
Your Word brings to us! Amen!

CROWN OF THORNS

The soldiers twisted a crown of thorns and put it on His head, and they put on Him a purple robe. Then they said, "Hail, King of the Jews!"

—JOHN 19:2; READ ALSO VV. 1–22

Kings wear crowns, but not crowns of torture. The specific thorn bushes of this region have long, hard, sharp thorns. This was a crown that cut, pierced, and bloodied the head of the King who wore it.

The crown of thorns was a public demonstration that Jesus was dying a cursed man. Remember the first mention of thorns in the Bible? Those thorns were part of the curse for Adam's disobedience. Long thorns were pressed into Jesus' skull. This is an illustration that much of the bondage of the curse is in your mind. God wants to deliver you from cursed thinking, which can give you as much pain as thorns buried into your skull.

You may be plagued with such thoughts as, "I'll never make it." "Things always turn out bad for me." "Our family has always been poor." "My dad was an alcoholic, so I guess I will be one too." "I guess I'm a loser." "I can't get ahead, I'm always behind." "No one likes me."

These can be painful thorns in your mind and your emotions. Jesus will heal you from these "griefs and sorrows," as well as from your physical pains and sicknesses (Isaiah 53:4). Jesus became a curse for you so that the blessing of Abraham would come to you, and to all peoples (Galatians 3:13–14).

Jesus was also crucified on Golgotha, the place of the skull. This place was named because David brought Goliath of Gath's head outside of Jerusalem. Some believe this is where the name originated. Jesus died for all forms of mental sickness and torment and trauma. He died so that our minds can be free to love and worship Him.

PRAYER: *Father in Heaven, thank You for Your Son wearing the crown of thorns and all that means to us. You truly took care of every weapon the enemy has against our minds. We ask for healing of our minds. In Jesus' name. Amen!*

June 11

IT IS FINISHED

So when Jesus had received the sour wine, He said, "It is finished!"
And bowing His head, He gave up His spirit.
—John 19:30; read also vv. 23–42

This is the most important moment in history for every person in the world, including you and me. What Jesus declared at this moment is the foundation of the Christian faith. What happened when Jesus shed His blood and His body was broken? Here is the Gospel on the five fingers of your hand to remember what was finished for us on the cross:[10]

1. Freedom from Sin. Jesus broke the power of sin, so that you can be forgiven and live a holy life (Ephesians 1:7–8).

2. Freedom from Sickness. Jesus broke the power of sickness so that you can be healed in your body, soul and spirit (Isaiah 53:5). *"By His wounds you have been healed."*

3. Freedom from Satan. Jesus broke the power of Satan and all demons, so that you can be free of all fear and live in the peace and joy of the Lord (Hebrews 2:14, 15). The fear of death is the root of all fears.

4. Freedom from the Curse. Jesus broke the power of the curse, so that you could be free from poverty and hopelessness, and so that you can live a fruitful and blessed life (Galatians 3:13, 14).

5. Freedom to Live in the Presence of God. Through His broken body and His shed blood, Jesus restored your fellowship with your Heavenly Father. When Jesus died, *"the veil of the temple was torn in two from top to bottom."* This made a way for us to have wide open access to our Heavenly Father.

Prayer: *Thank You Jesus for all You did for us on the cross. Thank You for freedom from sin, sickness, Satan, the curse and freedom to live in the presence of Father God. We give You praise! Help us to walk in these truths! Amen!*

RADICAL BELIEF

The other disciples therefore said to him, (Thomas), "We have seen the Lord." So he said to them, "Unless I see in His hands the print of the nails, and put my finger into the print of the nails, and put my hand into His side, I will not believe. Then He said to Thomas, "Reach your finger here, and look at My hands; and reach your hand here, and put it into My side. Do not be unbelieving, but believing." And Thomas answered and said to Him, "My Lord and my God!"
—JOHN 20:25, 27–28; READ ALSO JOHN 20

Thomas was not with the other disciples when Jesus came, but he was not criticized for his absence. He is often known as "Doubting Thomas." Here we can say that Thomas didn't doubt; he plainly and strongly refused to believe. He refused to believe the testimony of many witnesses and reliable witnesses.

In mercy and kindness, Jesus granted Thomas what he had asked for when he said, *"reach your finger here, and look at My hands; and reach your hand here, and put it into My side."* This shows He is full of love and graciousness and gentleness to His people.

Jesus commanded Thomas: *"Do not be unbelieving, but believing."* Because he did not believe in the resurrected Jesus, Jesus considered him unbelieving.

Thomas responded with radical belief: *"My Lord and my God"* (v. 28). Jesus accepted these titles. The Lord is so patient with us, not willing that any should perish! Thomas later was a missionary to India and ended up giving his life for Christ.

PRAYER: *Dear Heavenly Father, we praise You for Your mercy and kindness and power in winning a person of unbelief. We praise You that no one is too far away from You for You to bring him to Yourself and turn him to radical belief! Lord, we consider that it just took one encounter with You for Thomas to turn around. Your arm is not too short to reach any person! Amen!*

FEED MY LAMBS

So when they had eaten breakfast, Jesus said to Simon Peter, "Simon, son of Jonah, do you love Me more than these?" He said to Him, "Yes, Lord, You know that I love You." He said to him, Feed My lambs.
—JOHN 21:15; READ ALSO JOHN 21

Jesus wanted to give special attention to Peter to restore him after he denied Him three times. It is interesting that Peter was standing next to a fire when he denied Christ, and now he is standing next to a fire when Jesus restores him.

The large catch of fish points to a mighty harvest from among the people groups of the world. This great catch of fish begins the process of inner healing for Peter from the guilt and shame of his denial of Christ. Peter began to follow Jesus because of a great catch of fish (Luke 5:2–10), so Jesus now repeats that miracle, (v. 6), by inviting Peter to follow Him again.

Jesus asked Peter if he loved *(agape)* Him more than these. More than these could mean the fish and fishing, but more likely, it meant asking him if he loved Jesus more than the other disciples did. He had previously boasted that he loved Jesus more than the others did, and even though everyone else might leave Him, Peter said that he never would.

Yet, Peter did deny Jesus—three times, and now Jesus asked Peter three times if he loved Him. Jesus' compassion removed Peter's pain of denial. The first "love" was the Greek word *agape*—a God kind of love full of fire. Peter answered with the word *phileo*—the Greek word meaning a brotherly kind of love. This was repeated a second time. The third time, Jesus used the same word Peter had, *"phileo".* Peter three times makes his confession of his deep love for Christ. Jesus wanted to restore Peter.

Then Jesus said, *"Feed My lambs;" "Tend my sheep;"* and the third time, *"Feed My sheep."* Peter was commissioned to be a shepherd to the sheep. Men and women need to be cared for and fed by the leadership of Christ's church.

PRAYER: *Heavenly Father. We see that You want us restored to You after we blow it. You are awesome! Amen!*

BAPTIZED WITH THE HOLY SPIRIT

And being assembled together with them, He commanded them not to depart from Jerusalem, but to wait for the Promise of the Father, "which," He said "you have heard from Me; for John truly baptized with water, but you shall be baptized with the Holy Spirit not many days from now" (v. 4–5). "But you shall receive power when the Holy Spirit has come upon you; and you shall be witnesses to Me in Jerusalem, and in all Judea and Samaria, and to the end of the earth." Now when He had spoken these things, while they watched, He was taken up, and a cloud received Him out of their sight.
—ACTS 1:9; READ ALSO ACTS 1

Jesus commanded His disciples to wait in Jerusalem for the coming of the Holy Spirit. He knew they could do nothing effective for the Kingdom of God until the Spirit came. This is history's most powerful prayer meeting. The disciples engaged in persistent unified prayer, not knowing how long they would be waiting. Jesus ministered to them after the resurrection for forty days. They ended up waiting ten more days. The fiftieth day was the Day of Pentecost.

Jesus had prophesied this event in John 7:37–38. "On the last day, that great day of the feast (Tabernacles), Jesus stood and cried out, saying, 'If anyone thirsts, let him come to Me and drink. He who believes in Me, as the Scripture has said, out of his heart will flow rivers of living water.' But this He spoke concerning the Spirit, whom those believing in Him would receive; for the Holy Spirit was not yet given, because Jesus was not yet glorified."

Jesus said that this baptism of the Holy Spirit would bring power to be witnesses to the ends of the earth. Before this, Peter denied Jesus three times. After the baptism of the Holy Spirit he boldly preached on the Day of Pentecost and three thousand people were saved.

After giving them this assignment, Jesus was taken up to heaven while they watched. He will come back in like manner.

PRAYER: *Heavenly Father, we praise You for sending the fire of the Holy Spirit! Fill us again. Make us soul winners! Amen!*

June 15

FILLED WITH THE HOLY SPIRIT

When the Day of Pentecost had fully come, they were all with one accord in one place. And suddenly there came a sound from heaven, as of a rushing mighty wind, and it filled the whole house where they were sitting. Then there appeared to them divided tongues, as of fire, and one sat upon each of them. And they were all filled with the Holy Spirit and began to speak with other tongues, as the Spirit gave them utterance.
—ACTS 2:1–4; READ ALSO VV. 1–21

When the Holy Spirit becomes your friend, He brings four amazing benefits into your life:

1. *Power.* Sadly, many Christians struggle all their days to live the Christian life and they experience all kinds of failure because they try to live it in their own strength. The Holy Spirit brings that power we need to succeed.

2. *Love.* The famous love chapter, 1 Corinthians 13 is sandwiched between the two chapters that deal with the gifts of the Holy Spirit. The Holy Spirit fills us with love and gives us the power to love one another.

3. *Fruit.* According to Galatians 5:22, the Holy Spirit fills us with love, joy, peace, patience, kindness, gentleness, etc. This is the secret to not worrying about anything.

4. *Gifts.* Words of wisdom, knowledge, discerning of spirits, tongues, interpretations, prophecy, faith, healing and miracles. We can begin to hear God's voice clearly, speaking directly to us, and He quickens His Word to us in the Bible. We can now pray in the Spirit.

After being filled with the Holy Spirit, Robert Morris heard the Lord talk to him about a man in his church who felt like the prodigal son because he had been away from the Lord for a long time. The Lord told him to say to him, "Welcome home, son." When he did, the man's eyes filled with tears and the prodigal came back to the Lord.[11]

PRAYER: *Father in Heaven, help us to hunger after everything You have provided for us and not settle for less! Amen!*

June 16

THE EARLY CHURCH

So continuing daily with one accord in the temple, and breaking bread from house to house, they ate their food with gladness and simplicity of heart, praising God and having favour with all the people. And the Lord added to the church daily those who were being saved.
—Acts 2:46–47; read also vv. 22–47

Let's take a visit to the early church in Rome in A.D. 95. The time is Saturday evening. There appears to be some type of party going on. There is singing, dancing, clapping of hands, flutes, tambourines, etc. Exuberant praise. Most church services would begin with the people getting in a ring and dancing Jewish-style ring dances (like the Hora).

After much singing and dancing, food is brought out—yes, a meal right in the middle of the church service. During the meal a leader stands and reads a letter from an apostle named Junia. Yes, Junia is the woman apostle mentioned in Romans 16. The meal continues until there is a change in the atmosphere. A tangible Presence of God comes and rests in the place. In this Presence, sinners find salvation, backsliders find repentance, and the miraculous becomes commonplace.

At this point, the ministry begins. 1 Corinthians 14 describes the Holy Spirit sovereignly manifesting His gifts as His people assemble. A woman on the far side of the courtyard stands and gives a word of knowledge for healing. A man raises his hand for prayer, people cluster around him, and he is healed. Someone reads from Scripture, and another explains the passage. A woman sings a prophetic song. Prophetic words are given. There are tongues and interpretation.

A new family comes with a blind daughter. As they anoint her with oil, she cries, "I can see! I can see!" This is where the evangelism takes place. This is how half the Roman Empire converted to Christianity by the end of the third century.[12]

PRAYER: *In the Name of Yeshua, do it again, Father! Amen!*

June 17

GOD OF HEALING

Then Peter said, "Silver and gold I do not have, but what I do have I give you: In the name of Jesus Christ of Nazareth, rise up and walk."
—ACTS 3:6; READ ALSO ACTS 3

This is a true story of a teacher of mine who received an amazing miracle at a Kathryn Kuhlman meeting. My 7th and 8th grade teacher of science was Harold Selby. His wife, Arlene, was my music/piano teacher.

After they left my hometown of Plainfield, Iowa, they moved to their next town. It was there that he contracted multiple sclerosis. It was a very advanced case, and soon, he was walking with two canes and was blind. There was a pastor in town who gave him a book by Kathryn Kuhlman and told him to go to one of her meetings.

As a last resort, as his case was hopeless, he went to Pittsburg, Pennsylvania to a meeting. Since he couldn't see well, he wanted his wife to drive. She was afraid of driving, so she sat next to him and told him when to stop, start, turn, and all! Arriving safely was their first miracle.

At the meeting itself, Kathryn came out and asked everyone to join hands. Harold was standing next to an African-American woman, and he, unfortunately, was prejudiced. However, he realized this was a sin, and when he asked forgiveness, there was a giant bright light that came toward him and went up and down his body. At the same time, Kathryn Kuhlman said, "God is healing someone." He was able to get up, and as he was going, he didn't need his canes anymore. He literally ran up to the altar and was able to see! He was healed of M.S., blindness, and being lame. It was a miraculous healing. He was able to drive home and see normally. His students were shocked—he had been healed! He went back to school, but in order to renew his contract, he would have to stop talking about Jesus. He decided to resign! [13]

PRAYER: *Truly, Father, You are a God of miracles! Amen!*

JESUS, THE NAME THAT SAVES

Nor is there salvation in any other, for there is NO OTHER NAME UNDER HEAVEN GIVEN AMONG MEN BY WHICH WE MUST BE SAVED.
—ACTS 4:12; READ ALSO VV. 1–22

This verse is in agreement with what Jesus himself said: "I am the way, the truth, and the life. No man comes to the Father, EXCEPT THROUGH ME" (John 14:6).

And consider Matthew 7:13 where Jesus says: "Enter by the narrow gate; for wide is the gate and broad is the way that leads to destruction, and there are many who go in by it. Because narrow is the gate and difficult is the way which leads to life, and there are few who find it."

This is why Jesus commanded His disciples in Matthew 28:19: "Go therefore and make disciples of all the nations, baptizing them in the name of the Father and of the Son and of the Holy Spirit, teaching them to observe all things that I have commanded you; and lo, I am with you always, even to the end of the age." Amen.

Some may insist that all religions lead to God. But consider the fundamental law of logic. The law of non-contradiction says: "Two contradicting 'truths' cannot both be true."

In other words, Hindus believe in reincarnation and in millions of gods. The Christians say there is one God and "It is appointed unto man once to die, and after that the judgment" (Hebrews 9:27). Both beliefs cannot be true at the same time.

Muslims believe Jesus never died on the cross but, instead He climbed down off the cross and went out into the desert with Mary. They also believe there is no resurrection. Christians believe in the death and resurrection of Jesus Christ. The Koran says, "Kill the unbeliever." The Bible says we are to "love our enemies." These beliefs are in direct contradiction to each other, and they cannot both be true.

PRAYER: *Father in Heaven, reveal to each one who Your Son is, and why He died and rose from the dead. Reveal to all a Spirit of truth, wisdom, and revelation. Amen.*

June 19

UNITED PRAYER WITH BOLDNESS

Now, Lord, look on their threats, and grant to Your servants that with all boldness they may speak Your word, by stretching out Your hand to heal, and that signs and wonders may be done through the name of Your holy Servant Jesus. And when they had prayed, the place where they were assembled together was shaken; and they were all filled with the Holy Spirit, and they spoke the word of God with boldness.
—ACTS 4:29–31; READ ALSO VV. 23–37

Dr. A. T. Pierson once said, "There has never been a spiritual awakening in any country or locality that did not begin in united prayer." [14] In 1857 concerts of prayer began when Jeremiah Lamphier, a Manhattan businessman, invited people to join in a noon prayer meeting. By 1858, six thousand were involved in daily noon prayer meetings, and 10's of 1000's in evening prayer meetings. Ten thousand a week were converted.

In 1904 the Welsh revival under Evan Roberts was preceded by prayer. Historian J. Edwin Orr said that in five months, one million people came to Christ and started to attend church regularly. The social impact was unprecedented. Judges were presented with white gloves. They had nothing to try. No robberies, murders, embezzlements, rapes, nothing. The police were unemployed, so they basically controlled crowds at the churches, and the rest formed quartets and were singing at the churches. Drunkenness was cut in half. There was a tremendous wave of bankruptcies—all taverns. There was a slow down in the mines. Coal miners were saved and stopped using bad language. The horses that dragged the trucks in the mines couldn't understand the commands without profanity and had to be retrained.[15]

PRAYER: *Dear Father in Heaven, we pray in Jesus' name for another outpouring of Your Spirit and prayer with people getting up at five in the morning to pray, or having half-night prayer times, or giving up lunchtime to pray. Amen.*

PRICE OF REVIVAL

And believers were increasingly added to the Lord, multitudes of both men and women, so that they brought the sick out into the streets and laid them on beds and couches, that at least the shadow of Peter passing by might fall on some of them. Also, a multitude gathered from the surrounding cities to Jerusalem, bringing sick people and those who were tormented by unclean spirits, and they were all healed.
—ACTS 5:14–16; READ ALSO VV. 1–21

People were so convinced of the reality and power of what the Christians believed, they thought they could be healed by the mere touch of Peter's shadow. It seems even the shadow of Peter became a point of contact where people released faith in Jesus as healer.

The Bible says that they were all healed. We shouldn't miss the connection between the purity preserved in the first part of the chapter (with the death of Ananias and the fear of God among the Christians) and the power displayed here. God blessed a pure church with spiritual power. The sin of Ananias in lying to the Holy Spirit could have corrupted the entire church at its root, instead, God's judgment over that sin purified the church.

"Dr. J. Edwin Orr's last sermon was titled *Revival Is Like Judgment Day*. In it he describes how the coming of revival is almost always marked by a radical work of God in dealing with the sins of believers:"

William Castle, from Sichuan in China, said, 'Revival means judgment day.' That's what happened in Shantung. Judgment on missionaries, pastors, people, and then fear fell on the world and God's name was glorified. And people have such a wrong idea of what revival means…They think of revival as something triumphant and, shall we say, an overflow of great blessing. It's judgment day for the church. But after the judgment, and after things are settled, it's blessing abounding.[16]

PRAYER: *Lord, are we willing to pay the price for revival?*

CHRISTIAN PERSECUTION

…Look, the men whom you put in prison are standing in the temple and teaching the people!
—ACTS 5:25; READ ALSO VV. 22–42

What an amazing story! The high priest and all who were with him laid their hands on the apostles and put them in the prison. But at night, an angel of the Lord opened the prison doors and brought them out and said, "*Go, stand in the temple and speak to the people all the words of this life*" (v. 20).

There is another recent story of a release from prison by Chinese Brother Yun. The PSB (Public Security Bureau) had heard a report that the underground church leaders had gotten together in unity in 1997 in Zhengzhou City, China. They were waiting for the underground pastors to arrive. Brother Yun jumped from a window and badly injured his feet. PSB guards captured him and beat him mercilessly. They crushed the bones in his legs, destroying them, and then took an electric baton and tortured him.

After the court hearing, he was transferred to a maximum-security prison and placed in solitary confinement. They continued to interrogate him and beat him. He had no Bible, so he meditated on God's Word from memory. He sang loudly day and night.

Three circumstances in Brother Yun's life revealed that he was to escape: through God's Word in Jeremiah, through a vision, and through Brother Xu (a Christian brother in prison with him). He escaped from three different floors when the gates opened as he reached each one, and the two guards who were on both sides of the gates did not see him go through.

He escaped by taxi to a Christian family. The Lord had spoken to them he was coming, and they had already prepared a secret place for him to hide. He realized that his legs had been totally healed and he could walk, run, and ride a bike with no pain! [17]

PRAYER: *Lord, would Your Christians in the West survive this kind of persecution? Prepare us Lord, to give our lives! Amen!*

June 22

PRAYER OUTREACH

But we will give ourselves continually to prayer and to the ministry of the word.

—ACTS 6:4; READ ALSO ACTS 6

The Moravians picked up the torch to pray by following the example of the early church and the Old Testament Scripture, Leviticus 6:13: "*A fire shall always be burning on the altar; it shall never go out.*"

In 1727 Count Zinzendorf, a young, wealthy German nobleman committed his estate in Germany to a twenty-four-hour-a-day prayer ministry. He renamed it "Herrnhut," which means "the watch of the Lord."

In 1722 he met a Moravian preacher who told him about the persecuted Protestants in Moravia. So in response to this, about three hundred believers from Bohemia moved to his estate. These radical believers at Herrnhut covenanted to pray in hourly shifts around the clock, all day and all night, every day. This prayer went on, day and night for over one hundred years! "God gave them 'three strands' around which they wove their lives:

1. They had relational unity, and sacrificial living.

2. The power of their persistent prayer produced a divine passion and zeal for missionary outreach to the lost. Many even sold themselves into slavery in places like Surinam in South America so they could carry the light of the gospel into closed societies. They went to strange places like Greenland, Lapland and many places in Africa. As they left their family and friends, they said words like: "Don't weep for us. We want to 'reap the rewards for the suffering of the Lamb.'"

3. Their motto was: "No one works unless someone prays." They were committed to praying for their missionaries. They are credited for winning John Wesley to the Lord on a ship to America during a storm. He led in the first great awakening in America.[18]

PRAYER: *Lord, let the fire of this kind of prayer come again! Amen!*

June 23

EVIL ACT OF ABORTION

This man (Pharaoh) dealt treacherously with our people, and oppressed our forefathers, making them expose their babies, so that they might not live.
—ACTS 7:17–19; READ ALSO VV. 1–21

Satan has always been after the babies to kill them because they are made in the image of God, and because he wants to cut off their destiny on the earth and thwart God's amazing plan for His people.

We see this in Exodus 1:22 where Pharaoh commanded the Israelite midwives to cast all the baby boys into the river. The midwives refused to do it. During this time Moses was born and his mother hid him in a basket and placed it in the river. Pharaoh's daughter found the baby and raised him as her son. God had plans for Moses to be a deliverer of his people through whom the Savior would come.

The next place in which we see the Enemy trying to destroy the babies is in Jeremiah 32:35: *"They built high places for Baal in the Valley of Ben Hinnom to sacrifice their sons and daughters to Molech, though I never commanded nor did it enter my mind, that they should do such a detestable thing and so make Judah sin."* They were offering their children to idols.

Then in Matthew after Jesus was born, the wise men stopped to see Herod and ask where the King of the Jews was born. They had seen His star in the East and had come to worship Him. This prompted Herod to kill all the baby boys two years old and under, because that was the time the wise men had seen the star. Ultimately, the devil was trying to kill the Christ child, or the seed of the woman (Genesis 3:15).

Now today, we see that same Pharaoh/Herod spirit at work trying to kill our babies and obliterate their purpose and destiny before they even have a chance to be born. We are offering our babies to our idols of self in the name of "Choice."

PRAYER: *God, forgive this great sin of abortion! Amen!*

THE PROPHESIED PROPHET

This is that Moses who said to the children of Israel, "The LORD your God will raise up for you a Prophet like me from your brethren. Him you shall hear." This is he who was in the congregation in the wilderness with the Angel who spoke to him on Mount Sinai, and with our fathers, the one who received the living oracles to give to us, whom our fathers would not obey, but rejected. And in their hearts they turned back to Egypt, saying to Aaron, "Make us gods to go before us; as for this Moses who brought us out of the land of Egypt, we do not know what has become of him." And they made a calf in those days, offered sacrifices to the idol, and rejoiced in the works of their own hands.
—ACTS 7:37–41; READ ALSO vv. 22–43

In Stephen's address, rather than defending himself, he brought an indictment against his accusers. Instead of manifesting a true zeal for the temple and the Law in their opposition to the gospel, the Jews were displaying the same rebellious spirit of unbelief that characterized their forefathers who resisted the purposes of God. Also, in his review of Israel's history, he concluded that God's presence is not limited to a geographical place nor to a particular people.

Moses promised that there would come after him another *Prophet* and warned that Israel should take special care to listen to this One. But just like Israel rejected Moses in the wilderness, so they were rejecting Jesus, of whom the Prophet Moses spoke.

Moses, like Jesus, led the congregation of God's people, enjoyed special intimacy with God, and brought forth the revelation of God.

When Israel rejected Moses and God's work through him, they replaced Him with their own man-made religion—the calf. Just like Israel worshipped the calf, so now they were worshipping the works of their own hands. They worshipped the temple, rather than the God of the temple.

PRAYER: *Father, each person must now decide whether they will accept or reject Jesus. Let us not be like the Israelites who knew about the Prophet but didn't recognize Jesus. Amen!*

OBEDIENT UNTO DEATH

And they stoned Stephen as he was calling on God and saying, "Lord Jesus, receive my spirit." Then he knelt down and cried out with a loud voice, "Lord, do not charge them with this sin." And when he had said this, he fell asleep.
—ACTS 7:59–60; READ ALSO VV. 44–60

Stephen's life ended in the same way it had been lived: in complete trust in God, believing that Jesus would take care of him in the life to come. Stephen was a martyr before they stoned him. He was the first martyr to seal his testimony with his blood.

Stephen prayed that God would not charge them with this sin, and God answered Stephen's prayer. He used it to touch the heart of a man who agreed with this stoning—Saul of Tarsus, who became the Apostle Paul. We should thank Stephen when we get to heaven for every blessing brought through the ministry of Paul.

Augustine said, "If Stephen had not prayed, the church would not have had Paul."

Stephen displayed the same forgiving attitude that Jesus had on the cross (Luke 23:34). He asked God to forgive his accusers.

The Bible says that Stephen fell asleep. If there had been any rose-colored optimism about quickly winning the Jewish people to their Messiah, that was gone. The church could not expect triumph without a bloody battle.

Stephen wasn't a superman, but he was a man filled through all his being with the Holy Spirit, with wisdom, with faith and power, and one who did great signs and wonders among the people. Many have little idea of how greatly they can be used of God as they walk in the power of the Holy Spirit.

PRAYER: *Father, may we also be filled with faith and power like Stephen, and if necessary, be obedient unto death. May we be willing to forgive everyone that has hurt us in any way. Let there be no bitterness or unforgiveness in our hearts. Amen.*

DIFFERENT BAPTISMS

Now when the apostles who were at Jerusalem heard that Samaria had received the word of God, they sent Peter and John to them, who, when they had come down, prayed for them that they might receive the Holy Spirit. For as yet He had fallen upon none of them. They had only been baptized in the name of the Lord Jesus. Then they laid hands on them, and they received the Holy Spirit.
—Acts 8:14–18; read also vv. 1–25

There are at least three baptisms mentioned in this passage. In v. 12 we read: "But when they believed Philip as he preached the things concerning the kingdom of God and the name of Jesus Christ, both men and women were baptized."

+ When the people believed they were baptized into the body of Christ. 1 Corinthians 12:13 says, *"For by one Spirit we were all baptized into one body…"* The Holy Spirit baptizes us into the body of Christ when we are saved.

+ Then they were baptized in water.

+ When the apostles heard that Samaria had received the Word of God, they sent Peter and John to pray for them that they might receive the Holy Spirit for He had not fallen upon them. So, when they laid their hands on them, they were baptized in the Holy Spirit. Power was released because Simon the sorcerer wanted to buy that power in the next verse. In the Acts 10:46 and 19:6 passages concerning the baptism of the Holy Spirit, they all spoke with tongues when they received.

Robert Morris, in his book *"The God I Never Knew"* tells that in the early years of his Christian walk, he was taught that once he was saved and water baptized, he had everything he needed to live the Christian life. Of course, now he knows that without receiving the Holy Spirit, he was living a powerless and defeated life of minimal effectiveness in God's kingdom.[19]

PRAYER: *Father, may we be saved, water baptized, filled with the Holy Spirit, and turn our world upside down! Amen!*

June 27

THE GUARDIAN ANGELS

Now an angel of the Lord spoke to Philip, saying, "Arise and go toward the south along the road which goes down from Jerusalem to Gaza."
—ACTS 8:26; READ ALSO VV. 26–40

This chapter contains many supernatural happenings. In this passage, an angel tells Philip what to do. When he was obedient, he was able to lead a eunuch of great authority under Candace, the queen of the Ethiopians to Christ. The eunuch just "happened" to be reading from Isaiah 53 about the coming Messiah, but he didn't understand what he was reading. After Philip explained that he was reading about Jesus, he confessed his belief in Jesus and was baptized. Later the Spirit of the Lord caught Philip up and released him at Azotus.

The Bible in Psalm 91 promises that God gives angels charge over us to keep us in all our ways. In his book, *"Angels on Assignment,"* Pastor Roland Buck from Boise, Idaho, tells about the angel Gabriel visiting him. The angel came with a sermon and shared many events that would take place.

> One of those events was about a couple that would come for marital counselling. They had been at a hotel and the phone book was opened to an ad about church counselling so they had called Roland Buck. He ministered to them and said he was happy they had come, 'But before you leave, sister, I would suggest you give me that pistol you have in your handbag you brought to kill your husband with.' Immediately she burst into tears, reached into her handbag and handed a loaded 32 caliber pistol to Pastor Buck. An hour later, the tearful couple left his office having prayed the sinner's prayer. The angel had revealed all these things ahead of time to Pastor Buck.[20]

PRAYER: *Father in Heaven, help us to partner with angels on assignment on this earth. Help us remember that they are sent to "minister to the heirs of salvation." Amen. Pray Psalm 91.*

June 28

SAUL'S ARREST BY GOD

As he journeyed he came near Damascus, and suddenly a light shone around him from heaven. Then he fell to the ground, and heard a voice saying to him, "Saul, Saul, why are you persecuting Me?" And he said, "Who are You, Lord?" Then the Lord said, "I am Jesus, whom you are persecuting. It is hard for you to kick against the goads."
—ACTS 9:3–6; READ ALSO VV. 1–22

Saul thought he was doing God a favor by killing the Christians, and so did Kamal Saleem, born in Lebanon. He was born into a Muslim family and his parents taught him to hate Jews and Christians. He was taught that "If you kill a Jew, your hand will light up before Allah and the host of heaven will celebrate your killing." They practiced killing on the cats and dogs in the neighborhood.

He went to his first PLO camp at seven and met Yasser Arafat. After that he traveled around the world to kill Jews. He loved to watch the beheadings of the infidels in Saudi. Of course, the giant infidel was America, and he came here for cultural jihad.

One day he was involved in a severe car accident. One of the doctors took him into his home to recuperate. The children in the family loved him and were praying "Jesus" prayers in their little voices for him to recover and be healed. They were Americans and Christians, but they were not bad people as he had always believed. They loved everyone, even their enemies. They trusted him to babysit, and they had no idea that their deadly enemy was in their midst.

He tried to call on Allah, but Allah didn't answer. But, the God of Abraham spoke to him, and Kamal asked if he could know Him. Jesus came and revealed Himself and totally healed him. He called him to be an "ambassador for Christ." [21]

PRAYER: *Father, we love our brothers, the descendants of Esau and Ishmael, and pray that Your glory will visit them! Amen!*

TABITHA ARISE

*But Peter put them all out, and knelt down and prayed. And turning
to the body he said, "Tabitha, arise." And she opened her eyes, and
when she saw Peter she sat up. Then he gave her his hand and lifted
her up; and when he had called the saints and widows, he presented
her alive.*
—Acts 9:40–41; read also vv. 23–43

What an amazing account of Peter raising Tabitha back to life. He
put out all of them, so no doubters were present, and he ordered her
to arise. Jesus said in Matthew 10, we were to heal the sick, cleanse
the lepers, raise the dead and cast out demons.

A modern-day example of a miraculous healing was in Smith Wigglesworth's ministry. The Holy Spirit was teaching Smith that faith
could be created in others. A family had sent for Smith to pray for
their young boy who was dying. When he arrived, the mom said, "You
are too late. There is nothing that can be done for him." Smith replied,
"God has never sent me anywhere too late." He told the family to lay
out his clothes because the Lord was going to raise him up. They
refused at first, but then relented. Smith said to put only socks on his
feet. He put the rest of the family out of the room and told the lifeless
boy that when he placed his hands on him, the glory of God would
fill the place till he shouldn't be able to stand. He would be helpless
on the floor. He did, and God's glory fell. The boy yelled, "This is for
your glory Lord!" He got up and dressed himself. Such glory filled
the house the mother and father fell to the floor also. His sister, who
had been released from an asylum was instantly restored in her mind.
Revival came to their city! [22]

Prayer: *Father, let Your glory fall in this nation. Let the lost be saved
and the sick be healed and the demonized be set free. Use Your church
like You used Smith Wigglesworth and even greater! Amen!*

BREAKTHROUGH FOR THE GENTILES

And a voice came to him, "Rise, Peter; kill and eat." But Peter said, "Not so, Lord! For I have never eaten anything common or unclean." And a voice spoke to him again the second time, "What God has cleansed you must not call common." This was done three times. And the object was taken up into heaven again.

—ACTS 10:13–16; READ ALSO VV. 1–23

Cornelius, a Roman centurion from Caesarea, was a devout man and feared God. He gave alms generously to the people and prayed to God always. He was a "God-fearer," which means he was a Gentile who worshipped Jehovah, but one who had not become a Jewish proselyte. They were the most receptive Gentiles to the gospel. A Jewish proselyte was a person who was circumcised and was accepted as a Jew. Cornelius had a vision of an angel coming to speak to him and tell him to send men to Joppa to find Simon Peter. So, he did.

In the meantime Peter, about noon, went up on the housetop to pray and fell into a trance. This was also a regular Jewish prayer time. There is something about seemingly routine habits of prayer that especially pleases God. Peter saw heaven open and something like a great sheet coming down to earth. It had all kinds of four-footed animals, creeping things, birds, etc. in it. A voice came and said the words, "*Rise, Peter; kill and eat.*" He saw this vision three times.

While Peter was thinking about this, the men sent from Cornelius arrived. The Lord told Peter to go with them. This was a hard thing to do because no orthodox Jew would enter the home of a Gentile. But he began to understand that the vision pertaining to unclean food was expanded by the Holy Spirit's instructions to include unclean people as well. In other words, the Gentiles were no longer to be considered unclean. God's incredible sense of timing also helped Peter tremendously in making his decision. Inviting them into the house was a huge breakthrough for the Gentiles.

PRAYER: *Thank You Father for making a way to include the Gentiles in Your plan of salvation! Amen!*

July 1

POWER OF THE HOLY SPIRIT

While Peter was still speaking these words, the Holy Spirit fell upon all those who heard the word. And those of the circumcision who believed were astonished, as many as came with Peter, because the gift of the Holy Spirit had been poured out on the Gentiles also. For they heard them speak with tongues and magnify God. Then Peter answered, "Can anyone forbid water, that these should not be baptized who have received the Holy Spirit just as we have?"
—ACTS 10:44–47; READ ALSO VV. 24–48

Peter must have been shocked when he opened his door to see two servants and a soldier who were not Jews, and that the Lord had told him to go with them. The idea that God could send and use Gentiles was entirely new to Peter. Yet, here they were, wanting to hear his message! Peter inviting them in and hosting them was an "out of the box" idea for a Jew.

The following day they entered Caesarea where Cornelius was waiting for them. He fell down at Peter's feet to worship him. But Peter said, "Stand up! I am a man like you!"

He told them right away that God had shown him that He shows no partiality to anyone from any nation but accepts all who fear Him and work righteousness.

Next, he preached about Jesus and told *"how God anointed Jesus of Nazareth with the Holy Spirit and with power, who went about doing good and healing all who were oppressed by the devil, for God was with Him"* (v. 38). He also told them that the Jews killed him on a cross and the third day He rose from the dead! Jesus Christ was ordained by God to be Judge of the living and the dead.

While he was speaking, the Holy Spirit fell on them and they spoke in tongues and magnified God. Peter asked, *"Can anyone forbid water, that these should not be baptized who have received the Holy Spirit just as we have?"* So, they were baptized in water *after* they were baptized in the Holy Spirit.

PRAYER: *Father, we thank You for Jesus telling His disciples to wait in Jerusalem until they were filled with the Holy Spirit. We see that it turned timid men into firebrands for God. Do it with us also, we pray! In Your Name. Amen.*

BAPTISM OF THE HOLY SPIRIT

And as I began to speak, the Holy Spirit fell upon them, as upon us at the beginning. Then I remembered the word of the Lord, how He said, "John indeed baptized with water, but you shall be baptized with the Holy Spirit."
—ACTS 11:15–16; READ ALSO ACTS 11

Peter here is recounting the story of how the Gentiles also were given the gift of salvation and the baptism of the Holy Spirit.

Robert Morris tells about D. L. Moody and his baptism in the Holy Spirit. It was in the late 1800s and Moody was the pastor of a church in Chicago, which met in a rented room. There were two elderly Free Methodist women in his congregation who were praying for him to receive the baptism in the Holy Spirit. He explained to them that he'd received all the Holy Spirit there was to get when he got saved.

According to Moody, these women kept praying for him, and he realized he didn't have much in the way of supernatural power operating in his ministry—at least not like what he saw working in the lives of ordinary Christians found in his Bible. He needed that baptism in the Holy Spirit.

Moody had been invited to preach in England. While in New York City, a few days before he was to leave, he was on a walk when something remarkable happened. The power of God fell upon him and he had to hurry off to a friend's house to seclude himself. He stayed in that room alone for hours and the Holy Ghost came upon him and filled him with such joy, that he had to ask God to withhold His hand, lest he die on the spot. He went out from that place with the power of the Holy Ghost and when he got to London, the power of God worked through him mightily and hundreds were added to the church.[1]

PRAYER: *Father in Heaven, we love You and desire all that You have for us! We don't want to walk through this life missing out on anything You have for us, only to find in heaven we could have had so much more fruit. We want more of You! Amen!*

PRIESTLY AND KINGLY INTERCESSION

Peter was therefore kept in prison, but constant prayer was offered to God for him by the church.

And when Peter had come to himself, he said, "Now I know for certain that the Lord has sent His angel, and has delivered me from the hand of Herod and from all the expectation of the Jewish people."
—ACTS 12:5, 11; READ ALSO ACTS 12

Peter was freed from prison through the prayers of the saints. King Herod had just killed James, the brother of John, with the sword. Because that pleased the Jews, he put Peter in prison and planned to kill him, too. It looked like a hopeless situation. But the church prayed.

Acts 12 opens with James dead, Peter in prison, and Herod triumphing. It closes with Herod dead, Peter free, and the Word of God triumphing!

In Dutch Sheets book, *"Authority in Prayer,"* we see an amazing answer to prayer. He was teaching about priestly intercession and kingly intercession.

> Priestly intercession requires love, mercy and grace. Kingly intercession requires authority and power. Kings have a scepter that symbolizes authority; priests use a censer that symbolizes worship. Priestly intercession begins with *"Our Father in heaven, hallowed be Your Name."* Kingly intercession says, *"Your kingdom come, Your will BE DONE on earth as it is in heaven."* [2]

When Dutch Sheets and Chuck Pierce were on a prayer tour of America, they were in Texas December 13, 2003. They were praying for Saddam Hussein's capture. During the prayer time, Dutch turned from priestly intercession to kingly intercession, and began to command and decree that the demonic activity keeping Hussein hidden be broken. Other leaders came to the platform and offered similar prayers and decrees. Saddam Hussein was captured three days later!

PRAYER: *Father, teach us how to use both priestly and kingly intercession! Show us how to decree things in prayer using Job 22:28. Amen!*

July 4

SOURCE OF SALVATION

As they ministered to the Lord and fasted, the Holy Spirit said, "Now separate to Me Barnabas and Saul for the work to which I have called them." Then having fasted and prayed, and laid hands on them, they sent them away.
—ACTS 13:2–3; READ ALSO VV. 1–25

The phrase *"As they ministered to the Lord"* means that they were involved in worship, praise, prayer, listening to, and honoring God.

Then we see that a prophecy was given by the Holy Spirit through one of the prophets. So *"having fasted and prayed, and laid their hands on them they sent them away."* This was the beginning of Paul's first missionary journey.

The calling God had for the life of Paul had already been stated in Acts 9:15–16. *"He is a chosen vessel of Mine to bear My name before Gentiles, kings, and the children of Israel. For I will show him how many things he must suffer for My name's sake."*

When the church sent them out, they were supported and sent by a specific congregation. Many regard this as the first real known missionary effort of the church.

They went to Cyprus to a city called Paphos to preach the Gospel and met Elymas, the sorcerer there. He withstood them and tried to turn the proconsul, Sergius Paulus, away from the faith. After Paul rebuked him, he became blind for a time, and then the proconsul believed.

What is a sorcerer? A person practicing sorcery is practicing witchcraft. A male witch is a wizard, and a female witch is a sorceress. They cast spells, create potions, do transformations, and other occult practices. Their power comes from the devil. Exodus 22:18 says, *"You shall not permit a sorceress to live."* That is an Old Testament Scripture under the Old Covenant. Jesus paid the price for the sin of sorcery. Therefore, they are not to be put to death; they are to repent and find salvation in Jesus.

PRAYER: *We pray people everywhere will turn to the Lord. He alone is our source of salvation, power, and miracles. Protect Your people from deception in these last days. Amen!*

July 5

SALVATION FOR ALL

God has fulfilled this for us their children, in that He has raised up Jesus. As it is also written in the second Psalm: "You are My Son, Today I have begotten You." And that He raised Him from the dead, no more to return to corruption, He has spoken thus: "I will give you the sure mercies of David." Therefore He also says in another Psalm "You will not allow Your Holy One to see corruption."
—ACTS 13:33–35; READ ALSO VV. 26–52

This is Paul's sermon to the church in Antioch, Pisidia. After his overview of Jewish history that leads up to the death and resurrection of Jesus, he pointed out the prophecies in the book of Psalms that applied to Jesus. Even though David saw corruption in the grave, Jesus did not!

The thing that came as a shock to the Jews was that Paul declared his message of salvation was for both of his audiences, the Jews and the Gentiles (v. 26).

The Jews had believed that as the chosen people of God, they had been given an exclusive channel to God through the Mosaic law. Gentiles could find God only as they became Jews and agreed to adhere to the law. Paul was teaching that which would be an outright heresy to the Jewish rabbis, namely that Gentiles could be saved without becoming Jews first.

The second shock came in verses 38–39, where Paul stated that forgiveness comes from God through faith in Jesus Christ apart from keeping the Mosaic law. The Jews would think of forgiveness being granted on the Day of Atonement through the offering of blood sacrifices. Thus, Paul's emphasis is really the truth of justification by faith. Paul declared in verses 42–48 that everyone can be justified by their faith in Jesus.

In response, the Jewish leaders stirred up persecution against Paul and Barnabas. But the Gentiles were excited about the message and the whole city turned out to hear them speak the next Sabbath.

PRAYER: *Father in heaven, Your plan to include anyone who believes in You is so amazing. "God so loved the world, that He gave His only begotten Son…" We believe and so have everlasting life! Amen!*

July 6

FAITH TO BE HEALED

And in Lystra a certain man without strength in his feet was sitting, a cripple from his mother's womb, who had never walked. This man heard Paul speaking. Paul, observing him intently and seeing that he had faith to be healed, said with a loud voice, "Stand up straight on your feet!" And he leaped and walked.
—Acts 14:8–10; read also Acts 14

On Paul's 1st missionary journey, he preached the gospel in Iconium first, and then went on to Lystra. Paul's healing of a man lame from birth was the event that caught the attention of the crowd. Some form of preaching happened before this, since the man *"listened to Paul as he was speaking"* (v. 9). Paul perceived the man had faith for healing, so commanded him to stand up on his feet! God usually moves in His supernatural power in response to faith.

The magnitude of this miracle apparently led the Gentile crowd to believe that the very top-ranking Greek deities of Zeus and Hermes had come in the form of Barnabas and Paul, and they were therefore prepared to worship them. Demonic spirits were actually behind those beliefs which controlled the crowd.

Paul urged them to turn from *"these useless things"* to the living God, who made the heaven, the earth, the sea, and all things that are in them.

"Then Jews from Antioch and Iconium came and stoned Paul and dragged him out of the city, supposing him to be dead. However, when the disciples gathered around him, he rose up and went into the city. The next day he departed with Barnabas to Derbe" (v. 19–20).

PRAYER: *Father in Heaven, "strengthen us with all might, according to Your glorious power, for all patience and longsuffering with joy" (Colossians 1:11). Help us to be like Paul who said, "For to me, to live is Christ, and to die is gain" (Philippians 1:21). Amen.*

WISDOM

If any of you lacks wisdom, let him ask of God, who gives to all liber-
ally and without reproach, and it will be given to him. But let him
ask in faith with no doubting, for he who doubts is like a wave of the
sea driven and tossed by the wind. For let not that man suppose that
he will receive anything from the Lord; he is a double-minded man,
unstable in all his ways.
—JAMES 1:5–8; READ ALSO JAMES 1

James, who led the church in Jerusalem, was the half-brother of Jesus and brother of Jude. He did not introduce himself as "the brother of Jesus" but rather as a bondservant of God and of the Lord Jesus Christ. It is said in an early history of the church that James was such a man of prayer that his knees had large and thick calluses, making them look like the knees of a camel. It also says that James was martyred in Jerusalem by being pushed from a high point of the temple. Yet the fall did not kill him, and on the ground, he was beaten to death, even as he prayed for his attackers.

He begins his letter by exhorting us to *"count it all joy"* when we fall into various trials because the testing of our faith produces patience. Trials don't produce faith, but when trials are received with faith, they produce patience. Yet patience is not inevitably produced in times of trial. If difficulties are received in unbelief and grumbling, trials can produce bitterness and discouragement. This is why James exhorts us to *"count it all joy."* This is faith's response.

Trials bring a necessary season to seek wisdom from God. In trials, we need wisdom a lot more than we need knowledge. Knowledge is raw information; wisdom knows how to use it.

So, to receive wisdom, we simply ask of God who will give it to us liberally and won't despise our request! But we must ask in faith, not doubting God's ability or desire to give us His wisdom. Then we need to listen to His answer. How wonderful that Jesus has promised in John 10:4–5 that we can hear His voice when we listen.

PRAYER: *Jesus Christ is made unto us wisdom, righteousness, sanctifica-*
tion and redemption (1 Corinthians 1:30). Amen.

July 8

FAITH WITHOUT WORKS IS DEAD

You believe that there is one God. You do well. Even the demons believe—and tremble. But do you want to know, O foolish man, that faith without works is dead? Was not Abraham our father justified by works when he offered Isaac his son on the altar? Do you see that faith was working together with his works and by works faith was made perfect?
—JAMES 2:20–22; READ ALSO JAMES 2

This is the first time James speaks of a dead faith. Faith alone saves us, but it must be a living and active faith. We can tell if faith is alive by seeing if it is accompanied by works. If it does not have works, it is dead.

Living faith is simply a real faith. If we really believe something we will follow through and act upon it. If we really put our faith in Jesus, we will care for the widow and orphan. We will want to see to it that people have food and clothes, and that they will have a chance to hear the Gospel. Here are some marks of faith:[3]

+ It is faith that looks not to self but to Jesus Christ.
+ It is faith that agrees with God's word, both inwardly by believing and outwardly by actions.
+ It is faith that is grounded in what Jesus did on the cross and by the empty tomb.
+ It is faith that will naturally be expressed in repentance and good works.
+ Sometimes there are doubts, yet the doubts are not bigger than the faith. *"Lord, I believe; help my unbelief"* (Mark 9:24).
+ It is faith that longs for others to come to the same faith.
+ It is faith that not only hears the word of God but does it (Matthew 7:24–27).

The fallacy of faith without works is demonstrated by the demons; *"even the demons believe—and tremble"* (v. 19). It doesn't have any good works along with it.

PRAYER: *Lord Jesus, we long to have faith, for without faith, it is impossible to please God, but enable us by our actions to show that we have faith. In Jesus' name. Amen.*

POWER OF LIFE AND DEATH
IS IN THE TONGUE

And the tongue is a fire, a world of iniquity. The tongue is so set among our members that it defiles the whole body, and sets on fire the course of nature; and it is set on fire by hell.
—JAMES 3:6; READ ALSO JAMES 3

Let's look at a couple other scriptures about the tongue: "Death and life are in the power of the tongue, and those who love it will eat its fruit" (Proverbs 10:19).

"But I say to you that for every idle (unproductive) word man may speak, they will give account of it in the day of judgment. For by your words you will be justified, and by your words you will be condemned" (Matthew 12:36–37).

In the book, *Heavenly Visitation* by Kevin Zadai, he tells how during a surgical procedure to remove impacted wisdom teeth, he died for a short time. He was soon aware that Jesus Christ was in the room with him. As Kevin walked over to Him, Jesus greeted him, and he knew Jesus had something very important to discuss with him. Jesus immediately began teaching him about the importance of words.

Jesus boldly shared the Scripture from Matthew above. For a long moment, He just looked at Kevin in silence. Then suddenly, He stepped quickly toward Kevin and whispered in his ear, "You know, I meant that!"

During the time that Kevin was in heaven with the Lord, He spent much of the time talking to Kevin about the power of words. They are either passwords to access God's power to build His kingdom on earth, or they create roadblocks to His purposes. Our words create either blessings or curses that come our way in life. Words are never a neutral force.[4]

PRAYER: *Father in Heaven, teach us to think before we speak, and watch what we speak. We want to speak the truth in love and use words that edify and build others up. We want to speak life and not death. Help us to hide Your Word in our hearts and speak that Word. In Jesus' name. Amen.*

July 10

SUBMIT TO GOD

But He gives more grace. Therefore, He says: "God resists the proud, but gives grace to the humble." Therefore submit to God. Resist the devil and he will flee from you.
—JAMES 4:6–7; READ ALSO JAMES 4

God resists the proud, but He gives grace to the humble. Grace and pride are enemies of each other. Humility puts us in a position to receive the gift He freely gives. In light of the grace offered to the humble, there is only one thing to do: submit to God. This means to surrender to Him as a conquering King and start receiving the benefits of His reign.

+ We should submit to God because He created us.

+ We should submit to God because His rule is good for us.

+ We should submit to God because all resistance to Him is futile.

+ We should submit to God because it is the only way to have peace with God.

I desire to whisper one little truth in your ear, and I pray that it may startle you: *You are submitting even now.* You say, "Not I, I am lord of myself." I know you think so, but all the while you are submitting to the devil. If you do not submit to God, you never will resist the devil and you will remain constantly under his tyrannical power. Which shall be your master, God or the devil, for one of these must? No man is without a master.[5]

If we really want to stop having conflicts and quarrels with others, mentioned in the beginning of the chapter, we need to draw close to God, ask for His help and wisdom, and resist the devil and his deceptions, and he will flee!

James simply challenges individual Christians to deal with Satan as a conquered foe who can and must be personally resisted.

PRAYER: *Thank You, Father, for giving us the spiritual weapons we need to win any battle the enemy throws at us. Amen!*

July 11

ANOINTED WITH OIL IN THE
NAME OF THE LORD

*Is anyone among you suffering? Let him pray. Is anyone cheerful?
Let him sing psalms. Is anyone among you sick? Let him call for the
elders of the church, and let them pray over him, anointing him with
oil in the name of the Lord. And the prayer of faith will save the sick,
and the Lord will raise him up. And if he has committed sins, he will
be forgiven.*

—JAMES 5:13–15; READ ALSO JAMES 5

What a wonderful Scripture to stand on! It is a promise that if we
call for the elders and anoint the sick person with oil, the Lord will
raise him up AND if he has committed sins, he will be forgiven! We
have often prayed for people anointing them with oil and have seen
miraculous results.

Smith Wigglesworth, mighty healing evangelist, often used the
anointing of oil when he prayed for people. This story is in Smith
Wigglesworth's book, *Apostle of Faith*:

> Soon after he began preaching, the wife of a devoted friend was so
> ill that the doctors expected her to die during the night. Smith went
> to a minister who was opening the church and asked if he would go
> and pray with him. He wouldn't go. Smith talked another friend into
> going, but when the man prayed, he prayed for 'the family that would
> be left behind: and continued in prayers of unbelief. Smith cried out,
> "Lord, stop him!"
>
> He then pulled a bottle of oil out of his pocket and poured the
> entire bottle over the body of the woman, in the name of Jesus. Then
> standing at the head of her bed, Smith experienced his first vision. He
> said, "Suddenly, the Lord Jesus appeared. I had my eyes open gazing
> at Him. He gave me one of those gentle smiles....I have never lost
> that vision, the vision of that beautiful, soft smile." A few moments
> after the vision vanished, the woman sat up in bed totally healed.[6]

PRAYER: *How precious and true Your Word is! "He sent His Word
and healed them..." (Psalm 107:20). Amen!*

July 12

EVERYTHING IS TO THE GLORY OF GOD

After this I will return and will rebuild the tabernacle of David, which has fallen down; I will rebuild its ruins, And I will set it up; So that the rest of mankind may seek the LORD, Even all the Gentiles who are called by My name, says the LORD who does all these things.
—ACTS 15:16–17; READ ALSO VV. 1–21

This was quoted by James during the Jerusalem Council. At this time, the Jews' position concerning the Gentiles was that non-Jews were not fully acceptable to God and that Gentiles could not be saved without first becoming Jews through circumcision. James was using this prophecy from Amos 9:11–12 to show that God's bringing the Gentiles into the kingdom was planned long ago. James' conclusion was that *"Therefore I judge that we should not trouble those from among the Gentiles who are turning to God"* (Acts 15:19). *"They just need to abstain from things sacrificed to idols, from blood and from things strangled and from fornication."*

This Scripture also applies in a fresh way today. God through Amos was giving an indication that the end-time global prayer movement will operate "in the spirit of the tabernacle of David." David built a tent to house the ark of the covenant and then organized four thousand musicians and two hundred eighty-eight singers to stand before the ark to minister to God in shifts that continued day and night (1 Chronicles 6:31–33; 9:33; 15:16–22; and 23:4–6). As they did this, their prayer was combined with worship to God. This same kind of prayer and worship is activated today through 24/7 prayer teams around the world. These prayer warriors are contending night and day for all the fullness of God regarding the release of righteous government over the nations when Jesus comes to set up His rule on earth during the millennium.[7] Mike Bickle's International House of Prayer (*ihopkc.org*) has been going 24/7 since 1999.

PRAYER: *We long to see the earth be filled with the knowledge of the glory of the Lord as the waters cover the sea! Amen!*

July 13

RECONCILIATION

Then after some days Paul said to Barnabas, "Let us now go back and visit our brethren in every city where we have preached the word of the Lord, and see how they are doing."
—ACTS 15:36; READ ALSO vv. 22–41

The idea of visiting their brothers in every city seemed like a great idea at first, until Barnabas wanted to take John Mark with them. However, Paul did not want to take John Mark with them because he had deserted them at Pamphylia. The contention actually became so sharp that they parted from one another. Barnabas took John Mark, who was his cousin, with him to Cyprus and Paul took Silas with him to finish his 2nd missionary journey.

Yes, there were even dissensions among the apostles and prophets. The question is: How do we solve relationship problems? As Christians, we are commanded to resolve relationship problems with others before we present ministry to God. *"Therefore, if you bring your gift to the altar, and there remember that your brother has something against you, leave your gift there before the altar, and go your way. First be reconciled to your brother, and then come and offer your gift"* (Matthew 5:23–24).

Paul also writes in Romans 12:18–21: *"If it is possible, as much as depends on you, live peaceably with all men. Beloved, do not avenge yourselves, but rather give place to wrath; for it is written, 'Vengeance is Mine, I will repay,' says the Lord. Therefore, 'If your enemy is hungry, feed him; If he is thirsty give him a drink; For in so doing you will heap coals of fire on his head. Do not be overcome by evil, but overcome evil with good.'"*

We can see that John Mark and Paul later reconciled because Paul came to minister with him and to value his contributions to the work of God (Colossians 4:10; Philemon 1:24; 2 Timothy 4:11).

PRAYER: *Father, forgive us our sins, as we forgive those who sin against us. We want to totally forgive, so we can be totally forgiven also! In Jesus' name. Amen.*

UNDERSTANDING, LIVING, AND SHARING THE GOSPEL

I marvel that you are turning away so soon from Him who called you in the grace of Christ, to a different gospel, which is not another; but there are some who trouble you and want to pervert the gospel of Christ. But even if we or an angel from heaven, preach any other gospel to you than what we have preached to you, let him be accursed.

—GALATIANS 1:6–8; READ ALSO GALATIANS 1

Paul here is contending for the gospel of Christ. Paul wrote this letter about 50 A.D. and begins by giving his apostolic credentials. God commissioned him through the risen Lord.

He was saying that someone brought a false gospel to the Galatians. There is something about the message of the true gospel that is deeply offensive to human nature. To understand this, we should first understand what the true gospel is. This is stated succinctly in 1 Corinthians 15:1–4. The message of the gospel is what Jesus did on the cross for us as revealed by the Scriptures and proven by the resurrection.

When we understand how offensive the true gospel is to human nature, we better understand why someone would want to pervert it.[8]

+ The gospel offends our *pride*. It tells us we need a Savior, and that we cannot save ourselves. It gives no credit to us at all for our salvation; it is all the work of Jesus for us.

+ The gospel offends our *wisdom*. It saves us by something many consider foolish—God becoming man and dying a humiliating, disgraceful death on our behalf.

+ The gospel offends our *knowledge*. It tells us to believe something which goes against scientific knowledge and personal experience—that a dead man, Jesus Christ, rose from the dead in a glorious new body that would never die again.

PRAYER: *Father, give us spiritual understanding of the true gospel, that we will not pervert it but live it and share it! Amen!*

July 15

CHRIST IN ME

I have been crucified with Christ; it is no longer I who live, but Christ lives in me; and the life which I now live in the flesh I live by faith in the Son of God, who loved me and gave Himself for me.
—GALATIANS 2:20; READ ALSO GALATIANS 2

Before Paul became a Christian, he was "blameless" in observing the law. He followed it to the letter. He believed keeping the law would save him. But when He encountered the Risen Lord, everything changed.

"I have been crucified with Christ:...." Paul was saying "Christ died in my place on the cross, so it is like it was me up on the cross. He died, and I died to the law when He died."

"It is no longer I who live, but Christ lives in me." Paul realized that on the cross, a great exchange occurred. He gave Jesus his old, try-to-be-right-before-God-by-the-law life, and that old life was crucified on the cross. Then Jesus came to live in him, and his life wasn't his own anymore, it belonged to Jesus Christ!

And the life that we live in the flesh we live by faith. We can only manage the new life Jesus gave us by faith. You can't live the new life by following rules. You can only live it by faith.

When Paul said, *"I now live in the flesh,"* flesh here means the whole nature of man. Paul was saying that he now lived by faith in the Son of God. He and Christ became one person. So now the life we live in the flesh we live by faith in the Son of God. We can live this way because He loves us and gave Himself for us.

Dead people don't get offended. Dead people don't get prideful or rude or be self-seeking. Dead people don't quit and run away from problems. Dead people don't hate or gossip. Dead people hardly notice when others do them wrong. *"I have been crucified with Christ...."*

PRAYER: *Help us to live this verse, Father. What a powerful antidote to feeling sorry for ourselves and for self-pity! What a powerful antidote against taking offense! This gives us Your perspective on life! We love You Jesus! Amen!*

EQUALITY BEFORE GOD

There is neither Jew nor Greek, there is neither slave nor free, there is neither male nor female; for you are all one in Christ Jesus. And if you are Christ's, then you are Abraham's seed, and heirs according to the promise.

—GALATIANS 3:28–29; READ ALSO GALATIANS 3

At the time this was written, some Rabbis quoted a morning prayer that was popular among many Jews of that day. In the prayer the Jewish man would thank God that he was not born a Gentile, a slave, or a woman. Paul takes each of these categories and shows them to be equal in Jesus.

Sadly, some Christians still draw lines today between races, genders, denominations, nations, political parties, and economic classes. Paul is saying that when we are saved, we are brought into a marvelous unity.

An example of someone breaking down dividing walls between races is George Washington Carver, (1864–1943). Carver was born into slavery near Diamond Grove, Missouri. His master was Moses Carver, and after slavery was abolished, he and his brother were adopted by Mr. and Mrs. Carver who taught them how to read and write.

He was not allowed at the public school in Diamond Grove, so he walked ten miles to a black school in Neosho. Carver was the first black student at Iowa State University and ended up teaching at Tuskegee University for forty-seven years.

He tells about his conversion when he was ten. A little white boy told him about church and prayer and hymns. He didn't know what prayer was, but he knelt down and prayed, and Jesus came into his heart. (Blacks were not allowed to go to church at that time.) He viewed faith in Jesus Christ as a means of destroying barriers of racial disharmony.

He became an agricultural chemist who discovered three hundred uses for peanuts and hundreds more uses for soybeans, pecans, and sweet potatoes.[9]

PRAYER: *Thank You, Father, for this amazing example that in Christ, there is no slave or free or respecter of persons! Amen!*

July 17

THE FULLNESS OF TIME

But when the fullness of the time had come, God sent forth His Son, born of a woman, born under the law, to redeem those who were under the law, that we might receive the adoption as sons. And because you are sons, God has sent forth the Spirit of His Son into your hearts, crying out, "Abba, Father!" Therefore, you are no longer a slave but a son, and if a son, then an heir of God through Christ.
—Galatians 4:4–7; read also Galatians 4

The idea behind *"the fullness of time"* is "when the time was right." The time was right because the 483 years prophesied by Daniel were drawing to a close (Daniel 9:24–26). It is so amazing that Daniel the prophet who lived approximately six hundred years before Christ prophesied the exact year when the Messiah would be cut off (i.e. killed). In verse 25 of Daniel 9 he says that from the going forth of the command to restore and build Jerusalem until Messiah is cut off, there shall be seven weeks of years (49 years), and sixty two weeks of years (434 years). This adds up to four hundred and eighty three years, the year Jesus rode into Jerusalem (Zechariah 9:9).

At this time, God sent forth His Son, born of a woman to redeem us, or to purchase us out of the slave market.

John Newton, the man who wrote the most popular and famous hymn in America, *Amazing Grace*, remembered the horror of slavery. He was only seven when his mother died. He became a sailor and went out to sea at eleven years old. He became the captain of a slave ship and had an active hand in the horrible inhumanity of the slave trade. But when he was twenty-three, and his ship was in imminent danger of sinking off the coast of Newfoundland, he cried out to God for mercy, and he found it. He never forgot how amazing it was that God had saved him. He posted Deuteronomy 15:15 over his fireplace: *"You shall remember that you were a slave in the land of Egypt, and the LORD your God redeemed you."* [10]

Prayer: *Thank You for Your amazing prophecies! Amen!*

July 18

GOD'S MISSION FOR US ON EARTH

Stand fast therefore in the liberty by which Christ has made us free...
—GALATIANS 5:1; READ ALSO GALATIANS 5

President Harry Truman held office during the end of World War II, one of the most difficult periods of the twentieth century. He said:

> We have just come through a decade in which forces of evil in various parts of the world have been lined up in a bitter fight to banish from the face of the earth...religion and democracy. For these forces of evil have long realized that both religion and democracy are founded on one basic principle, the worth and dignity of the individual man and woman. Dictatorship, on the other hand, has always rejected that principle. Dictatorship, by whatever name, is founded on the doctrine that the individual amounts to nothing; that the State is the only thing that counts; and that men and women and children were put on earth solely for the purpose of serving the State.
>
> In that long struggle between these two doctrines, the cause of decency and righteousness has been victorious. The right of every human being to live in dignity and freedom, the right to worship his God in his own way, the right to fix his own relationship to his fellow men and to his Creator—these again have been saved for mankind....
>
> If men and nations would but live by the precepts of the ancient prophets and the teachings of the Sermon on the Mount, problems which now seem so difficult would soon disappear....
>
> This is a supreme opportunity for the church to continue to fulfill its mission on earth...no other agency can accomplish moral and spiritual awakening. Unless it is done, we are headed for the disaster we would deserve. Oh, for an Isaiah or a Saint Paul to reawaken this sick world to its moral responsibilities.[11]

PRAYER: *Father, may we see that we have an opportunity to fulfill our mission on earth which is to accomplish this great spiritual and moral awakening. We need it so much to avoid the disaster of which President Truman spoke. Amen.*

July 19

WE REAP WHAT WE SOW

Do not be deceived, God is not mocked; for whatever a man sows, that he will also reap.

—GALATIANS 6:7; READ ALSO GALATIANS 6

How does your heart feel about the laws of God? Do you feel like His laws are punishment? There are times when God does punish, but the law is not punishment. It is an impersonal force. God intended that Adam and Eve should reap only blessedness. Since the fall, we have also reaped evil.

We know that natural law is absolute, and we obey it. Gravity always works. The same is true with God's laws. We are subject to God's laws, whether or not we believe in them.

One of God's laws is the law of sowing and reaping.

+ If we sow unkind words, we will reap unkind words.

+ If we sow mercy, we will reap mercy.

+ If we sow the fruits of the Spirit in Galatians 5:22: love, joy, peace, patience, goodness, gentleness, kindness, faithfulness, and self-control, we will reap the same.

+ If we sow judgments of our parents, we will reap in like manner. For the Bible says in Romans 2:1: *"Therefore you are inexcusable, O man, for in whatever you judge another you condemn yourself; for you who judge practice the same things."* So, if we accuse parents of being unfaithful, critical, angry, abusive, unforgiving or bitter, etc., we will reap by being the same way ourselves, or possibly by marrying someone who has these characteristics.

+ If we honor parents, the Bible says things will go well for us and we will live a long life. If we sow dishonor, we will reap dishonor and life will not go well with us.

+ If we sow finances into the Kingdom of God, we will reap with all our needs being met.

PRAYER: *Lord, show us how we are reaping what we have sown. Help us to sow good seed. We ask forgiveness where we have sown bad seed, and we pray for that crop to fail! Help us to sow into the Kingdom and get 30-60-100-fold return. Amen.*

July 20

FOLLOWING GOD'S VISION FOR YOU

And a vision appeared to Paul in the night. A man of Macedonia stood and pleaded with him, saying, "Come over to Macedonia and help us." Now after he had seen the vision, immediately we sought to go to Macedonia, concluding that the Lord had called us to preach the gospel to them.
—ACTS 16:9–10; READ ALSO VV. 1–21

The Macedonian man wanted help, so Paul brought the gospel. This is the best type of help anyone could give. It is good for us to bring other help along with the gospel, but without the gospel, little real help for eternity is given.

So, after he had seen the vision, he did not hesitate to answer the call of the Macedonian man. God still calls people to the mission field, and He may call YOU. His call may come through unusual ways. When the call comes, it is important to respond the way Paul did. He immediately sought to go to Macedonia.

We see in verses six and seven of this chapter, that the Spirit did not permit Paul to go to Asia or Bithynia. The Lord has his reason for saying "No." Paul went instead to Troas and picked up Luke who ended up writing a gospel and the Book of Acts. Luke also was a doctor, so Paul had his personal physician along with him as well.

We lived in Minnesota for thirty-four years, and at one point in the night, I had a dream of a man on his knees asking us to come to Murray to help. It seemed to me that a pastor was on his knees praying and asking God to send him some help. We were led to a church in Murray and have been in that church now for the entire time. Also, while we have been at that same church, we have been called on mission trips to Nepal, India, Bangladesh, and Sweden. It is so wonderful to hear His voice and be obedient to His call.

PRAYER: *Father in heaven, I pray right now for all who are reading this devotional that they will hear Your voice calling them for their assignment on this earth. I pray they will be obedient and fulfill it with all their hearts. No excuses! Amen!*

BELIEVING IS NOT JUST FOR YOU BUT YOUR ENTIRE HOUSEHOLD

Believe on the Lord Jesus Christ, and you will be saved, you and your household.
—ACTS 16:31; READ ALSO VV. 22–40

This is a most wonderful passage of Scripture. After Paul cast the spirit of divination out of the slave girl, Paul and Silas were beaten with rods and thrown into prison because the girl's masters had lost their income. BUT, at midnight, instead of complaining to the Lord and saying: "Lord, here we are serving You, and You let them beat us and throw us into prison!" No, instead they were praying and singing hymns to God at midnight, and the prisoners were listening to them. Suddenly, there was a great earthquake and all the prison doors were opened and everyone's chains were loosed.

When the keeper of the prison saw this, he was about to kill himself. But Paul called with a loud voice, saying, "Don't do it! We are all here!" Then the jailor called for a light and fell down before Paul and Silas saying the memorable words: *"What must I do to be saved?"* He knew he had just witnessed a miracle and that Paul and Silas had a connection to God and he wanted it too. So, they gave the answer to the question of how one can be saved: *"Believe on the Lord Jesus Christ and you will be saved, and your house."*

How wonderful that believing is not just for yourself, but it is for your whole house. *You must claim this promise not only for yourself, but for your immediate family, and also for your entire bloodline.*

There is also another important thing to note about this story. What were they doing in prison? In spite of having beaten, bloody bodies in a filthy prison, they were singing praises. Praise and worship during our most trying times is probably the most powerful thing we can do. It is a sacrifice of praise, because we do not feel like doing it. But when we do, wonders happen. Prison doors open. People are set free. Whole families come to know the Lord. Miracles happen!

PRAYER: *Lord, teach us to praise at all times—in the good times and in the bad times. Then let us watch You work! Amen!*

July 22

PAUL'S TYPE OF PRAYER

And this is my prayer that your love may abound more and more in knowledge and depth of insight, so that you may be able to discern what is best and may be pure and blameless until the day of Christ, filled with the fruit of righteousness that comes through Jesus Christ—to the glory and praise of God.
—Philippians 1:9–11, niv; read also Philippians 1

What a wonderful prayer to pray daily for loved ones. I pray this often for my family. Paul's prayers are uplifting. "They are God-centered prayers: each one is addressed to God. Not one apostolic prayer is addressed to the devil. This is the model set forth in the New Testament used in resisting and dislodging demonic spiritual forces and cultural strongholds." [12]

The apostolic prayers are "positive" prayers: they ask God to release good qualities rather than asking Him to remove negative qualities.

For example, in the above prayer, Paul prayed for love to abound rather than asking the Lord to remove hatred. He prayed that we may be pure and blameless rather than praying that we stop lying, cheating, stealing, etc.

These kinds of prayers are so powerful in church prayer meetings. When we pray prayers that focus on sin in the church or its leadership, this promotes judgment and anger.

The Father knew that praying for the impartation of positive virtues instead of focusing on removing negative characteristics would unify intercessors and heal some of the negative emotions against the church in the person who is praying. As we pray these kinds of prayer, we will develop more mercy toward the weaknesses in people and the church.

"The positive focus of the apostolic prayers is also essential in helping us to operate in faith. The apostolic prayers in the New Testament provide us with good theology for a victorious church. Praying these prayers builds our faith for revival." [13]

Prayer: *Teach us how to pray, Father. Let us follow the example of Paul's prayers. Help us to memorize them! Amen!*

AT THE MENTION OF HIS NAME

And being found in appearance as a man, He humbled Himself and became obedient to the point of death, even the death of the cross. Therefore God also has highly exalted Him and given Him the name which is above every name, that at the name of Jesus every knee should bow, of those in heaven, and of those on earth, and of those under the earth, and that every tongue should confess that Jesus Christ is Lord, to the glory of God the Father.
—Philippians 2:8–11; read also Philippians 2

Jesus humbled Himself:[14] a) He was humble in that He took the form of a man, and not a more glorious creature like an angel. b) He was humble in that He was born into an obscure, oppressed place. c) He was humble in that He was born into poverty among a despised people. d) He was humble in that He was born as a child instead of appearing as a man. e) He was humble in the long wait until He launched out into public ministry. f) He was humble in the companions and disciples He chose. g) He was humble in His total obedience to His Heavenly Father. h) He was humble in the agony of His death.

"*Therefore God highly exalted Him and gave Him a name above every name, that at the Name of Jesus every knee should bow...*" This conveys the absolute totality of all creation recognizing the superiority of Jesus Christ. One day every knee will bow after the final judgment, and everyone will make his confession that Jesus is Lord.

Jesus' humility stands in stark contrast to the Roman emperors who expected all residents of the Empire to burn incense to their image and to declare that Caesar was God. Christians who refused to participate or bow their knee to Caesar often paid with their lives.

Prayer: *He is Lord. He is Lord. He is risen from the dead and He is Lord. Every knee will bow, every tongue confess, that Jesus Christ is Lord. Amen.*

THAT I MAY KNOW HIM

*That I may know Him and the power of His resurrection, and the
fellowship of His sufferings, being conformed to His death.*
—PHILIPPIANS 3:10; READ ALSO PHILIPPIANS 3

To know Jesus is not the same as knowing His historical life; it is not
the same as knowing correct doctrines, knowing His moral example,
or knowing His great work on our behalf.

How do you really know someone? We know someone because
a) we recognize him; b) because we are acquainted with what he
does; c) because we actually converse with him; d) because we spend
time in his house; e) because we have committed our life to him and
live with him every day, sharing every circumstance as in a marriage.
Spurgeon says:

> They tell me He is a refiner, that He cleanses from spots; He has
> washed me in His precious blood, and to that extent I know Him.
> They tell me that He clothes the naked; He has covered me with a
> garment of righteousness, and to that extent I know Him. They tell
> me that He is a breaker, and that He breaks fetters, He has set my
> soul at liberty, and therefore I know Him. They tell me that He is
> a king and that He reigns over sin; He has subdued my enemies
> beneath his feet, and I know Him in that character.... They say He is
> a door; I have entered in through Him and I know Him as a door.[15]

When Paul says that he wants to know the power of His resurrection, it means he wants to see people saved, healed, and delivered.
He wants to see the lame walk, the blind see, the deaf hear, and the
demonized set free.

We also join in the fellowship of His suffering. Not everyone is
pleased with the gospel. Persecution and even martyrdom can go
along with it. *"We are heirs of God and joint heirs with Christ, if indeed
we suffer with Him, that we may also be glorified together"* (Romans 8:17).

PRAYER: *Father, the desire of our hearts is that we might know Christ,
that we might represent His love and attributes faithfully on this journey
through life. In Jesus' name. Amen.*

DON'T WORRY ABOUT ANYTHING

Be anxious for nothing, but in everything by prayer and supplication, with thanksgiving, let your requests be made known to God; and the peace of God, which surpasses all understanding, will guard your hearts and minds through Christ Jesus.
—Philippians 4:6–7; read also Philippians 4

This Scripture is the key to a worry-free life. When the Bible says, *"Don't worry about anything,"* it means just that. Because it is a command, when we do worry it is a sin.

The secret to not having worry or being stress-filled is in the above verses. As soon as we are tempted to worry, we must pray with thanksgiving. We give thanks for how God is going to meet the need or crisis. When we do this, His peace floods our hearts and minds as we trust in Him.

Think about it. Isn't the God who created the universe and holds all things together with His word, big enough to answer any prayer?

I was just learning about these verses when my husband was graduating from Iowa State with a master's degree in math. He wanted to teach in college, but there were no openings. He had applied for jobs, but we hadn't heard anything from anyone. One day we got a yellow envelope in the mail. I thought it was junk mail and let our little four-year-old daughter carry it home. Here was an invitation for a job interview in Minneapolis. He ended up getting this job and we lived there for 34 years and raised our family there.

There were many times before cell phones when we didn't know where our children were. Once our youngest daughter was working in a church in the inner city, and she didn't come home at the appointed time. We were quoting this verse and praying for her protection. She had decided to visit a girlfriend in town and had forgotten to let us know! These verses have been a lifeline for producing peace in our lives.

Prayer: *Father God, You are faithful. Amen. (Pray about something that troubles you and turn it over to Him. Memorize this Scripture and quote it when you need it.)*

July 26

USE US, LORD

These who have turned the world upside down have come here too.
—Acts 17:6; read also vv. 1–15

My husband and I experienced the greatest revival when we went to India with a group from Cedar Valley Church from Bloomington, MN in the spring of 2006. We were teaching Elijah House to pastors from two different churches that had experienced a church split. There were still feelings of unforgiveness.

I told the testimony of the miracle healing of a church split in Minnesota led by a missionary from India. Because of the pastors repenting for what happened many years ago, both churches began to experience growth and prosperity.

After I shared this testimony, the worship leader of the one church in India got up and asked forgiveness for his bad attitude toward the other group. Then the worship leader from that other group extended forgiveness, and asked forgiveness for his bad attitude as well. Pretty soon, a real spirit of travail developed, and they were in each other's arms asking for forgiveness. There had also been tribal warfare and killing between the Karbi and Khasi tribes in NE India. These two groups of pastors stood in the gap and asked forgiveness with many tears of repentance for their tribes participating in this. One of the teachers who had come with us had brought a newspaper with him telling about the tribal warfare. He wadded up the paper, threw it against the wall, and said, "I declare in Jesus' name the warfare is over!" And it was!

We eventually heard that revival had broken out in that area and one thousand people were added to the church, broken families repaired and restored, alcoholics delivered and healed, churches overflowing, and lives being changed on a daily basis. The schools had turned into places of revival and children were having dreams and visions of Jesus, angels, being in heaven, seeing hell, etc. A very conservative church that was very closed to the work of the Holy Spirit experienced a great visitation of Holy Spirit.

Prayer: *Use us again to "turn the world upside down!"Amen!*

July 27

GOD THE CREATOR

Then Paul stood in the midst of the Areopagus and said, "Men of Athens, I perceive that in all things you are very religious; for as I was passing through and considering the objects of your worship, I even found an altar with this inscription: TO THE UNKNOWN GOD."

—Acts 17:22–23; read also vv. 16–34

Athens was filled with statues dedicated TO THE UNKNOWN GOD. Six hundred years before Paul, a terrible plague came on the city and a man named Epimenides had an idea. He let loose a flock of sheep through the town, and wherever they lay down, they sacrificed that sheep to the god that had the nearest shrine or temple. If a sheep lay down near no shrine or temple, they sacrificed the sheep TO THE UNKNOWN GOD.[16]

Paul goes on to tell them who this God is: He made the world and everything in it, since He is Lord of heaven and earth and does not dwell in temples made with hands. He's not worshiped with men's hands either. For it in Him we live and move and have our being.

In explaining God to them, he started at the beginning; God is the Creator, and we are His creatures. And He has made from one blood every nation of men. Paul told them that we are all descended from Adam through Noah, and that there is one God who created us all, and to whom we all are obligated. We need to seek this God.

Paul then goes from who God is, (our Creator), to who we are (His offspring), to our responsibility before Him (to worship Him in truth), to our accountability if we dishonor Him. *"God commands all men everywhere to repent, because He has appointed a day on which He will judge the world in righteousness by the Man whom He has ordained. He has given assurance of this to all by raising Him from the dead"* (v. 31).

Prayer: *We praise You God for the privilege of walking in the truth. We don't worship an UNKNOWN GOD, but You have revealed Yourself through Your Son, Jesus Christ. Amen.*

July 28

WORD OF GOD IN POWER AND
IN THE HOLY SPIRIT

For our gospel did not come to you in word only, but also in power,
and in the Holy Spirit and in much assurance, as you know what
kind of men we were among you for your sake. And you became fol-
lowers of us and of the Lord, having received the word in much afflic-
tion, with joy of the Holy Spirit, so that you became examples to all in
Macedonia and Achaia who believe.
   —1 THESSALONIANS 1:5–7; READ ALSO 1 THESSALONIANS 1

This same gospel that was preached in power in Paul's day is the
same gospel preached today. A wonderful example of this is Teresia
Wairimu who came to a Reinhard Bonnke meeting in Nairobi, Uhuru
Park, in 1988 where he preached.

Teresia had longed to serve the Lord from childhood, and against
her parents' wishes, married a European missionary. This marriage
ended in divorce, she was broken-hearted, and her dreams were shat-
tered. As she heard Reinhard preach the Word of God with power,
hope began to arise in her heart, that she could be used this way too.
She too could see the lame walk, the deaf hear, and the blind see.
She had prayed, "God if You can give Bonnke one hundred thousand
souls, give me one hundred and I'll be happy." She desperately wanted
Reinhard to lay his hands on her and pray.

That didn't happen at that meeting, but she went to hear him in
Oslo, Norway. He did lay his hands on her there, and the fire of God
hit her. The force of God threw her twenty yards through the air, and
both of her shoes flew off her feet. She never found one of her shoes.

When she got back home, she called her girl-friends to a prayer
meeting. She started out with seventeen people, but in a couple weeks
there were two hundred people coming. Next, she rented an audito-
rium for two thousand people. Finally, she asked to use Uhuru Park,
where Bonnke had preached. When Bonnke went to hear her in 1998,
two hundred thousand people had gathered, the gospel was preached
in power, and amazing healings manifested. She never knew he was
there.[17]

PRAYER: *All the glory goes to You God! In Jesus' name. Amen!*

BELIEVERS OF THE MESSAGE

For this reason we also thank God without ceasing, because when you received the word of God which you heard from us, you welcomed it not as the word of men, but as it is in truth, the word of God, which also effectively works in you who believe.

For what is our hope, or joy, or crown of rejoicing? Is it not even you in the presence of our Lord Jesus Christ at His coming? So you are our glory and joy.

—1 Thessalonians 2:19–20; read also 1 Thessalonians 2

By way of review, in Acts 17, Paul came to Thessalonica and preached Jesus. The Jews who didn't believe set all the city in an uproar and attacked the house of Jason. They accused them of turning the world upside down. So, the believers sent Paul and Silas away immediately to Berea.

Paul was telling the believers in Thessalonica that he thanked God that they really received the Word he preached as the Word of God, and not just as the word of men.

Not everyone receives this message as the Word of God, yet when they do not, it reflects upon them, not upon the message.

> That you have not perceived spiritual things is true; but it is no proof that there are none to perceive. The whole case is like that of the Irishman who tried to upset evidence by non-evidence. Four witnesses saw him commit a murder. He pleaded that he was not guilty and wished to establish his innocence by producing forty persons who did not see him do it. What good was that? So if forty people declare that there is no power of the Holy Ghost going with the word, this only proves that the forty people did not know what others do know.[18]

The Thessalonians believed the message and became imitators of others who had suffered for the gospel. The thing that had stirred up the Jews was jealousy over the knowledge that Gentiles could be saved without first becoming Jews.

Paul longed to see these precious believers again soon. He said they were his hope, joy, and crown of rejoicing.

Prayer: *Of all the gifts You could give us, Father, the gift of souls coming to You is the greatest! That is our joy! Amen!*

July 30

BLAMELESS IN HOLINESS

Now may our God and Father Himself, and our Lord Jesus Christ, direct our way to you. And may the Lord make you increase and abound in love to one another and to all, just as we do to you, so that He may establish your hearts blameless in holiness before our God and Father at the coming of our Lord Jesus Christ with all His saints.
—1 Thessalonians 3:11–13; read also 1 Thessalonians 3

Paul could barely endure the thought that the faith of the Thessalonians might crumble under this season of affliction, so he sent Timothy to both check on them and to help them. He knew that Satan wanted to tempt the Thessalonians to give up on God. He did not want his labor to be in vain.

Paul had to be patient to get the report. Remember, there was no E-mail, or cell phones in those days! When Timothy did return from his visit to the Thessalonians, he brought good news. He said they were doing well in faith and love. Paul was so thankful that they held them dear in their hearts and had not believed the vicious and false rumors about Paul (2:3–6). He said he felt alive again as long as he knew they were standing firm in the Lord.

Paul prayed that he would soon be reunited with the Thessalonians. One of Paul's top priorities for those he'd won to the Lord, was that their love would abound toward one another even as he loved them! And that they would be established in holiness—set apart from the world and unto God. He prayed they would be blameless in holiness before God at the coming of our Lord Jesus Christ. Nothing can encourage us to holiness like remembering that Jesus might come today. Think of this: if this were your last day on earth, how would you live it? What would you do?

Prayer: *Father in Heaven, we do pray that we would increase and abound in love to each other and to all. We pray You would establish our hearts blameless in holiness before You at the coming of our Lord Jesus Christ with all His saints! Amen!*

THE RAPTURE OF THE CHURCH

For the Lord Himself will descend from heaven with a shout, with the voice of an archangel, and with the trumpet of God. And the dead in Christ will rise first. Then we who are alive and remain shall be caught up together with them in the clouds to meet the Lord in the air. And thus we shall always be with the Lord. Therefore comfort one another with these words.
    —1 THESSALONIANS 4:16–18; READ ALSO 1 THESSALONIANS 4

In the few weeks, Paul was with the Thessalonians, he talked about the soon return of Jesus. They had questions about those Christians who died before Jesus' return. Paul did not want them to be ignorant about those who had fallen asleep (died) lest they sorrow as others who had no hope. For the Christian, death is like laying down for a nap and waking up in glory. As Christians, we may mourn the death of other Christians; but our sorrow is like the sadness of seeing someone off on a long trip, knowing you will see them again, but not for a long time.

God promises that just like Jesus died and rose from the dead, so we also will be raised. We will not enter into "soul sleep." The Bible says, *"To be absent from the body is to be present with the Lord."* We will go immediately to heaven and be with the Lord and receive a temporary body, which will be recognizable. When Jesus comes back, we will come with Him.

Paul wanted the Thessalonians to know that the Christians, who have died before Jesus returns, will by no means be at a disadvantage. The Lord will descend from heaven with a shout, the voice of an archangel, and with a blast from the trumpet of God. Then the dead in Christ will rise first. (Our dead bodies will be resurrected). Then those who are alive on the earth will be *caught up together with them in the clouds to meet the Lord in the air.* This is called the rapture of the church. Then we will always be with the Lord. We are to comfort one another with these words.

PRAYER: *"What a day, glorious day, that will be!"* Maranatha! O Lord, come! Amen!

THANK GOD IN ALL SITUATIONS

Rejoice always, pray without ceasing, in everything give thanks; for this is the will of God in Christ Jesus for you.
—1 THESSALONIANS 5:16–18; READ ALSO 1 THESSALONIANS 5

When we discover the power in praise, we have entered into an exciting journey! It is so amazing how God can turn any situation around when we rejoice, pray always and give thanks! Merlin Carothers shares about the power in praise:

When Ron came to see Merlin, he was desperate. His wife wanted to commit suicide when he was drafted into the army and received orders to Vietnam. His wife, Sue, had been adopted and was now estranged from her adopted family. She had no one but Ron. Merlin told them both that they needed to give thanks and trust the Lord. This advice left them incredulous. He gave them this verse: *"In everything give thanks, for this is the will of God for you."*

Sue remained in despair. However, when they returned to another counseling session, they decided to take the plunge and give thanks to God, even though it made no sense. The next day, a young soldier came for a counseling session concerning his own marriage and sat beside Sue in the waiting room. He showed Sue the pictures of his family, and of his mother. Sue screamed, "That is MY mother!" When she was a girl, she ran across a picture of her birth mom, and now she was looking at her face in the picture! As they checked into it, they found it was true. Now she had a real brother and a whole family!

That's not all. Ron "happened" to run into an old friend from law school who persuaded Ron to ask for a transfer so he could work with him in the legal office. His request was granted! Now they weren't going to be separated after all, and Sue had found her real family. Giving thanks in all situations is truly mind-bogglingly powerful.[1]

PRAYER: *Lovely Father, help us to remember not to grumble and complain but to thank You in everything! Amen!*

WORTHY OF HIS CALLING

With this in mind, we constantly pray for you, that our God may count you worthy of his calling, and that by his power he may fulfill every good purpose of yours and every act prompted by your faith. We pray this so that the name of our Lord Jesus may be glorified in you, and you in him, according to the grace of our God and the Lord Jesus Christ.
—2 THESSALONIANS 1:11–12, NIV; READ ALSO 2 THESSALONIANS 1

This is the example of Paul in prayer. He constantly prays for the church at Thessalonica. How does one pray constantly? In the Spirit. What does he pray? He prays that God would count him worthy of His calling.

God gives Christians a high calling. The calling is to see Him glorified in us at His coming.

We can live worthy of this calling when:

+ Every good purpose of ours is fulfilled by His power. This means we live lives touched by His goodness, and we display His goodness.

+ Every act prompted by our faith is fulfilled by Him. The NKJV says that we live worthy of His call when we fulfill the work of faith with power.

+ The name of our Lord Jesus Christ is glorified in us. This includes displaying His character in our lives as well.

+ We live worthy of His calling when we are glorified in Him, when He alone is our source of glory and exaltation, and who we are in Jesus is more important than anything else.

This great work of living worthy of His calling can only happen according to the grace of God. It happens by His power, His favor, and His acceptance at work in us. *"In Him we live and move and have our being"* (Acts 17:28).

PRAYER: *Father in Heaven, we pray that You would fulfill every good purpose of ours. We pray You would quicken us with faith to do great things for You. In Jesus' name. Amen.*

FREEDOM FROM DECEPTION

*Let no one deceive you by any means; for that Day will not come
unless the falling away comes first, and the man of sin is revealed,
the son of perdition, who opposes and exalts himself above all that is
called God or that is worshiped, so that he sits as God in the temple of
God, showing himself that he is God.*
—2 THESSALONIANS 2:3–5; READ ALSO 2 THESSALONIANS 2

Paul is not describing events which must precede the rapture, but
events that are evidence of the Great Tribulation—the day of Christ.[2]

+ *The falling away.* This indicated a rebellion, an apostasy, or a
  departure. (This does not contradict a great revival in the last
  days.)

+ *The man of sin revealed.* This is the "prince who is to come"
  (Daniel 9:26). He is a prominent figure in the Bible and the
  ultimate personification of the spirit of the Antichrist spoken
  of in 1 John 4:2–3.

+ *The son of perdition.* Perdition means destruction/the opposite
  of salvation. This man of sin opposes and exalts himself above
  all that is called God or is worshipped. He demands worship for himself. His demand for worship will be so extreme,
  he will set himself up as God in the temple at Jerusalem and
  demand this blasphemous worship from everyone (Revelation
  13:14–15; Matthew 24:15–16). He invades the most sacred
  place and there takes his seat. His action is a claim to deity.
  This is *"the abomination of desolation"* spoken of by both Daniel
  and Jesus.

+ *Showing himself that he is God.* Clearly, he mirrors the ministry
  of Jesus. However, the return of Jesus and the judgment of
  God show that He is not God at all.

PRAYER: *We thank You, Father, that Your Word keeps us from deception in these last days. We do not need to be shaken or troubled. You
will comfort our hearts and establish us in every good word and work. In
Jesus' name. Amen.*

August 4

WORLD PRAYER POINT

Finally, brethren, pray for us, that the word of the Lord may run swiftly and be glorified, just as it is with you, and that we may be delivered from unreasonable and wicked men; for not all have faith.
—2 Thessalonians 3:1–2; read also 2 Thessalonians 3

Here are three powerful prayer points requested by the apostle who wrote most of the New Testament. We would do well to pray these points for ourselves, our spiritual leaders, and our missionaries. This will have eternal consequences for ourselves, our families, and His church around the world.

+ *Finally, pray for me.* Paul was always asking for prayer because he knew that the success of his ministry was directly related to the prayer that went up on his behalf. Think of those people who worked behind the scenes that never got their names in the Bible, but who were praying for Paul. Think of their prayers in the Spirit that brought about the signs, wonders, miracles, and harvest of souls. Only eternity will tell of their deeds and their rewards.

+ *Pray that the Word of the Lord may run swiftly and be glorified.* If the Word runs freely with no hindrances with our prayers, how many times has our prayerlessness hindered God's Word from accomplishing what He desires? God has promised that *"My word shall not return to Me void, but it shall accomplish what I please, and prosper in the thing for which I sent it"* (Isaiah 55:11). We must work with these promises by doing our part in praying.

+ *That we may be delivered from unreasonable and wicked men.* We must pray that either God will deliver us from their plans or save them and bring them to work alongside of us. We must pray for the persecuted church who face death threats all the time.

Every Home for Christ has a World Prayer Map (ehc.org) that is a wonderful tool for praying for all the nations in one month.

Prayer: *Father, let each of us pray and do our part! Amen!*

REFUSE THE SPIRIT OF UNFORGIVENESS

Now the Lord spoke to Paul in the night by a vision, "Do not be afraid, but speak, and do not keep silent; for I am with you, and no one will attack you to hurt you; for I have many people in this city."
—ACTS 18:9–10; READ ALSO ACTS 18

Paul met Priscilla and Aquila in Corinth. They were likely already Christians before they left Italy at the command of Claudius. They were tentmakers, like Paul.

Paul went to the synagogue every Sabbath and persuaded both Jews and Greeks. When Silas and Timothy came to Corinth with an offering from Macedonia, it allowed Paul to devote himself exclusively to preaching (2 Corinthians 11:9).

But when the Jews opposed him and blasphemed, he shook his garments and said to them, *"Your blood be upon your own heads; I am clean. From now on I will go to the Gentiles."* Shaking his garments meant that he was rejecting their rejection, and he refused to carry unforgiveness with him. When we refuse to carry unforgiveness, God opens amazing doors.

Paul then went next door to Justus' house, and started a home church. Guess who came? Crispus, the ruler of the synagogue next door, and he gave his heart to the Lord. Many believed and were baptized. This is when the Lord spoke to him to not be afraid. This is a word to us also, to not be afraid to share the good news. So, he was there a year and six months.

The Jews did bring Paul to the judgment seat, but Gallio, the proconsul of Achaia spoke up, refused to take the case, and drove them out. He said Paul was participating in a legal religion. Then all the Greeks took Sosthenes, the new ruler of the synagogue who replaced Crispus, and beat him. Later, he also became a Christian! (1 Corinthians 1:1).

From there, Paul left for Ephesus, Jerusalem and Antioch. But he left Priscilla and Aquilla at Ephesus to prepare for his return trip.

PRAYER: *Thank You, Father, for this exciting record of the early church—its courage, prayer, miracles and obedience! Amen!*

GOD USES THE FOOLISH THINGS OF THE WORLD TO SHAME THE WISE

For you see your calling, brethren, that not many wise according to the flesh, not many mighty, not many noble, are called. But God has chosen the foolish things of the world to put to shame the wise, and God has chosen the weak things of the world to put to shame the things which are mighty; and the base things of the world and the things which are not, to bring to nothing the things that are that no flesh should glory in His Presence.
—1 CORINTHIANS 1:26–29; READ ALSO 1 CORINTHIANS 1

Warning: the Corinthians were not to consider themselves so great!

Paul challenged them to see their calling and that not many wise according to the flesh were called. It is significant that often the most educated people have the least regard for God. This is not always the case; some of the most brilliant men of history have been Christians, (such as Isaac Newton). But largely, the "smarter" one sees himself, the less regard he has for God. Human "wisdom" is constantly rejecting and opposing God. It ultimately shows itself foolish and prideful.

On the contrary, God has chosen the foolish things of the world to put to shame the wise. God often rebukes the idolatry of human wisdom by choosing and using the foolish things of the world. He is not saying that it's better to be foolish or uneducated. Rather he is saying that the world's wisdom does not bring us salvation in Jesus Christ.

This is the end result. No one will stand before God and declare, "I figured You out," or "You did it just like I thought You should." God's ways are greater and higher than ours and no flesh will glory in His presence.

True wisdom belongs to the believing. *"But of him are you in Christ Jesus, who became for us wisdom from God, and righteousness and sanctification and redemption—that, as it is written, 'He who glories let him glory in the LORD'"* (v. 30–31).

PRAYER: *What a wonderful promise, that Jesus Christ is made unto us wisdom, righteousness, sanctification and redemption. Amen.*

PREACHING AS A DEMONSTRATION OF THE SPIRIT AND POWER

And I, brethren, when I came to you, did not come with excellence of speech or of wisdom declaring to you the testimony of God. I determined not to know anything among you except Jesus Christ and Him crucified. I was with you in weakness, in fear, and in much trembling. And my speech and my preaching were not with persuasive words of human wisdom, but in demonstration of the Spirit and of power, that your faith should not be in the wisdom of men but in the power of God.
—1 Corinthians 2:1–5; read also 1 Corinthians 2

Paul did not come as a philosopher or salesman; he came as a witness. He didn't come to reason or debate. He determined to put the emphasis on Jesus Christ and Him crucified.

The message of the cross and crucifixion may sound noble to our twentieth century ears, but in the first century, to talk about crucifixion was like talking about the electric chair. It was a cruel, humiliating, death. The great Roman statesman Cicero said that the cross speaks of that which is so shameful, so horrible, that it should never be mentioned in polite society.

Paul was not brimming with self-confidence. Yet, knowing his weaknesses kept him dependent on God's strength. After all, he was beaten three times and stoned once. The persecutions he endured could cause fear. Yet God showed up with a demonstration of the Spirit and of power.

One example of this demonstration of power which we have looked at in Acts 16 was where the girl possessed with a spirit of divination kept crying out that these men were servants of the Most High God. Paul commanded the spirit to come out of her, and it did! Then they were thrown in prison, and while they were singing and praising God there was an earthquake. The whole jailor's family got saved as a result. These miracles were what caused the early church to grow exponentially.

Prayer: *Father in Heaven, we pray the words of Paul that our speech and preaching would not be in words of human wisdom, but in a demonstration of the Spirit and power! Amen!*

CHRIST IS THE ONLY TRUE FOUNDATION

For no other foundation can anyone lay than that which is laid, which is Jesus Christ. Now if anyone builds on this foundation with gold, silver, precious stones, wood, hay, straw, each one's work will become clear; for the Day will declare it because it will be revealed by fire; and the fire will test each one's work, of what sort it is.
—1 Corinthians 3:11–13; read also 1 Corinthians 3

When Paul founded the church in Corinth (Acts 18), he laid the foundation of Jesus Christ, which is the only true foundation. So, we can't build on any other foundation, but we can build it with inferior materials.

God will test the building work of all His fellow workers, and each one's work will become clear. Some will build with precious things like gold, silver, and precious stones; others will build with unworthy materials like wood, hay, and straw.

By using the words gold, silver and precious stones, Paul seems to have in mind the building materials used in the construction of the temple (1 Chronicles 22:14). Precious stones consist of fine stone materials like marble and granite, but not jewels. Now if we were to build the church using alternate layers of straw and marble, that would be like mixing the carnal wisdom of men with the wisdom of God. Straw is fine in the barn, but it is an inadequate building material. Human wisdom and fleshly attractions may have a place in life, but not in the building of the church.

A fire will test each one's work and that will reveal what kind of work it was. Fire will destroy wood, hay and straw, but will refine gold and silver.

It is a sobering thought, but many people who believe they are serving God, are using "unworthy materials", such as teaching unsound doctrine which compromises the truth. They may be saved, but with a life that was wasted, they will receive no crown to give Jesus for His glory.

Prayer: *Father, give us wisdom as to how to build on the true foundation of obedience to Your Word. We want our work to pass through the fire and bring glory to You! Amen!*

August 9

THERE IS NO REASON FOR PRIDE

For who makes you differ from another? And what do you have that you did not receive? Now if you did indeed receive it, why do you boast as if you had not received it?
—1 Corinthians 4:7; read also 1 Corinthians 4

Here are three questions to humble the proud. The puffed-up state of the Corinthian Christians meant there was a pride problem. Though the pride was evident in the cliques around the different apostles, the cliques were the problem as much as pride was the problem. Paul addresses their proud hearts with three questions:

1. For who makes you differ from another? If there is a difference between us, it is because of what God has done in us, so there is no reason for pride.

2. And what do you have that you did not receive? Everything we have has come from God, so there is no reason for pride.

3. Why do you glory as if you had not received it? If what you have spiritually is a gift from God, why do you glory in it as if it were your own accomplishment? There is no reason for this self-glorying pride.

These three questions could prompt other questions in our hearts:

1. Do I truly give God the credit for my salvation?

2. Do I live with a spirit of humble gratitude?

3. Seeing that I have received from God, what can I give to Him?

These questions give room for self-examination. So often, when we compare ourselves with others, we come up desperately short, or we look down on others as not measuring up to us. The Bible says in 2 Corinthians 10:12: *"For we dare not class ourselves or compare ourselves with those who commend themselves. But they, measuring themselves by themselves, and comparing themselves among themselves, are not wise."*

Prayer: *Father in Heaven, help us to realize that all we have and all we are come from You—even our very breath. Amen.*

SPEAK THE TRUTH IN LOVE

It is actually reported that there is sexual immorality among you, and such sexual immorality as is not even named among the Gentiles— that a man has his father's wife! (v. 1). In the name of our Lord Jesus Christ, when you are gathered together, along with my spirit, with the power of our Lord Jesus Christ, deliver such a one to Satan for the destruction of the flesh, that his spirit may be saved in the day of the Lord Jesus.
— 1 CORINTHIANS 5:4–5; READ ALSO 1 CORINTHIANS 5

There was a great sin going on in the Corinthian church—that a man had his father's wife. The term *"porneia"* is used for sexual immorality here, and refers to any kind of extramarital sex, including homosexuality. The ancient Roman writer, Cicero, said this type of incest was an incredible crime and practically unheard of. It was unnamed among the Gentiles. Remember that Corinth was a city notorious for sexual immorality, and the pagan religions did not value sexual purity.

The Corinthian Christians probably allowed this in the name of "tolerance." They probably said, "Look how open-minded we are." "Look how we LOVE one another." The truth is that Jesus said, *"If you love me you will keep my commandments."* His commandment is that sex outside of marriage is strictly forbidden, and that the sexually immoral will not inherit the kingdom of heaven (1 Corinthians 6:9–11).

> Paul said the man was to be put out of fellowship and delivered to Satan for the destruction of his flesh. This means they were to put him outside the church into the world, which is the devil's domain. The punishment is a removal of spiritual protection and social comfort, not to inflict evil. The purpose was the destruction of the rebellious flesh—not the body." [3]

Paul hopes this will lead to his repentance. The goal was the salvation of his soul.

PRAYER: *Father, give us the courage not to turn a blind eye to sin in the church, but rather speak the truth in love. Amen.*

August 11

FIDELITY IN MARRIAGE

Or do you not know that he who is joined to a harlot is one body with her? For "the two," He says, "shall become one flesh." But he who is joined to the Lord is one spirit with Him. Flee sexual immorality. Every sin that a man does is outside the body, but he who commits sexual immorality sins against his own body.

—1 CORINTHIANS 6:16–18; READ ALSO 1 CORINTHIANS 6

In other words, anyone who has had sex outside of marriage has become one flesh with that person. This can lead to a profound scatteredness and brokenness of your spirit. Our spirit was designed to become one with our mate and to bless and cherish our mate. If these soul/spirit ties are not broken through repentance and the blood of Jesus cleansing us from all sin, then our spirits are continually reaching out to the one we became one with, causing us to not be fully present to our spouse. Following is a prayer for separation of spirits:

PRAYER

Lord, I repent for the ways I gave to another what belongs only to my spouse. I have come to recognize this as sin, and I ask Your forgiveness, Lord. I renounce these spiritual ties, and I ask You to cut me free, to restore me to myself, to my spouse and to You. I also ask Your forgiveness for the times I did not heed those You have put in my life to speak truth to me. Amen.

PRAYER Minister

So, in the Name of Jesus with the sword of truth, separate the spirits of these people that have sinned. Fully cleanse and renew. Cause their spirits to feel whole again. We ask that You bring back the scattered portions that have been reaching out to the person(s) they joined with. Help them to restore their spouse's trust. Grant them to bear the pain of knowing the damage this sin has caused. Cause them to be fully present to their spouse and be able to cherish and nurture, and in return draw nurture from You. Bless that covenantal union. May it bring glory to You.[4] Amen.

GOD'S WORD FOR HEALTHY MARRIAGE

Let the husband render to his wife the affection due her, and likewise
also the wife to her husband. The wife does not have authority over
her own body but the husband does. And likewise the husband does
not have authority over his own body, but the wife does.
—1 Corinthians 7:2–4; read also vv. 1–19

These are wonderful words for a healthy marriage. If husbands and wives lived in obedience to the word of God, there would be no divorce, no broken homes, no devastated children who must overcome abandonment and rejection.

Paul talks here about the affection due to the wife. It's not only the young, pretty or submissive wives, but every wife has affection due to them because she is the wife of a Christian man.

This also means that what the woman needs is not merely sexual relations, but she needs affection. This is true even for couples that cannot have a complete sexual relationship.

Likewise, the wife must render affection to her husband. There is mutual sexual responsibility in marriage in that the husband has obligations to his wife and the wife has obligations to her husband.

The emphasis is on giving to each other, looking after each other, and preferring each other.

The wife does not have authority over her own body. And the husband does not have authority over his own body. This, of course, does not justify a husband abusing or coercing his wife, sexually or otherwise. The point is that we must serve our partner with physical affection.

It is such a wonderful privilege, that out of the billions of people on the earth, God has chosen one person to meet our sexual needs. There is to be no one else.

Prayer: *Heavenly Father, You created marriage and said that a man should leave his father and mother and cleave to his wife, and that the two should be one flesh. And this is to be a picture of Christ and the church. Forgive us where our marriages and homes have not reflected that picture. Jesus, help us to model the love and sacrifice You gave for Your bride, the church. Amen.*

August 13

BE CONTENT IN YOUR SITUATION

But as God has distributed to each one, as the Lord has called each one, so let him walk. And so I ordain in all the churches.
—1 CORINTHIANS 7:17; READ ALSO VV. 20–40

This verse is saying that no matter what your station is right now—married, single, divorced, widowed, remarried, whatever—God can work in your life. Instead of thinking that you can or will walk with the Lord when your station changes, walk with the Lord in the place you are right now. Be thankful in the station you are in. Look for the good things that God is doing where you are right now and be thankful for those things. Remember the verse: *"In everything give thanks...."* (1 Thessalonians 5:18).

This also is a warning about trying to undo the past in regard to relationships. God tells us to repent of whatever sin is there and then to move on. If you are married to your second wife, after wrongfully divorcing your first wife, and then become a Christian, don't think you must now leave your second wife and go back to your first wife, in an attempt to undo the past. As the Lord has called you, be content in that place right now.

This is also a warning to beware of the danger in thinking other people have it better than you do because of their different station in life. The most important thing for you is to have an on-fire-for-God walk right now whether you are married, single, divorced, or remarried.

"Not that I speak in regard to need, for I have learned in whatever state I am, to be content: I know how to be abased, and I know how to abound. Everywhere and in all things I have learned both to be full and to be hungry, both to abound and to suffer need. I can do all things through Christ who strengthens me" (Philippians 4:11–13).

Paul had to learn contentment, and so do we. We can only do this through Jesus who strengthens us.

PRAYER: *Lord, we are making a decision today to be content in our situation. We are going to look for the good things that are happening and give thanks to You! Amen!*

August 14

YOUR LIFE IS A SHINING
EXAMPLE TO OTHERS

Therefore, if food makes my brother stumble, I will never again eat meat, lest I make my brother stumble.
—1 Corinthians 8:13; read also 1 Corinthians 8

This verse is written in the context of food that has been offered to idols. Now some people knew that idols were nothing and that there was only one God. Therefore, their conscience was not bothered by eating that food. However, this was a bad example to a weak brother in Christ who would not eat meat offered to idols. Therefore, to influence the weak brother to go against his conscience was actually to sin against Christ. *"But when you sin against the brethren, and wound their weak conscience, you sin against Christ"* (v. 12).

Paul makes the principle clear. Our actions can never be based only on what we know to be right for ourselves. We also need to consider what is right towards our brothers and sisters in Jesus.

We had a family member who was married to an alcoholic. At that time my husband participated in "social drinking." I observed that their drinking together was only reinforcing his alcoholism. In Romans 14:21 we read: *"It is good neither to eat meat nor drink wine nor do anything by which your brother stumbles or is offended or is made weak."*

Because of these verses, my husband and I decided we would never participate in "social drinking" of any kind because of the bad example it would set. We may never have become alcoholics, but there would be those watching us who could become alcoholics.

It is easy for a Christian to say, "I answer to God and God alone" and to ignore his brother or sister. But we will answer to God for how we have treated our brother or sister.

PRAYER: *Lord, help us to consider what kind of example we are setting in what we eat and drink, what kind of entertainment we watch, what kind of music we listen to, etc. Help us never to put a stumbling block in front of anyone that would lead them down a wrong path away from You. Amen.*

BE DISCIPLINED TO ACHIEVE GOD'S PURPOSE

Do you not know that those who run in a race all run, but one receives the prize? Run in such a way that you may obtain it. And everyone who competes for the prize is temperate in all things. Now they do it to obtain a perishable crown, but we for an imperishable crown. Therefore, I run thus: not with uncertainty. Thus I fight: not as one who beats the air. But I discipline my body and bring it into subjection, lest, when I have preached to others, I myself should become disqualified.
—1 Corinthians 9:24–27; read also 1 Corinthians 9

Since Corinth was the center for Isthmian Games, second in prestige to the ancient Olympics, Paul uses words that athletes understand. He tells us to train and compete as athletes who really want to win. Without effort, nothing can be won in a sporting event. To compete as an athlete, one must be temperate. Roman athletes had to train for ten months before being allowed in the games. An athlete must refuse things that may be fine in themselves but would hinder the pursuit of his goal. That goes for Christians. We may have to say no to things that hinder the pursuit of the imperishable crown.

> Paul disciplined his body. Discipline means "to strike under the eye; to give a black eye." Paul didn't want his body to lord it over his entire being. He wanted his body to be the servant, not the master; the desires of his body were not going to rule over his entire self.[5]

This did not mean that he thought the body was evil. We are created in the image of God and our body belongs to Jesus. But he disciplined his body lest when he had preached to others, he would become disqualified. Paul saw himself as one who announced the rules of the game, and then had to follow them himself. He wanted to win the prize of the high calling of God in Christ and win an imperishable crown.

Prayer: *Lord, help us to be Your disciples: disciplined in prayer, fasting, church attendance, witnessing, and all things. Amen.*

GOD MAKES A WAY OF ESCAPE

Therefore, let him who thinks he stands take heed lest he fall. No
temptation has overtaken you except such as is common to man; but
God is faithful, who will not allow you to be tempted beyond what you
are able, but with the temptation will also make the way of escape,
that you may be able to bear it.
—1 Corinthians 10:12–13; read also vv. 1–18

With all the preceding examples of Israel's temptations and how they
fell to lust and idolatry, the Corinthian Christians needed to understand that they were also vulnerable. The person who thinks he is
strong enough to withstand temptation will not be on his guard. As
a result, he may easily fall.

While walking on our way home from school, my brother and I
faced the temptation of stealing peanuts from the grocery store. After
we were caught and disciplined, we never did it again. The temptation
was still there, but we took the way of escape after that!

No temptation has overtaken us except such as is common to
man. We often want to excuse our particular tempting circumstance
as "very unique" or as a "special exception," but God reminds us that
our temptation is *not* unique at all. Many other men and women of
God have faced the same or similar temptations and have found the
strength in God to overcome the temptation. This means that we can
be victorious also—in the strength of Jesus, not in our own strength.
We fight temptation with Jesus' power, like the girl who explained
what she did when Satan came with temptation at the door of her
heart: "I send Jesus to answer the door. When Satan sees Jesus, he
says, 'OOPS, sorry, I must have the wrong house.'"

God has promised to supervise all temptation that comes at us
through the world, the flesh, or the devil. He promises to limit it
according to our capability to endure it—that is, as we rely on Him.
Then He provides a way of escape for us. It is then up to us to take
that way of escape.

Prayer: *Thank You Lord that You make a way of escape for us, and*
when we blow it, there is forgiveness. In Your mercy You give us other
chances to do the right thing. Amen.

August 17

SEEK ALSO THE BENEFIT OF OTHERS

*All things are lawful for me, but not all things are helpful; all things
are lawful for me, but not all things edify. Let no one seek his own, but
each one the other's well-being.*
—1 CORINTHIANS 10:23–24; READ ALSO VV. 19–33

We could focus on our own rights and ask only one question: "What's
the harm to me?" Instead of that, we need to also ask, "What good
can this be for me?" Just because something is permitted does not
mean it is beneficial.

For example, I may be "permitted" to go to an "R" rated movie, but
will it be beneficial to me? Will it edify me? Will it lead someone else
astray?

Do I want to go forward with Jesus, or do I want to see how much
I can get away with and still be a Christian? The Hebrew mind-set
is to draw fences that are proper and safe, and not have your foot
standing on the boundary itself.

Just because something is fine for me does not mean I should do
it. My own "rights" or what I know to be permitted for myself are not
the standards by which I judge my behavior. I must consider what is
the loving thing to do toward my brothers and sisters in Jesus.

The concluding principle is in verses 31–33: *"Give no offense, either
to the Jews or to the Greeks or to the church of God, just as I also please
all men in all things, not seeking my own profit, but the profit of many,
that they may be saved."*

The purpose of our lives is to glorify God, not to see how much we
can get away with. We are to give no offence to anyone. An offense is
an occasion to stumble, leading someone else into sin. More than anything, we want to lead people to salvation. More often than we think,
poor conduct in Christian living is connected to little regard for the
lost. Jesus came to *"seek and to save the lost."*

PRAYER: *Father in heaven, help us to influence people toward You by
our behavior, and not lead them away from You. Help us to live lives
that are pleasing to You and lives that will produce eternal fruit for Your
Kingdom! In the Name of Jesus Christ of Nazareth, we pray. Amen.*

HEADSHIP AND AUTHORITY

But I want you to know that the head of every man is Christ, the head of woman is man, and the head of Christ is God.
—1 Corinthians 11:3; read also vv. 1–16

This verse has had a tremendous impact on our marriage and home. My husband many years ago went to a Bill Gothard seminar and learned that the man was to be the spiritual head of the home. That revelation went deep into his spirit. This meant that his family was not going to go deeper spiritually than he did. When I (Jacqie) was filled with the Spirit, Jim knowing that he was my head or authority had two choices: either he could squelch me, or he could seek to be filled with the Spirit himself. Praise the Lord forevermore—he chose to be filled with the Spirit himself.

In its full sense, "head has the idea of headship and authority." It means to have the appropriate responsibility to lead, and the matching accountability. It is right and appropriate to submit to someone who is our head.

In this passage, we see Paul describes three "headship" relationships: Jesus is head of every man, man is the head of woman, and God is the head of Christ.

This is a wonderful model for marriage. The following principles for the husband-wife relationship are illustrated in the relationship of Jesus and the Father:

+ Husband and wife are to share a mutual love (John 13:34).

+ Husband and wife have different roles and accomplish different functions in the marriage (John 10:17).

+ Though having different roles, the husband and wife are equal and live in unity. The husband as head of the wife does not ascribe inferiority to her. It recognizes God-ordained order of authority to be respected. Jesus was totally under the authority of God, yet He is equally God (John 1:1).

+ Husband and wife live in unity, mutual respect and love (John 5:20).

Prayer: *May our homes reflect biblical order and love! Amen!*

THE SACRIFICE ON THE CROSS

For I received from the Lord that which I also delivered to you: that the Lord Jesus on the same night in which He was betrayed took bread; and when He had given thanks He broke it and said, "Take, eat; this is My body which is broken for you; do this in remembrance of Me." In the same manner He also took the cup after supper, saying, "This cup is the new covenant in My blood. This do, as often as you drink it, in remembrance of Me." For as often as you eat this bread and drink this cup, you proclaim the Lord's death till He comes.
—1 CORINTHIANS 11:23–26; READ ALSO VV. 17–34

We remember that the Last Supper was actually a Passover meal when Jesus celebrated the remembrance of Israel's deliverance from Egypt to the Promised Land.

The unleavened bread had the scorch-mark stripes and the holes from baking that looked like "pierce" marks. In the same way Jesus' body was broken for us. It was broken for our healing. 1 Peter 2:24 says: *"who Himself bore our sins in His own body on the tree, that we, having died to sins, might live for righteousness—by whose stripes you were healed."* This is a quote from Isaiah 53:4–6 which foretold the crucifixion, and what Jesus' work on the cross would mean. His body was whipped, beaten, and striped for me, and by His stripes, I was healed. When we receive the bread, we receive by faith the healing that it provided. We will no longer be weak, sick, and we won't die early.

In the same manner, He took the cup saying it was the new covenant in His blood. We recognize the juice represents His blood that was shed for the remission of sins. And *"without the shedding of blood there is no remission (of sin)"* (Hebrews 9:22). Now, because of the blood He shed, we can be born again and receive the righteousness of God in Christ (2 Corinthians 5:21).

We do this to proclaim the Lord's death and look forward to the coming of Jesus and the marriage supper of the Lamb!

PRAYER: *Father in heaven, thank You for sending Your only Son to die for our sins and purchase healing for us as well! We will never forget the sacrifice on the cross! Amen!*

GIFT OF THE HOLY SPIRIT

But the manifestation of the Spirit is given to each one for the profit of all....
—1 Corinthians 12:7–10; read also 1 Corinthians 12

Following is a definition of each gift of the Spirit:

+ *Word of wisdom:* supernatural wisdom that gives a person wisdom in making decisions given supernaturally in the moment. It is not wisdom gained through experience and knowledge.

+ *Word of knowledge:* a supernatural knowledge of facts that does not come through study, research or experience.

+ *Faith:* an unshakeable conviction given by God that He is going to act supernaturally in a particular situation. *"Have faith in God."* It is different than saving faith.

+ *Gifts of healing:* supernatural action to bring a sick person to physical, emotional or spiritual health. It is not something we can do in our own strength or ability.

+ *Working of miracles:* God uses us to bring about a miracle by His divine power.

+ *Prophecy:* Speaking a message inspired by the Holy Spirit, especially for the "edification, exhortation and comfort of others."

+ *Tongues:* speech inspired by the Holy Spirit in a language the speaker does not understand and has not learned.

+ *Interpretation of tongues:* a supernatural ability to understand the message and to proclaim it in a language understood by the listeners.

Randy Clark gave this testimony of the gifts in one of his meetings in Ukraine. "There was a Jewish man who was a Holocaust survivor. He came in a wheelchair, having been unable to walk for some years. There was a word of knowledge for the man. He stood in response. When he did, he was healed. Later he accepted Yeshua as his Messiah."[6] Here we see the gifts of a word of knowledge, healing, and miracles."

Prayer: *Praise You Lord, that Your gifts are for today! Amen!*

LOVE FOR ONE ANOTHER

Love bears all things, believes all things, hopes all things endures all things. Love never fails.
    —1 Corinthians 13:7; read also 1 Corinthians 13

Really. Who has this kind of love? We might have hoped that Paul would have chosen anything but *"bears ALL things." "All things"* covers everything! God calls us farther and deeper into love for Him, for one another, and for a perishing world.

+ Love bears all things. Love covers. As it is said in 1 Peter 4:8: *"And above all things, have fervent love for one another, for love will cover a multitude of sins."* This means that it never proclaims the errors of good men.
    + I would, my brothers and sisters, that we could all imitate the pearl oyster. A hurtful particle intrudes itself into its shell, and this vexes and grieves it. It cannot eject the evil, and what does it do but cover it with a precious substance extracted out of its own life, by which it turns the intruder into a pearl.[7]

+ Love believes all things: We, of course, will not believe a lie, but will we receive or believe an evil report? We must believe the best of people and not pass along an evil report. If someone comes with an evil report, ask how you can be a part of the solution.

+ Love hopes all things: Love has confidence in the future and puts its trust in God for His solution. Love is never pessimistic. It doesn't see the glass as half empty, but it sees it half full. *"Now may the God of hope fill you with all joy and peace in believing, that you may abound in hope by the power of the Holy Spirit"* (Romans 15:13).

+ Love endures all things: Most of us can bear all things, and believe all things, and hope all things, but only for a while! Agape love (the God kind of love) doesn't give up. Love never fails.

PRAYER: *"And now abide faith, hope, and love, these three; but the greatest of these is love"* (v. 13). Help us to love! Amen!

MIGHTY TOOL IN INTERCESSION

I wish you all spoke with tongues....
—1 Corinthians 14:5; read also vv. 1–20

The gift of tongues is speech inspired by the Holy Spirit in a language the speaker does not understand. In First Corinthians, Paul seems to speak about two different forms of this gift: tongues as a language for personal prayer and praise, and tongues as a public message for the congregation.

Tongues as a prayer language is a means by which the Holy Spirit enables a person to praise and thank God in a way that bypasses the mind and comes directly from the heart. It is a gift given when we are baptized in the Holy Spirit (Acts 2:4). Paul says in 1 Corinthians 14:2, *"For one who speaks in a tongue speaks not to men but to God, for no one understands him, but he utters mysteries in the Spirit."* "One of the most beautiful forms of this gift is when a whole congregation is singing in tongues together, in a rising and falling harmony inspired by the Holy Spirit, worshiping God with one voice."[8]

Tongues as a prayer language is the only spiritual gift that Paul notes as being beneficial to the one using it (1 Corinthians 14:4). It also is a mighty tool in intercession—in praying for others. Sometimes we don't know how to pray as we ought, but the Spirit intercedes through us with deep groanings (Romans 8:26–27).

The gift of tongues in the second sense can be a message for the church. It must be followed by an interpretation, so people can understand it and be built up by it. *"One who speaks in a tongue should pray that he may interpret"* (1 Corinthians 14:13). This then becomes a form of prophecy.

Paul said in verse 18 that *"I thank my God I speak with tongues more than you all."* If he needed it, so do we!

Prayer: *We thank You Lord for these beautiful and wonderful and useful gifts You have given us! More, Lord! Amen!*

USE YOUR GIFT AT THE RIGHT TIME

How is it brethren? Whenever you come together, each of you has a psalm, has a teaching, has a tongue, has a revelation, has an interpretation. Let all things be done for edification. If anyone speaks in a tongue, let there be two or at the most three, each in turn, and let one interpret. But if there is no interpreter, let him keep silent in church and let him speak to himself and to God. Let two or three prophets speak, and let the others judge...For you can all prophesy one by one, that all may learn and all may be encouraged. And the spirits of the prophets are subject to the prophets.
—1 CORINTHIANS 14:26–29; READ ALSO VV. 31–32, 21–40

Paul sees the gathering of the church as a time when people come to participate and to give to one another, not merely to passively receive. In the small groups someone might contribute by reading or singing a psalm. Another might offer a word of teaching. Someone might pray in a tongue and another give the interpretation. Someone else might have a revelation, a word from God's heart.

The goal of coming together as a church is not to be entertained, nor even to receive a blessing, but we gather for edification. We are built up so we can live lives that glorify Jesus Christ outside the walls of the church.

Paul gives instructions for proper order in the church. If someone speaks in a tongue (this is a message for the body, not private tongues), then there must be an interpreter. If not, don't give the message. Also limit prophecies to two or three.

This is wonderful. You can all prophesy one by one, that all may learn and all be encouraged. In fact, Paul has said in 1 Corinthians 1:1, *"Pursue love and desire spiritual gifts, but especially that you may prophesy."* We are to desire and ask for the gifts! He ends this section by saying that the spirits of the prophets are subject to the prophets. That means you are in control. You can pray and prophesy whenever it is the right time. The exercising of the gift is under your control.

PRAYER: *Thank You, Lord, that we submit to You in the gifts. When You prompt, we speak. We bring glory to You. Amen.*

August 24

THE MYSTERY OF CHRIST

*For I delivered to you first of all that which I also received: that Christ
died for our sins according to the Scriptures, and that He was buried,
and that He rose again the third day according to the Scriptures.*
—1 CORINTHIANS 15:3–4; READ ALSO VV. 1–28

This is a most amazing Scripture and is well worth memorizing in
order to share the core of the gospel concisely and powerfully. This
gospel is not just insightful teaching or good advice. At the core of it
are things that happened—actual, real, historical events. Our faith is
not based upon opinions, but upon facts.

Christ died: This is the center of the gospel. How did He die?
The Roman government executed Him by one of the most cruel and
excruciating forms of capital punishment ever devised: crucifixion.
The stripes on His back, His hands and feet nailed to the crossbeam:
these things caused excruciating pain.

He died for our sins. The Father laid upon Him all the guilt and
wrath our sin deserved and satisfied the wrath of the Father against
sin. *"He was wounded for our transgressions, He was bruised for our
iniquities; the chastisement for our peace was upon Him, and by His
stripes we are healed"* (Isaiah 53:5).

He was buried: This is a very important part of the gospel. It is
positive proof that He really died. It also fulfilled Scripture that *"they
made His grave with the wicked; but with the rich at His death"* (Isaiah
53:9).

He rose again the third day according to the Scriptures: Jesus proclaimed He would rise three days after His death (Matthew 16:21;
17:23; 20:19). *"And if Christ is not risen, then our preaching is empty
and your faith is also empty"* (v. 14). Then He was seen by Cephas,
then by the twelve, then by over five hundred brothers at once, by
James, and then by Paul himself.

PRAYER: *Hallelujah for the resurrection! And now He goes to prepare a
place for us and will come again for us soon. Amen.*

GOD CONQUERED DEATH

...Death is swallowed up in victory. O Death, where is your sting? O Hades, where is your victory? The sting of death is sin, and the strength of sin is the law. But thanks be to God, who gives us the victory through our Lord Jesus Christ. Therefore, my beloved brethren, be steadfast, immovable, always abounding in the work of the Lord, knowing that your labor is not in vain in the Lord.
—1 CORINTHIANS 15:54b–58; READ ALSO VV. 29–58

Because of the resurrection, Paul can almost taunt death, because death has no power over the person found in Jesus Christ. Death has no sting to the believer. For those not in Christ, death still has its sting.

> The sting of death lay in this, that we had sinned and were summoned to appear before the God whom we had offended. This is the sting of death to you, unconverted ones, not that you are dying, but that after death is the judgment, and that you must stand before the Judge of the quick and dead to receive a sentence for the sins which you have committed in your body against him.[9]

The strength of sin is the law, but we are not under the law any longer. We are no longer subject to the penalty of the law and we are set free from sin. It is Jesus who gives us the victory! Death is swallowed up in victory!

Because we know death is defeated and we have an eternal, resurrected destiny with Jesus Christ, we should stand all the more firm and unshakable for Him right now. We must not let discouragements cause us to want to quit. We must always remember that our labor is never in vain in the Lord. We don't need to waver, or give up, but instead, we must remain steadfast to the end. *"For our light affliction, which is but for a moment, is working for us a far more exceeding and eternal weight of glory"* (2 Corinthians 4:17). We must finish strong! We have His promises of victory!

PRAYER: *O victory in Jesus, our Savior forever. You sought us and You bought us, with Your redeeming blood! Amen!*

August 26

BLESSING IN TITHING

Now concerning the collection of the saints, as I have given orders to the churches of Galatia, so you must do also: On the first day of the week let each one of you lay something aside, storing up as he may prosper, that there be no collections when I come. And when I come, whomever you approve by your letters I will send to bear your gift to Jerusalem.
—1 CORINTHIANS 16:1–3; READ ALSO 1 CORINTHIANS 16

The Bible teaches us about tithing and giving. In the above passage the saints were asked to give to the church of Jerusalem. This is an offering. Offerings are to be above and beyond the tithe. There is a great blessing in giving to the poor. *"He who has pity on the poor lends to the Lord, and He will pay back what he has given"* (Proverbs 6:38). *"Give and it shall be given to you: good measure, pressed down, shaken together, and running over will be put into your bosom. For with the same measure that you use, it will be measured back to you"* (Luke 6:38).

We are taught about tithing in the book of Malachi: *"'Bring all the tithes into the storehouse, that there may be food in My house, and try Me now in this,' says the Lord of hosts, 'If I will not open for you the windows of heaven and pour out for you such blessing that there will not be room enough to receive it. And I will rebuke the devourer for your sakes, so that he will not destroy the fruit of your ground, nor shall the vine fail to bear fruit for you in the field,' says the Lord of hosts"* (v. 9–11).

Bringing the tithes into the storehouse is bringing the tenth of all your income into the church where you attend. The church we attend is our storehouse from which we are fed. Jesus says we cannot serve both God and mammon. When we give the tithes and offerings, we will be protected from serving the god of mammon and the snare of materialism. If we put the Lord first in this, He promises He will rebuke the devourer for us. In other words, when others have financial woes, sickness, lawsuits, break downs of appliances and machinery, we will be protected from this. We will walk in God's blessing.

PRAYER: *We love the blessings in tithing! We love to be cheerful givers and have an unselfish and giving heart. Amen.*

August 27

GOD OF ALL COMFORT

Blessed be the God and Father of our Lord Jesus Christ, the Father of mercies and God of all comfort, who comforts us in all our tribulation, that we may be able to comfort those who are in any trouble, with the comfort with which we ourselves are comforted by God.
—2 CORINTHIANS 1:3–4; READ ALSO 2 CORINTHIANS 1

Our God is a Father of mercies and a God of all comfort. Comfort comes from the Greek word *paraklesis*. The idea behind this word in the New Testament is always more than just sympathy. It means strengthening, helping, making strong. The Latin word for comfort also means "brave." [10]

We also know that the Holy Spirit is a Comforter (John 14:16). And Jesus is our Comforter and Strengthener in temptations (Hebrews 2:18).

We receive this comfort and help so that when others are going through trials, we can comfort them with the comfort that we ourselves have received. I know after my mother died, I was able to give comfort and peace to those who also had lost loved ones.

Mr. Knox, (Scottish preacher during the Reformation) a little before his death, rose out of his bed; and being asked wherefore, being so sick, he would offer to rise? He answered that he had had sweet meditations of the resurrection of Jesus Christ that night, and now he would go into the pulpit, and impart to others the comforts that he felt in his soul.[11]

PRAYER: *Father in Heaven, as we are going through this global coronavirus "Divine Pause," what a perfect time to reach out to bring strength, help and comfort to those around us! What an important time to pray for those affected by this sickness for their peace, healing and protection. What a wonderful time to draw close to You, our Comforter. Help us not to miss opportunities to bring comfort to others. Amen.*

IN CHRIST, WE ARE MORE
THAN CONQUERORS

Now thanks be to God who always leads us in triumph in Christ,
and through us diffuses the fragrance of His knowledge in every place.
For we are to God the fragrance of Christ among those who are being
saved and among those who are perishing.
—2 Corinthians 2:14–15; read also 2 Corinthians 2

Jesus is our victorious, conquering general in a triumphal parade. A
Roman triumphal parade was given to successful generals as they
returned from their conquests.

> In a Triumph the procession of the victorious general marched
> through the streets of Rome to the Capitol…First came the state
> officials and the senate. Then came the trumpeters. Then were car-
> ried the spoils taken from the conquered land…. Then came the pic-
> tures of the conquered land and models of conquered citadels and
> ships. Then followed the white bull for sacrifice which would be
> made. Then there walked the captive princes, leaders and generals in
> chains, shortly to be flung into prison and in all probability almost
> immediately to be executed…. Then they were followed by the musi-
> cians with their lyres; then the priests swinging their censers with
> the sweet-smelling incense burning in them. After that came the gen-
> eral himself….Finally came the army wearing all their decorations
> and shouting their cry of triumph! As the procession moved through
> the streets, all decorated and garlanded, amid the cheering crowds, it
> made a tremendous day which might happen only once in a lifetime.[12]

That is the picture that is in Paul's mind. He sees Christ marching
in triumph through the world, and himself in that conquering train.

Incense was common in these parades. To Paul, this fragrance is
like the sweet perfume of our lives. It is the breath and fragrance of a
life hidden with Christ in God.

Prayer: *Lord, thank You that You always lead us in a triumphal*
procession. We are more than conquerors in You! Amen!

TRANSFORMED PEOPLE OF GOD

But we all, with unveiled face, beholding as in a mirror the glory of the Lord, are being transformed into the same image from glory to glory, just as by the Spirit of the Lord.
> —2 CORINTHIANS 3:18; READ ALSO 2 CORINTHIANS 3

Paul invites every Christian to a special, glorious intimacy with God. This is a relationship and transforming power that is not just for a few privileged Christians, but it can belong to all.

What is an unveiled face? *"When one turns to the Lord, the veil is taken away"* (2 Corinthians 3:16). If we will turn to the Lord, He will take away the veil and we can behold His glory.

We can see the glory of the Lord but not perfectly. A mirror in the ancient world did not give nearly as good a reflection as our mirrors do today. Ancient mirrors were made of polished metal, and gave a clouded, fuzzy, somewhat distorted image.

There may be another thought here also.

Now as mirrors, among the Jews, Greeks, and Romans, were made of highly polished metal, it would often happen, especially in strong light, that the face would be greatly illuminated by this strongly reflected light; and Paul seems to allude to this circumstance.[13]

In any case, as we behold the glory of God, we will be transformed from the inside out. Though the old covenant had its glory, it could never transform lives through the law. God uses the new covenant to make us transformed people, not just nice people. The more time we spend in His word and in His presence and in prayer, the more we will look like Him and be transformed into His glory. When we look into "God's mirror," it shows us what we are becoming. This is the key to "being changed" from glory to glory.

PRAYER: *Lord, we call forth the glory of God to arise, shine, and appear on us as Isaiah prophesied in Isaiah 60 and as was seen on both Jesus and Moses. In Jesus' name. Amen.*

August 30

BLESSED TO BE CALLED

But we have this treasure in earthen vessels, that the excellence of the power may be of God and not of us. We are hard-pressed on every side, yet not crushed; we are perplexed, but not in despair; persecuted, but not forsaken; struck down but not destroyed—always carrying about in the body the dying of the Lord Jesus, that the life of Jesus also may be manifested in our body.
—2 Corinthians 4:7–10; read also 2 Corinthians 4

We have had the privilege of taking many mission trips and most recently have gone to minister in Bangladesh. An example of a man from Bangladesh who lived the above verses was Abdul Wadud Munshi, who was the son of a Muslim priest. He became a Christian as a boy and received his theological training in a mission school.

Upon conversion, Abdul was rejected by his own family. His parents and brother, soon after his profession of faith, tied him to bamboos and put him in a pond for three days. His own mother mocked him and told him that his "Jesus" would allow him to die if he didn't renounce this new religion. He told them that he was ready to die, but he would not denounce his Lord. The rest of the family finally intervened.

One day Abdul chanced to read a book by Mrs. Woodworth-Etter describing the outpouring of the Holy Spirit throughout the world. Abdul received the infilling or baptism of the Spirit after coming in touch with Assemblies of God missionaries in Purulia, India. He returned to Bangladesh and had a powerful Pentecostal ministry among Muslims, Hindus, and nominal Christians and established several churches.[14]

We have had the honor and privilege of ministering with his grandson, Jonathan Munshi, General Superintendent of the Bangladesh Assemblies of God. We have been a part of seeing thousands of people come to Christ in Bangladesh.

Prayer: *We are declaring that everyone that reads this devotional will be used in missions somewhere in some way! Amen!*

AMBASSADORS FOR CHRIST

Now then, we are ambassadors for Christ, as though God were pleading through us: we implore you on Christ's behalf, be reconciled to God. For He made Him who knew no sin to be sin for us, that we might become the righteousness of God in Him.
—2 CORINTHIANS 5:20–21; READ ALSO 2 CORINTHIANS 5

Just think of it, dear ones. We are ambassadors for Christ! An ambassador does not speak to please his audience, but the King who sent him. An ambassador does not speak on his own authority; his own opinions or demands mean little. He simply says what he has been commissioned to say. He is a representative of the King and the honor and reputation of his country are in his hands. We are representatives for Christ! As His ambassadors we implore others to be reconciled to God. We do not speak to please our audience, but our King Jesus who sent us. We need to lead others to make things right with God, not the other way around.

How did God make reconciliation possible? He made Him who knew no sin to be sin for us. Jesus was not a sinner, even on the cross. On the cross, the Father treated Him as if He were a sinner, yet all the while, sin was "outside" of Jesus not "inside" Him and it was not a part of His nature (as it is with us).

When we accept the payment He made for our sins, we become the righteousness of God in Christ. Righteousness simply defined is RIGHT STANDING WITH GOD. It gives us the ability to be free of guilt, condemnation, and shame. Guilt says, "I *made* a mistake." Shame says, "I *am* a mistake."

Righteousness is actually received at salvation. Because many have not understood the righteousness of God, which is by faith, they have failed to experience the full joy of God's gift.

PRAYER: *Thank You Lord that in our spirit man, we are fully righteous and made in the image and likeness of Christ. His nature, character, power and glory have been given to us. Amen.*

September 1

AVOID UNGODLY INFLUENCE

Do not be unequally yoked together with unbelievers. For what fellowship has righteousness with lawlessness? And what communion has light with darkness? And what accord has Christ with Belial?... Therefore come out from among them and be separate, says the Lord.
—2 Corinthians 6:14–15, 17a; read also 2 Corinthians 6

These are verses that will protect one from a lifelong disaster in marriage. The idea of being unequally yoked comes from Deuteronomy 22:9 which prohibited yoking together two different animals. It speaks of joining two things that should not be joined.

If a man or woman marries an unconverted person, the outcome could affect them in two ways: they will either compromise on their beliefs and become backslidden, or they will carry a very heavy cross all their lives as they try to please the Lord and try to please their spouse. Then there is the matter of the children. Will the spouse allow them to be brought up to serve the Lord, or will the spouse's influence in the ways of darkness be the thing the children want to follow? Will the converted spouse always be the one to lead in prayer at mealtime, or will family devotions and prayers be done away with? The Bible says the spiritual head of the house should be the man. Will the woman have to take that over if the husband is unsaved? What will the relationship be with the grandparents and extended family? Will they be in unity? How will it affect family conversations? Will it be acceptable to talk about the Lord or spiritual things, or will that subject have to be avoided because it makes the unconverted person uncomfortable? What about the choice of church? Will the converted spouse be able to choose a Bible-believing, Spirit-filled church? Will the spouse even want to go to church?

This unequal yoke could also come through a book, a movie, a T.V. show, a magazine, or even through worldly Christian friends. We can't let ungodly things influence our minds. "Evil company corrupts good habits." (1 Corinthians 15:33).

PRAYER: *Father give us discernment in these important matters! We pray for Christian spouses for our families! Amen!*

TRUE REPENTANCE

For godly sorrow produces repentance leading to salvation, not to be regretted; but the sorrow of the world produces death.
—2 Corinthians 7:10; read also 2 Corinthians 7

What is real repentance? The Greek word for repentance is *metanoia*: a change of mind or purpose. It is fully turning to God without reservation or excuse. Godly sorrow leading to repentance is a gift of God's grace based on love for God and other people, and recognition and sorrow for the wounding we have caused.

We read about true repentance in 2 Samuel 12. In this chapter, David sinned with Bathsheba, and a child was conceived. Then David had her husband sent to the front lines of battle where he would be killed. When David was confronted for his sin, he accepted the truth and made no excuses. He didn't blame someone else for his sin. He took responsibility for his actions and was willing to face the consequences and change one hundred and eighty degrees. He wrote in Psalm 51:17, "*The sacrifices of God are a broken spirit; a broken and contrite heart, O God, You will not despise.*"

The opposite of repentance is remorse which produces death. Saul is an example of this in 1 Samuel 15. In this chapter, Saul didn't wait for the priest Samuel to give the sacrifice, but offered it himself. Only priests were allowed to give sacrifices. Saul was sorry but didn't face his own sin. He wanted to cover his tracks with pride and self-exaltation (v. 12). He blamed others (v. 15a) and offered "good reasons" for disobedience (v. 15b). Remorse is feeling sorry that you "got caught." The result was that Saul lost his mind, his kingdom, and lived the rest of his life in disillusionment.

Prayer: *Father, we ask for the gift of true heartfelt repentance to follow David's example, and make no excuses for our sin. Amen.*

WE ARE RICH BECAUSE WE HAVE CHRIST

But as you abound in everything—in faith, in speech, in knowledge, in all diligence, and in your love for us—see that you abound in this grace (of giving) also. For you know the grace of our Lord Jesus Christ, that though He was rich, yet for your sakes He became poor, that you through His poverty might become rich.
—2 Corinthians 8:7, 9; read also 2 Corinthians 8

We begin our services at Hope Harbor Church in Murray, KY with saying: "This is my Bible. I am what it says I am. I have what it says I have. I can do what it says I can do." We *"abound in everything."* We have all we need in every area.

Through the grace of the Lord Jesus, though He was rich He became poor. The Greek word for poor here means to be destitute, reduced to extreme poverty. He did this that we might be rich; that we would always have what we need.

Marilyn Hickey in her book, *"It's Not Over Until You Win,"* tells a story about her first huge budget shortfall when they were airing on four hundred and eighty eight stations across the US and airing their daily program on television. They were behind seventy thousand dollars on their bills. She said it might as well have been seventy million dollars, because it looked so impossible.

While she was trying to figure this out, she was asked to preach at a church in New York in order to raise money for the Teen Challenge ministry. The amount they needed to raise was seventy thousand dollars. She was asking God why He asked her to raise for someone else what she needed! God reminded her of Daniel 6:16 where the Scripture showed how Daniel served God faithfully, right up to the point he was thrown into the lion's den. He was asking her to obey Him. God gave her the gift of faith, and special anointing, and they raised seventy thousand dollars! Several days later, seventy thousand dollars came in to meet her need also! Through His becoming poor, we became rich![1]

Prayer: *We praise You that You are the God of miracles and provision. Nothing is too hard for You! Amen!*

September 4

SOW GENEROUSLY

Remember this: Whoever sows sparingly will also reap sparingly, and whoever sows generously will also reap generously. Each man should give what he has decided in his heart to give, not reluctantly or under compulsion, for God loves a cheerful giver. And God is able to make all grace abound to you, so that in all things at all times, having all that you need, you will abound in every good work.
—2 Corinthians 9:6–8, niv; read also 2 Corinthians 9

This means that if we sow (give) with a teaspoon, we will reap with a teaspoon. If we sow by the truckload, we will reap by the truckload.

My husband's mother, Emma Kruger, was a tither. She was the church's financial secretary. In those days, churches allowed the offering money to be taken home to be counted. So, my husband and his siblings helped their mom count the money.

There were doctors and lawyers in the congregation, but the kids noticed their mom was giving more than they were on her tithe. This was a matter of faith for her, as her husband had died of cancer, and she was raising six children on her own. She looked to the Lord as her provider.

Then one day, one of the boys needed his appendix to be removed. There was no money in the family's bank account to pay for this operation. Jim's mom went to the hospital to come up with a payment plan for the bill. But upon her arrival, she was told that someone had already paid it!

We have always paid our tithe and have seen how God has "rebuked the devourer" for us (Malachi 3:10–11). We have been healthy and protected from many accidents that could have been fatal. Our car would break down as we were pulling into our driveway or right by a station where it could be repaired. We don't owe debts because the Lord has always supplied our needs! We have always been able to give to those in need as well. We realize it is by His grace.

Prayer: *Thank You, Lord, for the example of godly parents who obeyed Your Word, and the blessings have come down through the generations. Amen.*

September 5

ELIMINATING STRONGHOLDS

For the weapons of our warfare are not carnal but mighty in God for pulling down strongholds, casting down arguments and every high thing that exalts itself against the knowledge of God, bringing every thought into captivity to the obedience of Christ.
—2 Corinthians 10:4–5; read also 2 Corinthians 10

Mike Bickle in his book *Growing in Prayer* gives excellent definitions for three types of "strongholds," which are lies that are against God's truth. Here is a paraphrase of these three:[2]

+ Personal strongholds of the mind that bind people in sinful mind-sets and lifestyles. An example would be alcohol and drug addiction, pornography, etc.

+ Cultural strongholds, or values in our society, that are in agreement with darkness. Cultural strongholds are agreements with Satan's values in our society at large. Examples of this would be Charles Darwin's theory of natural selection which opposes biblical creation.

+ Cosmic strongholds are demonic powers and principalities that control whole nations. Examples are abortion and gay marriage (Exodus 20:13; Jude 7).

We dismantle these strongholds by agreeing with God and renouncing the enemies' lies through prayer and action. This includes:

+ Worship and praise (Psalm 149; 2 Chronicles 20:15–29).
+ Fasting (Isaiah 58:6).
+ Binding and Loosing (Matthew 18:18–19).

Binding the enemy is like a cowboy in a rodeo roping a calf, jumping off the horse and tying up its legs so it cannot move. Then he throws up his hands in victory. We bind (forbid) the enemy by speaking the Word of God. Example: "Satan, I bind you in the Name of Jesus from bringing strife." Then we lose (permit) peace. *"For he himself is our peace who has made both one and broken down the middle wall of partition…"* (Ephesians 2:14).

Prayer: *Help us to use Your weapons, Lord! In Jesus' Name!*

DISCERNING THE THINGS OF GOD

For if he who comes preaches another Jesus whom we have not preached, or if you receive a different spirit which you have not received, or a different gospel which you have not accepted—you may well put up with it.
—2 CORINTHIANS 11:4; READ ALSO VV. 1–15

It was right that Paul was afraid that the serpent might deceive them away from simple truth of the gospel by preaching another Jesus.

This actually happened in 1913 at a Maria Woodworth-Etter meeting in Los Angeles. A businessman had invited her to come and speak after he visited her healing meetings in Dallas. When she came, thousands poured into the area for these meetings. The results were phenomenal, but it also birthed an issue that split the early Pentecostal Movement.

Early one morning John G. Scheppe, after praying through the night hours, received what he believed to be a new revelation concerning the power resident in the name of Jesus. He ran through the camp, waking everyone with this good news. Another man after searching the Scriptures, made the observation that the apostles baptized converts only in the name of Jesus. (This is in direct conflict with Matthew 28:19.) This started the "Jesus Only" or "Oneness movement."

Soon large groups were rebaptized in the name of Jesus even if they had already been baptized in the Trinity. This soon evolved into a denial of the Trinity. The result of this led to the Assemblies of God developing the "Sixteen Fundamental Truths" to give guidance to the church's teaching and protect from doctrinal errors and heresy. Sister Etter later called the "oneness" position "the biggest delusion the devil ever invented." [3]

PRAYER: *Father, sometimes the devil comes as "an angel of light." Give us, Your church, discerning of spirits to understand what is of You and what is not! In Jesus' name, Amen.*

THE PRICE OF SUFFERING
AND PERSISTENCE

From the Jews five times I received forty stripes minus one. Three times I was beaten with rods; once I was stoned; three times I was shipwrecked; a night and a day I have been in the deep; in journeys often, in perils of water, in perils of robbers, in perils of my own countrymen, in perils of the Gentiles, in perils in the city, in perils in the wilderness, in perils in the sea, in perils among false brethren; in weariness and toil, in sleeplessness often, in hunger and thirst, in fastings often, in cold and nakedness....
—2 CORINTHIANS 11:24–27; READ ALSO VV. 16–33

In this passage, Paul describes his own qualifications for ministry. Five times he was beaten with stripes. Deuteronomy 25:3 says: "Forty blows he may give him and no more...." Actually, the rabbis restricted the number of stripes to 39 because they feared there might be a miscount. The ancient Jewish writing tells how very cruel this was. "The scourge was made of leather divided into four tails. He who scourges lays one third on the criminal's breast, another third on his right shoulder, and another on his left...."[4]

This is the price that Paul paid for the gospel. How do we react to it? Perhaps one week of living this kind of life and we would be done, but he went through it for his whole life, and gloried in his tribulations. Do we take the Word of God for granted? Considering that Paul was beaten, stoned, shipwrecked, and still persevered, do we complain about our own trials? About church letting out late? About the color of the carpet?

When Paul said he gloried in tribulations, he truly lived it. In 2 Corinthians 4:17–18 he writes: "*For our light affliction, which is but for a moment, is working for us a far more exceeding and eternal weight of glory, while we do not look at the things which are seen, but at the things which are not seen. For the things which are seen are temporary, but the things which are not seen are eternal.*"

PRAYER: *Thank You for all those who have gone before us and paved the way through much suffering and persistence. Amen.*

September 8

HE HAS GONE TO PREPARE A PLACE FOR US

I know a man in Christ who fourteen years ago—whether in the body I do not know or whether out of the body I do not know, God knows—such a one was caught up to the third heaven. And I know such a one...how he was caught up into Paradise and heard inexpressible words, which it is not lawful for a man to utter.
—2 Corinthians 12:2–3a, 4; read also 2 Corinthians 12

These verses are about Paul's trip to the 3rd heaven.

Following is a testimony of another man's trip to heaven: Dr. Percy Collet had spent fifty years as a missionary to South America. He'd had many poisoned darts thrown at him, was attacked by wild animals and was forced to drink poison. In all these things, God saved him. When he was eighty two years old, he told how he had been taken to heaven for 5 ½ days and then experienced a 6 hour return trip to earth.

His soul body was transported to heaven by his guardian angel. He was ushered into the throne room where he could see the Throne of God from any place in heaven. The Throne is two thousand miles from the base to the top. The City foursquare is one thousand five hundred miles each way you look at it (Revelation 21:16).

He had many discussions there with Jesus, Paul, and John the Baptist. He saw different departments. The Pity Department was the place where the souls of aborted babies went and also severely retarded babies. Here they receive training before going to the Throne Room. There was also the Record Room, an immense area where all the "idle" words spoken by Christians are being retained until after Christians give an account of them or are judged.

Our mansions are beautiful and studded with diamonds and precious stones. The size of them is determined by how many souls are won to the Lord. Jesus is building mansions now. He said He was going to prepare a place for us (John 14).[5]

Prayer: *May we all have big mansions to meet with all the souls that You have enabled us to win to You! Amen!*

JESUS IN OUR HEART

Examine yourselves as to whether you are in the faith. Test yourselves. Do you not know yourselves, that Jesus Christ is in you?—unless indeed you are disqualified.
—2 Corinthians 13:5; read also 2 Corinthians 13

What are we to look for when we examine and test ourselves? We are to see if Jesus is in us. The true Christian carries the Cross in his heart. If the Cross is there, then all the crosses of this world's troubles will seem to you to be light enough, and you will be able to bear it. What does it mean to have Jesus in your heart? It means that you believe in Jesus as your Savior, that you love Him and trust Him. It means He is your daily bread and that you are the temple of the Holy Spirit. As the old hymn *"In the Garden"* says: *"And He walks with me and He talks with me. And He tells me I am His own."*

Am I really in the faith? Here are some questions to ask:

+ Have I asked Jesus to be my Lord, as well as my Savior?

+ Do I love Him? If I love Him, I will obey His commands. Do I love my neighbor as myself?

+ Do I love His church? He said not to forsake the gathering together of believers (Hebrews 10:25).

+ Do I give tithes to the church? Do I give to the poor?

+ Do I love to spend time with Him in His Word every day?

+ Do I pray without ceasing?

+ Have I asked Jesus to baptize me in the Holy Spirit? He said: *"Be filled with the Spirit, speaking to yourselves in psalms and hymns and spiritual songs* (Ephesians 5:18).

+ Do I have His peace? *"Peace I leave with you. My peace I give to you. Not as the world gives, give I unto you. Let not your heart be troubled, neither let it be afraid"* (John 14:27).

Prayer: *Create in me a clean heart, O God. And renew a right spirit within me. Cast me not away from Your presence and take not Your Holy Spirit from me. Restore to me the joy of my salvation and renew a right spirit within me (Psalm 51:10–12). Amen.*

September 10

PAUL'S TEACHING ON BAPTISM

Did you receive the Holy Spirit when you believed?
—ACTS 19:2; READ ALSO VV. 1–18

Here we have one of the clearest teachings from Paul about the different kinds of baptisms. Paul doesn't seem to have any doubt in his mind that someone can come to saving faith in Jesus Christ yet not receive the fullness of the Holy Spirit. In other words, Paul knows that a person can be baptized by the Spirit into Christ (salvation), yet not be baptized by Jesus into the Holy Spirit. Paul asked the Ephesians about their baptism. Into what were you baptized?

- John's baptism. It was a baptism of repentance. Even Jesus in setting an example, was baptized by John.
- Water baptism. Then Paul baptized them in water in the name of Christ Jesus. This is a work of grace, in and upon the heart of man. Of course, being baptized in water doesn't save us. Rather the act of being immersed in water is symbolic in an outward way of what has happened to us inwardly, symbolizing the death and burial of our old sinful self and the raising up of the "new creation" mentioned in 2 Corinthians 5:17.
- Baptism in the Holy Spirit. When Paul laid his hands on them, they were filled with the Holy Spirit and they all spoke with tongues and prophesied. This was the baptism of power. This was the common New Testament pattern of baptisms.

Marilyn Hickey has a powerful testimony along these lines. At first, she was not interested in being Spirit-filled. God told her one night that He had dealt with her for four years about being Spirit-filled. If you resist, you'll never marry Wally Hickey or fulfil what I have for you. She repented and was gloriously filled with the Holy Spirit and spoke in tongues. This was the door to the miracle ministry that has taken the gospel of salvation and the healing power of God to millions of people in hundreds of nations.[6]

PRAYER: *Father, what an example of fruitfulness! Amen!*

September 11

POWER OF GOD OVER HIDDEN
THINGS OF THE DARKNESS

Also, many of those who had practiced magic brought their books together and burned them in the sight of all. And they counted up the value of them, and it totaled fifty thousand pieces of silver. So the word of the Lord grew mightily and prevailed.
—Acts 19:19–20; read also vv. 19–41

Before the incident of the book burning, we see that God worked unusual miracles by the hands of Paul, so that even handkerchiefs from him, when laid on the sick, would bring healing. The seven sons of Sceva tried to perform these acts of power, but when they tried to cast out demons by the Name of Jesus whom Paul preaches, the demons jumped on them and they ran away naked. They did not have a personal relationship with Christ, so the demons declared: *"Jesus I know, and Paul I know; but who are you?"* (v. 15).

In other words, the name of Jesus could not be used as some magic formula. This defeat for the sons of Sceva was really a defeat for magic in general because it resulted in a great public book burning by the converted sorcerers of the city. "The value of the burned books was about fifty thousand days' wages or four million dollars in today's economy at ten dollars an hour."[7] Verse 20 again reports on church growth associated with the Holy Spirit's power ministries. *Note:* Perhaps there are books, CD's, video games that we need to get rid of. One example could be the Harry Potter books. Harry Potter learns he is a wizard (male witch) and is accepted into Hogwarts School of Witchcraft and Wizardry. This is introducing readers to such things as witchcraft, sorcery, spells and spiritual power apart from God. It presents occult practices as normative and good. Reports have shown that young people after reading these books are going to Google to inquire how they can become a witch.

Prayer: *Father, thank You for bringing hidden things of darkness to light and bringing truth to Your children! Amen!*

September 12

DO NOT TROUBLE YOURSELF

*And in a window sat a certain young man named Eutychus, who
was sinking into a deep sleep. He was overcome by sleep; and as Paul
continued speaking, he fell down from the third story and was taken
up dead. But Paul went down, fell on him, and embracing him said,
"Do not trouble yourselves, for his life is in him."*
—ACTS 20:9–10; READ ALSO VV. 1–16

Paul certainly did not have a boring life! After the incidence of the
burning of books, etc., something really astounding happened at
Ephesus. A man by the name of Demetrius, who made silver shrines
of Diana (the Greek god of love and fertility) started having worries.
He was concerned that his livelihood would cease to exist if Paul kept
turning people from false gods to Jesus. He said, *"So not only is this
trade of ours in danger of falling into disrepute, but also the temple of
the great goddess Diana may be despised and her magnificence destroyed,
whom all Asia and the world worship"* (Acts 19:27). The temple of
Diana was one of the seven wonders of the world and was four times
the size of the Parthenon. So, a riot occurred, and the people shouted
for about two hours, *"Great is Diana of the Ephesians."* The city clerk
quieted the crowd down, and Paul left for Macedonia.

While he was in Troas, he was preaching late into the night when
Eutychus fell out the window and died. What can we learn from
this? (If you can't stay awake, don't sit in the back row—especially
the window.) Paul simply went down and raised him from the dead.

God still raises people from the dead who die in church. In March
2020, an older man died in our church service at Hope Harbor
Church in Murray. The people at church gathered around him and
prayed while the doctors did CPR, and he was raised from the dead!
Nothing is impossible for God!

PRAYER: *Father in heaven, we thank You for Your Word and for the
price Your servants paid to follow Christ and write the Word down.
Thank You that it is a plumb line for truth! Amen!*

September 13

ATTITUDE OF GIVING

And remember the words of the Lord Jesus, that He said, "It is more blessed to give than to receive."
—Acts 20:5b; read also vv. 17–38

"The evidence of God's grace," said the Presbyterian revivalist Charles G. Finney, "was a person's benevolence toward others," and this principle was borne out of the Second Great Awakening (1800–1830's) in the United States.[8]

During the powerful evangelical revivalism of these years, church growth was stimulated, particularly in America's main-line denominations. From the extraordinary energies generated by the evangelical movement, numerous benevolent societies emerged. Originally devoted to the salvation of souls, the mission of some of these societies eventually expanded to the eradication of every kind of social ill, such as drinking and gambling, slavery, no voting rights for women, and freemasonry. Finney and Nash actually attributed the outpouring of the Awakening to entire denominations recanting of freemasonry. Freemasonry is a Secret Society which is very occultic; in the very first, or Blue Lodge degree, they kneel to the "Great Architect of the Universe," who is revealed in the 33rd degree as Lucifer.

It is interesting to note that when revivals take place, and people come to Christ, there is also a springing up of creativity to solve problems in society. The earliest and most important of these organizations included the American Education Society (1815), the American Bible Society (1816), the American Sunday School Union (1824), the American Tract Society (1825), and the American Home Missionary Society (1826). This powerful network of benevolent organizations had local branches existing in almost every town and city, especially in the Northeast.

Prayer: *May Your church, Father, be known as those who give, but may we also have the humility to receive as well. May we find the solutions to our social problems today, such as abortions, teen pregnancies, suicide, racism, drugs, and alcohol! Amen!*

POWER OF APOSTOLIC PRAYER

...that the God of our Lord Jesus Christ, the Father of glory, may give to you the spirit of wisdom and revelation in the knowledge of Him, the eyes of your understanding being enlightened; that you may know what is the hope of His calling, what are the riches of the glory of His inheritance in the saints and what is the exceeding greatness of His power toward us who believe, according to the working of His mighty power which He worked in Christ when He raised Him from the dead and seated Him at His right hand in the heavenly places, far above all principality and power and might and dominion, and every name that is named, not only in this age but also in that which is to come. And He put all things under His feet, and gave Him to be head over all things to the church, which is His body, the fullness of Him who fills all in all.
—EPHESIANS 1:17–23; READ ALSO EPHESIANS 1

This is called an "Apostolic Prayer." These prayers of the apostles are valuable gifts to the church because they reveal God's burning heart for His people. They give us the language of His heart, and because God never changes, we can be assured that they are still burning in His heart today. These prayers are God-centered, positive and powerful. It is a very good idea to memorize this prayer and other Apostolic Prayers found in the New Testament. To make these prayers personal, put your name in each sentence where you see the word "you."

Paul prays that God would give us a spirit of wisdom and revelation in the knowledge of Him. Revelation knowledge is a gift from God. He also prays that we would know the hope of our calling. God has a calling for each of us. He planned this calling before the foundation of the earth (2 Timothy 1:9). As we seek Him, He will reveal it to us. He also prayed that we might know His power which is the same power that raised Christ from the dead. He is giving us revelation as to where Christ is seated, and the power He has. And since we are seated with Him; we are where He is, and then He delegates to us His power.

PRAYER: *Father in Heaven, teach us how to pray using these prayers. Give us revelation as to how powerful they are! Amen!*

SAVED BY GRACE

For by grace you have been saved through faith, and that not of your-selves; it is the gift of God, not of works, lest anyone should boast.
—Ephesians 2:8–9; read also Ephesians 2

Verse 1 in this chapter says we were dead in trespasses and sins. This means we were spiritually dead. We were also: *blind* (2 Corinthians 4:3–4); *a slave to sin* (Romans 6:17); *a lover of darkness* (John 3:19–20); *sick* (Mark 2:17); *lost* (Luke 15); *an alien, a stranger, a foreigner* (Ephesians 2:12, 2:19); *a child of wrath* (Ephesians 2:3); and *under the power of darkness* (Colossians 1:13).[9] We needed lots of help!

But, in these wonderful verses, we are saved by grace, through faith. It is not about how many works we have done. Salvation is a gift of God. If we could have worked our way to heaven through good works, then we could boast. But it is a gift of God, so we cannot boast. Here is a question to consider: If you were to die tonight, and God were to ask you why He should let you into heaven, what would you say? Many would say "It is because I have been a good person. I didn't kill anyone, I went to church, or even that I have been baptized or confirmed." We can see from this answer that they are depending on their good works to get them to heaven, but that will not work.

The Bible says, *"all have sinned and come short of the glory of God"* (Romans 3:23). It also says in James 2:10, *"For whoever shall keep the whole law, and yet stumble in one point, he is guilty of it all."* This means that if you have ever told one lie, you are guilty of breaking all of the ten commandments (Exodus 20). Jesus said, *"Except a man be born again, he cannot see the kingdom of God."* We must be born again. We must confess our sins and ask Jesus to be the Lord of our lives and follow Him. Following is a prayer you can pray to be born again.

Prayer: *I call upon You Lord today and ask that You will save me. I do confess my sins and invite You to be Lord of my life. I choose to follow You and be Your disciple. In Jesus' name. Amen.*

September 16

DEEPER EXISTENCE OF GOD'S LOVE

That He would grant you, according to the riches of His glory, to be strengthened with might through His Spirit in the inner man, that Christ may dwell in your hearts through faith; that you, being rooted and grounded in love, may be able to comprehend with all the saints what is the width and length and depth and height—to know the love of Christ which passes knowledge; that you may be filled with all the fullness of God. Now to Him who is able to do exceedingly abundantly above all that we ask or think, according to the power that works in us, to Him be glory in the church by Christ Jesus to all generations, forever and ever. Amen.
—EPHESIANS 3:16–21; READ ALSO EPHESIANS 3

This is a powerful prayer for supernatural strengthening of the heart, and a deeper experience of God's love.

First of all, we are praying for strengthening of the spirit in the inner man. There is an inner man just as real as our physical body. We know the importance of strength in our physical body, but we are not aware of developing strength in the inner man. This strength gives us peace in turbulent times, hope in times of despair, solutions when we can't figure things out, patience when we are tempted to be angry, the ability to focus when we are distracted, love when we are irritated, etc.

We are praying for Christ to dwell in our hearts by faith. We want Jesus to live in our hearts, not just visit as a stranger. As a community of believers, we want to know that Jesus' love has width—it covers over our sin. It has length—it is everlasting. It has depth—He died for us. It has height—we are seated with Him in heavenly places (Ephesians 2:6). We want to know the love of Christ; and be filled with the fullness of God. This is SO BIG it confounds our understanding.

PRAYER: *Lord, we pray that You would do exceedingly abundantly ABOVE all we could ever ask or even think according to the power that works in us. Help us to understand that this power is available now—this power that raised Jesus from the dead! Lord, we want to give You glory in the church forever and ever, world without end. Amen!*

FIVE-FOLD MINISTRY GIFTS

And He Himself gave some to be apostles, some prophets, some evangelists and some pastors and teachers, for the equipping of the saints for the work of ministry, for the edifying of the body of Christ, till we all come to the unity of the faith and of the knowledge of the Son of God to a perfect man, to the measure of the stature of the fullness of Christ.
—Ephesians 4:11–13; read also Ephesians 4

These are offices of spiritual leadership in the church that Jesus established. He chooses specific people for an office. We can't call ourselves to these positions. The five-fold ministry gifts are:

+ Apostles—These are special ambassadors of God's work. They move in signs and wonders and mighty deeds (2 Corinthians 12:12).

+ Prophets—These speak God's messages to the people and are in complete agreement with the Old and New Testaments. Sometimes they speak in a predictive sense, but not always. They are always subject to the discernment of the church leadership. *"God does nothing unless He reveals His secret to His servants the prophets"* (Amos 3:7).

+ Evangelists—These are specifically gifted to preach the good news of salvation in Christ.

+ Pastors and teachers—These are shepherds of the flock of God primarily through teaching the Word of God.

The purpose of these gifts of leadership is so the saints might be equipped for the work of ministry so that the body of Christ would be built up and strengthened.

The first goal of God's work through these offices is that we would come to the unity of the faith and come to a knowledge of Christ. The goal is maturity in intimacy with Christ, and that, as verse 16 says, each part would do their share to make the body of Christ strong and healthy.

Prayer: *Thank You, Father, for these wonderful gifts to the church. We do bless and honor these men and women of God who sacrificially serve us that we might grow in You and become who we are supposed to be in Your church. Amen.*

DRUNK ON HOLY SPIRIT

And do not be drunk with wine, in which is dissipation (excess); but be filled with the Spirit, speaking to one another in psalms and hymns and spiritual songs, singing and making melody in your heart to the Lord, giving thanks always for all things to God the Father in the name of our Lord Jesus Christ.
—EPHESIANS 5:18–20; READ ALSO VV. 1–20

In contrast to the world which gets drunk on wine, we are to be filled with the Holy Spirit. *"Wine is a mocker, strong drink is a brawler, and whoever is led astray by it is not wise* (Proverbs 20:1). We, on the other hand, are to be constantly filled with the Holy Spirit. Whereas alcohol is a depressant and depresses people's self-control, wisdom, balance and judgment, the Holy Spirit is a stimulant; He moves us to better performance.

The Spirit-filled life is marked by worship and gratitude. When we are truly filled with the Spirit, we want to worship God and to encourage others in their worship of God. We naturally want to praise.

God gives such variety as we praise Him: psalms and hymns and spiritual songs. Spiritual songs are the spontaneous songs that we sing. They are new songs that just arise from our hearts. God does give us beautiful melodies in our hearts that He longs for us to sing to Him. He may even give us new songs that we are to write down for others to sing. Other times we may want to sing songs in our prayer language that we receive when we are baptized in the Holy Spirit. There is nothing more beautiful than when a whole congregation sings these songs in the Spirit together. It is as a choir of angels is singing.

When we are filled with praise, we are also filled with thanksgiving. "A complaining heart and the Holy Spirit just don't go together."

PRAYER: *Expand our words, our melodies, and our praise to please You, Lord. Expand our hearts to praise You **always**! Amen!*

WHAT MARRIAGE SHOULD BE

Husbands, love your wives, just as Christ also loved the church and gave Himself for her, that He might sanctify and cleanse her with the washing of water by the word, that He might present her to Himself a glorious church, not having spot or wrinkle or any such thing but that she should be holy and without blemish.

—Ephesians 5:25–27; read also vv. 21–33

What a wonderful verse following the verses on submission to one another. It is easy to recognize the husband as head of the wife as Christ is the head of the church, when he lays down his life for her as Christ did for the church. The marriage is a picture of Christ being the Bridegroom and the church being the bride.

The word Paul used for love was *agape*, which is the God kind of love, based on decision, not on feelings. It is a self-giving love that gives without demanding or expecting repayment. It is love so great following that it can be given to the unlovable or unappealing. It is love that loves even when it is rejected.

Jesus' attitude toward the church is a pattern for the Christian husband's love to his wife. Paul is teaching here about the nature of a relationship between husband and wife, and about Christ's relationship with His church. This is the strongest kind of love there ever was.

When Jesus gave Himself for the church on the cross, He also provided cleansing from every stain of sin. His Word as we read it, speak it, and obey it, cleanses us from every sin. It washes and purifies our soul. As we look into the law of liberty, it points out where we fall short, and teaches us how to get back on the path of truth and excellence and fruitfulness. Jesus Christ's goal is not only that His church would be spotless, wrinkle free, and without any stain, but that there would not even be a blemish! This desire is for us now, but also when we are joined to Christ in heaven for the glorious wedding feast of the Lamb!

Prayer: *Maranatha! (Come Lord Jesus!) We long for that glorious Day! Amen!*

WEAPONS OF SPIRITUAL WARFARE

Stand and gird your waist with truth....putting on the breast-
plate of righteousness....having shod your feet with the gospel of
peace....taking the shield of faith....take the helmet of salvation and
the sword of the Spirit which is the word of God....praying with all
prayer in the Spirit...
—EPHESIANS 6:14–18; READ ALSO EPHESIANS 6

This is Paul's spiritual warfare chapter and is worth memorizing.
Since we are fighting against enemies in the spirit world, we need special equipment for both offense and defense.

+ The girdle of truth. This part holds all the other parts of the
  armor together. The girdle also holds the sword of the Spirit.
  Satan is a liar, but the Truth will defeat him!

+ The breastplate of righteousness. This piece of armor, made of
  metal plates or chains, covered the body from the neck to the
  waist, both front and back. When we accept Christ, we receive
  the gift of righteousness.

+ The shoes of the Gospel. Roman shoes were hobnails to give
  better footing. Because we have God's peace that comes from
  the Gospel, we need not fear Satan or men. We bring peace.

+ The shield of faith. This shield was large, usually about four feet
  by two feet, made of wood and covered with tough leather. This
  protected the soldier from the fiery darts of the enemy. The
  shields could interlock with others and march into the enemy
  like a solid wall. The "faith" mentioned here is faith in the
  promises and power of God. Our shield blocks lies and doubts.

+ The helmet of salvation. It protects our mind. We must fill our
  minds with the Word of God.

+ The sword of the Spirit. This is the Word of God.

+ Praying in the "Spirit. This is praying in tongues (1 Corinthians 14:14). This is how we can "pray always." We are to pray
  to the Father through the Son in the Holy Spirit.

PRAYER: *Father, thank You that Your weapons are not carnal, but*
mighty through God to pull down strongholds! Amen!

September 21

EXCHANGE OF TRUTH TO LIES

For this reason God gave them over to their own disgraceful and vile passions. Enflamed with lust for one another, men and women ignored the natural order and exchanged normal sexual relations for homosexuality. Women engaged in lesbian conduct, and men committed shameful acts with men, receiving in themselves the due penalty for their deviation.
—Romans 1:26–27, tpt; read also Romans 1

The Passion Translation continues:

Throughout human history the fingerprints of God were upon them, yet they refused to honor Him as God or even be thankful for His kindness. Instead, they entertained corrupt and foolish thoughts about what God was like. Although claiming to be super-intelligent, they were in fact shallow fools....So God lifted off His hand and let them have full expression of their shameful desires. They exchanged the truth of God for a lie. They worshipped and served the things God made rather than the God who made all things (v. 21–23, tpt).

Paul wrote to a culture where homosexuality was accepted as a part of life for both men and women. "For some two hundred years, the men who ruled the Roman Empire openly practiced homosexuality often with young boys. Legal marriage between same gender couples was recognized and even some of the emperors married other men. At the very time Paul wrote, Nero was emperor. He took a boy named Sporus and married him with a full ceremony and made the boy his "wife." Later Nero lived with another man and Nero was the "wife." [10]

Many historians say that the gross immorality of the Roman Empire brought its destruction. Civilizations are destroyed from within. When America legalized "gay marriage" in June 2015, we were following in Rome's footsteps.

Prayer: *Father forgive us for exchanging the truth for a lie in America! Bring a great awakening with repentance! Bring a mass exodus out of the "gay" lifestyle. Amen.*

JUDGING OTHERS

*Therefore you are inexcusable, O man, whoever you are who judge,
for in whatever you judge another, you condemn yourself; for you who
judge practice the same things.*
—Romans 2:1; read also Romans 2

Remember the old saying "When you point your finger at someone,
you have three pointing back at yourself. So true.

Not understanding or following this important verse can have far
reaching consequences in our lives, especially when you combine it
with: "Honor your father and your mother, which is the first commandment with promise, that it may be well with you and you may
live long on the earth" (Ephesians 6:2–3). And also, consider the law
of sowing and reaping, *"that whatsoever a man sows, that will he also
reap"* (Galatians 6:7). This is a spiritual law and will always work like
physical laws work. Gravity is an example.

Consider how these verses can work together. If you judge a parent,
for example, of being critical, you are judging them in an unfavor-
able way. You are planting a seed of judgment and seeing yourself as
better. Unforgiveness is always part of judgment. This is dishonoring
your parent.

So, when we sow this judgment, we are due to reap in some way.
The Bible then says in Romans 2:1 that when we judge someone, we
are guilty of doing the same thing. When we judge a parent of being
critical, or of being angry, we will often reap by being critical or angry
ourselves. Another way we can reap is by marrying someone like the
parent we judged.

One lady judged her dad of being an alcoholic and couldn't forgive
him for the way he had mistreated her. She reaped from her judgment by being an alcoholic herself. She had to repent of judging her
father and ask forgiveness for herself. Unforgiveness is always part of
the problem, so the person needs to forgive the person that hurt them,
and then ask for forgiveness themselves for their judgments.

Prayer: *Father, help us to remember that along with forgiving the
person that hurt us, we need to ask forgiveness for our own sins of
judging others. Amen.*

BE AT PEACE WITH GOD

For all have sinned and come short of the glory of God.
—ROMANS 3:23; READ ALSO ROMANS 3

Following are STEPS TO PEACE WITH GOD[11] If you learn these and memorize them, you can lead many to Christ:

STEP 1: GOD'S PURPOSE: PEACE AND LIFE

We have peace with God through Jesus Christ.

"For God so loved the world that He gave His only begotten Son, that whoever believes in Him should not perish but have everlasting life" (John 3:16).

STEP 2: THE PROBLEM: OUR SEPARATION

"For all have sinned and fall short of the glory of God" (Romans 3:23).

"For the wages of sin is death, but the gift of God is eternal life in Christ Jesus our Lord" (Romans 6:23).

"But your iniquities have separated you from your God; and your sins have hidden His face from you, so that He will not hear" (Isaiah 59:2).

STEP 3: GOD'S BRIDGE: THE CROSS

"For there is one God and one Mediator between God and men, the Man Christ Jesus" (1 Timothy 2:5).

"But God shows his love for us in that while we were still sinners, Christ died for us" (Romans 5:8, ESV).

STEP 4: OUR RESPONSE: RECEIVE CHRIST

"Behold, I stand at the door and knock. If anyone hears My voice and opens the door, I will come in to Him and dine with Him, and He with Me" (Revelation 3:20).

"If you confess with your mouth that Jesus is Lord and believe in your heart that God raised him from the dead, you will be saved." (Romans 10:9, ESV).

PRAYER: *Dear Father, I know that I am a sinner. I ask for Your forgiveness. I believe Your Son, Jesus, died for my sins and You raised Him to life again. I want You Jesus to come into my heart and be my Savior. I want to follow You as my Lord from this day on. In Jesus' name. Amen.*

ASK WITH ABRAHAM KIND OF FAITH

God who gives life to the dead and calls those things which do not exist as though they did; who contrary to hope, in hope believed, so that he became the father of many nations.... And not being weak in faith, he did not consider his own body, already dead (since he was about a hundred years old), and the deadness of Sarah's womb. He did not waver at the promise of God through unbelief, but was strengthened in faith, giving glory to God, being fully persuaded that what He had promised He was also able to perform.
—ROMANS 4:17, 20–21; READ ALSO ROMANS 4

It looked like a hopeless situation. God had promised him a son, but Sarah's womb was barren. They waited and waited and waited for this child. He was now a hundred years old and Sarah was ninety years old. God had told him back in Genesis 15 that one coming from his own body would be his heir. God then brought him outside and said, "*Look now toward the heaven, and count the stars if you are able to number them.*" And He said to him, "*So shall your descendants be.*" Abraham did not waver at the promise of God, and this is a perfect example of how we also are not to waver with unbelief at the promise of God. Our God is a God of miracles. Isaac was born to Abraham and Sarah just as God promised.

What is the greatest desire of your heart? A job? A college education? A spouse? A child? A healing? A healing of marriage? A prodigal child? A house? Souls for Jesus? Begin to speak God's Word into that situation. We have a precious friend whose wife left him. God had promised that she would come back and their marriage would be healed. It looked hopeless, but we quoted this verse over and over along with other verses and were strengthened in faith. We were fully persuaded that what God had promised us, He was able to perform. We worshipped Him for how He was going to bring a solution. We spoke to the mountain of divorce and said, "No!" God is faithful! She came back, and their marriage was restored. Nothing is too hard for the Lord.

PRAYER: *Father, grant us the Abraham kind of faith! Amen!*

MADE A SINNER FOR OUR SAKE

For as by one man's disobedience many were made sinners, so also by one Man's obedience many will be made righteous. Moreover the law entered that the offense might abound. But where sin abounded, grace abounded much more, so that as sin reigned in death, even so grace might reign through righteousness to eternal life through Jesus Christ our Lord.
—ROMANS 5:19–21; READ ALSO ROMANS 5

Adam's disobedience makes mankind sinners. Jesus' obedience makes many righteous. Looking at the fruits of people's lives, it becomes evident Whom they are following.

At the root of all this, we were made sinners by the work of Adam. However, we can be made righteous by the work of another man, Jesus.

If I robbed a bank and was found guilty of the crime, a friend could not say to the judge, "Your honor, I love my friend and I want to serve his prison time. I will stand in his place and receive the punishment he deserves." The judge would reply, "Nonsense. We will not punish you for his crime. That wouldn't be fair. He did the crime, so he has to pay the penalty." And yet, that is just what Jesus did. He stepped down off the judge's bench and paid for the crimes each of us committed.

The purpose of the law is to make man's sin clearer and greater by contrasting it with God's holy standard. The law makes sin abound because it draws clear lines between right and wrong that our sinful hearts want to break. This reminds me of our three-year-old daughter who was told not to eat something. But, lo and behold, when I looked in the refrigerator, it was gone. When I asked her if she ate it, she said, "I did—but I didn't." She was overcome by the temptation but didn't want the punishment! But where sin abounds, grace does much more abound. She was forgiven!

PRAYER: *Thank You for stepping down off the judge's bench, taking our offense as Yours and paying the fine. Amen.*

BELIEVE AND BE BAPTIZED

Therefore we were buried with Him through baptism into death, that just as Christ was raised from the dead by the glory of the Father, even so we also should walk in newness of life.
—Romans 6:4; read also Romans 6

The ordinance of baptism by immersion in water is commanded in the Scriptures. All who repent and believe on Christ as Savior and Lord are to be baptized. Thus, they declare to the world that they have died with Christ and that they also have been raised with Him to walk in newness of life. *"All authority has been given to Me in heaven and on earth. Go therefore and make disciples of all the nations, baptizing them in the name of the Father and of the Son and of the Holy Spirit, teaching them to observe all things that I have commanded you; and lo, I am with you always, even to the end of the age. Amen"* (Matthew 28:18–20).

Water baptism symbolizes the beginning of a new spiritual life. It is a public declaration of our faith in Jesus Christ, and that we identify with Him in His death and resurrection. When we go down under the water in immersion, this symbolizes that our old life has died. When we come up out of the water, it symbolizes the new resurrection life we have in Christ. It is a most amazing, meaningful experience.

The New Testament teaches that water baptism is for believers only. *"He who believes and is baptized will be saved; but he who does not believe will be condemned"* (Mark 16:16). Peter says in Acts 2:38, *"Repent and be baptized,"* so according to the Bible, repentance precedes baptism. For the one who is truly born again (cleansed by His blood and justified), baptism becomes not only a testimony but also the pledge that we will continue to live a new life in the risen Christ.

When our children were small, we attended a church that baptized infants, so our children were baptized as infants. But when they received Christ later, they were immersed.

Prayer: *Father, in this great awakening, may we see repentance, baptism, and infilling of the Holy Ghost! Amen!*

BATTLE AGAINST SIN

*For I delight in the law of God according to the inward man. But I see
another law in my members warring against the law of my mind, and
bringing me into captivity to the law of sin which is in my members. O
wretched man that I am! Who will deliver me from this body of death?
I thank God—through Jesus Christ our Lord! So then, with the mind
I myself serve the law of God, but with the flesh the law of sin.*
—ROMANS 7:22–25; READ ALSO ROMANS 7

Paul is talking about the battle between the "old man" which is his
flesh, and the "new man." When Paul was "born again" his spirit
became totally new. The problem is that his flesh was not made new,
and his mind was not renewed. Anyone who has tried to do good is
aware of this struggle. We never know how hard it is to stop sinning
until we try. C. S. Lewis once said that no man knows how bad he is
until he has tried to be good.

We cannot battle sin in our own strength and power. If we try to
live up to the law in our own strength, we will always fail. Paul is desperate in this battle over sin when he says, "O wretched man that I am!"
But when he says this, he is beginning to look to God for the answer
rather than finding the answer within himself. When he says, "Who
will deliver me from this body of death?", he is referring to how ancient
kings used to torment their prisoners.

> It was the custom of ancient tyrants, when they wished to put men
> to the most fearful punishments, to tie a dead body to them, placing
> the two back to back; and there was the living man, with a dead body
> closely strapped to him, rotting, putrid, corrupting, and this he must
> drag with him wherever he went."[12]

Paul longed to be free from the wretched body of death clinging to
him. When he finally looked from himself to Jesus, he thanked God
that it is in Jesus that we have victory!

PRAYER: *We know that You, Lord, are our victory; Your Word delivers
us and renews our minds and sets us free. Amen.*

THE HOLY SPIRIT IS OUR PRAYER ASSISTANT

Likewise the Spirit also helps in our weaknesses. For we do not know what we should pray for as we ought, but the Spirit Himself makes intercession for us with groanings which cannot be uttered. Now He who searches the hearts knows what the mind of the Spirit is, because He makes intercession for the saints according to the will of God. And we know that all things work together for good to those who love God, to those who are the called according to His purpose.
—ROMANS 8:26–28; READ ALSO VV. 1–28

The Spirit helps us in our praying. Sometimes we do not know what to pray for, but the Spirit always does. He makes groanings which cannot be uttered. This help from the Spirit may include praying with the spiritual gift of tongues (1 Corinthians 14:2, 14–15), but it is not limited to praying in an unknown tongue. It seems that the verse refers to sighs, groans, loud "cries and tears" and other expressions of our hearts and spirits in prayer that are taken by the Holy Spirit and made into effectual intercession before the throne of God.

> There definitely are similarities, though, between speaking in tongues and the activity Paul describes here, for speaking in tongues is often prayer or praise in syllables the speaker does not himself understand, and both kinds of speech are made effective by the Holy Spirit.[13]

And God is able to work all things, not some things, out for good for those who love the Lord. This wonderful and amazing promise follows the Scripture about the Spirit helping us in our prayers. It is after our prayers in the Spirit according to the will of God that all things work together for our good to those who love God. We are the called according to His purpose. He has a purpose and a calling for each one of us and we know that this calling and purpose is far beyond anything we can ask or imagine (Ephesians 1:18–19).

PRAYER: *Father, You are a good God, and we know that all things in our life work together for good, for we love You! Amen!*

UNSPEAKABLE LOVE OF GOD

Yet in all these things we are more than conquerors through Him who loved us. For I am persuaded that neither death nor life, nor angels nor principalities nor powers, nor things present nor things to come, nor height nor depth, nor any other created thing, shall be able to separate us from the love of God which is in Christ Jesus our Lord.
—ROMANS 8:37–39; READ ALSO VV. 29–39

This passage is such a wonderful tribute to God's everlasting love. As it asks in the 33rd verse: "*Who shall bring a charge against God's elect? It is God who justifies.*" Who, then, can condemn us? We are secure from every charge against us. If we are declared "not guilty" by the highest Judge, who can bring an additional charge? Christ is at the right hand of God making intercession for us. Nothing shall separate us from His marvelous love. Nothing. No tribulation. No distress or persecution. Not famine or nakedness or sword. Nothing.

Therefore, "We've been made more than conquerors, overcomers in this life. We've been made victorious, through the Blood of Jesus Christ.

"*If trouble comes knockin' at your door. Don't be afraid, it's not like before. Don't you give in, don't let it bring you down. You don't have to worry anymore. We've been made more than conquerors....*" (song by Janny Grein).[14]

How are we more than a conqueror? We overcome with a greater power, the power of Jesus. We overcome with a greater motive, the glory of Jesus. We overcome with a greater love, conquering enemies with love and patience and prayer.

No created thing, whether good or evil, can separate us from this unspeakable love of God, either in the present, or in the future.

PRAYER: *Our Father who is in heaven, we thank You for Your amazing love and promises to us that nothing can ever separate us from Your love. We pray that we might know this love that passes knowledge so we might be filled with Your fullness. In Jesus' name. Amen.*

September 30

THE OLD COVENANT

O Israel, my Jewish family, I feel such great sorrow and heartache for you that never leaves me! God knows these deep feelings within me as I long for you to come to faith in the Anointed One. My conscience will not let me speak anything but the truth. For my grief is so intense that I wish that I would be accursed, cut off from the Messiah, if it would mean that you, my people, would come to faith in Him!
—ROMANS 9:1–3; READ ALSO VV. 1–15

How Paul longed for "his people" the Israelites to come to faith in Christ. After all, they were the ones that had God's glorious presence and the covenants. The Old Covenant was the Ten Commandments found in Exodus 20:

1. You shall have no other gods before Me.
2. You shall not make for yourself a carved image.
3. You shall not take the name of the Lord in vain.
4. Remember the Sabbath day, to keep it holy.
5. Honor your father and mother, that your days may be long upon the land which the Lord your God is giving you.
6. You shall not murder.
7. You shall not commit adultery.
8. You shall not steal.
9. You shall not lie.
10. You shall not covet.

To the Israelites belonged the covenants, the Torah (first five books of the Old Testament), the temple with its sacrifices, and the promises of God. To them belong the patriarchs, and through their bloodline is the genealogy of the Messiah, who is God over everything (v. 4–5).

Paul would have given his life for them to come to faith. This was his great passion. Lesser things did not trouble him. However, just being an Israelite, did not guarantee their inheritance. In the same way, just calling oneself a Christian doesn't mean you are a true disciple of Christ either. All must be *"born again"* to enter the kingdom of God (John 3:3).

PRAYER: *We pray that all Israel will be saved! Amen!*

RIGHTEOUSNESS THROUGH FAITH

What shall we say then? That Gentiles, who did not pursue righteous-
ness, have attained to righteousness, even the righteousness of faith;
but Israel, pursuing the law of righteousness has not attained to the
law of righteousness. Why? Because they did not seek it by faith, but
as it were, by the works of the law. For they stumbled at that stum-
bling stone.
  —ROMANS 9:30–31; READ ALSO VV. 16–33

By all appearances, the Gentiles found righteousness even though it
did not seem that they really looked for it. On the other hand, even
though the Israelites strenuously worked for the righteousness of
God, they did not find it.

We may ask what the difference is. Why did the unlikely Gentiles
find righteousness, when the Jews did not? The reason is because the
Gentiles pursued righteousness that comes by faith and the Jews pursued the law of righteousness. The Gentiles who were saved came to
God through faith, receiving His righteousness as a gift of grace. The
Jews, who seem to be cast off from God for a time, tried to justify
themselves before God by performing works according to the law.

The Jews stumbled at that stumbling stone. In other words, they
were offended by how they would obtain it, just as it was written of
them by the prophet Isaiah. *"Behold, I lay in Zion a stumbling stone*
and rock of offense, and whoever believes on Him will not be put to
shame" (v. 33; Isaiah 28:16). The stumbling stone and rock of offense,
prophesied by Isaiah, is the Messiah, Jesus Christ.

But God in His extreme mercy, wrote of the Jews and the Gentiles,
"I will call them My people, who were not My people, and her beloved,
who was not beloved." "And it shall come to pass in the place where it was
said to them, 'You are not My people,' There they shall be called sons of
the living God" (v. 25–26).

PRAYER: *Father, thank You for calling us Your people, and Your*
beloved; sons and daughters of the living God. Thank You for the Good
News that "the just shall live by faith!" Amen! (Habakkuk 2:4).

CONFESSING OUR SALVATION

But what does it say? "The word is near you, in your mouth and in your heart" (that is, the word of faith which we preach): that if you confess with your mouth the Lord Jesus and believe in your heart that God has raised Him from the dead, you will be saved. For with the heart one believes unto righteousness, and with the mouth confession is made unto salvation.

—ROMANS 10:9–10; READ ALSO ROMANS 10

Romans 10:9–10 is really "Romans TNT." This is the dynamite power of the Gospel, and assurance of salvation.

+ First, if we confess with our mouth the Lord Jesus...We have been speaking of the power of words. The power of life and death is in the tongue, and the power of words directs our whole life; it sets the whole course of nature on fire (James 3:6).

+ If we believe in our hearts that God has raised Him from the dead...Do you believe that God raised Jesus from the dead? Do you believe in the resurrection?

+ If so, you will be saved.

+ For with the heart one believes unto righteousness. As we saw in Chapter Nine, the Jews tried to find righteousness through works, but that did not work. The Gentiles found righteousness through faith. *"Not by works of righteousness that we have done, but according to His mercy He saved us, by the washing of regeneration, and renewing of the Holy Ghost"* (Titus 3:5).

+ And with the mouth confession is made unto salvation. So, when we confess this, or speak this out loud, it seals our salvation. It is important here to see the role of the tongue in speaking what has happened in the heart. There is no place for closet Christians. We must be vocal about our faith in Christ. This is a powerful promise of God. This truly is a TNT verse.

PRAYER: *We pray Father, today that You will bring someone to mind, to whom we can confess our faith in Christ. Amen.*

October 3

THE HOLY ROOT

For if their being cast away is the reconciling of the world, what will their acceptance be but life from the dead? For if the firstfruit is holy, the lump is also holy; and if the root is holy, so are the branches. And if some of the branches were broken off, and you, being a wild olive tree were grafted in among them, and with them became a partaker of the root and fatness of the olive tree, do not boast against the branches. But if you do boast, remember that you do not support the root, but the root supports you.
—Romans 11:15–18; read also vv. 1–18

"In Chapter 11 we can see the general progression of the last days." [1]

When the Gentile believers manifest the gifts and power of the Holy Spirit, the Jews will be provoked to jealousy. Paul said he hoped that he could somehow arouse his own people to envy and save some of them. This jealousy leads to a saved remnant from Israel (Romans 11:14). That saved remnant from Israel, along with the saved Gentiles, will manifest the Kingdom of God in the John 17 fulfillment of Yeshua's prayer for unity.

"*If the firstfruit is holy, the lump is also holy*" (v. 16). This means that the lump, or unbelieving Israel, is holy because of the firstfruit of Israel who believe, (the remnant). The Passion Translation says it like this: "*Since Abraham and the patriarchs are consecrated and set apart for God, so also will their descendants be set apart. If the roots of a tree are holy and set apart for God, so too will be the branches*" (v. 16).

Paul is saying that if the Gentiles, (we), being a wild olive tree were grafted into the true olive tree, we should not think we are better than the original branches, (the Jews). The new branches don't support the root, but we owe our life to the root that supports us!

Prayer: *Father, we do thank You that we are the seed of Abraham and grafted into the true olive tree of salvation. Amen.*

GOSPEL OF THE KINGDOM

For I do not desire, brethren, that you should be ignorant of this mystery, lest you should be wise in your own opinion, that blindness in part has happened to Israel until the fullness of the Gentiles has come in. And so all Israel will be saved, as it is written: "The Deliverer will come out of Zion, And He will turn away ungodliness from Jacob; For this is My covenant with them, When I take away their sins."
—ROMANS 11:25–26; READ ALSO VV. 19–36

Asher Intrater and Dan Juster, Messianic Jews, in their book write that the *"fullness of the Gentiles"* means that the full number of Gentiles will come to faith in Jesus Christ.

The Kingdom witness that Jesus commanded in Matthew 24:13–14 will be fulfilled. This Gospel of the Kingdom will be preached in all the world as a witness, and then the end will come. The Gospel of the Kingdom has miraculous signs following it: the blind see, the deaf hear, the lame walk, the dead are raised and those with skin diseases (and all diseases) are healed. This is the Gospel that will get the attention of the world. This is partly what the *"fullness of the Gentiles"* means. They will be full of power. Then the deliverer will come from Zion; He will turn godlessness away from Jacob. This is one of the covenants that God has promised them, that He would take away their sins.

Some people say that all Israel being saved means that all people, Jew and Gentile who are born again will be saved. We do not believe that is what it means, but rather that the text means what it says, that the whole nation will be saved.[2]

God has committed Jew and Gentile alike to disobedience, that He may have mercy on them all!

"Oh the depth of the riches both of the wisdom and knowledge of God! How unsearchable are His judgments and His ways past finding out! For of Him and through Him and to Him are all things, to whom be glory forever. Amen" (v. 34, 36).

PRAYER: *Lord, when we see Your plan, it brings us to our knees! All Israel will be saved. Glory to Your Name! Amen!*

October 5

GIFT OF A CHRISTIAN

Having then gifts differing according to the grace that is given to us, let us use them: if prophecy, let us prophesy in proportion to our faith; or ministry, let us use it in our ministering; he who teaches, in teaching; he who exhorts, in exhortation; he who gives, with liberality; he who leads, with diligence; he who shows mercy, with cheerfulness.
—Romans 12:6–8; read also Romans 12

Which gift(s) do you have? Characteristics of these ministry gifts are:[3]

+ *Prophecy:* People with this motive have insight into what motivates others. They see things in black and white and are frank and direct. They are protective of God's program and want to see born-again Christians living righteous lives.
+ *Ministry (Serving):* These folks are hard workers almost to the point of exhaustion. They want immediate results. They remember people's preferences. They need recognition.
+ *Teaching:* These take great delight in studying the Word of God and doing biblical research. They are very watchful that others who teach the Word don't deviate from the truth. They use biblical examples and value clarity and accuracy.
+ *Exhortation:* Exhorters prescribe "steps of activity" for others to follow so they may come out of their misery, trials, and tribulations. They like to relate personal examples to biblical truths. They love to counsel others.
+ *Giving:* People with this gift have an ability to generate income and like to give their money away. They motivate others to give. They want to see the church's needs met.
+ *Organization:* They can visualize the overall picture and plan long-range goals. They are aware of the resources needed to complete a task. When the job is done, they move on.
+ *Mercy:* Merciful people are very sensitive to words and actions that could wound. They are sensitive to others' reactions to spiritual happenings. They discern true motives.

PRAYER: *Father, help us to use our gifts to their fullest. Amen.*

October 6

OBEDIENT TO THOSE IN AUTHORITY

Let every soul be subject to the governing authorities. For there is no authority except from God, and the authorities that exist are appointed by God. Therefore whoever resists the authority resists the ordinance of God, and those who resist will bring judgment on themselves. For rulers are not a terror to good works, but to evil. Do you want to be unafraid of the authority? Do what is good, and you will have praise from the same. For he is God's minister to you for good. But if you do evil, be afraid; for he does not bear the sword in vain; for he is God's minister, an avenger to execute wrath on him who practices evil.
—ROMANS 13:1–4; READ ALSO ROMANS 13

We are not to seek vengeance ourselves or take the law into our own hands, but this does not take away the government's authority to punish wrongdoers. They do not bear the sword in vain.

David Guzik says, "God appoints a nation's leaders, but not always to bless the people. Sometimes it is to judge the people or to ripen the nation for judgment."[4]

We must remember that Paul wrote this during the reign of the Roman Empire. It was no democracy and certainly was no special friend to Christians. Jesus suffered under Pontius Pilate, one of the worst Roman governors Judea ever had. Paul suffered under Nero, the worst Roman emperor. And neither Jesus nor Paul denied their authority.

Since governments have authority from God, we are bound to obey them—unless of course they ask us to disobey God's laws; God's laws are higher.

We as Christians should be the best citizens of all, because we are honest, pay taxes, pray for our leaders, and do not give trouble to the state.

PRAYER: *Father in heaven, we do pray for our leaders. We thank You for our president and pray blessings upon him and his family. Protect him from evil. Give him wisdom. Amen.*

October 7

OUR SINS WERE JUDGED ON THE CROSS

But why do you judge your brother? Or why do you show contempt for your brother? For we shall all stand before the judgment seat of Christ. For it is written: "As I live, says the LORD, every knee shall bow to Me, And every tongue shall confess to God." So then each of us shall give account of himself to God.
—ROMANS 14:10–12; READ ALSO ROMANS 14

We will all stand before the righteous Judge to give an account of our lives. Hebrews 9:27 says, *"It is appointed once to die and after that the judgment."* In other words, there is no such thing as reincarnation and cycling back through life in another form. After death, we will face judgment.

The judgment seat of Christ is for believers only. It is not a judgment on sin, because our sins were judged at the Cross already. This judgment is a matter of appropriate reward for what we have done for Jesus. As we read in 1 Corinthians 3:11–15, it was pointed out that all believers are building a building, some of permanent material: gold, silver, and precious stones; and some of material that is not permanent: wood, hay and stubble. Our deeds will be examined by the fire of God's judgment. Especially our motives will be judged. We read in 1 Corinthians 13:3, *"And though I bestow all my goods to feed the poor, and though I give my body to be burned, but have not love, it profits me nothing."*

If we are responsive to the gentle voice of the Holy Spirit and try our best to allow Christ to live through us, *"we may be confident and not be ashamed before him at his coming"* (1 John 2:28).

But one thing we can be sure of, there is coming a time when *every* knee shall bow and *every* tongue shall confess to God. The prophet Isaiah said this about Christ seven hundred years before He was born (Isaiah 45:23).

PRAYER: *Our Father who is in heaven, Yours is the Kingdom, and Yours is the Power, and Yours is the Glory forever and ever. Amen.*

October 8

APOSTOLIC PRAYER MODEL

Now may the God of patience and comfort grant you to be like-minded toward one another, according to Christ Jesus, that you may with one mind and one mouth glorify the God and Father of our Lord Jesus Christ.

—ROMANS 15:5–6; READ ALSO VV. 1–13

This is another example of a powerful apostolic prayer. As a rule, our prayers should be God-centered prayers, rather than demon-centered or sin-focused prayers. This is the New Testament model of prayer set forth by Paul. Below are some ways to pray for the church using the apostolic prayers.[5]

+ Pray for the church to be like-minded toward each other, and that with one mind and one mouth we would glorify the God and Father of our Lord Jesus Christ (Romans 15:5–6).

+ Pray that love will abound and that believers will approve the things that God calls excellent (Philippians 1:9–10).

+ Pray that the anointing of conviction will rest on the preaching of the Word so that both believers and unbelievers are impacted greatly (John 16:8).

+ Pray for a great increase of the gifts of the Spirit in the church and the manifestation of these gifts through words of knowledge, words of wisdom, discerning of spirits, healing, miracles, and so on.

+ Pray for a prophetic spirit to rest on preachers, worship teams, and ministry leaders (Acts 2:17).

+ Pray that the Spirit will open more doors to minister to unbelievers and that He will prepare them to receive the gospel (Colossians 4:3; 2 Thessalonians 3:1).

+ Pray that the Spirit will motivate believers to share the gospel (Matthew 9:37–38).

+ Pray for a spirit of wisdom and revelation in the knowledge of God to be given to the leaders and all (Ephesians 1:17).

+ Pray for every family member to be saved, healed, and to prosper with secure, steady jobs (3 John 2).

PRAYER: *Begin to pray the above prayers regularly. Amen.*

October 9

FULLNESS OF THE BLESSING

But I know that when I come to you, I shall come in the fullness of the blessing of the gospel of Christ.
> —ROMANS 15:29; READ ALSO VV. 14–33

Fullness here is from the Greek word, *pleroma*. It means full number, full complement, full measure, copiousness, plenitude, that which has been completed. The word describes a ship with a full cargo and crew, and a town with no empty houses. *Pleroma* strongly emphasizes fullness.[6]

In Deuteronomy 28, Moses says that if the people of Israel would carefully observe all His commandments the Lord would set them high above all nations on the earth and all these blessings would overtake them:

Blessed shall you be in the city and blessed in the country.

Blessed shall be the fruit of your body, the produce of your ground and the increase of your herds.

Blessed shall you be when you come in and blessed shall you be when you go out.

Your enemies who rise against you will be defeated before you.

Blessed will you be in your storehouses and in all to which you set your hand.

The Lord will establish you as a holy people to Himself.

The Lord will open to you His good treasure, the heavens, to give the rain to your land in its season and bless all the work of your hand. You shall lend to many nations, but you shall not borrow.

The Lord will make you the head and not the tail, you shall be above only, and not be beneath.

The Aaronic blessing is in Numbers 6:24: "*The Lord bless you and keep you; the Lord make His face shine upon you and be gracious to you....and give you peace.*"

PRAYER: *In Christ, the fullness of the blessing is ours! Amen!*

ROLE OF WOMEN IN THE SCRIPTURE

I commend to you Phoebe, who is a servant of the church of Cenchrea...Greet Priscilla and Aquila...Greet Andronicus and Junia...Greet Tryphena and Tryphosa; and beloved Persis...Greet Philologus and Julia.
—ROMANS 16:1, 3a, 7a, 12, 15a; READ ALSO ROMANS 16

We will be taking a look at the roles of women in Scripture. In verse 1, Phoebe is commended and was classified as a *diakonos*, here translated *servant*. It is rendered *minister* when applied to Paul and Apollos (1 Corinthians 3:5) and deacon when used of other male officers of the church (1 Timothy 3:10, 12–13). So she could just as well be called, Phoebe, a minister, or a deacon. Ministers and deacons led and taught in the church.

An early third-century writing called the *Didascalia* (teaching), said that persons being baptized came up from the water and were received and taught by the women deacons. Clearly Paul held Phoebe and other female fellow-workers in high esteem. In fact, of the twenty-nine people Paul greets in Romans 16, ten of them are women.

In the city of Ephesus, Priscilla, along with her husband Aquila, both well known to Paul, taught Apollos. The fact that Priscilla's name is mentioned first, indicates that she was the primary teacher of Apollos, a Christian leader.

In the Romans 16:7 passage, we see Junia and Andronicus were "of note" among the apostles. John Chrysostom (337–253 A.D.) said the name was a variant of Julia, and said, "Oh how great is the devotion of this woman that she should be counted *worthy of the appellation of apostle.*"[7]

Tryphena, Tryphosa, and Persis in verse 12 also were women who labored with Paul in the Lord. Julia and her husband are mentioned in verse 15. These women played a key role in leadership in ministry in the early church.

PRAYER: *Thank You Lord, that in You there is no male or female. Amen.*

ROLE OF WOMEN PART 2

Now this man had four virgin daughters who prophesied.
—Acts 21:8–9; read also vv. 1–17

This is a continuation of women in ministry in the New Testament from yesterday's devotional.

> This reference to Philip's daughters' each exercising the gifts of prophecy, makes it clear that women did bring God's Word by the power of the Holy Spirit and that such ministry was fully accepted in the early church. This is reinforced by Paul in 1 Corinthians 11:5, where he directs: 1) that a woman may "prophesy," but 2) that she must be properly "covered," that is, rightly related to her husband or other spiritual authority. This is a regulation incumbent upon all spiritual leaders—male or female (see 1 Timothy 3:1–13).
>
> It is puzzling why the place of women in ministry is contested by some in the church. Women had an equal place in the Upper Room, awaiting the Holy Spirit's coming and the birth of the church (Acts 1:14). Then Peter's prophetic sermon at Pentecost which affirmed the Old Testament promise was now to be realized: "your daughters" and "maidservants" would now share fully and equally with men in realizing the anointing, fullness, and ministry of the Holy Spirit, making them effective in witness and service for the spread of the gospel.[8]

One of Satan's greatest fears has to do with women. The threat is recorded in Genesis 3:15. "The seed of the woman (Jesus) will defeat Satan, who will have his head bruised while inflicting minor damage to the heel of the woman doing the bruising."[9] Satan has tried to keep women down, but as it says in Psalm 68:11, at a strategic time, God will give a command, and a company of women who proclaim the good news will rise up and defeat His enemies. Look out when she rises up to fight!

Prayer: *Father, women are Your secret weapon. We have a decisive role in winning the final battle! Amen!*

October 12

PERSONAL PROPHECY

Then the commander came near and took him, and commanded him to be bound with two chains; and he asked who he was and what he had done.
—Acts 21:33; read also vv. 18–40

The trip to Jerusalem marks the beginning of the end of both Paul's ministry and his life. Paul had entered the temple with others who had taken a purification rite. But when Jews from Asia saw him in the temple, they stirred up the whole crowd and laid hands on him. They thought he had taken a Gentile into the temple with him, which was not true. They dragged him out of the temple and sought to kill him, beating him until the commander of the garrison and some soldiers came and stopped them. Then the commander ordered that he be bound with two chains.

The prophetic word about this came from verses 10–11 of this chapter, where Agabus came to Paul, and took Paul's belt and bound his own hands and feet, and said, *"Thus says the Holy Spirit, 'So shall the Jews at Jerusalem bind the man who owns this belt, and deliver him into the hands of the Gentiles.'"*

This is personal prophecy. The Bible clearly allows for personal prophecy. Nathan brought David a word from God. (2 Samuel 12:13); Isaiah predicted Hezekiah's death (Isaiah 38:1); and here Agabus told Paul he faced trouble in Jerusalem. Here are some safeguards: 1) The "word" will usually not be new to the mind of the person, but it will confirm something God is already speaking to him. 2) The character of the person bringing the word is to be weighed. 3) It is not to be considered controlling. 4) All prophecy is "in part", which means that as true as that "part" is, it does not give the whole picture. 5) We must prayerfully consider the word. We must pray and wait on God.[10]

Prayer: *We ask for wisdom in evaluating prophecy. You said in John 10:4–5 that "the sheep…know his voice. Yet they will by no means follow a stranger, but will flee from him for they do not know the voice of strangers." Amen.*

THE EFFICACY OF TESTIMONY

Now it happened, as I journeyed and came near Damascus at about noon, suddenly a great light from heaven shone around me. And I fell to the ground and heard a voice saying to me, "Saul, Saul, why are you persecuting Me?" So I answered, "Who are You Lord?" And He said to me, "I am Jesus of Nazareth, whom you are persecuting."
—ACTS 22:6–8; READ ALSO ACTS 22

Paul gives his testimony here to the Jews of how he was born a Jew and had persecuted the church. On the way to Damascus a great light from heaven shone around him and he fell to the ground. Jesus said, "*Saul, Saul, why are you persecuting Me?*" He was blinded by the light, led to Damascus where Ananias prayed for him, and he received the Holy Spirit and regained his sight. Ananias prophesied to him that God had chosen him to know His will, to see Jesus and to hear the voice of His mouth. He would be a witness to all men. Following this Paul was baptized, and the Lord sent him to the Gentiles. After this account in Acts 22 Paul was in custody the rest of his life, although God still used him mightily.

Paul's testimony is shared four times in the New Testament. There is great power in a testimony. It says in Deuteronomy 6:16–17 that we are to keep His commandments and His testimonies. How do we keep a testimony? We keep a record of the supernatural interventions of God and tell others about them. This brings angelic involvement because Jesus is lifted up. It increases faith greatly. In Revelation 19:6 it says: "*The testimony of Jesus is the spirit of prophecy.*" In other words, when we give our testimony, it increases people's faith to believe for the same thing. When a person gives a testimony of healing, others say, "If He did it for them, He will do it for me." When we give our testimony of salvation, others get saved. "*They overcame him by the Blood of the Lamb and the word of their testimony!*" (Revelation 12:11).

PRAYER: *Father, help us to remember our answers to prayer and give our testimonies. They will bring great results. Even the smallest testimony brings praise to You! Amen!*

October 14

GOD'S PROMISE TO STAND BY US

But the following night the Lord stood by him and said, "Be of good cheer, Paul; for as you have testified for Me in Jerusalem, so you must also bear witness at Rome."
—ACTS 23:11; READ ALSO VV. 1–15

Paul had had a difficult day! He had tried to preach to a huge crowd on the temple mount and it ended in failure. He was sharing his testimony, but when he got to the part of being sent to the Gentiles, a riot erupted with them tearing their clothes and throwing dust into the air! Then he was called to speak to the Sanhedrin, but when he mentioned "resurrection" another fight broke out between the Pharisees and Sadducees. The commander thought they would tear him apart, so he was removed to the barracks. These two opportunities of preaching the gospel seemed to come to nothing.

But Jesus comforted him and said, *"Be of good cheer."* The Lord stood by him, even as He promises to stand by us. He promised that He will never leave us or forsake us. Praising Him helps us see the bigger picture.

> Jesus knew where Paul was; He had not lost sight of Paul because he was in jail. When John Bunyan, author of *Pilgrim's Progress*, was in jail, a man visited him and said, "Friend, the Lord sent me to you, and I have been looking in half the prisons in England for you." John Bunyan replied, "I don't think the Lord sent you to me, because if He had, you would have come here first. God knows I have been here for years."[11]

No matter what our circumstances are, Jesus tells us to *"be of good cheer."* Why? Not because everything is fine; but because God is still on His throne, and He still holds to His promise that *"all things work together for good to those who love God, to those who are the called according to His purpose"* (Romans 8:28). Anyone can be of good cheer when everything is great; but the Christian can be of good cheer when everything looks rotten, because God is good and will help us.

PRAYER: *We want to praise You Jesus for showing up during our dark night and saying, "Be of good cheer." Amen.*

CONSPIRACY AGAINST THE GOSPEL

And when it was day, some of the Jews banded together and bound themselves under an oath, saying that they would neither eat nor drink till they had killed Paul. Now there were more than forty who had formed this conspiracy.
—Acts 23:12–13; read also vv. 16–35

The enemies of Paul had bound themselves under this oath and hatched the plan that the Sanhedrin suggest to the commander that Paul be brought down to them so they could inquire of him more fully. However, Paul's nephew heard of it and told Paul, who then had him inform the commander about the plot. The commander then had two centurions prepare two hundred soldiers, seventy horsemen, and two hundred spearmen to take Paul to Caesarea at the third hour of the night. The next day he was presented to Felix the governor in Caesarea. God had supernaturally protected Paul.

Marilyn Hickey escaped a very real threat to her life while in Pakistan in 2005. They had several nights of healing meetings planned in Islamabad at a stadium. However, before the start of the meeting, they were informed that sixteen members of a thirty two member terrorist cell had just been arrested. They found in the terrorist compound blueprints of the stadium with six large red Xs marked on the stadium, two of which were on the platform. These were to direct the placement of bombs. They also found four pictures that represented people who were to be killed; each had a red X on their face. Marilyn Hickey's picture was one of those pictures. It was a life or death situation. They posted a guard 24 hours a day at her hotel room. She decided to go ahead with the meetings, and said "If I die, I die." The Lord opened up another venue, as the stadium had been shut down. The meetings were a huge success and thousands came and were saved. The Lord had protected her and her team! [12]

Prayer: *Father, thank You for Psalm 91 protection! Thank You for brave servants who risk death to share the gospel in unreached places! Amen!*

RESPONDING TO GOSPEL

And after some days, when Felix came with his wife Drusilla, who was Jewish, he sent for Paul and heard him concerning the faith in Christ. Now as he reasoned about righteousness, self-control, and the judgment to come, Felix was afraid and answered, "Go away for now; when I have a convenient time, I will call for you."
—ACTS 24:24–25; READ ALSO ACTS 24

Here is a wonderful example of the boldness of the preaching of Paul, and his refusal to be intimidated by those in high positions of leadership.

Felix was the governor, and he wanted his wife to hear Paul's testimony. Drusilla was Jewish and also related to Herod Agrippa II. She was about twenty years old. Felix seduced her away from her husband and made her his third wife.

Paul reasoned about righteousness, self-control, and the judgment to come, which were very convicting topics. Had not the Lord told Paul in Acts 18:9, *"Do not be afraid, but speak, and do not keep silent?"* We admire Paul's bold preaching which was directed right to the issues of Felix's life.

Felix had begun life as a slave. It was through his brother, who was a friend of the emperor, that he rose in status. Tacitus, the Roman historian, described Felix as "a master of cruelty and lust who exercised the powers of a king with the spirit of a slave."[13] In particular, he ordered a massacre of thousands of Jews in Caesarea, with many more Jewish homes looted by the Roman soldiers.

After Felix heard Paul, he said, *"Go away for now; when I have a convenient time, I will call for you."* Many respond to the gospel in this way; their rejection is expressed through delay. The Bible says, *"Behold, now is the accepted time; behold, now is the day of salvation"* (2 Corinthians 6:2). If we "wait for a convenient time" we may wait for an eternity.

PRAYER: *Father, help us never to put off what You are calling us to do today, especially witnessing. Amen.*

OPPORTUNITY TO SPEAK GOD'S TRUTH

So Paul said, "I stand at Caesar's judgment seat, where I ought to be judged. To the Jews I have done no wrong, as you very well know."
—Acts 25:10; read also Acts 25

Paul was kept in prison for two years at Caesarea until Felix was succeeded as governor by Porcius Festus. Festus, being a better man than Felix, went up to Jerusalem to investigate the charges against Paul. The Jews tried to convince Festus to transfer Paul back to Jerusalem. Again, there was a plot against his life to be carried out during the transfer. However, Festus wanted the trial to be held at Caesarea. Later, Festus wanted Paul to return to Jerusalem to face the Sanhedrin, but Paul realized that would not be safe, so he appealed his case to Caesar.

It was the right of every Roman citizen to have his case heard by Caesar himself, after initial trials and appeals failed to reach a conclusion. This was like appealing to the Supreme Court of the Roman Empire. He was appealing to Nero, who was later a notorious enemy of Christians.

Now Paul stood before the next in line of the Herods: Herod Agrippa. His wife Bernice was also his sister. Agrippa told Festus that he wanted to hear Paul himself.

This gave Paul an opportunity to speak God's truth to a Gentile ruler. He already had the opportunity to speak to Felix and Festus. The next day Agrippa and Bernice came to the "hearing" with much pomp. All the commanders and prominent men were there—what a tremendous opportunity for Paul. This event illuminates who is important in God's eyes. Sometimes those whom the world thinks are important, and those whom God thinks are important, are two different things. All these "important" people would have been surprised to see the estimates that later generations would form of them and of their prisoner. *"Do nothing out of selfish ambition or vain conceit, but in humility consider others better than yourselves"* (Philippians 2:3).

Prayer: *Father, thank You for opening doors for us to speak Your words. Amazing doors. Amazing grace. Amen.*

OPPORTUNITY TO HEAR THE GOSPEL

"King Agrippa, do you believe the prophets? I know that you do believe." Then Agrippa said to Paul, "You almost persuade me to become a Christian."

—ACTS 26:27–28; READ ALSO ACTS 26

It is not God's will that any should perish and go to hell. Regardless of how evil and wicked someone may be, God will give them an opportunity to accept the Cross.

There was never a family more demonically controlled than Herod the Great and his sons.

+ Herod the Great received a witness when the wise men came to look for Jesus. Instead of listening, he had two thousand babies killed in an effort to destroy Jesus. Herod was so wicked he even drowned one of his own sons. At the time of his death he ordered that in every village and town, the most beloved people should be arrested. These fifteen thousand people were killed. All Israel went into mourning, but they didn't mourn over Herod's death!

+ Herod Antipas was his son. John the Baptist witnessed to him. He had John the Baptist beheaded and gave the bloody head to his half-daughter.

+ Herod Agrippa I was king during the early church. Many miracles were happening with signs and wonders in the streets. Even though he didn't believe, he had James the brother of John arrested and beheaded. Then he arrested Peter, but an angel helped Peter escape from prison.

+ Herod Agrippa II was witnessed to by Paul, but he didn't believe either. He "almost believed."

Herod's family rejected every opportunity. When they fell out of favor with Rome, they were settled in Italy by Mount Vesuvius. In 79 A.D. a volcanic eruption killed everyone in the area. Today there are no members of the ancient Herod family left.[14]

PRAYER: *Thank You Father for giving everyone a chance to hear the gospel. Help us to obey the Great Commission. Amen.*

October 19

ANGELIC INTERVENTION

For there stood by me this night an angel of the God to whom I belong and whom I serve, saying, "Do not be afraid, Paul; you must be brought before Caesar; and indeed God has granted you all those who sail with you."
—Acts 27:23–24; read also Acts 27

On the trip to Rome, Paul warned them not to leave Fair Havens because the voyage would end in disaster. They did not listen to Paul, and the majority advised them to set sail again and try to reach Phoenix, another harbor of Crete. But not long after, a "tempestuous head wind called Euroclydon arose, and the ship was caught in it. They were driven up and down in the sea for 14 days. Miraculously they made it to Malta. An angel appeared to Paul and told him not to be afraid because it was God's plan that he be brought before Caesar. The best news of all was that the angel said that God had granted everyone life.

We also have a testimony of angelic intervention and preservation of life. My husband, Jim, was driving to a softball game in our little VW bug when an oncoming Mercury station wagon crossed over the center line and crashed into him. The last thing he remembered was turning his wheel to the left. The accident took place totally in his lane. They needed to peel back the top of the car to get him out. Sadly, the man riding next to him, our wonderful friend and director of the St. Olaf orchestra, was killed. Jim had five broken ribs, but it was as if an angel had laid over him because that was the only part of the car that was not destroyed.

When he left home in the morning, I prayed protection for him. After lying down, I had a dream of him in our 5th grade elementary room in Plainfield, Iowa. This was the room we used during fire drills. He was feeling around, and I was praying Psalm 91 protection over him—praying that God would give His angels charge over him and praying in the Spirit as well. I woke up when a lady from Divine Redeemer hospital called, saying he'd been in a terrible accident. He recovered, and we give the glory to God for His protection!

PRAYER: *Thank You Jesus for Your angels on duty! Amen!*

THE SICK WERE ALL HEALED

But when Paul had gathered a bundle of sticks and laid them on the fire, a viper came out because of the heat, and fastened on his hand. So when the natives saw the creature hanging from his hand, they said to one another, "No doubt this man is a murderer, whom, though he has escaped the sea, yet justice does not allow to live." But he shook off the creature into the fire and suffered no harm.
—ACTS 28:3–5; READ ALSO VV. 1–14

After Paul's ship was shipwrecked on Malta, they all made it safely off the ship to land by swimming, some on boards, and some on parts of the ship.

The natives showed kindness to them and kindled a fire, but when Paul gathered sticks, the viper fastened onto him. The natives expected he would swell up and die, but when he didn't, they thought he was a god.

The Lord provided ministry and miracles there, because the leading citizen of the island, Publius, had a father who was sick of a fever and dysentery. Publius was the highest-ranking Roman official on the island. When Paul laid his hands on his father, he was healed. Then the rest of the people on the island brought their sick to him and they were all healed.

This healing ministry was an example of Mark 16:17: *"And these signs will follow those who believe: In My name they will cast out demons; they will speak with new tongues; they will take up serpents; and if they drink anything deadly, it will by no means hurt them; they will lay hands on the sick, and they will recover."*

These divine healings happened here in spite of the fact that Luke, a physician, accompanied Paul. Of course, they lost everything on the ship when it was destroyed, but Jesus saw to it that everyone on the island was healed by the laying on of hands. This was to the glory of God, and undoubtedly resulted in many salvations as well. God cares about souls more than earthly treasures!

PRAYER: *Thank You Father, that Your word is true today if we will believe and not doubt. You are Jehovah Rophe. Amen.*

October 21

FINISHING OUR RACE WELL

Now when we came to Rome, the centurion delivered the prisoners to the captain of the guard, but Paul was permitted to dwell by himself with the soldier who guarded him. And it came to pass after three days that Paul called the leaders of the Jews together.
—ACTS 28:16; READ ALSO VV. 15–31

Paul took courage when the Christians from the city came out to meet him walking about 43 miles to the Appii Forum to welcome him and his companions.

At the very end of Acts he comes to Rome as Jesus had promised him that he would (Acts 23:11).

Paul was not in a normal prison but was allowed to dwell by himself and provide his own living space in a rented house. Yet he was constantly under the supervision of a Roman guard, and often chained. The rotation of the guard gave him a constant supply of people to talk to. In Philippians 1:13, Paul told how his message reached the palace guards of Rome.

Paul called the leaders of the Jews together, following his practice of going first to the Jews in every city. He told them that he had done *"nothing against our people or the customs of our fathers"* (v. 17). He told them it was for the hope of Israel that he was bound with the chain. They told him they didn't know anything about Paul, but they had heard that Christianity was spoken against everywhere.

Paul spoke to the Jewish community for one full day about the kingdom of God, persuading them concerning Jesus from the Law of Moses and the Prophets. Some believed and some didn't. He shared from Isaiah 6:9–10 about the rejection of the gospel, and that the gospel of salvation had been sent to the Gentiles. That caused, as usual, a great dispute.

Paul lived two years in his rented house and received all who came to him and preached Jesus and the kingdom.

PRAYER: *Paul preached the gospel faithfully to the end. May we do likewise. May we all "fight the good fight and finish the race." (1 Timothy 6:12). In Jesus' name. Amen.*

October 22

FILL US WITH THE KNOWLEDGE
OF YOUR WILL

For this reason we also, since the day we heard it, do not cease to pray for you, and to ask that you may be filled with the knowledge of His will in all wisdom and spiritual understanding; that you may walk worthy of the Lord, fully pleasing Him, being fruitful in every good work and increasing in the knowledge of God; strengthened with all might, according to His glorious power, for all patience and longsuffering with joy; giving thanks to the Father who has qualified us to be partakers of the inheritance of the saints in the light. He has delivered us from the power of darkness and conveyed us into the kingdom of the Son of His love.
—COLOSSIANS 1:9–13; READ ALSO COLOSSIANS 1

We should pray the things mentioned in this apostolic prayer for all people, even those we don't know. Paul himself did not know the Colossians, but he prayed for them always. He prayed for all of us:

+ That we be filled with the knowledge of Him in all wisdom and spiritual understanding. This is not about seeking the accumulation of knowledge; that in itself is empty (Gnosticism). God's knowledge leads to a changed life. Paul wanted them to know God better and please Him. He wanted them to be fruitful in every good work. Jesus said in John 15:5: *"I am the vine, you are the branches. He who abides in Me, and I in him, bears much fruit; for without Me you can do nothing."*

+ That we be strengthened in our inner man to endure and overcome problems with people or circumstances. We must be patient and longsuffering and have an attitude of joy at all times. His joy is our strength.

+ We are to give thanks because He has qualified us to be partakers of the inheritance of the saints in light. We don't earn it; it is the Father who qualifies us. This is a powerful reason to give thanks every day, because He has transferred us out of the kingdom of darkness into the kingdom of light.

PRAYER: *Father, we do pray to be filled with the knowledge of Your will, and that we'd walk worthy of You. Amen.*

October 23

STANDING AND BELIEVING IN TRUTH

As you therefore have received Christ Jesus the Lord, so walk in Him, rooted and built up in Him and established in the faith, as you have been taught, abounding in it with thanksgiving. Beware lest anyone cheat you through philosophy and empty deceit, according to the tradition of men, according to the basic principles of the world, and not according to Christ. For in Him dwells all the fullness of the Godhead bodily; and you are complete in Him, who is the head of all principality and power.
—COLOSSIANS 2:6–9; READ ALSO COLOSSIANS 2

The problem that Paul was combatting in the Colossian church (v. 4ff) was similar to Gnosticism (Greek word for knowledge). This heresy undermined Christianity in several basic ways: 1) It insisted that important secret knowledge was hidden from most believers. Paul said Christ provides all the knowledge we need. 2) It taught that the body was evil. Paul countered that God himself lived in a body (Jesus). 3) It contended that Christ only seemed to be human, but was not. Paul insisted that Jesus was fully human and fully God.[15]

In order to stand for truth and against heresies, we must be rooted and built up in Him through the knowledge of the Word of God. Receiving Christ as Lord of your life is the beginning of life with Christ; after this we must seek to learn from Him, His life, and His teachings. We must be filled with the Holy Spirit, because He leads us into truth, and opens our eyes to the meaning of the Word. He is our Teacher and our Guide.

Without the Word of God as our plumb line, it is easy for the devil to deceive us into believing a lie—especially when "everyone else" is saying or doing something.

PRAYER: *Father, send Your Spirit to us to lead us into all truth. Help us not to skim over parts of Your Word that we don't want to listen to. Help us to read with understanding, and then obey what You show us! In Jesus' name. Amen.*

PUT ON LOVE AND BE THANKFUL

But above all these things put on love, which is the bond of perfection.
And let the peace of God rule in your hearts, to which also you were
called in one body and be thankful. Let the word of Christ dwell in you
richly in all wisdom, teaching and admonishing one another in psalms
and hymns and spiritual songs, singing with grace in your hearts to the
Lord. And whatever you do in word or deed, do all in the name of the
Lord Jesus, giving thanks to God the Father through Him.
—COLOSSIANS 3:14–17; READ ALSO COLOSSIANS 3

Put on love. Just like we put on clothes in the morning for the day, we
should put on love. We decide what we want to wear, and in the same
manner, we should decide to put on love. The Bible also says we have
not, because we ask not. We must remember to ask for God's love to
shine through us each day.

And we are to let the peace of God rule in our hearts. We are to let
Christ's peace be the umpire or referee in our heart. Our heart is the
center of conflict, because there our feelings and desires clash—our
fears and hope, distrust and trust, jealousy and love. Paul says we
must decide between things that conflict by using the rule of peace.
We need to make choices in our thinking that promote peace.[16]

We must live by the word J O Y. Jesus first, **O**thers second, and
Yourself last. Our selfishness helps promote the conflict.

And be thankful. As we start listing all the things for which we
are thankful, a shift occurs in our thinking. The more we sing and
praise, the more those things that were troubling us seem smaller and
smaller!

We must honor the Lord in whatever we say or do, knowing we are
His representatives. What impression do people have of Christ when
they see or talk with us?

PRAYER: *This is such beautiful and practical wisdom for having a good*
attitude, and peaceful relationships. Father, we thank You for Your
mirror showing us our hearts. Amen.

October 25

WAYS TO PRAY FOR THE CHURCH

Continue earnestly in prayer, being vigilant in it with thanksgiving; meanwhile praying also for us, that God would open to us a door for the word, to speak the mystery of Christ, for which I am also in chains, that I may make it manifest, as I ought to speak.
—Colossians 4:2–6; read also Colossians 4

Paul requested prayer that the Spirit would open more doors to minister to unbelievers and that he would present the gospel clearly, as well as prepare the people to receive it.

Following are additional suggested ways to pray for the church:[17]

+ Pray that we would sense the glory of God. Glory is the visible manifestation of the splendor, power, and radiance of God. Whenever God's presence comes down within the church, His people are uplifted spiritually. His presence manifests in awesome worship, and this worship brings miracles. The gifts of the Spirit are released (John 17:22).

+ Pray that we would follow the Word of God. Jesus said: *"For I gave them the words you gave Me and they accepted them"* (John 17:8). When the people in the church are in the Word, they begin to change; their lives take on new meaning.

+ Pray that we would be united in the love of God. When the church is unified through the love of God, they can do anything. They can shake the very gates of hell (John 17:21).

+ Pray that we would go forth in the mission of God, and that all His church would be soul winners.

+ Pray that we would experience the joy of God! Jesus prayed that His church would have His joy (John 17:13).

PRAYER: *Pray the John 17 prayer for the church! Amen!*

GOD SPOKE THROUGH HIS SON

God, who at various times and in various ways spoke in time past to the fathers by the prophets, has in these last days spoken to us by His Son, whom He has appointed heir of all things, through whom also He made the worlds; who being the brightness of His glory and the express image of His person, and upholding all things by the word of His power, when He had by Himself purged our sins, sat down at the right hand of the Majesty on high.
—HEBREWS 1:1–4; READ ALSO HEBREWS 1

God has spoken through the prophets in various ways, such as dreams (Daniel 2:3), visions (Ezekiel 8:4), angels (Zechariah 1:9) and direct speech (Genesis 12:1). Now He speaks through His Son, and this passage describes the sevenfold excellencies of Jesus:[18]

+ He is heir of all things. He inherited it all.

+ It was through Jesus that God created the worlds, "the panorama of all things and all time."[19] Not only is Jesus the exact representation of God, but He is God himself—the very God who spoke in Old Testament times.

+ He is the brightness of His glory, "the dazzling radiance of God's splendor."

+ He is the express image of His person, "the exact expression of God's true nature."

+ He upholds all things by the word of His power; "He upholds and expands it by the mighty power of His spoken Word."

+ He, by Himself, purged our sins. "The complete cleansing of our sins."

+ He sat down at the right hand of the Majesty on high. "He took his seat on the highest throne at the right hand of the majestic One."

PRAYER: *Praise the Lord for His beauty and majesty. Meditate upon these truths, and spend time worshipping Him. Amen.*

October 27

DO IT AGAIN, JESUS

How shall we escape if we neglect so great a salvation, which at the first began to be spoken by the Lord, and was confirmed to us by those who hear Him, God also bearing witness both with signs and wonders with various miracles, and gifts of the Holy Spirit, according to His own will.
—Hebrews 2:2–4; read also Hebrews 2

This is a great salvation: a) We are saved by a great Savior. b) We are saved at a great cost. c) We are saved from a great penalty.

This Word was spoken by the Lord and was confirmed with signs, wonders, miracles, and gifts of the Holy Spirit given by God. Jesus said that miraculous signs would follow those who believe (Mark 16:17). "If there is no element of the miraculous, one may question whether there is true belief in Jesus or if the Word of God is truly being preached. The preacher must give God something to confirm." [20]

Once James Maloney was ministering in Colorado. He was on his way out to catch a plane after the service, when a woman seated in one of the chairs had a baby girl on her lap. She reached out and asked if he would pray for her. He said he felt really rushed, but bent down, laid his hand on her, and prayed, "Lord, just do the creative miracle that she needs."

It turns out the child had been born with no pupils or irises—nothing but white eyeballs. The next day she was crying in her crib. When the parents went in, she had brilliant, sparkling blue eyes! God had created irises and pupils for her overnight! [21]

PRAYER: *Do it again, Jesus! We invite You to come! So many people need healing. So many people need salvation. Let faith arise in our hearts to believe You for signs, wonders and miracles. Let this 3rd Great Awakening be a combination of the Book of Exodus and the Book of Acts! In Your Name. Amen.*

ENCOURAGE ONE ANOTHER IN FAITH

Beware, brethren, lest there be in any of you an evil heart of unbelief in departing from the living God; but exhort one another daily, while it is called "Today," lest any of you be hardened through the deceitfulness of sin. For we have become partakers of Christ if we hold the beginning of our confidence steadfast to the end while it is said: "Today, if you will hear His voice, Do not harden your hearts as in the rebellion."

—HEBREWS 3:12–15; READ ALSO HEBREWS 3

We are told to encourage one another in the faith, because we can be hardened through the treachery and lies of sin and turn away from the living God.

Dr. Bob Rodgers told a story about that very thing in his devotional.[22] There was a young preacher who lived near Lexington, Kentucky. He married a young girl from his local church and God opened a door for them to minister in Independence, Missouri.

The New Hope Baptist church began to grow. It opened a Bible school and other ministries and became one of the largest churches in the territory. However, when they began to have tensions in the church, he became so upset that he resigned.

At that time, they had discovered gold at Colonel Sutter's sawmill in California. He told his family that he was going to California to find gold, and after he got established, he would send for them. Because of the unsanitary conditions there, disease was rampant. Pastor James became ill and died.

The family back home was devastated with the news. His two older sons, Frank and Jesse James, became the most famous outlaws in American history.

Both Frank and Jesse could quote the Bible and no doubt had the call to preach that had been upon the father. When the father got out of the will of God through the deceitfulness of sin, he caused the whole family to fall.

PRAYER: *We pray especially for leaders to stand strong. Amen.*

October 29

THE POWER OF GOD'S WORD

For the word of God is living and powerful, and sharper than any two-edged sword, piercing even to the division of soul and spirit, and of joints and marrow, and is a discerner of the thoughts and intents of the heart.
—HEBREWS 4:12; READ ALSO HEBREWS 4

The Word of God lays open the heart and accurately discerns spiritual health. When the Word exposes our weakness and unbelief, it shows its inherent power, accuracy and sharpness. When we read the Word, it is for far more than Bible knowledge. We do it for the ministry of the Word itself: [23]

+ God's Word brings true health, fruitfulness, prosperity and success to what we do (Psalm 1:3).
+ God's Word has healing power and the power to deliver from oppression (Psalm 107:20).
+ God's Word cleanses us (John 15:3).
+ God's Word, hidden in our hearts, keeps us from sin (Psalm 119:11).
+ God's Word is a counselor (Psalm 119:24).
+ God's Word is a source of strength (Psalm 119:28).
+ God's Word imparts life (Psalm 119:93; Matthew 4:4).
+ God's Word is a source of illumination and guidance (Psalm 119:105).
+ God's Word gives peace to those who love it (Psalm 119:165).
+ God's Word when heard and understood and obeyed, brings fruit (Matthew 13:23).
+ God's Word, when we abide in it, is evidence of true discipleship (John 8:31).
+ God's Word is Jesus (John 1:1).
+ God's Word has inherent power and authority against demonic powers (Luke 4:36).

PRAYER: *Father, Your Word is a lamp to our feet and a light unto our path. Give us the desire to hide it in our hearts. Amen.*

DISCERNING BETWEEN GOOD AND EVIL

But solid food belongs to those who are of full age, that is those who by reason of use have their senses exercised to discern both good and evil.
—HEBREWS 5:14; READ ALSO HEBREWS 5

Our senses are trained by how we use them to discern both good and evil. The plumb line for determining good and evil is the Word of God. If the Bible says it is right and good, it is right and good. If the Bible says it is wrong and evil, it is wrong and evil. We need to be biblically literate to know what is actually written in the Bible to be able to discern what is good and what is evil. If we don't know what is written in the Bible, how will we know what is right or wrong?

In these last days, we need wisdom to discern what is good and what is evil. Isaiah 5:20–23 applies to today: "Woe to those who call evil good, and good evil; Who put darkness for light, and light for darkness; Who put bitter for sweet, and sweet for bitter! Woe to those who are wise in their own eyes, and prudent in their own sight! Woe to men mighty at drinking wine, Woe to men valiant for mixing intoxicating drink, Who justify the wicked for a bribe, And take away justice from the righteous man!"

When we see Christians voting for those who support abortion, do they know Exodus 20:13? "You shall not murder." When we see people voting for those who support gay marriage, do they know Leviticus 18:22? "You shall not lie with a male as with a woman. It is an abomination."

When we see people living together without benefit of marriage, do they know Galatians 5:19 which says that those who practice fornication will not inherit the kingdom of God? In fact, do they know all the sins listed in Galatians 5:19?

Our Scripture says that solid food belongs to those who practice righteousness and know the difference between right and wrong. They are the ones who get it. They are the ones who get revelation from the Word.

PRAYER: *Father in heaven, we ask for Your help in discernment between good and evil! Let us be a light for You! Amen!*

October 31

TREASURING OUR SALVATION

For it is impossible for those who were once enlightened, and have tasted
the heavenly gift, and have become partakers of the Holy Spirit, and
have tasted the good word of God and the powers of the age to come,
if they fall away, to renew them again to repentance, since they crucify
again for themselves the Son of God, and put Him to an open shame.
—Hebrews 6:4–6; read also Hebrews 6

This seems to be a clear passage, a) against eternal security, and
b) that it is not possible for one to repent IF:

+ If they were once enlightened, or the true light of Christ has
  shined on them.

+ If they have tasted or have had a full and real experience of the
  heavenly gift, or the gift of salvation.

+ If they have become partakers of the Holy Spirit. This means
  they have received and fellowship with the Holy Spirit. They
  were used in the gifts of the Spirit.

+ If they have tasted the good Word of God. This means they
  have experienced the goodness of the Word of God.

+ If they have experienced the powers of the age to come—God's
  supernatural power.

+ If they fall away, to renew them again to repentance. This refers
  to Christians. Demas is an example of this type of person. He
  was a Christian (Colossians 4:14). He is called a fellow worker
  (Philemon 24). Yet Paul said Demas had forsaken him having
  loved this present world (2 Timothy 4:10). Falling away is not
  the same as falling. Falling means you sinned. Falling away is
  departing from Jesus Himself. The former is represented by
  Peter, who was forgiven; the latter is represented by Judas.

+ If they *"crucify again for themselves the Son of God, and put*
  Him to an open shame."

They can't repent because they don't want to. Anyone that wants
to repent can do that!

Prayer: *Father, help us not to ever take this gift of salvation for*
granted. Help us to treasure it for eternity! Amen!

CHRIST IS BOTH PRIEST AND KING

For He testifies: "You are a priest forever according to the order of Melchizedek."... Therefore He is also able to save to the uttermost those who come to God through Him, since He always lives to make intercession for them.

—HEBREWS 7:17, 25; READ ALSO HEBREWS 7

Melchizedek is a type of Christ in His high priestly ministry. He is mentioned in Genesis 14:18–20 and Psalm 110:4.

"Like Melchizedek, Jesus Christ is a universal priest, and He is both priest and king. The silence surrounding Melchizedek's ancestry, his priestly pedigree, his birth and death illustrates the eternal and changeless priesthood of Christ" (v. 3).[1]

The fact that Abraham paid tithes to Melchizedek and was blessed by him establishes his superiority over the Levitical priests (v. 4–7).

The Levitical priests were mortal and subject to death, but no mention is made of Melchizedek's death (v. 8).

Even Levi paid tithes to him *while he was still in Abraham's loins.* This speaks loudly that what we do impacts our children and future generations (v. 9–10).

The fact that Christ was born of the tribe of Judah, not Levi, emphasizes the beginning of a new priestly order (v. 13–14.) We needed a new priesthood because the old one failed.

Jesus is "another priest" which supersedes the Levitical priesthood. The first covenant had to be annulled because it didn't provide full access to God's presence (v. 15–18). Jesus made a way when He died and the veil was torn, giving us unlimited access into the Holy of Holies.

The Levitical priests died, and their office had to be filled by another. But Jesus permanently holds His priestly office (v. 22–24). He is able to save fully both now and forever everyone who comes to God through Him, because He lives to pray continually for them. He doesn't need to offer up daily sacrifices, for He offered up Himself once and for all (v. 25–27).

PRAYER: *Lord, You are able to save to the uttermost! Amen!*

November 2

THE NEW COVENANT

For this is the covenant that I will make with the house of Israel after those days, says the LORD: I will put My laws in their mind and write them on their hearts; and I will be their God, and they shall be My people. None of them shall teach his neighbor, and none his brother saying, "Know the LORD," for all shall know Me, from the least of them to the greatest of them. For I will be merciful to their unrighteousness and their sins and their lawless deeds I will remember no more.
—HEBREWS 8:10–12; READ ALSO HEBREWS 8

This is part of a quote from Jeremiah 31:31–34, which states the heart of the new covenant will be through the blood of Jesus. The new covenant is not like the old one (the Law of Moses), and under its power God will change you. God will write His law on your heart. You will have a new heart that wants to serve God. He will put His laws in your mind, as well as write them on your heart. The words *"written on your heart"* states the difference between the old and the new covenants. In the old covenant He wrote the commandments on the stones (not on the heart) and said, "Now you do these." But the old covenant made no one righteous. There would need to be a new covenant.

The new covenant is also called the gospel of Jesus Christ, which is the power of God for salvation (Romans 1:16). When God writes His laws on our hearts and Jesus comes in, He changes us.

Under the law, you would try to do your part, and (outside of you) God would do His part. In the new covenant, God moves inside of you, and He becomes everything you need to do your part! *"Christ in you, the hope of glory"* (Colossians 1:28).

He is not outside of you telling you what to do. You are His home. His mind becomes your mind. His desires become your desires. You and God become one (1 Corinthians 6:17). That is the miracle of your salvation. This is the new covenant.

PRAYER: *What a powerful Scripture to pray for our relatives and friends, that You will write Your laws on our hearts, and You will be merciful to us! You can pray this prayer, that God will take out hearts of stone and put in hearts of flesh. Amen.*

THE OLD TESTAMENT TABERNACLE

*For a tabernacle was prepared: the first part, in which was the
lampstand, the table, and the showbread, which is called the sanctuary;
and behind the second veil, the part of the tabernacle which is called the
Holiest of All, which had the golden censer and the ark of the covenant
overlaid on all sides with gold, in which were the golden pot that had
the manna, Aaron's rod that budded, and the tablets of the covenant;
and above it were the cherubim of glory overshadowing the mercy seat.*
—HEBREWS 9:1–5; READ ALSO HEBREWS 9

The Old Testament tabernacle was built on a pattern of the true tabernacle in heaven. It is all a type and shadow of Jesus.

The first piece in the OUTER COURT was the *Bronze Altar*. This is where the animals would be sacrificed. Watching it burning on the altar above your own reflected image in the bronze plate of that altar, would leave a strong impression of the cost of your sin. The bronze altar was a picture of the cross and every animal that shed its blood was a prophecy of the Lamb of God.

The Laver was next, and the priests used it for washing the blood of the animals off before going into the Holy Place. It is a picture of Jesus. He washes us with His word (Ephesians 5:26).

In the HOLY PLACE, the *Golden Lampstand* was on the left and gave light to the priests. Jesus is the light of the world.

Next is the *Table of Showbread* on your right. It was called the Bread of His Face. Jesus is the Bread of life (John 6:51).

The *Golden Altar* was straight ahead in front of the curtain. It burned perpetual incense. The priest prayed for people at this altar. Jesus is our High Priest who prays for us.

The HOLY OF HOLIES was behind the curtain and held the Ark of the Covenant. On it was the Mercy Seat which had two gold cherubim. In it were the ten commandments, manna, and Aaron's rod that budded. The High Priest went in once a year to put blood on the altar to cover sins.

PRAYER: *Jesus, You tore the veil when You died and now we can enter the Holy of Holies anytime! You put Your blood on the mercy seat to pay for our sins once and for all. Amen!*

OBEDIENCE

*Therefore, when He came into the world, He said: "Sacrifice and
offering You did not desire, but a body You have prepared for Me.
In burnt offerings and sacrifices for sin You had no pleasure." Then I
said, "Behold, I have come—In the volume of the book it is written of
Me—to do Your will, O God."*
—HEBREWS 10:5–7; READ ALSO VV. 1–18

Jesus came to do the Father's will in obedience. In fact, the Bible says
in 1 Samuel 15:22: *"To obey is better than sacrifice."*

The agony in the Garden of Gethsemane (Matthew 26:36–39),
proved He struggled with the difficulty of obedience. "When He had
offered up prayers and supplications, with vehement cries and tears to
Him who was able to save Him from death, and was heard because
of His godly fear, though He was a Son, yet He learned obedience by
the things which He suffered" (Hebrews 5:7–8).

This is how Jesus knows what we are going through, and He ever
lives to make intercession for us according to the will of God (Romans
8:27). "For we do not have a High Priest who cannot sympathize with
our weaknesses, but was in all points tempted as we are, yet without
sin" (Hebrews 4:15).

Jesus modeled obedience in everything He did. He says in John
15:10, "If you keep My commandments, you will abide in My love,
just as I have kept My Father's commandments and abide in His love."
These are His commands: we are to give thanks in everything, pray
always, and forgive.

Obedience is also connected with answered prayer: "And whatever
we ask we receive from Him, because we keep His commandments and
do those things that are pleasing in His sight. And this is His commandment: that we should believe on the name of His Son Jesus Christ
and love one another, as He gave us commandment" (1 John 3:22–23).

It was by Jesus' obedience that we could be saved. It is also by our
obedience that people are saved, because we share the Gospel with
them at the prompting of the Holy Spirit.

PRAYER: *Father, we ask for help in obeying, doing what You ask
without procrastinating. We desire death to self and life to You! Amen!*

ASSEMBLY OF CHRISTIANS

And let us consider one another in order to stir up love and good works, not forsaking the assembling of ourselves together, as is the manner of some, but exhorting one another and so much the more as you see the Day approaching.
—HEBREWS 10:23–25; READ ALSO VV. 19–39

When we come together, Jesus is there as He said, "*For where two or three are gathered together in My name, I am there in the midst of them*" (Matthew 18:20). When we come together we can stir up one another to love and good works. Love is possible only in community and won't happen on a desert island.

Forsaking the assembling of ourselves together will foster discouragement and a feeling of being unneeded and unwanted. One pastor we had many years ago said, "It only takes missing church three weeks in a row to become backslidden." Some only go to church if they feel they "need it" at the time. But our motivation for fellowship must be to obey God and to give this fellowship to others. We should gather with believers to encourage someone who needs to stand strong against a tide of discouragement.

+ We gather to give and receive something from God.
+ We gather to encourage each other by our shared faith and values.
+ We gather to bless one another and share our gifts.
+ We gather together because we are commanded to do it by the Lord. The warning is that "the banana that leaves the bunch gets peeled."
+ We need to gather together especially as we see the soon return of Christ.
+ We gather together to pray and become that healing, evangelizing army of God.
+ We gather together to worship together and sense the joy and power of a corporate anointing.

PRAYER: *Jesus, You gave Yourself that Your church would be a bride without spot or wrinkle or any such thing. Amen.*

WITHOUT FAITH, NO MAN CAN PLEASE GOD

*By faith Abel offered to God a more excellent sacrifice than Cain,
through which he obtained witness that he was righteous, God testi-
fying of his gifts; and through it he being dead still speaks.*
—HEBREWS 11:4; READ ALSO VV. 1–19

This is the astounding chapter on the faith of the giants of the Bible.
And we know that *"Without faith it is impossible to please Him"* (v. 6a).

While Dick Eastman, well known prayer leader, was speaking at
North Central University (his alma mater), God showed him that
there would be a wave of sacrifice on the campus unlike anything
they had ever witnessed. It would be the beginning of a life of total
discipleship. The chapel and evening services were amazing. He was
concluding what he felt were his final remarks when a startling thing
occurred. A student who had left five minutes earlier returned and
was heading straight to the platform with her wallet in her hand. She
told all the students that God had told her to get this from her room,
and it was all that she had.

> Suddenly a strong wind of conviction settled upon the four hundred
> students. Students were coming from everywhere toward the plat-
> form. They were emptying their wallets; the majority giving every-
> thing they had.
>
> Dollars however, were not the only things given that night. Stu-
> dents began leaving the chapel moments after conviction settled. Again,
> only the Holy Spirit prompted them. Within two hours the plat-
> form looked like a junkyard—televisions, instruments, albums, radios,
> sports equipment, photographs, a rifle, and a mink-trimmed coat.[2]

It took faith for Dick Eastman to share before the whole college
what the Lord had showed him, about the wave of sacrifice never witnessed before. *"God is a rewarder of those who diligently seek Him"* (v. 6b).

PRAYER: *Lord, use us as a spark for others' faith! In Jesus' name.
Amen!*

THROUGH FAITH, WE SUBDUE KINGDOMS AND OBTAIN PROMISES

And what more shall I say? For the time would fail me to tell of Gideon and Barak and Samson and Jephthah, also of David and Samuel and the prophets: who through faith subdued kingdoms, worked righteousness, obtained promises, stopped the mouths of lions.
—HEBREWS 11:32–33; READ ALSO VV. 20–40

When we think of Elijah, we think of him calling down fire on the sacrifice and killing the prophets of Baal. The drought ended when he prayed for the rain to come and he saw the clouds rising (1 Kings 18).

Cindy Jacobs, a modern-day prophet, also has a testimony of God answering prayer concerning the weather.

It was July 7, 2007 and more than seventy thousand adults and youth gathered for The Call, led by Lou Engle, at the large Nissan stadium in Nashville. (We were also there.) The fight to end abortion was the main theme.

It was so very hot, and many people were passing out. Lou Engle asked Cindy to do something about it, so she and a radical-looking young man of prayer knelt down and prayed. They pointed to the sky and commanded the clouds to come.

This was their proclamation: "In the name of Jesus, we command the clouds to come from the four corners of the earth and cover this stadium. We speak to the north, the south, the east, and the west. *Clouds come!*"³

And of course, the clouds came! I remember being so thankful that the clouds came and covered the stadium.

Then she told her young prayer warrior they were going to command the winds to blow—and they did! I remember being so thankful for the beautiful breeze and knowing it was entirely supernatural!

PRAYER: *Father, in the Name of Jesus we call forth an army of prayer warriors who, like those of Hebrews 11, will rise up and through faith subdue kingdoms and obtain promises! Amen!*

SHAME IS THE TOOL OF THE ENEMY

Let us lay aside every weight and the sin which so easily ensnares us, and let us run with endurance the race that is set before us, looking unto Jesus, the author and finisher of our faith, who for the joy that was set before Him endured the cross, despising the shame, and has sat down at the right hand of the throne of God.
—HEBREWS 12:1–2; READ ALSO HEBREWS 12

One of the tools of the enemy to hold God's people bound is shame. Jesus took not only all our sins, but He took our shame.

Guilt is not the same as shame. Guilt is what we should experience as soon as we sin. Shame is the real problem. It inspires fear of being found out, humiliated, and/or rejected or abandoned.

Guilt says, "I made a mistake." Shame says, "I am a mistake." Shame is a lie we believe about who we are.

The remedy for guilt is the Cross.

The remedy for shame is God's truth.

Shame can develop: a) through demands of performance and unrealistic expectation; b) through words that pronounce a curse; c) through rejection, abandonment and neglect; d) through physical or sexual abuse which brings the most severe kind of shame; or e) through family dysfunction such as alcoholism. Shame is the core of all addictions.

To receive healing from shame, we must recognize the fruits of it in 1) the fear of isolation or difficulty in making friends; 2) self-loathing; 3) addictive habits; 4) the stigma of "badness."[4]

PRAYER: *God wants to heal you! Repent of foundational lies and speak the truth of God's Word over you. Forgive those who have hurt you. Take shame and lies to the cross. Come out of agreement with the lies! You are loved! You are accepted in the Beloved! You have value and purpose! Amen!*

PRAISE GOD ALWAYS

Therefore by Him let us continually offer the sacrifice of praise to God, that is, the fruit of our lips, giving thanks to His name.
—Hebrews 13:15; read also Hebrews 13

Praising the Lord is not always easy. It is a sacrifice because it costs us something. We do not necessarily praise God because we feel like doing it. In fact, we do it out of obedience because God said to do it. And we do it because of what He has done for us.

Thanksgiving is directly commanded by God. It is the way into God's presence. "Enter His gates with thanksgiving and His courts with praise; give thanks to Him and praise His name" (Psalm 100:4, niv).

"Let the high praises of God be in their mouth, and a two-edged sword in their hand to execute vengeance on the nations, and punishments on the peoples; to bind their kings with chains, and their nobles with fetters of iron; to execute on them the written judgment—This honor have all His saints. Praise the LORD!" (Psalm 149:6–10). This is spiritual warfare praise as when Jehoshaphat sent out the singers ahead of the army. As they sang and praised the Lord, the Lord sent ambushments against their enemies. They did not even have to fight the battle because the enemy defeated each other.

When our children were moving from Indianapolis to Florida, they were trying to sell their house. They had bought a house in Florida, so they were having two house payments. A big storm came, and the creek behind their Indiana house rose until the whole yard was flooded. It looked like the "For Sale" sign was floating in the yard, and that you would have to get in a rowboat to get to the front of the house. Who would want to buy a house like that? We praised and prayed for a change in the weather, and for the sale of the house. The Lord heard us and answered, and the house was sold! Praise the Lord!

Prayer: *Let us not be moved by what we see or moved by what we feel. Let us praise You, Lord, at all times, trusting that You are working all things out for our good! Amen!*

PASTORS NEED PRAYERS

For this reason I left you in Crete, that you should set in order the things that are lacking, and appoint elders in every city as I commanded you—.
—Titus 1:5; read also Titus 1

Paul told Titus to appoint elders, who are also called bishops in verse 7. Elders and bishops are terms describing pastors over congregations in different cities in Crete.

Pastors aren't perfect—Except for this one:

He preaches twenty minutes and then sits down. He condemns sin, but never steps on anybody's toes. He works from eight in the morning to ten at night, doing everything from preaching to sweeping. He makes four hundred dollars a week and gives one hundred dollars to the church, drives a late model car, buys lots of books, wears fine clothes and has a nice family....He is thirty-six years old and has been preaching forty years. He is tall, on the short side; heavyset, in a thin sort of way; and handsome....He has a burning desire to work with the youth and spends all his time with the senior citizens. He smiles all the time while keeping a straight face....He makes fifteen calls a day on church members, spends all his time evangelizing nonmembers, and is always found in his study if he is needed. Unfortunately, he burnt himself out...[5] I guess he's not perfect after all!

Pastors need prayer! *Prayer for personal needs*: 1) humility which includes a servant's heart, 2) wisdom to know God's agenda, 3) positive relationships, 4) the fruit of the Spirit, 5) health. *Prayer for family needs*: 1) the priority of family, 2) provision for family. *Prayer for spiritual needs*: 1) time alone with God, 2) anointing, 3) integrity, 4) protection from spiritual warfare and discouragement, 5) accountability. 6) intercessors. *Prayer for congregational needs*: 1) evangelism 2) personal growth, 3) mobilization of the laity, 4) intercession.

PRAYER: *Father, we pray that our congregations will raise up a prayer shield for all pastors and their families. Amen.*

LOVE OF HUSBAND AND CHILDREN

The older women likewise, that they be reverent in behavior, not slanderers, not given to much wine, teachers of good things—that they admonish the young women to love their husbands, to love their children, to be discreet, chaste, homemakers, good, obedient to their own husbands, that the word of God may not be blasphemed.
—TITUS 2:3–5; READ ALSO TITUS 2

"Few portions of the New Testament excel this chapter. It may well form the creed, system of ethics, and textbook of every Christian preacher."[6]

First, Titus deals with the older women, or women elders. They are to be reverent in behavior, not slanderers. They are not to be involved in any kind of gossip, or false accusation, for this is the work of the enemy. Reverent behavior means behavior that is holy; they view life as sacred in all aspects. They were also not to be drinkers of wine and involved in drunkenness. This was a problem in Crete (Titus 1:5).

Then, these women were admonished to use their wisdom and experience in teaching *the younger women to love their husbands and children.* They are to build them up and say good things about them and to them. One of the best ways to build up husbands and children is to lift them up daily before the throne of God in prayer. Pray the Lord's prayer over them. Pray these apostolic prayers for them: Ephesians 1, 3, 6; Colossians 1; 1 Thessalonians 1; 2 Thessalonians 3; Philippians 1; etc. Wives and mothers, you determine the spiritual atmosphere of your home through your prayers and love.

We are admonished to be chaste, innocent, pure, modest; we are to be obedient to our husbands in the Lord (Ephesians 5:22). When others see our homes, they should see Christ as the Bridegroom, and us as the Bride, living as though He might come anytime.

PRAYER: *Thank You Lord for entrusting our husbands and children to us! Help us to see You and them and love them the way that You do! Amen!*

SALVATION IS NOT DEPENDENT ON OUR WORK

But when the kindness and the love of God our Savior toward man appeared, not by works of righteousness that we have done, but according to His mercy He saved us, through the washing of regeneration and renewing of the Holy Spirit.
—TITUS 3:4–5; READ ALSO TITUS 3

God is so good! God is kind and full of love for us! His kindness and love appeared to us as a man, and Jesus is His name. There is no one so kind and good as God.

It's *"not by works of righteousness that we have done."* In other words, our salvation is not based on our works.

+ Church attendance does not save us.

+ Giving does not save us.

+ Reading the Bible does not save us.

+ Going to the altar and praying does not save us.

+ Baptism does not save us.

+ Confirmation and communion do not save us.

"He saved us through the washing of regeneration and renewing of the Holy Spirit."

This washing of regeneration is the spiritual cleansing by the Word of God. Jesus says in John 15:3: *"You are already clean because of the word which I have spoken to you."* Also, Ephesians 5:26 says: *"That He might sanctify and cleanse her with the washing of water by the word."*

Regeneration means spiritual rebirth. It means being *"born again"* (John 3:3). Jesus said we must be *"born again"* to inherit the kingdom of God. Renewing means being made new by the Holy Spirit. When we are *"born again"* the Holy Spirit comes inside and transforms us into a *"new creature in Christ."* Water baptism is then an outward sign of what the Holy Spirit did on the inside of us. Then, after we are saved, we want to do good works because we are thankful for what God has done. Then our motive for good works is entirely different than if we were doing it to be saved.

PRAYER: *Father, we declare that by Your mercy You have saved us and made us righteous. Amen.*

WHO WE ARE IN CHRIST

... That the sharing of your faith may become effective by the acknowledgment of every good thing which is in you in Christ Jesus.
—PHILEMON 1:6; READ ALSO V. 4

Paul prayed for Philemon and desired that the sharing of his faith would become effective as he understood the work God did in him, and as he understood who he was in Christ.

Knowing who we are in Christ makes us overcomers.

I AM SIGNIFICANT:

I am God's child (John 1:12; Romans 8:14–16); I am God's workmanship (Ephesians 2:10); I am a saint (Ephesians 1:1); I am Christ's friend (John 15:15); I am a citizen of heaven and sit with Christ in the heavenly places (Ephesians 2:6); I am the salt of the earth (Matthew 5:13); I am the light of the earth (Matthew 5:14); I have been chosen and appointed to bear fruit (John 15:16).

I AM ACCEPTED:

I have been justified (Romans 5:1); I have been made righteous (2 Corinthians 5:21); I have been redeemed and forgiven of all my sins (Colossians 1:14); I have direct access to God through the Holy Spirit (Ephesians 2:18); I may approach God with boldness and confidence (Ephesians 3:12); I am complete in Christ (Colossians 2:10).

I AM SECURE:

I have been justified (Romans 5:1); I am free from condemnation (Romans 8:1); I have been given the Holy Spirit as a pledge guaranteeing my inheritance to come (Ephesians 1:12, 14); I am hidden with Christ in God (Colossians 3:3); I know that all things work together for good for me (Romans 8:28); I have not been given a spirit of fear (2 Timothy 1:7); God will complete His good work in me (Philippians 1:6).

I AM OF VALUE:

I am chosen, holy and dearly loved (Colossians 3:12).

PRAYER: *These words are so powerful, Father, give us a spirit of wisdom and revelation to take them all in and apply them to our lives. Thank You that we are chosen, and not forsaken, that we are adopted, and not orphans. Amen.*

November 14

GOD ALONE DESERVES OUR WORSHIP

Now to the King eternal, immortal, invisible, to God who alone is wise, be honor and glory forever and ever. Amen.
— 1 TIMOTHY 1:17; READ ALSO 1 TIMOTHY 1

This is Paul's praise to the God who saved him. Sometimes we can lose sight of the awe and reverence that should be a part of our worship of Him. Following is a wonderful hymn based on this text by Walter Chalmers Smith, a pastor and important leader of the Free Churches of Scotland. It was published in 1867. Meditate on these words:

> Immortal, invisible, God only wise,
> In light inaccessible hid from our eyes,
> Most blessed, most glorious, the Ancient of Days,
> Almighty, victorious—Thy great name we praise.
>
> Unresting, unhasting, and silent as light,
> Nor wanting, nor wasting, Thou rulest in might;
> Thy justice, like mountains, high soaring above
> Thy clouds, which are fountains of goodness and love.
>
> To all, life Thou givest—to both great and small,
> In all life Thou livest—the true life of all;
> We blossom and flourish as leaves on the tree,
> And wither and perish—but naught changeth Thee.
>
> Great Father of glory, pure Father of light,
> Thine angels adore thee, all veiling their sight;
> All praise we would render—O help us to see
> Tis only the splendor of light hideth Thee!

PRAYER: *Jesus, You are beautiful beyond description—too marvelous for words. Too wonderful for comprehension, like nothing ever seen or heard. Who can grasp Your infinite wisdom, Who can fathom the depths of Your love? You are beautiful beyond description. Majesty enthroned above. I stand, I stand in awe of You. Holy God to whom all praise is due, I stand in awe of You.[7] Amen.*

November 15

INTERCEDE FOR THE GOVERNMENT

*Therefore I exhort first of all that supplications, prayers, interces-
sion, giving of thanks be made for all men, for kings and all who are in
authority, that we may lead a quiet and peaceable life in all godliness and
reverence. For this is good and acceptable in the sight of God our Savior,
who desires all men to be saved and to come to the knowledge of the truth.*
—1 Timothy 2:1–4; read also 1 Timothy 2

Of primary importance to Paul was prayer for all who are in authority,
starting with the king. Consider making a list of those people and
putting their names in a prayer notebook. In our nation, we can
start with the president and vice president, and then those in the
White House including his cabinet. Pray much for the judges on the
Supreme Court. Also, we must pray for national and state senators
and representatives, judges and governors. On the city level, there are
mayors and city council members, as well as leaders in our schools.

Suggestions for praying for the mountain of government:

1. Pray God would mobilize intercessors for them.
2. Pray that God will call and empower men and women to be
   national and state leaders who are humble, willing to intercede and even to lay their lives down on behalf of our nation as
   Moses did for Israel (James 4:6; Exodus 32).
3. Pray God will raise up leaders like King David who boldly
   worship God and acknowledge His sovereignty (1 Chronicles
   29:10–13).
4. Pray our leaders will rule the people with justice under the fear
   of the Lord (2 Samuel 23:3).
5. Thank God for leaders like King Solomon who have great
   wisdom and knowledge and who will release blessings on their
   people (2 Chronicles 1:12).
6. Pray God will use men like Joseph who will have wisdom,
   knowledge, and understanding to protect and provide for
   nations in seasons of famine (Genesis 41).

PRAYER: *Thank You, Father, for enlightening our people to vote for
godly men and women who love and fear You. May there be unprecedented numbers of people coming to the polls. We ask for people who
value their freedom to vote for those who are running for office and take
advantage of that right! Amen.* 319

STRONG FAMILIES MAKE STRONG NATIONS

Let deacons be the husbands of one wife, ruling their children and their own houses well.
—1 Timothy 3:12; read also 1 Timothy 3

We have heard, "As goes the family, so goes the nation." Strong and loving marriages and homes built upon God's word are the foundation of a strong society.

Ronald Reagan, fortieth President of the United States wrote:

> The family has always been the cornerstone of American society. Our families nurture, preserve, and pass on to each succeeding generation the values we share and cherish, values that are the foundation for our freedoms. In the family, we learn our first lessons of God and man, love and discipline, rights and responsibilities, human dignity and human frailty.
>
> Our families give us daily examples of these lessons being put into practice. In raising and instructing our children, in providing personal and compassionate care for the elderly, in maintaining the spiritual strength of religious commitment among our people—in these and other ways, America's families make immeasurable contributions to America's well-being.
>
> Today more than ever, it is essential that these contributions not be taken for granted and that each of us remember that the strength of our families is vital to the strength of our nation.[8]

Make these decrees over your marriage and family:

+ "For richer or poorer, in sickness and in health, to love and to cherish...till death do us part."
+ *"As for me and my house, we will serve the Lord"* (Joshua 24:15).

Prayer: *Bless this house, O Lord, we pray. Make it safe by night and day. Bless these walls so firm and stout, keeping want and trouble out. Bless the roof and chimneys tall. Let thy peace lie over all. Bless this door that it may prove, ever open to joy and love. Amen.*[9]

REVIVALS

Let no one despise your youth, but be an example to the believers in word, in conduct, in love, in spirit, in faith, in purity.
—1 TIMOTHY 4:12; READ ALSO 1 TIMOTHY 4

In every generation God has been faithful to bring revival, and in almost all cases, the revival started with young people. The following men used mightily in revivals were in their 20's.[10]

1. John Calvin in the Great Reformation, 1500's.

2. George Whitefield in the Great Awakening, 1700's.

3. Zinzendorf of the Moravians who started the 100-year prayer meeting and won John Wesley to Christ, 1700's.

4. Barton Stone, Cane Ridge Revival in 1801, and Charles Finney mightily used in the 2nd Great Awakening.

5. C. T. Studd together with D. L. Moody, won 1000's in 1857 revival.

6. Evan Roberts began the Welsh Revival that swept around the world in the power of the Holy Spirit, 1900s.

7. Billy Graham/Jesus People/Charismatic renewal 1950—today.

8. Prophets today like James Goll have seen visions of stadiums filled with youth worshipping God. These new songs and new sounds will rock nations for Jesus. The 24/7 Tabernacle of David style worship with prayer and the Word, started by Mike Bickle in Kansas City in 1999 has sent music missionaries around the world. *(ihopkc.org).* Power worshippers will arise as a new generation moves into cities and regions and breaks open the heavens through worship and prayer.

PRAYER: *"In the last days, I will pour out My Spirit on all flesh and your sons and daughters shall prophesy." (Joel 2:28). In Jesus' name. Amen.*

REWARD FOR THOSE WHO
LABOR IN GOD'S VINEYARD

Let the elders who rule well be counted worthy of double honor, espe-
cially those who labor in the word and doctrine. For the Scripture
says, "You shall not muzzle an ox while it treads out the grain," and,
"The laborer is worthy of his wages."
—1 TIMOTHY 5:17–18; READ ALSO 1 TIMOTHY 5

Elders are the ones in leadership in the church. If they labor and work
hard in the Word and doctrine, they are worthy of double honor. In
this case, double honor means financial support.

The Scripture says in Deuteronomy 25:4 that we should not
muzzle an ox while it treads out the grain. In other words, we should
let him eat because he is working and needs nourishment. It also says
in Luke 10:7 that the laborer is worthy of his wages.

The Bible teaches that a person can find special favor with God by
giving and helping those in ministry and missions. Following is a list
of six ways you will be blessed for giving from 2 Corinthians 9:

+ Sowing bountifully causes you to reap bountifully (v. 6).
+ God will make all grace abound to you (v. 8). *"He who is kind*
  to the poor lends to the Lord and He will reward him for what he
  has done" (Proverbs 19:17, NIV).
+ You will have an abundance for every good work (v. 8).
+ God will multiply your seed sown and the fruits of your righ-
  teousness (v. 10).
+ Your giving will supply the needs of the saints (v. 12).
+ Your giving shows obedience to the gospel and will be a cause
  for people's hearts to be softened and many will be saved (v. 13).

PRAYER: *Father, we count it a privilege to sow into the kingdom and*
bless Your servants who work hard in the word and doctrine. They
spend countless hours studying and working on sermons and teachings.
They pray for us and sacrifice in many ways. Bless them financially and
in every way. May they have more than enough. Amen.

November 19

THE LOVE FOR MONEY

But those who desire to be rich fall into temptation and a snare, and into many foolish and harmful lusts which drown men in destruction and perdition. For the love of money is a root of all kinds of evil, for which some have strayed from the faith in their greediness and pierced themselves through with many sorrows.
—1 Timothy 6:9–10; read also 1 Timothy 6

The desire for riches tempts our heart away from eternal riches and ensnares us in a trap few can escape. The desire to be rich can really only be satisfied in Jesus Christ.

The fate of those who live for the love of money (which is the root of all evil) can be exemplified by J. Paul Getty, the oil baron who many believed was the richest man in the world.

This man was so stingy that he had payphones installed in his mansion for his house guests to use.

His grandson, J. Paul Getty III was kidnapped when he was sixteen years old. The kidnappers demanded seventeen million dollars from the oil baron. Not only did Getty refuse to pay, but said, "I have fourteen grandchildren and if I pay anything for his release, I'll have to pay for the others too."

Eventually, the kidnappers lowered their demands to three million dollars. It wasn't until they cut off the ear of the grandson did Getty agree to give anything. Then he would only come up with two million, two hundred thousand dollars the maximum amount that his accountants said would be tax-deductible. The boy's father paid the rest, though he had to borrow it from his father—at four percent interest. The teenager, malnourished, bruised and missing an ear, was released on December 15th.

Even though J. Paul Getty was the richest man in the world, he was despised and hated by not only the public, but also by his own family.[11]

Prayer: *Where our riches are, that's where our heart is. Amen.*

PREACH GOD'S WORD WITHOUT FEAR

*For God has not given us a spirit of fear, but of power and of love
and of a sound mind. Therefore do not be ashamed of the testimony
of our Lord, nor of me in the sufferings for the gospel according to the
power of God, who has saved us and called us with a holy calling, not
according to our works, but according to His own purpose and grace
which was given to us in Christ Jesus before time began.*
—2 TIMOTHY 1:7–9; READ ALSO 2 TIMOTHY 1

The body of Christ is rising up in this hour in boldness to share
Christ. We are not ashamed of the testimony of Christ, for it is *"the
power of God unto salvation for everyone who believes, for the Jew first
and also for the Greek"* (Romans 1:16). We will not fear, for Christ
has promised us in these verses that we were given power, love and a
sound mind.

For God has given us a holy calling to know Him and the power of
His resurrection (Philippians 3:10). We are called to walk with Him,
live with Him, and reign with Him. We are called to share His Word
and His love with everyone. We are called to share the gifts He has
given us, both natural and spiritual, as He leads us.

This calling has nothing to do with our works, but is according
to His own purpose and grace *which was given to us in Christ before
time began* (v. 9). Before time began we were in His mind and He gave
us this calling, purpose and gifts even then. As it also says in Psalm
139:16: *"Your eyes saw my substance, being yet unformed and in Your
book they all were written, the days fashioned for me, when as yet there
were none of them."*

*"Oh the depths of the riches both of the wisdom and knowledge of God.
His ways are beyond finding out"* (Romans 11:33).

PRAYER: *Father, help us to treat all life from conception onward as
precious. Help us to see ourselves through Your Word as precious, gifted
and called with a unique purpose that no one else can fulfill. We pray
this in Jesus' name. Amen.*

FAITHFUL STUDENTS OF
THE WORD OF GOD

*Be diligent (or study) to present yourself approved to God, a worker
who does not need to be ashamed, rightly dividing the word of truth.*
—2 TIMOTHY 2:15; READ ALSO 2 TIMOTHY 2

The way to healthy, successful living is through *"rightly dividing"* the
word of truth. A correct and accurate application of God's Word is
the result of diligent study. We are not to make the Bible say what we
want it to say, but rather know that the Bible means what is says and
says what it means.

Two of America's spiritual fathers practiced this diligently. John
Wesley arose at four AM for over sixty years to pray and study. For
over fifty years he preached at five A.M.

> On an average day John preached three times, traveling about twenty
> miles on horseback. Every morning he began preaching at five o'clock
> in order to reach the workers on their way to the fields. He preached
> again at noon, when the workers broke for lunch, followed often by
> two more times in the evening.[12]

Jonathan Edwards also, another of our early spiritual fathers, once
carefully disassembled one of his Bibles and sewed a sheet of blank
paper between each pair of pages to allow him to record his notes.
This is one of his resolutions:

"Resolved to study the Scriptures so steadily, constantly and frequently, as that I may find, and plainly perceive myself to grow in the
knowledge of the same." [13]

The Great Awakening certainly saw a display of God's glory. New
England is reported to have had as many as fifty thousand people
converted to Christ, with the total population at only about three
million. One hundred and fifty new churches were established.

PRAYER: *Help us to be faithful students in Your Word. Help us to
treasure it. Help us to desire Your Word more than gold; let it be more
precious than silver. Let it be a lamp to our feet and a light to our path,
showing us the way to heaven. Amen.*

PERILOUS TIMES IN THE LAST DAYS

But know this, that in the last days perilous times will come: For men will be lovers of themselves, lovers of money, boasters, proud, blasphemers, disobedient to parents, unthankful, unholy, unloving, unforgiving, slanderers, without self-control, brutal, despisers of good, traitors, headstrong, haughty, lovers of pleasure rather than lovers of God, having a form of godliness but denying its power. And from such people turn away!
—2 TIMOTHY 3:1–5; READ ALSO 2 TIMOTHY 3

We see this in the LGBTQ movement. Kids are given transition drug treatment to change sexes beginning in elementary school.[14] We see ordaining of homosexuals in mainline churches. We see the extreme feminism movement tearing marriages and homes apart. We see living together without benefit of marriage. We see abortion and infanticide. We see Planned Parenthood at work destroying lives. We also see racism and the connection with Planned Parenthood as it was started by Margaret Sanger as a means to prevent the African Americans from growing numerically. We see the rise of witchcraft in movies, games, cartoons, Harry Potter as well as yoga based on the Hindu religion coming into schools and churches. We see a new interest in the Greek gods and goddesses.

We see the church keeping silent about addressing social issues from the biblical perspective.

This is what William Booth said in the mid 1850's: "The chief danger of the twentieth century will be religion without the Holy Ghost, Christianity without Christ, forgiveness without repentance, salvation without regeneration, politics without God, and Heaven without Hell." [15]

PRAYER: *We cry out to You, Lord, to forgive us for turning to false gods and doing wicked and perverse things in Your sight. Forgive us and lead us back to Your Word and following Your laws. Your Word is a lamp unto our feet and a light unto our path giving us wisdom as to what is right, and what is wrong; what is light and what is dark; what is sweet or bitter. Amen.*

November 23

BE READY AT ALL TIMES

Preach the word! Be ready in season and out of season. Convince, rebuke, exhort, with all longsuffering and teaching (v. 2)....But you be watchful in all things, endure afflictions, do the work of an evangelist, fulfill your ministry. For I am already being poured out as a drink offering, and the time of my departure is at hand. I have fought the good fight, I have finished the race, I have kept the faith. Finally, there is laid up for me the crown of righteousness, which the Lord, the righteous Judge, will give to me on that Day, and not to me only, but also to all who have loved His appearing.
—2 TIMOTHY 4:5–8; READ ALSO 2 TIMOTHY 4

One example of the fulfillment of this Scripture, which is written to all of us, is one of God's generals, Dwight L. Moody. One of Moody's critics may have summed up his life when he admitted,

> In his rage to save souls he traveled more than a million miles, addressed more than a hundred million people, and personally prayed and pleaded with seven hundred and fifty thousand sinners. All in all, it is very probable, as his admirers claim, that he reduced the population of hell by a million souls.[16]

> Of his own death, Moody had stated earlier, "Someday you will read in the papers that D. L. Moody, of East Northfield, is dead. Don't you believe a word of it! At that moment, I shall be more alive than I am now. I shall have gone up higher, that is all out of this old clay tenement into a house that is immortal; a body that death cannot touch, that sin cannot taint, a body fashioned like unto His glorious body. I was born of the flesh in 1837. I was born of the Spirit in 1856. That which is born of the flesh may die. That which is born of the Spirit will live forever."[17]

PRAYER: *Father, help us, like this general, be able to say at the end of our lives, "I have fought the good fight. I have finished the race; I have kept the faith." Amen.*

THE BIBLE WILL NEVER PASS AWAY

All flesh is as grass, and all the glory of man as the flower of the grass. The grass withers, and its flower falls away, but the word of the LORD endures forever.
—1 Peter 1:24–25; read also 1 Peter 1

One of the claims which the Bible makes for itself is that it can never be destroyed. The abundance of copies of the Scriptures now available is abundant proof that it has made good its claim. Jesus also said, "Heaven and earth shall pass away, but my words shall not pass away" (Matthew 24:35).

The Bible is a very ancient book. Its antiquity is a wonder. The first five books of the Old Testament were written by Moses about 1500 B.C. making them nearly three thousand five hundred years old; the book of Job was probably written about 2000 B.C.

The enemies of Christianity have tried to destroy the Bible. The Roman emperor, Diocletian (284–316), sent out "royal edicts commanding that the churches be leveled to the ground and the Scriptures destroyed by fire."[18] He also went on to say that if anyone had a copy of the Scriptures and did not surrender it to be burned, he would be killed. However, the next emperor had Eusebius, the historian, copy fifty copies of the Bible!

Voltaire, the French infidel made the prediction that within hundred years, the Bible and Christianity would be swept into oblivion. But, in fact, the very printing press upon which Voltaire had printed his infidel literature was being used to print copies of the Bible. And afterward, the very house in which Voltaire had lived was literally stacked with Bibles prepared by the Geneva Bible Society. Voltaire died in 1778, and the Bible and Christianity live on.

The above Scripture also points to the fleetingness of life. I have a saying on the wall of my prayer room, "Only one life, so soon it will pass. Only what's done for Christ will last."

Prayer: *May we "hide Your Word" in our hearts, Father, and never take it for granted. It is a treasure! Amen!*

November 25

HAPPY TO BE CHOSEN

*But you are a chosen generation, a royal priesthood, a holy nation,
His own special people, that you may proclaim the praises of Him
who called you out of darkness into His marvelous light.*
—1 Peter 2:9, read also 1 Peter 2

We are a chosen generation. He has "picked or gathered" us out from among the larger group for special service or privileges. Say, "I am chosen." "I am royalty."

We are a royal priesthood. It was the priests in the Old Testament that were chosen to offer the sacrifices to the Lord. No one else could do that. King Uzziah tried offering sacrifices and became leprous (2 Chronicles 26:16–21). The priests offered incense or prayers for the people. We are kings and queens—royalty—a royal priesthood. Whereas priests "offer up" to heaven, kings "proclaim" downward to earth.

What do we proclaim? We proclaim the praises of God. The Greek word translated "praises" also means "excellencies" of God. It also means "manliness, valor, superiority." We proclaim the superiority of God.

So as a "royal priesthood" we pray, exercising both the priestly and kingly dimensions of prayer. We can see this in The Lord's Prayer (Matthew 6:9–13). The priestly dimension is saying "Holy is Your Name." We then shift to the kingly dimension when we say, "Your kingdom come. Your will be done." These verbs are in the command form (imperative). The prayer then shifts back to the priestly petitioning asking for provision, forgiveness, and freedom from temptation.[19]

We give praise that He has called us out of darkness into His marvelous light. Jesus is the light of the world (Matthew 5:14).

PRAYER: *We do praise You that You chose us and that we are a royal priesthood. We praise You that You brought us out of darkness into Your marvelous light! Amen.*

BE READY TO GIVE A REASON
FOR THE HOPE IN YOU

*But sanctify the Lord God in your hearts, and always be ready to give
a defense to everyone who asks you a reason for the hope that is in
you, with meekness and fear.*
—1 Peter 3:15; read also 1 Peter 3

I had a precious neighbor in Minnesota whose name was Gayle who
has gone on to be with the Lord now. When I first met her, they
had just moved in across the street. I brought over some cookies and
asked how they were doing. She said the sale of their previous house
had just fallen through, and now they were making two house payments. She told me she was a nervous wreck and was smoking three
packs of cigarettes a day, and taking three nerve pills a day, plus blood
pressure medication. I told her I would go home and pray. She said,
"Don't bother. I don't believe in God." I said, "Well, I do, and I'm
going home to pray."

I did just that and knelt down in front of the window facing their
home and prayed that God would intervene in the sale of their previous home. I went into a time of travailing prayer. When the burden
lifted, I stood up and looked out the window. They were coming out
of the house. She yelled across the street, "The house just sold, and
we're going to close on it!"

When I went over to their house later, she said, "Okay, I'm ready to
listen. Tell me about your faith." So, I told her about Jesus and being
"born again." She accepted Christ as her Savior.

We were having special meetings at our church and I invited her.
She went and was prayed for and received deliverance of some things.
She had such peace, she stopped taking her nerve pills, and cut her
blood pressure medicine in half.

I then gave her a book, "Seven Vital Steps to Receiving the Holy
Spirit" by Kenneth Hagin and she was filled with the Holy Spirit!
After this, she brought her cigarettes over and we took authority over
the nicotine and threw them away. She never smoked another ciga-
rette. Praise the Lord!

Prayer: *Help us to share the hope that is within us! Amen!*

ALWAYS BE WATCHFUL IN PRAYER

But the end of all things is at hand; therefore be serious and watchful in your prayers. And above all things have fervent love for one another, for "love will cover a multitude of sins."
—1 PETER 4:7–8; READ ALSO 1 PETER 4

Every believer is called to be a watchman. What is a watchman? They are intercessors; they are worshippers; they wait on and listen to the Lord. Often, they are prophetic. Here are aspects of being a watchman:

+ We watch the Lord! We gaze on His beauty (Song of Solomon 2:8–11; 5:10–16). Our lover is outstanding among ten thousand!
+ We watch His Word. We meditate upon His Word day and night (Psalm 1:2–3; Joshua 1:8; John 15:7–8).
+ We watch with thanksgiving (Colossians 4:2).
+ We praise and worship Him (Psalm 100). It is eternal.
+ We pour out our heart like water (Lamentations 2:19).
+ We wait upon the Lord (Isaiah 40:31). It renews our strength so that we mount up on wings as eagles.
+ We listen to the Lord and write what He tells us (Habakkuk 2:1; John 10:27–28).
+ We keep watch and do not allow our houses to be broken into (Matthew 24:42–44).
+ We watch and pray that we do not enter into temptation (Matthew 26:37–39; Matthew 26:40–41).[20]

Above all things we must have a fervent love for one another, because this love covers a multitude of sins. As we enter into these last days and see the troubles around us, even as we are in the middle of a world-wide pandemic right now, it is easy to point fingers and place blame on others. More than ever we need to stand in love and unity in our families and churches. *"Let the words of our mouths, and the meditations of our heart be acceptable in His sight"* (Psalm 19:14).

PRAYER: *Jesus, we want to be able to say "Yes," when You ask: "Could you not watch with me one hour?" Amen.*

THE HUMBLE SHALL BE EXALTED

Therefore humble yourselves under the mighty hand of God, that He may exalt you in due time, casting all your care upon Him, for He cares for you. Be sober, be vigilant; because your adversary the devil walks about like a roaring lion, seeking whom he may devour. Resist him, steadfast in the faith.
—1 Peter 5:6–9a; read also 1 Peter 5

We are to be "clothed with humility" (v. 5). Here are some marks of humility:[21]

* The willingness to perform the lowest and littlest services for Jesus' sake.
* Consciousness of our own inability to do anything apart from God.
* The willingness to be ignored of men.
* Not self-hating, but instead being truly others-centered instead of self-centered.

True humility is being able to cast all our cares on Him. It is presumption on our part that we must worry about and take responsibility for things God has promised to take care of for us.

"*Casting*" is a word to consider. He didn't say, "Lay your cares on Me," but rather cast them on Me. In other words, we are to throw them on Jesus, and then leave them there. We cast them on Him, because He cares for us! The fact that God cares for us sets us apart from all other religions. When a child of God is full of worry and fear, this reflects poorly upon our Father in heaven who even knows when a sparrow falls.

Next, we are told to be sober and vigilant because the devil seeks to devour us. "*Pride goes before destruction and a haughty spirit before a fall*" (Proverbs 16:18). Walking in humility and seeking God in prayer and His Word, protects us from the devil. We are to resist him, steadfast in the faith.

Prayer: *Lord, as we humble ourselves, You will lift us up over our troubles and temptations and trials and make us victorious and triumphant in Jesus' name. Amen.*

BELIEVE THE BIBLE WITHOUT DOUBT

Knowing this first, that no prophecy of Scripture is of any private interpretation, for prophecy never came by the will of man, but holy men of God spoke as they were moved by the Holy Spirit.
—2 PETER 1:20–21; READ ALSO 2 PETER 1

We need to settle once and for all in our hearts that God's Word is true. If we start questioning parts of the Bible, then eventually, the whole Bible and its authority and accuracy will be questioned.

The most popular and well-known evangelist of America, Billy Graham faced such a questioning. After he became president of Northwestern School in Minneapolis, Minnesota, a fellow evangelist, Charles Templeton, advised him to work toward a Ph.D. at Princeton. Tem-pleton was beginning to struggle with some theological issues related to the authority and accuracy of the Bible. He began to read the Bible as metaphor rather than literal truth. Charles told Billy that, *"People no longer accept the Bible as being inspired the way you do. Your faith is too simple. Your language is out of date. You're going to have to learn the new jargon if you're going to be successful in your ministry."* [22] (Charles Tem-pleton, in his autobiography, "Farewell to God" rejected the Christian faith when he began to doubt the truth of the inspiration of the Bible).

One night Billy opened his Bible and told God there were many things in the Bible he did not understand and some things that didn't seem to correlate with modern science, but that he was going to accept His Word by faith and believe it was His inspired Word. He got up from his prayer and sensed the presence of God for the first time in months. The battle in his spirit was over.

Billy Graham went on to be America's most well-known evangelist for six decades. He preached in person to nearly two hundred and fifteen million people in more than one hundred and eighty countries and territories. In April 1996, the Billy Graham Evangelical Association sponsored a rebroadcast of one of Billy's sermons to an audience of 2.5 billion people in 48 languages and 160 countries.

PRAYER: *Lord, I choose to believe Your Word. I choose to believe Your Word is inspired and will show me the way and the truth about how to live this life and get to heaven. Amen*

LORD, SAVE ME FROM MY SIN

For if God did not spare the angels who sinned, but cast them down to hell and delivered them into chains of darkness, to be reserved for judgment;...

—2 PETER 2:4; READ ALSO 2 PETER 2

Jesus speaks very plainly about the reality of hell. In Mark 9:47, He says, *"And if your eye causes you to sin, pluck it out.* (This is a hyperbole to show how purposeful we must be to avoid sin). *It is better for you to enter the kingdom of God with one eye, rather than having two eyes, to be cast into hell fire—where 'Their worm does not die, and the fire is not quenched'"* (v. 47–48).

Dr. Mary Kathryn Baxter has been a minister of the gospel since 1983 after she received a Doctor of Ministry degree from Faith Bible College, an affiliate of Oral Roberts University. She was literally taken to view the reality of hell with Jesus in 1976 for thirty days. Afterwards she was taken to heaven and was told to write about these things so that everyone would know about the reality of heaven and hell. She entered with Jesus into a gateway to hell and encountered the sights, sounds, and smells of that dark place of torment, including its evil spirits, cells, fire pits, jaws, and heart. She could tell as she passed the fire pits that they felt the fire, the worms, the pain, and the hopelessness. They knew there was no way out of the flames and that they were lost forever. Yet they still cried out to Jesus as He passed by. As they passed one woman in a cell, she said,

> Lord, when I was on earth, I worshipped the Hindu gods and many idols. I would not believe the gospel the missionaries preached to me, although I heard it many times. One day I died. I cried for my gods to save me from hell, but they could not. Now, Lord, I'd like to repent." "It's too late," Jesus said. Flames covered her form as we walked by; her cries still fill my soul even now. Satan had deceived her.[23]

PRAYER: *Lord, I repent of my sins. Please save me! Amen!*

THE KING IS COMING

> *But the day of the Lord will come as a thief in the night, in which*
> *the heavens will pass away with a great noise, and the elements will*
> *melt with fervent heat; both the earth and the works that are in it will*
> *be burned up Therefore since all these things will be dissolved, what*
> *manner of persons ought you to be in holy conduct and godliness.*
> —2 PETER 3:10–11; READ ALSO 2 PETER 3

Though the Lord's longsuffering love to the lost makes it seem like He is delaying His coming, the truth is He will indeed come. He doesn't want anyone to perish so He is giving more time for everyone to repent. But the day of the Lord will come as unexpectedly as a thief. It will surprise many. This is amazing, but the heavens will pass away with a great noise. The solar system and the great galaxies and all the elements which make up the physical world will be dissolved by heat and utterly melt away. And the earth and everything on it will be burned up.

> This world, so far as we know, will not cease to be; it will pass through
> the purifying flame, and then it may be the soft and gentle breath of
> Almighty love will blow upon it and cool it rapidly, and the divine
> hand will shape it as it cools into a paradise more fair.[1]

And so, since everything around us is going to melt away, what holy, godly lives we should be living! Realizing that the earth is going to be burned up, we should put our confidence in what is lasting and eternal and not be bound to earth and its treasures or pursuits. Do we spend more of our time piling up possessions or striving to develop Christlike character?

"The King is coming; He is coming to His throne, and to His judgment. The King is almost here; you are at His door; He is at yours. How can we sin against One who is so close at hand?"[2]

PRAYER: *Father, we want to grow in the grace and knowledge of our Lord and Savior, Jesus Christ. Amen.*

December 2

FATHER, I HAVE SINNED

If we say that we have no sin, we deceive ourselves, and the truth is not in us. If we confess our sins, He is faithful and just to forgive us our sins and to cleanse us from all unrighteousness.
—1 John 1:8–9; read also 1 John 1

The first thing to realize here is that we have sinned. Without the Holy Spirit convicting us of our sins, there can be no repentance and there can be no salvation. Whoever believes they have not sinned and, therefore, do not even need a Savior, are deceived and the truth is not in them.

My husband had a colleague who spent the night at our house. When we shared these Scriptures with him, he said he was a good person and he was not going to have anybody die for his sins. He would be responsible for dealing with his sins himself.

Even a child can be deeply convicted of sin. When I got saved at ten years old, I wept hours on end with the realization that I was a sinner who needed a Savior and that I couldn't make it to heaven by myself. I received forgiveness and salvation. In the Bible we see that those who came to Jesus were deeply convicted of sin. Consider Zacchaeus, and how he received salvation (Luke 19:1–10):

+ He was looking for Jesus. He climbed up in the tree to see Him.

+ Jesus told him to come down and said He would stay at his house. He obeyed the Word of the Lord.

+ Zacchaeus *received Him* at his house, joyfully. I believe this is a sign of his conversion.

+ He gave half of his goods to feed the poor and restored fourfold of what he had wrongfully taken. This restitution is sign of his repentance.

+ Jesus said that "salvation had come to his house" because he was a son of Abraham. Jesus said, "He had come to seek and to save that which was lost."

Prayer: *Father, may we experience true repentance and forgiveness and salvation, even as Zacchaeus did! Amen!*

December 3

TRUE PRIORITIES

*Do not love the world or the things in the world. If anyone loves
the world, the love of the Father is not in him. For all that is in the
world—the lust of the flesh, the lust of the eyes, and the pride of life—
is not of the Father but is of the world. And the world is passing away,
and the lust of it; but he who does the will of God abides forever.*
—1 JOHN 2:15–17; READ ALSO 1 JOHN 2

What is loving the world? This is not a warning against loving the
beauty of the world God created. (Although we must always love the
Creator, not the creation). Instead, this is a warning against loving the
material things which characterize the world system. The answer is
in verse 16:

+ The lust of the flesh. This would include giving an inordinate
  priority to the way we look, with exercising, dieting, etc. Eve
  went after the fruit of the Garden of Eden because it was good
  to eat. We need to take care of ourselves, while not neglecting
  the true priorities of spending time on developing the "incor-
  ruptible beauty of a gentle and quiet spirt which is precious in
  the sight of God" (1 Peter 3:4).

+ The lust of the eyes. This would include loving the things we
  can buy such as cars, homes, or gadgets, and the status that
  goes with all of them. Eve went after the fruit of the Garden
  because it was pleasant to her eyes (Genesis 3:6).

+ The pride of life is desiring superiority over others, mostly by
  impressing others through outward appearances—even if by
  deception. It is the superiority we feel when we have advanced
  degrees, high places in government, or riches and fame. Eve
  went after the pride of life when she thought how smart the
  fruit would make her! How her husband would admire her!

PRAYER: *Thank You, Father, for helping us focus on true priorities
because this world will pass away and the lusts in it, but if we follow
after You, we will live forever! Amen!*

December 4

SEEING THE LORD AS HE IS

Beloved, now we are children of God; and it has not yet been revealed what we shall be, but we know that when He is revealed, we shall be like Him, for we shall see Him as He is.
—1 JOHN 3:2; READ ALSO 1 JOHN 3

We can have an assurance that we are among the children of God. "The Spirit Himself bears witness with our spirit that we are children of God" (Romans 8:16). However, we know that "when He is revealed, we shall be like Him, for we shall see Him as He is."

"For whom He foreknew, He also predestined to be conformed to the image of His Son, that He might be the firstborn among many brethren" (Romans 8:29). This means we will be like Jesus while maintaining our own personalities!

Actually, as Christians, we long to be like Jesus, but God will never force us to be like Jesus unless we want that to happen. He has given us a free will. The good news is that when we finally see Him face to face, then we shall be like him for we shall see Him as He really is. "For now we see in a mirror, dimly, but then face to face. Now I know in part, but then I shall know just as I also am known" (1 Corinthians 13:12).

Heaven is precious to us for many reasons. We long to be with loved ones who have passed before us and whom we miss dearly, as well as great men and women of God. We want to walk the streets of gold, see the pearly gates, and see the angels round the throne of God worshipping Him day and night.

But really what we are longing for more than anything is the presence of our Lord and to see Him as He is. In Revelation 1:13–16, He was dressed in a long robe with a golden breastplate. His head and His hair were white as snow. A sharp two-edged sword came out of His mouth and His face was ablaze like the sun at its height.

PRAYER: *Lord, we long to see You as You really are and be like You in every way! In Jesus' name. Amen.*

TO KNOW GOD, YOU MUST LOVE

Beloved, let us love one another, for love is of God; and everyone who loves is born of God and knows God. He who does not love does not know God, for God is love.
—1 JOHN 4; READ ALSO VV. 7–8

The following story exemplifies the sacrificial love of God flowing through one person, changing the life of another.

David Attah was raised as an only child in a Muslim home in Nigeria. He never had a relationship with his father, and when he was only a child, his mother died. This made him very lonely.

He went to college where he reached out to people and became very popular. While there, he went to hear an evangelist and became a Christian. Oh, how wonderful it was to hear of Jesus' love!

After this, he was struck down by a vehicle. The driver was intoxicated. A neurosurgeon tested David's speech, and though he could write, he had totally lost the ability to make his mouth utter or whisper a single word. Through weeks of rehabilitation, he regained use of his right hand to write.

He became so desperate that he decided to take his life. He wrote a good-bye letter to the staff and put it inside his Bible. That night Rita who was a Christian, training to be a nurse, came into his room. She read his suicide note. She said he must NEVER do this, and if he would promise her this, she *promised him and God that she would always stand by him.*

Rita went away to nursing school. She had decided she would never marry but that she would stick by David's side as she promised. She believed he would talk again. After completing her nurses training, she continued to care for him and encourage him in his faith.

In 2003, Reinhard Bonnke came to their town for a crusade. To make a long story short, David was miraculously healed and could speak perfectly. His first word was "Jesus." Rita had stood by him for *eight long years.* They are now married and in ministry full time.[3]

PRAYER: *Father, teach us what Your kind of love is like. Amen.*

DO YOU KNOW THE WILL OF GOD?

Now this is the confidence that we have in Him, that if we ask any-thing according to His will, He hears us. And if we know that He hears us, whatever we ask, we know that we have the petitions that we have asked of Him.

—1 JOHN 5:14–15; READ ALSO 1 JOHN 5

What wonderful promises we have in prayer! If we ask according to His will, He hears us, and He grants our petitions. Now the big ques-tion is: What is His will? How can we know for sure what His will is? The Bible is very clear on what His will is. It is His will that we:

- Love the Lord with all our heart, soul, and mind; and love our neighbor as our self (Matthew 22:37–39).
- Be saved (1 Timothy 2:4; 2 Peter 3:9).
- Prosper (3 John 2; Philippians 4:19).
- Be in health (1 Peter 2:24; Matthew 8:17; Psalm 103:3; Exodus 15:26; James 5:14).
- Have peace (Philippians 4:6–8; John 14:27).
- Have no fear (2 Timothy 1:7).
- Have wisdom (Ephesians 1:17–23; James 1:5–8).
- Know God's love (Ephesians 3:14–21).
- Be protected (Psalm 91; Ephesians 6:13–18).
- Have strong marriages (Matthew 19:5–6).
- Have children that honor parents (Ephesians 6:1–4).
- Meditate in His Word and be successful (Joshua 1:8; Psalm 1)
- Forgive those who sin against us (Matthew 6:12).
- Be filled with the Spirit (Ephesians 5:18–20).
- Fulfill the Great Commission (Matthew 28:19–20).
- Attend church regularly and tithe (Hebrews 10:25; Malachi 3:10–12).
- Watch what we say—life and death is in the power of the tongue (Proverbs 18:21).

PRAYER: *Father, thank You that all Your promises listed above are "Yes and Amen" to the glory of God! Amen!*

THE DOCTRINE OF CHRIST

*Whoever transgresses and does not abide in the doctrine of Christ
does not have God. He who abides in the doctrine of Christ has both
the Father and the Son. If anyone comes to you and does not bring
this doctrine, do not receive him into your house nor greet him.*
—2 JOHN 9–10; READ ALSO 2 JOHN

We are to be knowledgeable of the antichrist spirit, and not to be
deceived by it. Following are some common doctrines that are of the
antichrist spirit. 2 John says, *"Do not receive him into your house nor
greet him."* All of these cults deny the divinity of Christ.

+ Jehovah's Witnesses—a) They believe Jesus was really the archangel Michael. b) They deny the bodily resurrection of Christ.

+ Mormons—a) They believe in many gods and faithful Mormons will become gods. b) They deny the virgin birth of
  Christ. c) Their book is equal with the Bible.

+ Freemasonry—a) It is a secret society that worships Baal and
  Lucifer. b) They take gruesome death oaths.

+ Wicca/witchcraft—a) The goddess (lady) and god (lord) created the human race, but it needed healing, so they created
  witches. It is mainstreaming worship of gods and goddesses.
  b) Witchcraft promotes spells, curses, and spiritual power
  apart from God. The Bible condemns it (1 Samuel 15:23; Deuteronomy 18:10–12).[4]

+ Yoga—a) The goal of yoga is to become one with the universal
  soul to stop the endless cycle of reincarnations. (Hebrews
  9:27). b) The god of yoga is shiva, a Hindu god whose name
  means "the destroyer."

+ Socialism/communism/globalism—a) It is an involun-
  tary redistribution of wealth. Governmental control of our
  resources is not biblical (Exodus 20:15). b) There is no God in
  these forms of government (Exodus 20:3).

PRAYER: *We ask for protection against these antichrist agendas especially in our schools and universities! Amen!*

GOD WANTS US TO PROSPER

*Beloved, I pray that you may prosper in all things and be in health,
just as your soul prospers. For I rejoiced greatly when brethren came
and testified of the truth that is in you, just as you walk in the truth. I
have no greater joy than to hear that my children walk in truth.*
—3 JOHN 2–4; READ ALSO 3 JOHN

This is a prayer showing clearly that the will of God is to prosper. In
this text the word "prosper" literally means "to help on the road" or
"succeed in reaching." This shows that divine prosperity is not just a
fleeting or passing thing, but it is an ongoing, progressing state of success and well-being. This prosperity is intended for every area of life,
the spiritual, the physical, emotional, and material. However, God
does not want us to emphasize any one area. We must maintain a
balance.[5]

This is also a prayer that we be in health. It is God's will that we be
healed and whole and be protected from sickness and disease.

God wants our mind, will and emotions (soul) to prosper as well.
He wants us to have a clear mind, a will submitted to His purposes,
and experience life through healthy emotions of love, joy, peace, etc.
It is not His will that we be depressed, hopeless, and sad. The joy of
the Lord is our strength (Nehemiah 8:10).

John knew that Gaius (to whom the letter was written) was
walking in truth, and nothing pleased him more than to know that.
This is more than just believing correct doctrine. To walk in truth
means to walk consistent with the truth of the Bible. If you believe
you are a sinner (after receiving the righteousness of Christ in salvation), you will reflect that belief. If you believe you are a child of God,
you will have a totally different viewpoint of yourself and your worth.

PRAYER: *We are so thankful for these powerful promises. We can know
that it is Your will that we have all our needs met, spirit, soul, and body.
If we walk in faith, we will walk in victory and joy! Amen!*

DOXOLOGY FOR KEEPING US FROM FALLING

Now to Him who is able to keep you from stumbling, and to present
you faultless before the presence of His glory with exceeding joy, To
God our Savior, Who alone is wise, be glory and majesty dominion
and power, both now and forever. Amen.
—JUDE 24–25; READ ALSO JUDE

Jude mentions that he is a "brother of James," which also means he
was a half brother of our Lord Jesus. He identified himself as a *"bond-*
servant of Jesus Christ, and brother of James."

He closes his letter with a doxology, which is a declaration of praise
to God. Hallelujah! He is able to keep us from stumbling. After Jude
had warned his readers of false teaching and immorality, he wanted
to encourage them that the answer lies in the power of God. He is
able to keep us!

In verse 20, He tells us how we can work with God in this process. We are to *"build yourselves up on our most holy faith, praying*
in the Holy Spirit." As we learned in 1 Corinthians 14:14, praying in
the Spirit means praying in other tongues. This baptism of the Holy
Spirit and praying in the Spirit is a powerful way to keep ourselves
and our faith always growing.

"Just like in mountain climbing, the beginning hiker attaches himself to the expert so that if he loses his footing he won't stumble and
fall to his death. In the same manner, if we stay connected with God,
we cannot fall. He keeps us safe." [6]

Because God is faithful, we won't have to slink shamefacedly into
the presence of God. We can be presented before Him with exceeding
joy, with ecstatic delight because we have stayed connected to Him!

These outstanding qualities of God that Jude mentions are breath-
taking. He is all wise, glorious, majestic, and has great power and
authority—from before He created time, for now, and throughout all
the ages of eternity. Amen.

PRAYER: *Father, this doxology is our prayer today! We thank You that*
you are able to keep us from falling and present us blameless with joy
before God our Savior. Amen!

December 10

WHEN HE COMES, EVERYONE WILL KNOW

Behold, He is coming with clouds, and every eye will see Him, even they who pierced Him. And all the tribes of the earth will mourn because of Him. Even so, Amen. "I am the Alpha and the Omega, the Beginning and the End," says the Lord, "who is and who was and who is to come, the Almighty."

—REVELATION 1:7; READ ALSO REVELATION 1

Revelation was written by John on the Isle of Patmos directly west of Ephesus. He was banished there in 95 A.D. by the Emperor Domitian and was released eighteen months later.

Our Scripture gives an opening description of the return of Jesus. John begins the chapter by praising Jesus as the faithful witness, the firstborn from the dead, and the ruler over the kings of the earth. He washed us from our sins in His blood.

Next, John says to *"behold"* or look for His coming. When He comes he will be surrounded by clouds. When He ascended, He was taken up in a cloud (Acts 1:9–11). Two men like angels were standing there and said He would return in like manner.

When Jesus comes, it will not be a secret coming. Every eye will see Him. Everyone will know. The ones who pierced Him will see His pierced hands and feet. The Bible says in Zechariah 12:10 that they (who pierced Him) will mourn for Him as one mourns for his only son. And all the tribes of the earth will mourn because of Him.

Next, Jesus introduces Himself as *"the Alpha and the Omega"*— the beginning and the end, *"who is and who was and who is to come."* The idea behind this is that Jesus is before all things and will always be beyond all things. He is Yahweh the eternal One. *"The Almighty"* means, "the one who has his hand on everything: past, present and future.

PRAYER: *Jesus, Your head and hair are white like wool, as white as snow, and Your eyes are like a flame of fire; Your feet are like fine brass and Your voice as the sound of many waters (v. 14–15). No wonder John fell at Your feet as dead! You deserve all honor, glory, power and praise! Amen!*

December 11

BE PREPARED FOR PERSECUTION

Do not fear any of those things which you are about to suffer. Indeed, the devil is about to throw some of you into prison, that you may be tested, and you will have tribulation ten days. Be faithful until death, and I will give you the crown of life.
—REVELATION 2:10; READ ALSO REVELATION 2

Jesus begins by addressing the Persecuted Church at Smyrna. The other three were the Loveless Church, in Ephesus; the Compromising Church, in Pergamos; and the Corrupt Church, in Thyatira. These churches have counterparts in today's church.

Our friends Nick and Marcae Robertson, missionaries to India, and now at North Central University in Minneapolis, tell this story of one of their students in India—Yadav, from Nepal.

He was an officer in the Nepali army, married with two children. He drank a lot, and then heard about Jesus and gave his life to Him. His wife, seeing the big change in him, followed suit and gave her life to Christ as well.

When the Nepali army became aware of Yadav's decision, he was given a choice of denying Christ or execution. He refused to deny Christ. He hugged his family good-bye and got in the back of an army truck for transport to where he would be executed. His family prayed for God to intervene. He did.

The truck carrying him had two other vehicles traveling with it along the winding roads of the Himalayas. One of the vehicles hit another vehicle and all the vehicles crashed. Everyone was killed or immobilized—except for Yadav. Instead of running away, he stayed to help the ones he could by trying to stop their bleeding.

When help finally arrived, he was taken to prison. The guards and officials came to see him and asked why he stayed to help. He told them Jesus told us to love our enemies. Instead of being executed, he was set free and discharged from the army!

PRAYER: *Father, we pray today for the persecuted church around the world. Deliver them like You did Yadav! Also, we pray that we might be prepared for any future persecution. Amen.*

CHRIST HAS THE KEY TO THE KINGDOM

And to the angel of the church in Philadelphia write, "These things says He who is holy, He who is true, He who has the key of David, He who opens and no one shuts, and shuts and no one opens."
—REVELATION 3:7; READ ALSO REVELATION 3

This is written to the Faithful Church in Philadelphia. He told them to persevere and He would keep them from the hour of trial that shall come upon the whole world, to test those who dwell on the earth.

The above verse is a verse displaying the authority of Jesus. "He is the One who has the key of David, and He has the authority to shut doors, and the authority to open doors."

Jesus' authority is described in Isaiah 22:22: "*Then I will set the key of the house of David on his shoulder, when he opens no one will shut, when he shuts no one will open.*" As Christ's ambassadors under His direction we also operate in this authority.

Dutch Sheets was given this verse in January 2003 and was to "close the door to the counsel currently coming to the president that is not My will. Then open the door for My counsel to come to him." He was by the White House and was praying that verse in total unbelief, and was going to leave, when a young mom strolling her baby came up to him and asked him if he were Dutch Pierce. (She confused him with Chuck Pierce, a different prophet.) She said the Lord told her to come to the White House, find you, and "remind you of Isaiah 22:22, and that you really do have the keys to open and close doors in the Spirit." He said "thanks," and told her to get her baby back home out of the cold. He received quite a reprimand from the Lord about that— that he shouldn't have to go through Faith and Obedience 101 again![7]

PRAYER: *Lord, You hold the keys to the kingdom and You have given us authority to use these keys to open and close doors in the spiritual realm, under Your direction. Amen.*

SING UNTO THE LORD A NEW SONG

Now when He had taken the scroll, the four living creatures and the twenty-four elders fell down before the Lamb, each having a harp and golden bowls full of incense, which are the prayers of the saints. And they sang a new song, saying: "You are worthy to take the scroll, and to open its seals for You were slain, and have redeemed us to God by Your blood out of every tribe and tongue and people and nation, and have made us kings and priests to our God and we shall reign on the earth."
—Revelation 5:8–10; read also vv. 4–5

John was taken up to the throne room of heaven, and oh, the glorious things he saw:

+ He who sat on it was like a jasper and a sardius stone.
+ Twenty-four elders were sitting on twenty-four thrones.
+ These elders were clothed in white robes.
+ From the throne proceeded lightnings and thunders.
+ Seven lamps of fire burned before the thrones which were the seven Spirits of God.
+ A sea of glass like crystal was there.
+ Four living creatures like a lion, calf, man, and eagle were singing, *"Holy, Holy, Holy."*

At first, it looked like no man was worthy to open the seven-sealed scroll from the hand of God. But the Lion of the Tribe of Judah, the Root of David, was counted worthy!

Now when He had taken the scroll, the four living creatures and the twenty-four elders fell down, having a harp and bowls full of incense which are the prayers of the saints.

This is the model for prayer and worship in use by the 24/7 house of prayer established in Kansas City and which is spreading around the world. The songs are intermingled with the prayers, as they are in the throne room. The prayers are modeled on the apostolic prayers from the Bible, followed by spontaneous singing of words from the prayers. This is a powerful and effective means for worship and prayer.[8]

PRAYER: *Blessing and honor and glory and power be unto the Ancient of Days! Every nation will bow before You! Amen!*

HIS DEATH SAVED US FROM GREAT TRIBULATION

I looked when He opened the sixth seal, and behold, there was a great earthquake; and the sun became black as sackcloth of hair, and the moon became like blood. And the stars of heaven fell to the earth, as a fig tree drops its late figs when it is shaken by a mighty wind. Then the sky receded as a scroll when it is rolled up, and every mountain and island was moved out of its place.
—Revelation 6:12–14; read also Revelation 6

Chapter six begins with the breaking of the seven seals. The breaking of each seal brings a tragedy on the earth. With the breaking of each seal, the redemption of the earth draws one step closer. The "scroll" contains the history and destiny of mankind and creation, and only Jesus—the Lamb—has the right to loosen the seals on this scroll thereby culminating all of history. When the seal is opened, the sentence is executed. This is the beginning of the Tribulation.

+ The first seal reveals the rider on the white horse. Many believe this is the antichrist, who imitates Jesus.
+ The seventieth week of Daniel 9 (last seven years) begins with this leader making a covenant with the Jewish people.
+ The second seal reveals a red horse taking peace from the earth.
+ The third seal reveals a black horse—famine on earth.
+ The fourth seal reveals a green horse. Death sat on him, and he had power to kill one-fourth of the earth.
+ The fifth seal brings forth the cry of the martyrs.
+ The opening of the sixth seal brings cosmic disruption: the earthquake, the sun becoming black, the moon becoming like blood, the stars falling, and the sky receding. (See also Luke 21:25–26.) This judgment is the wrath of the Lamb during the Great Tribulation. Who can stand? The true believer can, because Jesus already bore the wrath the believer deserved.

Prayer: *Worthy are You, O Lord, for Your blood was shed and You took our punishment, so that we might escape this Great Tribulation. We pray for the Great Awakening! Amen!*

A GREAT MULTITUDE IN WHITE
ROBES WORSHIPPING

After these things I looked, and behold, a great multitude which no one could number, of all nations, tribes, peoples, and tongues, standing before the throne and before the Lamb, clothed with white robes, with palm branches in their hands, and crying out with a loud voice, saying, "Salvation belongs to our God who sits on the throne and to the Lamb!" These are the ones who come out of the great tribulation, and washed their robes and made them white in the blood of the Lamb.
—REVELATION 7:9–10, 14; READ ALSO REVELATION 7

The four angels at the corners of the earth were told to wait until the one hundred and forty four thousand were sealed. It is best to see these as specifically chosen Jewish people who come to faith in Jesus. They are protectively sealed throughout the Tribulation as a sign.

After these things, a great multitude from all nations out of the Great Tribulation, were seen before the throne clothed in white, worshipping God and the Lamb with palm branches in their hands. The white robes are an emblem of righteousness, and the palms are emblems of victory. This great diversity of people is evidence that the Great Commission of Matthew 28:18–20 will be fulfilled before the end.

This great throng of people and angels and elders and living creatures fall on their faces before the throne and worship saying: *"Amen! Blessing and glory and wisdom, thanksgiving and honor and power and might, be to our God forever and ever. Amen"* (v. 12).

The throngs in heaven are able to see the great power and wisdom and majesty of God! Oh, that we, while we are still on the earth, could join with the angels and the heavenly host and worship God with all our hearts. Oh, that we could *"Worship the Lord in the beauty of holiness"* (Psalm 29:2).

PRAYER: *"Ascribe to the LORD, O families of nations, ascribe to the LORD glory and strength, ascribe to the LORD the glory due his name. Tremble before him, all the earth! Let the heavens rejoice, let the earth be glad; let them say among the nations, 'The LORD reigns!'"* (1 Chronicles 16:28–31, NIV) Amen!

JUDGMENT TO COME

Then another angel, having a golden censer, came and stood at the altar. He was given much incense, that he should offer it with the prayers of all the saints upon the golden altar which was before the throne. And the smoke of the incense, with the prayers of the saints, ascended before God from the angel's hand. Then the angel took the censer, filled it with fire from the altar, and threw it to the earth. And there were noises, thunderings, lightnings, and an earthquake.
—Revelation 8:3–5; read also Revelation 8

The sealed scroll was introduced in Revelation 5 and the seals were opened one by one up to the sixth seal in Revelation 6. We had a pause in Revelation 7 with the revealing of the one hundred and forty four thousand, and the great multitude out of the Great Tribulation.

Now when He opened the seventh seal, there was silence in heaven for about half an hour. This silence perhaps demonstrates an awestruck silence at the judgments to come. *REMEMBER, the purpose of the judgments are to strike hard at Satan and his kingdom.*

Next John saw seven angels standing before God and they were given seven trumpets. Then another angel came with a golden censer, and he was given much incense in order to offer it with the prayers of the saints. So, before anything else happens at the opening of the seventh seal, the prayers of the people come before the Lord God. Just as incense is pleasant, so are our prayers as they rise to God.

Now the seven angels prepared themselves to sound. These are the first four of the trumpet judgments: 1) The vegetation was struck and a third of the trees and green grass was burned up. 2) The seas were struck and a third of the sea became blood. 3) The waters were struck and a third of the waters became wormwood or bitter. 4) The heavens were struck and a third of the sun, a third of the moon, and a third of the stars were darkened. There are three trumpet judgments to go.

PRAYER: *As we see these things that are prophesied to come to pass, help us make the most of every opportunity to rescue people from the fiery darts of the enemy. Help us to redeem the time and make the most of every opportunity! Amen!*

December 17

GOD'S WRATH

They had as king over them the angel of the bottomless pit, whose name in Hebrew is Abaddon, but in Greek he has the name Apollyo.
—REVELATION 9:11; READ ALSO REVELATION 9

The 5th angel sounded and a star fell from heaven and he was given the key to the bottomless pit. Who was this angel? This angel is possibly Satan himself. Jesus said in Luke 10:18: *"I beheld Satan as lightning fall from heaven."*

When the bottomless pit is opened, hideous, demonic locusts come out. Men do not die from the pain of the locusts' sting, but they want to. The bottomless pit is a temporary prison house. Demons didn't want Christ to send them there (Luke 8:27–31).

This trumpet judgment lasted five months. Who was the king over these demon locusts? He has two names: Abaddon, ("Destruction"), and Apollyon ("Destroyer").

The 6th trumpet judgment is when the four evil angels bound in the river Euphrates are loosed (Jude 6; 1 Peter 3:19–20). Very possibly, these are angels who cohabited with the daughters of men. Their seed were called Nephilim, which means "fallen ones." These angels loose judgment upon the whole world. They kill a third of mankind.

The number of the army of horsemen was two hundred million. The heads of the horses were like the heads of lions and out of their mouths came fire, smoke and brimstone. The sad thing is that the rest of the people who were not killed by these plagues, did not repent of the works of their hands, or repent of worshipping demons and idols of gold, silver, brass, etc. They didn't repent of murders or sorceries or immorality. The great moral sin that will be involved here is fornication or sexual sins. This will be the same as the period preceding the flood and Sodom and Gomorrah. It will be a terrible day of devastation—the Day of the Lord, or the Day of God's wrath.

PRAYER: *Lord, this list of sins is an accusation against our present age. We ask for forgiveness and repent of these sins. Send a supernatural repentance to Your church. Amen.*

GOD'S RESTORATION PLAN

I saw still another mighty angel coming down from heaven, clothed with a cloud. And a rainbow was on his head, his face was like the sun, and his feet like pillars of fire. He had a little book open in his hand. And he set his right foot on the sea and his left foot on the land, and cried with a loud voice, as when a lion roars.
—Revelation 10:1–3a; read also Revelation 10

Who is the mighty angel who stands on the sea and the earth? This refers to Jesus Christ or His special envoy. He is clothed with a cloud, which refers only to deity. God came down to the Israelites *"in a thick cloud and the voice of the trumpet, so that all the people that were in the camp trembled"* (Exodus 19:16). Revelation 1:7 says: *"Behold, He is coming with clouds, and every eye will see Him, even they who pierced Him. And all the tribes of the earth will mourn because of Him."*

His face is described like the sun. Christ's countenance was described as "the sun shining in its strength" (Revelation 1:16). His feet were "like fine brass, as if refined in a furnace" (Revelation 1:15).

He is, of course, the Lion of the tribe of Judah: *"Behold, the Lion of the tribe of Judah, the Root of David, has prevailed to open the scroll and to loose its seven seals"* (Revelation 5:5). *"He cried with a loud voice, as when a lion roars"* (v. 3).

What is the little book? It is the title deed to the earth. The book's contents will not only be sweet to John when he eats it, but it will also be bitter because he has to be a part of setting the earth in order by way of the judgments.[9]

God gave the dominion of the earth to Adam, but Adam committed high treason, and Satan became the god of this earth. Now the earth will be reclaimed, and man will be given dominion of the earth again; the saints are destined to inherit the earth. This is fulfilled at the sounding of the 7th trumpet. (See Revelation 11:15 and Daniel 7:27.)

Prayer: *Father, Your plans of restoration are amazing! Amen!*

December 19

JESUS CHRIST SHALL REIGN
FOREVER AND EVER

Then the seventh angel sounded: And there were loud voices in heaven, saying, "The kingdoms of this world have become the kingdoms of our Lord and of His Christ, and He shall reign forever and ever!"
—REVELATION 11:15; READ ALSO REVELATION 11

The temple spoken of in the beginning of this chapter is the Tribulation temple. The plan for the first temple began with David who prepared for it. His son, Solomon, later built the temple in 959 B.C. This temple was destroyed by Nebuchadnezzar in 586 B.C. Seventy years later when they returned from Babylon, they built another temple, called Zerubbabel's temple. About forty years before Jesus was born Herod renovated it, and it was called Herod's temple. This temple was destroyed in 70 A.D. by Titus, a Roman general.

However, there was to be another temple in the end times. Jesus prophesied that an abomination would stand in the Holy of Holies (Matthew 24:15; Daniel 9:27). The Jews, under the Antichrist will rebuild their temple and offer sacrifices again. In the midst of the Tribulation (7 years), Antichrist will break his agreement with the Jews and set up his idol in the temple. This is the beginning of the last three years which is called the Great Tribulation. The Jews flee into the wilderness at this time.

Before the 7th trumpet is sounded, two witnesses are sent from God who will harass the Antichrist. Many scholars believe these men will be Moses and Elijah. They will reenact the life, death and resurrection of Jesus by themselves being killed, raised to life and ascending to heaven.

Now comes the 7th trumpet judgment, and voices in heaven speak "the Hallelujah Chorus" words. "Some Messianic Jews believe this is the last trump of God (1 Corinthians 15; 1 Thessalonians 4:16), and that this rapture is mid-tribulation." [10] Others believe the rapture occurs before the Tribulation; some believe it will take place after the Tribulation.

PRAYER: *We give You thanks, O Lord God Almighty, the One who is and who was and is to come. Amen.*

December 20

THE SAINTS' VICTORY OVER SATAN

And they overcame him by the blood of the Lamb and by the word of their testimony, and they did not love their lives to the death.
—REVELATION 12:11; READ ALSO REVELATION 12

In Revelation 12, 13, and 14, the main figures of the Great Tribulation are described: a) the *woman*, representing Israel; b) the *dragon*, representing Satan; c) the *man-child*, referring to Jesus; d) the *angel Michael*, head of the angelic host; and e) the *offspring of the woman*, representing Gentiles who come to faith in the Tribulation.

In verse 5, Jesus' ministry is described. He was the male child who was to rule all nations with a rod of iron. He was caught up to the throne upon His resurrection and ascension. In verse 6, the woman fled into the wilderness. She is being persecuted by the dragon. This is Israel during the last three and a half years of the Great Tribulation.

In verses 7–9 we see Michael and his angels fighting with the dragon (Satan). At the mid-point of the Great Tribulation, God will turn the tide against Satan, and he will no longer have any access to heaven. Up to that point, he did have access. The accuser of the brethren who has accused us (the church) day and night was cast down in this war and his angels were cast out with him. (These are fallen angels, or demons.)

Then there was (and will be) great rejoicing in heaven! Our opening verse gives us three keys to the saint's victory over Satan: 1) *the blood of the Lamb*; His blood speaks of His death in our place and the judgment He bore on our behalf. That is what saves us. Because Jesus overcame and defeated Satan, we overcame and defeated him. 2) *the word of our testimony*; our testimony tells of the wonderful things God has done for us. This builds up our faith, and others' faith. It is powerful because no one can deny it by saying, "That never happened to you!" 3) *we did not love our lives unto death*; if we do not cling to our lives, Satan can't bring a threat against us (Philippians 1:21).

PRAYER: *Thank You for these three weapons You gave us! Amen!*

THE MARK OF THE BEAST

He causes all, both small and great, rich and poor, free and slave, to receive a mark on their right hand or on their foreheads, and that no one may buy or sell except one who has the mark or the name of the beast, or the number of his name. Here is wisdom. Let him who has understanding calculate the number of the beast, for it is the number of a man: His number is 666."
—REVELATION 13:16–18; READ ALSO REVELATION 13

John saw a beast rising up out of the sea. The sea is symbolic of humanity in prophetic literature. This beast here has all the attributes of the beasts/kingdoms described in Daniel 7:4–6: Babylon is like a lion; Medo-Persia is like a bear; and Greece is like a leopard. The beast of Revelation 13 combines the ferocity of all three. He is like the dragon (Satan) because he also has seven heads and ten horns. The ten horns represent ten kingdoms according to Daniel 7:7. This beast is the Antichrist, and he was given authority to continue for forty-two months. John also wrote about this Antichrist in 1 John 2:18: *"Little children, it is the last hour; and as you have heard that the Antichrist is coming."* The person indwelt by Satan during the Tribulation is the Antichrist. There is also a "spirit of antichrist;" both are in rebellion against God.

In verse 3 we see that this Antichrist was wounded in his head, died, and came back to life. The world worshipped the dragon which gave power to the beast. The beast blasphemed God, and all those whose names are not written in the Lamb's Book of Life worshipped him.

Then the false prophet arose in verse 11 and had great power to do miracles and caused the earth to worship the beast. He gave life to the image of the beast, and all who did not worship him were killed. He required all to receive a mark in the right hand or in their foreheads, so that no one could buy or sell without the mark. The number of the mark was 666.

PRAYER: *Father, thank You for the anointing that abides in us and teaches us the truth, that we will not be deceived in these last days (1 John 2:28). Amen.*

THOSE WHO DIE IN THE LORD

Then I heard a voice from heaven saying to me, "Write: Blessed are the dead who die in the Lord from now on." "Yes, says the Spirit, that they may rest from their labors, and their works follow them."
—REVELATION 14:13; READ ALSO REVELATION 14

The one hundred and forty four thousand Jewish male virgins follow the Lamb wherever He goes. They sang a new song before the throne. These are the ones who miraculously made it through the Great Tribulation and preached the gospel. They were marked with the Father's name on their foreheads.

Then we see the proclamation of three angels: 1) of the everlasting gospel to all those who dwell on the earth. 2) to Babylon that is fallen. 3) to warn against taking the mark of the beast. Those who do so will be tormented with fire and brimstone in the presence of the holy angels and the Lamb. They will have no rest day or night.

On the contrary, those who die in the Lord will rest from their labors and their works will follow them.

The patient endurance and work of these saints is remembered in heaven. Our work for Jesus and His Kingdom goes with us into heaven, giving dignity and significance to all work here below.

Next, we see the Son of Man on a white cloud wearing a golden crown and holding a sickle. He reaps the harvest of the earth. According to Daniel Juster, Messianic Jew, this is the rapture of the church mid-tribulation.[11] Others say it is the final judgment.

Another harvest is spoken of next and this is the harvest of all the wicked that are thrown into the great winepress of the wrath of God. The blood in this battle, Armageddon, came up to the horses' bridles, for a distance of about 184 miles.

PRAYER: *Thank You for the cross, Lord, and for the price You paid for our salvation and our revelation to walk in the truth! Amen!*

SEVEN ANGELS WITH SEVEN PLAGUES

They sing the song of Moses, the servant of God, and the song of the Lamb, saying: "Great and marvelous are Your works, Lord God Almighty! Just and true are Your ways, O King of the saints! Who shall not fear You, O Lord, and glorify Your name? For You alone are holy. For all nations shall come and worship before You, For Your judgments have been manifested."
—REVELATION 15:3–4; READ ALSO REVELATION 15

Chapter 15 is the shortest chapter in Revelation and is a preparation for the last seven plagues. These seven last plagues are God's judgment on a disobedient and contrary world.

John saw something like *"a sea of glass mingled with fire."* The sea mingled with fire suggests divine judgment proceeding from God's holiness.[12]

Those standing on the sea of glass are the Tribulation martyrs, described in Revelation 7:9–17. Even though the Antichrist kills them, they have victory over the beast. Many believe that the sea of glass is a physical representation of the Word of God, and the washing of water by the Word (Ephesians 5:26). They are standing on the Word.

They have harps and are worshipping God as they sing the song of Moses and the song of the Lamb.

Then John saw the temple of the tabernacle of the testimony in heaven. Exodus 25:8–9 and Hebrews 8:9 remind us that the tabernacle Moses built was modeled on the heavenly pattern.

Out of the temple came the seven angels having the seven plagues. They do not act on their own authority, but God's. One of the four living creatures gave to the seven angels the seven golden bowls full of the wrath of God. The temple was filled with smoke from the glory of God, and no one was able to enter the temple until the seven plagues of the seven angels was complete. This declares the judgment was irreversible.

PRAYER: *Your mercy is in the heavens. Your faithfulness reaches to the clouds. Your judgments are a great deep. Amen.*

December 24

THE BOWLS

Behold, I am coming as a thief. Blessed is he who watches, and keeps his garments, lest he walk naked and they see his shame.
—Revelation 16:15; read also Revelation 16

God's loud voice from the temple initiates the horrific judgments of the bowls. These bowls are the third woe mentioned in Revelation 11:14. They are described as the wrath of God. He tells the seven angels to go and pour out the bowls of wrath of God on the earth:

1. The first bowl: foul and loathsome sores coming upon those who had the mark of the beast.
2. The second bowl: the sea turned to blood.
3. The third bowl: fresh waters became blood.
4. The fourth bowl: the sun scorches men. They did not repent but blasphemed the Name of God.
5. The fifth bowl: a plague of darkness. Jesus described hell as outer darkness.
6. The sixth bowl: the great river Euphrates was dried up, so that the way of the kings and their armies from the east might be prepared. This is the battle of Armageddon.
   - Three unclean spirits like frogs came out of the mouth of the dragon, the beast, and the false prophet. They are demons performing signs.
   - There is a warning here by Jesus to watch and put on righteousness as a garment.
7. The seventh bowl: the final judgments.

   "It is done. No more judgments."
   - Great earthquake as has never occurred before.
   - Great Babylon was given the cup of the fierceness of His wrath and divided into three parts.
   - Great hail fell—up to one hundred pounds.

Prayer: *Father, help us always to watch and pray as Jesus commanded us, and to remember to put on the whole armor of God, and having done all to stand (Ephesians 6:13). Amen.*

HAPPY BIRTHDAY, JESUS CHRIST

Glory to God in the highest, and on earth peace, goodwill toward men!
—MATTHEW 1:14; READ ALSO LUKE 2

What marvelous revelation Charles Wesley had when he wrote this hymn:

Hark! The herald angels sing, Glory to the newborn King;
Peace on earth, and mercy mild, God and sinners
    reconciled!
Joyful, all ye nations, rise, Join the triumph of the skies;
With the angelic host proclaim, "Christ is born in Bethlehem!"
Note: Jesus brought reconciliation between God and man.

Christ, by highest heaven adored; Christ, the everlasting Lord!
Late in time behold Him come, Offspring of the Virgin's
    womb:
Veiled in flesh the Godhead see; Hail the incarnate Deity,
Pleased as man with men to dwell, Jesus, our Emmanuel.
*Note: He was born of a virgin. He is Deity. Emmanuel—God
    with us.*

Hail the heaven born Prince of Peace! Hail the Sun of
    Righteousness!
Light and life to all He brings, Risen with healing in His
    wings.
Mild He lays His glory by, Born that man no more may die,
Born to raise the sons of earth, Born to give them second birth.
*Note: He brings peace. He is our healer. He came to redeem us
    and take us to heaven. He came so that we might be "born
    again."*

Chorus: Hark the Herald Angels sing, Glory to the Newborn
    King!

PRAYER: *We remember Your birth today and all You have done for
us. We invite You into our celebrations today! As we gather with family,
may You be in the center of it all! May Your love bind our families
together forever! Amen!*

THE LAMB

These will make war with the Lamb, and the Lamb will overcome them, for He is Lord of lords and King of kings; and those who are with Him are called, chosen, and faithful.
—Revelation 17:14; read also Revelation 17

The great harlot sitting on many waters is Babylon. This was a literal city on the Euphrates River. According to religious history and legend, the Babylonian religion was founded by the wife of Nimrod (great-grandson of Noah) named Semiramis. She was a high priestess of idol worship and gave birth to Tammuz whom she claimed was conceived miraculously. Baal was the Canaanite name for the Babylonian god Tammuz. The woman on the scarlet beast pictures false religion that will dominate the world in the tribulation period.[13]

Religious Babylon intoxicates kings and peoples. The fact that she is riding on the beast, symbolizes that she is supported by the political power of the beast. There is a stark contrast between her and the woman of Revelation 12, who represents Israel and God's people. Mystery Babylon, on the other hand, represents all idolatry and false worship.

The seven heads are the seven mountains on which the woman sits. Rome sits on seven hills, but this religious Babylon is much bigger than Roman Catholicism. We do see tendencies for Roman Catholicism's ultimate partnership with a one-world religion. This became evident in Pope John Paul II's approval of and unity with, other anti-Christian religions.

The ten kings may allude to a ten-nation confederation. The European Union itself claims to be a successor to the ancient Roman Empire. These nations will join with the Antichrist in the war against Christ. Ultimately the Antichrist will not tolerate any worship except of himself. The war with the Lamb is the battle of Armageddon.

Prayer: *The Lamb has overcome for He is the King of kings, and Lord of lords. Amen.*

December 27

MYSTERY BABYLON

Rejoice over her, O heaven, and you holy apostles and prophets, for God has avenged you on her!
—REVELATION 18:20; READ ALSO REVELATION 18

Most Bible scholars believe that mystery Babylon, the religious system, is destroyed in Chapter 17. Chapter 18 is concerned with commercial Babylon. Religious Babylon of Revelation 17 is judged at the midpoint of the Tribulation. Commercial Babylon is judged at the end of that period.

Another voice from heaven said, "Come out of her, my people, lest you share in her sins." Commercial Babylon, with its lure to materialism, is a constant threat to be guarded against. We are commanded in Ephesians 5:11 *"And have no fellowship with the unfruitful works of darkness, but rather expose them."*

God will give Babylon exactly what she deserves. She will be repaid double according to her works. Double restitution was required in the Old Testament in cases of theft (Exodus 22:4–9). Perhaps this is how she made her wealth.

The kings of the earth who lived in luxury with her will weep and wail when they see the smoke of her burning. In just one hour, her judgment came. There was mourning at the loss of luxuries, not of necessities. These kings sold the bodies and souls of men. Today we see this in the form of sex trafficking, prostitution, and pornography. Their sorrow at commercial Babylon's fall was very selfish.

We are to rejoice over this, not in the destruction that God's judgment brings, but we rejoice in God's righteous resolution.

A mighty angel then took up a great millstone and threw it into the sea, and said, "Thus with violence the great city Babylon shall be thrown down and shall not be found anymore" (v. 21).

The ultimate reason for her judgment was that she had killed the prophets and saints. Their blood still cries out.

PRAYER: *May we not love the world or anything in it! May we instead love the Lord our God with all our hearts! Amen!*

December 28

THE GLORY OF JESUS' RETURN TO EARTH

Now I saw heaven opened, and behold, a white horse. And He who sat on him was called Faithful and True, and in righteousness He judges and makes war. His eyes were like a flame of fire, and on His head were many crowns. He had a name written that no one knew except Himself. He was clothed with a robe dipped in blood, and His name is called The Word of God.... And He has on His robe and on His thigh a name written: KING OF KINGS AND LORD OF LORDS"
—Revelation 19:11–13, 16; read also Revelation 19

A great multitude in heaven rejoice over the judgment of Babylon who had corrupted the earth with her fornication and defiled the earth with the blood of His servants. They sang with unrestrained worship and praise, *"Alleluia! Salvation and glory and honor and power belong to the Lord our God!"* (v. 1).

One reason this great multitude is so filled with praise is because the time has come for the marriage supper of the Lamb. In biblical times a marriage involved two major events: the betrothal and the wedding. These were separated by a period of time. The wedding began with a procession to the bride's house and was followed by a return to the house of the groom for the marriage feast. Jesus will return at the rapture for His church and return to heaven for the marriage feast which lasts throughout eternity. The Bride, (His church), is dressed in fine linen which are the righteous acts of the saints.

Oh, the glory of Jesus' return to earth! Meditate on verses 11–16. This time He doesn't return as a Baby in a manger, but with a sword in His mouth on a white horse with many crowns on His head! And we will also come with Him on white horses. At this time Israel will cry out to Jesus their Savior for deliverance! All Israel will be saved! He is KING OF KINGS AND LORD OF LORDS!

The beast and his armies, gathered together at Armageddon, will be defeated and the beast and the false prophet will be thrown into the lake of fire.

Prayer: *Maranatha! Come Lord Jesus, Come! Amen!*

THE LAMB'S BOOK OF LIFE

Then I saw a great white throne and Him who sat on it, from whose face the earth and the heaven fled away. And there was found no place for them. And I saw the dead, small and great, standing before God and books were opened. And another book was opened, which is the Book of Life. And the dead were judged according to their works, by the things which were written in the books.
—Revelation 20:11–12; read also Revelation 20

Satan will be bound for a thousand years in the bottomless pit, and he will deceive the nations no more during that time.

This thousand-year period is known as the Millennium and Jesus will rule and reign on the earth during this time. During the Millennium, the citizens of the earth will acknowledge and submit to the Lordship of Jesus. There will be no more war. During the Millennium, animals relate to each other and to humans differently. A little child will lead a wolf or a leopard or lion or bear. The nursing child will play by the cobra's hole (Isaiah 11:6–9). There will be blessing and security for national Israel. There will be a rebuilt temple and restored temple service as a memorial of God's work in the past (Ezekiel 37:26–28). During this time, the saints will live and reign for the one thousand years. Saints who were raptured will administrate the kingdom of Jesus Christ over the earth, reigning over those who passed through the earth during the Great Tribulation into the earth of the Millennium.

When the one thousand years are over, Satan will be released for a time to deceive the nations and will gather them together for a final battle against Christ. Fire will come from heaven and devour them. The devil will then be thrown into the lake of fire and brimstone.

At the end of the Millennium, there will be the great white throne judgment and the resurrection of the wicked dead. They will be judged for their works and will be cast into the lake of fire; their names are not found in the Book of Life.

Prayer: *How we praise You that when we repent and ask You to be the Lord of our lives, our names are written in the Lamb's Book of Life! Amen!*

NEW HEAVEN AND NEW EARTH

Then I, John, saw the holy city, New Jerusalem, coming down out of heaven from God, prepared as a bride adorned for her husband. "Come I will show you the bride, the Lamb's wife." And he carried me away in the Spirit to a great and high mountain, and showed me the great city, the holy Jerusalem, descending out of heaven from God.
—Revelation 21:2, 9b–10; read also Revelation 21

All things will be made new: a new heaven, a new earth and there will be no more sea. The new heaven is not referring to God's heaven (the 3rd heaven), but to the 1st heaven which is our atmosphere, and the 2nd heaven which is where Satan and his demons are currently. Jesus said that heaven and earth shall pass away, but His Word would live forever (Luke 21:33). Also, in Isaiah 65:17 God said that He would create a new heaven and earth.

The New Jerusalem coming down out of heaven is the place of our true citizenship (Philippians 3:20). It will be beautiful. "The most beautiful thing a man will ever see is his bride coming down the aisle, ready to meet him." This is how beautiful the New Jerusalem will be. And here there will be no more death, nor sorrow, nor crying, nor pain.

This beautiful city will be one thousand five hundred miles square, high and wide and long—a perfect cube. The wall is two hundred and fifty feet high and has twelve gates. Each gate is guarded by an angel named after one of the tribes, and each gate is made of pearl. A pearl is a living organism, created by an irritant or wound. Jesus was wounded for our sin.

The city is of pure gold. The twelve foundations are of beautiful stone: jasper, sapphire, chalcedony, emerald, sardonyx, sardius, chrysolite, beryl, topaz, chrysoprase, jacinth, amethyst.

The city has no temple for the Lord God Almighty and the Lamb are the temple. It has no need of sun or moon, for the glory of God illuminates it. Only those in the Lamb's Book of Life are there.

PRAYER: *The breath of heaven in this chapter is sweet; the magnificence of heaven, incomprehensible! PTL! Amen!*

December 31

GOD IS COMING QUICKLY

And behold, I am coming quickly, and My reward is with Me, to give to every one according to his work. I am the Alpha and the Omega, the Beginning and the End, the First and the Last.
—Revelation 22:12–13; read also Revelation 22

In the interior of the New Jerusalem we see a river flowing from the throne of God. It is a pure river of the water of life. On either side of the river was the tree of life which bore twelve fruits, each tree yielding its fruit every month. The leaves of the tree were for the healing of the nations.

In Genesis, the Bible begins with a tree of life which man was not allowed to eat from after the sin at the tree of the knowledge of good and evil. Now we see the tree of life again and we are invited again to eat of its fruit.

The leaves of the tree were for the healing of the nations. This word can also mean "health-giving."

In heaven the curse described in Genesis 3:16–19 is gone. The throne of God and of the Lamb shall be there and we will see His face; His Name will be on our foreheads.

Jesus' parting words are *"Behold, I am coming quickly!"* The word here could also be translated "suddenly." God wants all generations to be expectant, watching and ready for His return. We can never miss the note of urgency and warning in all that Jesus tells us about His coming. His message always is: "Be ready!"

We are admonished to not seal up the words of this book. We are admonished to keep His commandments that we can enter the city. The dogs (morally impure) are outside the city.

Jesus is the Root and the Offspring of David, the Bright and Morning Star. He closes Revelation by warning us not to add to or take away from the words of this book. The Spirit and the bride say, "Come!" Whoever desires can come!

Prayer: *Thank You that the grace of our Lord Jesus Christ is with us all! We will see Your face, and Your name shall be on our foreheads. We will reign with You forever! Amen!*

SCRIPTURE INDEX

This scripture index does not include the Bible reading plan scriptures that are listed for daily reading at the top of each page.

1 CORINTHIANS

2 CORINTHIANS

NOTES

JANUARY

1. Dr. Richard G. Lee, ed., *The American Patriot's Bible*, (Nashville, Tennessee: Thomas Nelson, Inc., 2009), 6.

2. Ibid., 1096.

3. Ibid., I-6.

4. www.guideposts.org

5. Lee, *The American Patriot's Bible*, 623.

6. Mildred Martin, *Missionary Stories with the Millers*, (Mifflin, PA: Green Pastures Press, 1993), 62–66.

7. Mike Bickle, *Growing in Prayer*, (Lake Mary, FL: Charisma House, 2014), 225–226.

8. Brian Simmons, The Passion Translation, (Broadstreet Publishing Group, LLC, 2017), 291.

9. Lee, *The American Patriot's Bible*, I-28.

10. Ibid.

11. Paraphrased from Faisal Malick, *10 Amazing Muslims Touched by God*, (Shippensburg, PA: Ambient Press, 2012), 145ff.

12. James Goll, *The Lost Art of Intercession* (Shippensburg, PA: Destiny Image Publishers, 2007), 64.

13. Ibid., 72–73.

14. *En.wikipedia.org/wiki/Lincoln%27s_House_Divided_Speech*

15. Interview on Sid Roth's *It's Supernatural Network* (ISN).

16. Marilyn Hickey, *It's Not Over Until You Win*, (Englewood, CO, Marilyn Hickey Publ., 2019), 230–232.

17. Wikipedia, George Müller from Steer, Roger (1997). *George Müller: Delighted in God*. Tain, Rosshire: Christian Focus, 131.

18. Dutch Sheets, *Authority in Prayer*, (Minneapolis, MN: Bethany House, 2006), 21.

19. James W. Goll, *Prayer Storm Study Guide*, (Shippensburg, PA: Destiny Image Publishers, Inc., 2008), 69.

20. Andrew Murray, *The Believer's School of Prayer*, (Minneapolis, MN: Bethany House Publishers, 1982), 88.

21. *www.frc.org/8/27/2019.*

22. Andrew Murray, *Humility*, (New Kensington, PA: Whitaker House, 1982), 51.

February

1. www.youtube.com/watch?v=3RJ3Wa5NeU

2. Myron S. Augsburger, *Mastering the New Testament—Matthew*, (Dallas, Texas: Word Publishing, 1982), 265.

3. Lee, *The American Patriot's Bible*, 1125.

4. Elijah House School of Ministry, *Training Course 201: Level 1 Prayer Ministry*, (Coer d'Alene, ID: Elijah House, Inc., 2011), 95.

5. Augsburger, *Mastering the New Testament—Matthew, Vol. 1*, 311.

6. Cindy Jacobs, *Women of Destiny Bible*, (Nashville, TN: Thomas Nelson Publishers, 2000), 1314.

7. Lee, *The American Patriot's Bible*, 1131.

8. *www.youtube.com/watch?v=vP4iY1TtS3s*

9. James Maloney, *The Dancing Hand of God*, (Argyle, Texas: Answering the Cry Publications, 2008), 32–33.

10. Lee, *The American Patriot's Bible*, 1136.

11. Sheets, *Authority in Prayer*, 22.

12. *Miller, S.M. (2013). Jim Elliot: Missionary Martyr. Barbour. ISBN 978-1-62416076-9. Retrieved 13 September 2015.*

13. David L. McKenna, *Mastering the New Testament—Mark, Vol 2*, 92.

14. Lee, *The American Patriot's Bible*, 1140.

15. Jack Hayford, ed., *New Spirit-filled Life Bible*, (Kingdom Dynamics) (Nashville, TN: Thomas Nelson Publishers, 2002) 1357.

16. *Youtube.com/watch?v=g1CekJrJpp8*

17. *en.wikipedia.org/wiki/Polycarp*

18. Paraphrased from Sandford, *Elijah House School of Ministry, Training Course 201,* 3–4.

MARCH

1. www.blessitt.com

2. Paraphrased from Joyce Booze and Cathy Ketcher, Sacrifice and Triumph, (Springfield, MO: Assemblies of God World Missions, 2003), 171–177.

3. Lee, *The American Patriot's Bible*, 1149.

4. www.ihopkc.org

5. Lee, *The American Patriot's Bible*, 1151.

6. Martin, *Missionary Stories with the Millers*, 92–93.

7. www.ehc.org

8. Simmons, The Passion Translation, 472.

9. Ibid., 474.

10. www1.cbn.com/secret-reinhard-bonnkes-success-fire-holy-spirit.

11. Lee, *The American Patriot's Bible*, 1160.

12. Women of Destiny Bible, (Nashville, TN: Thomas Nelson, Inc., 2000), 1228.

13. Lee, *The American Patriot's Bible*, 1164.

14. Enduringword.com (Spurgeon)

15. Paraphrased from Lee, *The American Patriot's Bible*, 1171.

APRIL

1. David Guzik, enduringword.com

2. Pierre Bynum, frc.org 12/11/19.

3. Sandford, *Elijah House School of Ministry, Training Course 201*, 184–187.

4. Bill Johnson, *When Heaven Invades Earth*, (Shippensburg, PA: Destiny Image Publishers, Inc., 2003), 69.

5. Cindy Jacobs, *Women of Destiny*, (Ventura, California: Regal Books, 1998), 115–116.

6. Enduringword.com (Clarke)

7. Ed Silvoso, *Prayer Evangelism*, (Ventura, CA: Regal Books, 2000), 39.

8. Goll, *The Lost Art of Intercession*, 91.

9. Mike Bickle, *Growing in Prayer*, (Lake Mary, FL: Charisma House, 2014), 140–144.

10. David Guzik, enduringword.com

11. Enduringword.com (Spurgeon).

12. David Guzik, enduringword.com

13. Johnson, *When Heaven Invades Earth*, 26–27.

14. David Guzik, enduringword.com

15. Enduringword.com (Morrison)

16. Cindy Jacobs, *Women of Destiny*, (Ventura, CA: Regal Rooks, 1998), 124–126.

17. Paraphrased from David Guzik, enduringword.com

18. Ibid.

19. Paraphrased from Dutch Sheets, Intercessory Prayer, (Ventura, California: Regal Books, 1996), 16–19.

20. Paraphrased from Maloney, *The Dancing Hand of God*, 110.

21. David Guzik, enduringword.com

22. Dr. Paul Cho, *Prayer*

23. *Key to Revival*, (Waco, Texas: Word Books, 1984), 15.

24. David Guzik, enduringword.com

May

1. David Guzik, enduringword.com

2. Paraphrased from John F. Matthews, *The Covenant in Jesus' Blood*, (Coon Rapids, MN: Scarlet Thread Ministries, 2013), 11–12.

3. Enduringword.com (Spurgeon)

4. Enduringword.com (Spurgeon)

5. David Guzik, enduringword.com

6. Paraphrased from Cindy Jacobs, *Women of Destiny*, (Ventura, California: Regal Books, 1998), 111–112.

7. David Guzik, enduringword.com

8. Paraphrased from Hickey, *It's Not Over Until You Win*, 187–188.

9. John F. Matthews, *The Covenant in Jesus' Blood*, (Coon Rapids, MN: Scarlet Thread Ministries, 2013), p. 10–11.

10. Paraphrased from Robert Heidler, *The Messianic Church Arising*, (Denton, TX: Glory of Zion International Ministries, Inc., 2006), 211–212.

11. Paraphrased from Simmons, *The Passion Translation*, 608.

12. Lee, *The American Patriot's Bible*, I-13.

13. Enduringword.com (Bruce)

14. David Guzik, enduringword.com

15. Ibid.

16. Josh McDowell, *A Ready Defense*, (Nashville, Tennessee: Thomas Nelson Publishers, 1993), 215.

17. David Guzik, enduringword.com

June

1. Enduringword.com (Spurgeon).

2. Maloney, *The Dancing Hand of God*, 313–314.

3. Lee, *The American Patriot's Bible*, 1226.

4. Paraphrased from Lee, *The American Patriot's Bible*, 1228.

5. Enduringword.com, (Tenney).

6. Ibid., (J. Edwin Orr).

7. Simmons, *The Passion Translation*, 634.

8. Lee, *The American Patriot's Bible*, I-22.

9. Paraphrased from David Guzik, enduringword.com

10. Matthews, *The Covenant in Jesus' Blood*, 4.

11. Robert Morris, *The God I Never Knew*, (Colorado Springs, CO: Waterbrook Press, 2011), 25.

12. Robert Heidler, *The Messianic Church Arising*, (Denton, TX: Glory of Zion International Ministries, Inc., 2006), 22–23.

13. Paraphrased from Kathryn Kuhlman, *God Can Do It Again*, (Alachua, FL: Bridge-Logos, 1969), 103–109.

14. James Goll, *Prayer Storm*, (Shippensburg, PA: Destiny Image Publishers, Inc., 2008), 176.

15. Ibid., 176–181.

16. Enduringword.com (Orr).

17. Paraphrased from Paul Hattaway, *The Heavenly Man*, (United Kingdom: Monarch Books, 2002), 251–260.

18. Goll, *The Lost Art of Intercession*, 24.

19. Paraphrased from Robert Morris, *The God I Never Knew*, (Colorado Springs, CO: Waterbrook Press, 2011), 103–104.

20. Bob Rodgers, *A Daily Guide to Miracles*, March Vol 3, (Louisville, KY: Bob Rodgers Ministries, 2020), 42–43.

21. Paraphrased from Malick, *10 Amazing Muslims Touched by God*, 30ff.

22. Paraphrased from Roberts Liardon, *God's Generals, Why They Succeeded and Why Some Failed*, (New Kensington, PA: Whitaker House, 1996), 214.

JULY

1. Paraphrased from Morris, *The God I Never Knew*, 95–96.

2. Sheets, *Authority in Prayer*, 84, 88.

3. David Guzik, *enduringword.com*

4. Paraphrased from Kevin Zadai, *Heavenly Visitation: A Guide to Participating in the Supernatural*, (Nashville, TN: Thomas Nelson, Inc. 2015) Location 166.

5. *Enduringword.com* (Spurgeon).

6. Stanley Howard Frodsham, *Smith Wigglesworth: Apostle of Faith*, (Springfield, MO: Gospel Publishing House, 1948), 35–36.

7. Paraphrased from Bickle, *Growing in Prayer*, 234.

8. David Guzik, *enduringword.com*

9. *Wikipedia.org*

10. Paraphrased from Kenneth W. Osbeck, *Amazing Grace 366 Inspiring Hymn Stories for Daily Devotions*, (Grand Rapids: Kregel Publications, 1990), 170.

11. Lee, *The American Patriot's Bible*, 1333.

12. Bickle, *Growing in Prayer*, 78.

13. Paraphrased from Bickle, *Growing in Prayer*, 79.

14. Paraphrased from David Guzik, *enduringword.com*

15. *Enduringword.com* (Spurgeon).

16. David Guzik, *enduringword.com*

17. Paraphrased from Bonnke, *Even Greater,* (Orlando, FL: Full Flame, 2004), 19

18. *Enduringword.com* (Spurgeon).

AUGUST

1. Paraphrased from Merlin Carothers, *Prison to Praise,* (Escondido, CA: Merlin Carothers, 1970), 83–92.

2. David Guzik, *enduringword.com*

3. David Guzik, *enduringword.com*

4. Paraphrased from John and Paula Sandford, *Elijah House School of Ministry, Training Course 202* (Elijah House, Inc., 2011), 248.

5. David Guzik, *enduringword.com*

6. Randy Clark and Mary Healy, *The Spiritual Gifts Handbook,* (Minneapolis, MN: Chosen, 2014), 161–162.

7. *Enduringword.com,* (Spurgeon).

8. Clark and Healy, *The Spiritual Gifts Handbook,* 178–179.

9. *Enduringword.com,* (Spurgeon).

10. James Strong, *Strong's Exhaustive Concordance of the Bible* (Grand Rapids, MI: Zondervan), 55.

11. *Enduringword.com* (Trapp).

12. *Enduringword.com,* (Barclay).

13. *Enduringword.com* (Clarke).

14. Paraphrased from Larry R. Smith, *Bangladesh Must Be Saved,* (Dhaka, Bangladesh: Larry R. Smith, 2016) 16–17.

SEPTEMBEr

1. Paraphrased from Marilyn Hickey, *It's Not Over Until You Win,* (Englewood, CO: Marilyn Hickey Publisher, 2019), 116–117.

2. Paraphrase from Bickle, *Growing in Prayer,* 98.

3. Paraphrased from Liardon, *God's Generals, Why They Succeeded and Why Some Failed*, 65–66.

4. *Enduringword.com* (Mishna, fol.22,2, Clarke).

5. Paraphrased from Charles Brown, *Evangelist tells of trip to heaven*, (Montgomery, AL: The Journal and Advertiser, Aug. 1984), 3–8.

6. Paraphrased from Hickey, *It's Not Over Until You Win*, 33–35.

7. C. Peter Wagner, *Blazing the Way*, (Ventura, California: Regal Books, 1995) 169.

8. Lee, *The American Patriot's Bible*, 1266.

9. David Guzik, *enduringword.com*.

10. Paraphrased from David Guzik, *enduringword.com*.

11. *PeaceWithGod.net/peace*.

12. *Enduringword.com* (Spurgeon).

13. Hayford, *New Spirit-filled Life Bible*, 1562.

14. Youtube.com/watch?v=cDM76laYPLY.

OCTOBER

1. Paraphrased from Asher Intrater and Dan Juster, *Israel, the Church, and the Last Days*, (Shippensburg, PA: Destiny Image Publishers, Inc., 2003), 84–87.

2. Ibid., 86–88.

3. Marilyn Hickey and Sarah Bowling, *Know Your Ministry*, (New Kensington, PA: Whitaker House, 1986), 1–93.

4. David Guzik, *enduringword.com*.

5. Bickle, *Growing in Prayer*, 81.

6. Jack W. Hayford, *New Spirit Filled Life Bible, Word Wealth*, (Nashville, TN: Thomas Nelson 2002), 1649.

7. Paraphrased from Jacobs *Women of Destiny*, 181, 183–185.

8. Hayford, *New Spirit Filled Life Bible, Kingdom Dynamics*, 1531.

9. Ed Silvoso, *God's Secret Weapon*, (Minneapolis, MN, Chosen, 2001), 13–15.

10. Hayford, *New Spirit Filled Life Bible, Kingdom Dynamics*, 1531.

11. David Guzik, *enduringword.com*.

12. Paraphrased from Hickey, *It's Not Over Until You Win*, 230–232.

13. David Guzik, *enduringword.com*.

14. Paraphrased from Rodgers, *A Daily Guide to Miracles, March—Volume 3*, 43–44.

15. Ronald A. Beers, ed., *Life Application Study Bible*, (Wheaton, IL: Tyndale House Publishers, 1996), 1903.

16. Ibid., 1906.

17. John Maxwell, *Partners In Prayer*, (Nashville, TN: Thomas Nelson Publishers, 1996), 96–102.

18. Hayford, *New Spirit-filled Life Bible*, 1730.

19. Brian Simmons, *The Passion Translation*, 1000. (#1–7, parts in quotes).

20. David Guzik, *enduringword.com*.

21. Paraphrased from Maloney, *The Dancing Hand of God*, 235.

22. Paraphrased from Bob Rodgers, *A Daily Guide to Miracles, February—Volume 2* (Louisville, KY: Bob Rodgers Ministries, 2020), 48–49.

23. David Guzik, *enduringword.com*.

November

1. Hayford, *New Spirit-filled Life Bible*, 1736.

2. Cindy Jacobs, *The Power of Persistent Prayer*, (Minneapolis, MN: Bethany House, 2010), 156–157.

3. Ibid., 152–153.

4. Paraphrased from *Elijah House School of Ministry, Training Course 201*, 152–155.

5. John Maxwell, *Partners in Prayer*, (Nashville, TN: Thomas Nelson, 1996), 81–82, 87–88.

6. *Enduringword.com*, (Clarke).

7. *www.youtube*.com.

8. Lee, *The American Patriot's Bible*, 1367.

9. *www.youtube*.com/watch?v=es_Q0Pc614E.

10. htttp://www.youthnow.org.

11. Paraphrased from Rodgers, *A Daily Guide to Miracles, February—Volume 2*, 43–44.

12. Roberts Liardon, *God's Generals—The Revivalists*, (New Kensington, PA: Whitaker House, 2008), 67.

13. Ibid., 140.

14. Tony Perkins, frc.org, 2/27/2020, (Rob Hoogland testimony).

15. Liardon, *God's Generals—The Revivalists*, 388.

16. Roberts Liardon, *God's Generals—The Revivalists*, 385.

17. Ibid.

18. *www.truthmagazine*.com/archives/volume19/TMO19211.html.

19. Paraphrased from Sheets, *Authority in Prayer*, 21.

20. Tom Hess, *The Watchmen*, (Charlotte NC: Morning Start Publications, 1998), 57–70.

21. David Guzik, *enduringword.com*.

22. Liardon, *God's Generals, The Revivalists*, 464.

23. Mary K. Baxter, *A Divine Revelation of Heaven & Hell*, (New Kensington, PA: Whitaker House, 2019), 267–268.

December

1. *Enduringword.com* (Spurgeon).

2. Ibid.

3. Paraphrased from Reinhard Bonnke, *Even Greater*, (Orlando, FL: Full Flame, 2004), 151.

4. Cindy Jacobs, *Deliver Us From Evil*, (Ventura, CA: Regal Books, 2001), 76–78.

5. Hayford, *New Spirit-filled Life Bible*, 1797.

6. David Guzik, *enduringword.com*.

7. Paraphrased from Sheets, *Authority in Prayer*, 77–78.

8. *www.ihopkc.org*.

9. Marilyn Hickey, *The New Millennium & End-time Prophecy*, (Denver, CO, Marilyn Hickey Ministries, 1999), 96–99.

10. Intrater and Juster, *Israel The Church, and the Last Days*, 237.

11. Ibid., 240–241.

12. *Enduringword.com* (Walvoord).

13. David Guzik, *enduringword.com*.